MW01153455

GANDOLFINI

ALSO BY THE AUTHOR:

Fun City Cinema: New York City and the Movies That Made It

It's OK with Me: Hollywood, the 1970s, and the Return of the Private Eye

Richard Pryor: American Id

The Ultimate Woody Allen Film Companion

Pulp Fiction: The Complete Story of Quentin Tarantino's Masterpiece

GANDOLFINI

JIM, TONY, AND THE LIFE OF A LEGEND

JASON BAILEY

ABRAMS PRESS, NEW YORK

Published in 2025 by Abrams Press, an imprint of ABRAMS.

Library of Congress Control Number: 2024948413

ISBN: 978-1-4197-6769-2
eISBN: 979-8-88707-009-4

Printed and bound in the United States
10 9 8 7 6 5 4 3 2 1

ABRAMS The Art of Books
195 Broadway, New York, NY 10007
abramsbooks.com

CONTENTS

INTRODUCTION

JAMES

THE NEW YORK TABLOIDS COVERED his death with all the respect and nuance with which they'd covered his life—which is to say, none. TONY SOPRANO DEAD, read the front-page headline of the *New York Post*, with an interior article hed of LAST ACT FOR TONY SOPRANO, while the *New York Daily News* went with the simpler TONY'S DEAD on the cover and 'MOB' STAR'S SHOCK END: TOP 'SOPRANO' FELLED BY HEART ATTACK ON ITALY TRIP on page 2. It was one last indignity from the papers that had treated him so balefully, especially in those early years of the show, the Beatlemania years, when *The Sopranos* was the new sensation, when every Sunday night airing was an event, and when his every move (every night out, every fan interaction, every business deal, and then the divorce, dear God, the divorce) had been chronicled, analyzed, and sensationalized by those second-rate rags.

And now here they were, sticking it to him again. He hadn't been Tony Soprano for six years—six years almost to the day, the tenth day of June 2007, the cut to black heard 'round the world—but that's what they were still calling him, alongside cover photos of him in his Tony duds, his clean-shaven face a menacing scowl. Yet that wasn't who he was, not then, and certainly not now. "You can't go on saying we lost Tony Soprano," his co-star and friend Vinny Pastore pointed out, not long after. "We didn't lose Tony Soprano. We lost James Gandolfini."

But over the course of eighty-six hours of television spread across nine years, people felt like they knew Tony Soprano, the anxiety-prone mob boss and family man at the center of HBO's *The Sopranos*, a series that one can say, without hesitation, changed American popular culture. This deeply complicated, frequently monstrous, yet oddly sympathetic antihero was one of the great characters in television history, and as most of the show's viewers had no previous recognition or understanding of James Gandolfini, the actor and the character fused into one.

For a time, that was how he liked it. When the show took off, he decided that press overexposure of James Gandolfini would make the audience less likely to believe him as Tony Soprano; he wanted them to focus on the character, not the actor. But after a time, it became clear that he just didn't like sitting for interviews and profiles. "I'm not trying to be difficult," he said in a rare one, with the *Newark Star-Ledger*'s Matt Zoller Seitz. "It's not that I'm afraid to reveal personal stuff. . . . It's just that I really, genuinely don't see why people would find that sort of thing so interesting."

So if James Gandolfini wasn't Tony Soprano, then . . . who was he?

IT'S THE MOST BASIC QUESTION a biographer must ask, and one that Gandolfini, in his lifetime (and, somehow, after it), didn't make easy to answer. His all-out resistance to interviews softened somewhat in the post-*Sopranos* years, in which he realized that the anti-Tony roles he desired were mostly found in meaningful but low-budget indie films, so his personal press availabilities helped to get the work seen. But he still gave precious few in-depth, long-form interviews—an *Esquire* profile here, a sit-down for *Inside the Actors Studio* there—and the people he worked with kept a code of silence around their patriarch that rivaled that of the crime family they portrayed.

His friends remain fiercely protective; to give just one example, *Sopranos* co-star Steve Schirripa began our interview by demanding, "Now, this ain't a hatchet piece, is it?" The subject's surviving family politely declined to participate in this biography, or did not respond to requests to do so. His son, Michael, thanked me for assembling several of these interviews, in their embryonic form, for a *Vanity Fair* tribute on the tenth anniversary of Gandolfini's death, while emphasizing that his father would have appreciated the piece "because it focused on the work" (though that was not, in fact, the primary focus). His widow, Deborah, explicitly instructed one longtime friend who had worked with Gandolfini late in his career to answer only my questions about their professional relationship ("she would prefer I respect that Jim always kept personal stuff private," he explained).

In both cases, the attempt to compartmentalize the actor and his work, the art and the artist, is as ill-advised as it is impossible. Those who worked with Gandolfini remember him fondly not because of the brilliance of his acting (or at least not solely), but because of his personal and professional grace. "He was everything," Joe Pantoliano says, "pragmatic and hardworking, and he devoured life." Viewers who find his performance as Tony Soprano spellbinding are often doubly impressed to discover how far removed he was from the character—that in real life, he was a soft-spoken, kindhearted, genuinely modest average Joe. "He would say to me, before the season, 'Let's go down to Little Italy, have dinner,'" Schirripa recalls.

"'I want to just be around, kind of get the feel of things again, you know.' Jim was not Tony Soprano. He was a Birkenstock-wearing, music-loving guy. He was kind of a hippie. He was not that guy *at all*." And so a curious viewer might want to know how such a teddy bear created such a monster, and how his warm personality may have contributed to the otherwise inexplicable affection they feel toward this amoral gangster.

Yet it's also difficult to know who James Gandolfini really was because, like many complicated men of a certain age, he was different things to different people. Some didn't even know him by the same name. "It's funny because you can tell when somebody met him by what they call him," explains his longtime acting partner and coach, Susan Aston. "When I met him, he was James, and he didn't start going by Jim till later." Throughout his fifty-one years, he was known by a variety of monikers, in varying circles of friends, family, and collaborators—Jamie, Bucky, James, Jimmy, Jim—his rotation of affectionate nicknames a handy symbol of his ability to shed and shift skins while remaining, all the while, the same shy kid from Jersey underneath. Crossovers could get confusing. "One of my best friends is Aida Turturro," says Gandolfini's high school classmate Karen Duffy, "and she was doing *Streetcar*, and she kept telling me about James. And then when I saw it, I was like, 'Ooooh, OK'—I didn't put it together, that *her* James was *my* Jimmy. Or my other friend Vince, we worked together as oyster shuckers, and he was roommates with a guy named Bucky who also was from New Jersey. And I was like, 'Yep, don't know a Bucky.'" Gandolfini's eventual (and, it seems, preferred) nomenclature of "Jim" became known outside of his orbit during the run of *The Sopranos*, when any scrap of information was welcomed and scrutinized.

Jim.

Jim.

It seemed so uncharacteristic, so entirely at odds with the man on our televisions week after week; Jim was your milquetoast uncle, your rec center volleyball coach, your best friend's dad who wore those awful tube socks with loafers. This man on HBO every Sunday, this king of crime, dressed to the nines, puffing on a Cuban, making men quake in their boots with a word or merely an impatient glance—that was not a *Jim.*

But it was. And as he embarked on a life and career beyond that iconic character, James Gandolfini was faced with something actors must often conquer: an identity crisis. He wanted to play characters who were as divergent from Tony as he was (and when he did play criminals after, they would pointedly not recall Tony Soprano; if anything, they would subvert the image of power and cool he'd defined in that role).

And so, to understand Jim, one must first grapple with the gulf between Jim and Tony—and how its depth and breadth were often variable.

THE SAINTHOOD OF JAMES GANDOLFINI began almost immediately after his death. Two days hence, Schirripa penned a heartfelt testimonial in the *New York Post*, telling (among other tidbits) the story of how, after a bitter and public salary renegotiation with HBO, Jim wrote giant checks sharing the raise with several of his co-stars. It became a key piece of Gandolfini lore, and a quintessential Jim story: an act of jaw-dropping generosity, done without fanfare, and to be kept between the giver and the receiver (if not in total anonymity). In the passing years, similar stories would surface, bound by the common thread of Gandolfini's kindness, consideration, and modesty.

In the dozens of interviews conducted for this book, I would hear these stories and more, tales of actorly camaraderie, friendly encouragement, and financial munificence. But the portrait of Jim Gandolfini as selfless martyr is as simplistic and unrealistic as that of Jim Gandolfini as Tony Soprano. As I spoke to additional friends and collaborators, a more complicated portrait emerged, of a man whose personal magnanimity often coexisted uneasily with professional selfishness, and whose (to borrow the most oft-intoned term) "demons" resulted in a recklessness that sometimes frightened those around him.

He was not simply one thing or another—neither a saint nor a sinner, but a *guy*, an uncommonly talented, undeniably complex, warm, self-lacerating, accommodating, short-fused, charitable, working-class, free-spending, hard-drinking, hard-partying, hardworking, hard-living twenty-first-century man. "He was a searcher, really," said *Sopranos* creator David Chase. "Whatever the opposite of bullshit is, that's what I think Jim Gandolfini was searching for."

CHAPTER 1

FINI

HIS SEARCH BEGAN IN NEW JERSEY.

To be more accurate, it started in Jersey, since nobody who spent any time there or knew a damn thing about the place used the "New." Tony Soprano is perhaps the fictional character most identified with Jersey; James Gandolfini is likely the real person second-most associated with the Garden State, behind only Bruce (whose last name is as unnecessary to its denizens as the aforementioned "New").

And to be more precise, his journey started in Westwood, a New York City suburb located in nearby Bergen County, with a population just over nine thousand, per the 1960 census. James Joseph Gandolfini Jr. appeared the following year, on September 18. His father, James Sr., was forty; his mother, Santa Gandolfini (née Penna) was thirty-seven. Both had strong roots in the old country. "My father was born in Italy, in a place called Borgotaro," according to Jim, "and then when he was two or three, he came here. My mother was born in America and moved back to Italy when she was six months old, and then came back when she was about twenty."

James the elder was living with his family on 64th Street in Brooklyn when he registered for the draft at age twenty-one; the registrar noted his height as 5 feet 8 1/2 inches tall and his weight as 151 pounds, and under "other obvious physical characteristics that will aid in identification," he noted, "Nose broken at one time." He served in World War II—fighting, in a peculiar twist of fate, against Italy—and received a Purple Heart, then came to Jersey after the war to find work. "In his youth he was a bricklayer who helped build Shea Stadium," his son said in 2009, still beaming with pride. When the senior Gandolfini got too old to work construction, he became head custodian of Paramus Catholic High School, where yearbook photos reveal a thin, stern-looking man who would pass on to his son a notably receding hairline. "He talked about 'the War' late in life," Jim said. "There was so much I didn't know. You can have a vision of your father, but it can never be complete. He's not just the guy who drove me around when I was a kid, and yelled at me for not doing yard work."

Santa was the cafeteria manager over at Immaculate Heart Academy in nearby Washington Township, New Jersey. She's seen in the school's 1971 yearbook holding a bowl of ingredients, her dark hair piled in a bun atop her head, her full and smiling face undeniably foreshadowing that of her son. The photo is captioned: "'Mama Mia, that's a spicy meatball,' teases Mrs. Gandolfini."

The family took to calling the younger James "Jamie," which was his nickname of choice until high school; his sisters continued to refer to him as such throughout the rest of his life. Johanna Gandolfini (later Antonacci) was thirteen years his senior, while Leta Gandolfini was ten years older than Jamie, who was the baby of the family and frequent center of attention.

At home, James Sr. and Santa mostly spoke English, saving Italian for "when they didn't want us to know what they were talking about," Jim recalled. "So they didn't teach it to my sisters or myself." His parents' Italian roots were a strong component of his childhood, however: "I didn't know anything else, so I can't really compare it. I mean, you know, the big Thanksgiving dinners, the big Christmas dinners, Italian food." His old man loved to play music from the old country, what his son would call "a lot of like, *da da da da, da da, da da da*, stuff like that. My father used to wear sandals with black socks and shorts, and these boxer pants that went up to here, no shirt, and a hat. And he would put the tarantella on and go out and cut the grass. The speakers would be outside. My mother's horror . . . was pretty good."

Jamie would recall his "most Italian quality" as "loyalty to friends and family, I think. I guess you'd have to ask them. Stubbornness. I don't know. I think I'm very Italian. I communicate a little bit through yelling. A lot of our family does that. I've been working on that." From his father, he inherited a quick temper: "I yell when I can't put shit together. When you've got to screw little fucking screws into little things, like putting a table together. I start screaming, 'This fucking crap . . . this shit . . . fucking Japanese shit. . . .' Like that." He made this confession in 2004, long past the point when he could afford to hire out this sort of busy work; it was more of a haunted memory. "I used to have to put Ikea furniture together when we were first married and had the baby," he recalled. "All that Ikea shit. I used to swear and yell. So occasionally I'll have that Italian fucking fit. Which is funny. I mean, I've had some good laughs at my father's fits. But then, some ain't so funny."

One thing Jamie didn't inherit from James Sr. was respect for money. "There were things I did that drove my father nuts, I know." He laughed. "Lying on the couch and then getting up, and 35 cents would have fallen out of my pocket and just be lying there on the cushions. Drove him crazy. He said it showed I had no respect for money. Maybe I didn't. Maybe I still don't. Or me taking forever in the shower, leaving water all over the floor. Not turning off the lights when I left the room. . . .

"Look, our parents, that generation, the Depression, the war, they had really tough lives, a lot tougher than ours were."

His mother was "introspective, depressed, a little judgmental, kind of smart about people," qualities he'd say he inherited. "My mother had an opinion about everything, man," he'd say. "She came from old-school Italian [culture], where you sum up somebody in about five seconds. They walk in the door, they're summed up, and that is it. . . . Doesn't matter what he does or what he says. It's, 'Look at the shoes.'"

The family had landed in Westwood as part of a working-class migration from Newark to the suburbs in the 1950s. When Jamie was entering grade school, the family moved again, to the slightly smaller (just shy of 6,400 residents in the 1960 census) borough of Park Ridge. "Park Ridge, New Jersey, is a great little town," says Elizabeth Forsyth, a classmate whose family were neighbors to the Gandolfinis. "I like to refer to it as Mayberry." If you're looking for a more contemporary pop-culture comparison, Park Ridge today is something akin to Stars Hollow on *Gilmore Girls*—a cozy, homey, tree-lined suburban community of wide streets, friendly neighbors, and comfortable homes.

"It's somewhat of a commuter town," says Karen Duffy, who graduated from Park Ridge High School with Jim's class of 1979 and went on to a career as a model, actress, writer, and MTV personality. "When we were there in the '70s it was, I would say, a more scrappy, blue-collar community. There's an immense amount of pride from being from Park Ridge, because it's essentially like two miles square. That's what my mother would always say, as she'd make us walk back from swim team practice." (Duffy and Gandolfini aren't the only celebrities associated with the area. "Richard Nixon and his wife, Pat, were not accepted at any co-ops in New York," Duffy says, "so they moved into the Bears Nest," a Park Ridge town house community, in 1991.)

The family fit right in, making lifelong friends in town and at Our Lady of Mercy Roman Catholic Church, where they attended mass. "I think the thing about New Jersey is you have a lot of regular people doing regular jobs," Jim explained. "There are a few rich places, rich enclaves, and half an hour away, you have the greatest city in the world. But it's basically a middle-class, working-class state, so you have normalcy, that foundation of a regular outlook on life. That's why a lot of people who come out of New Jersey are successful, you know, they can look at things from a lot of different ways. I think it's an exceptional place to grow up. But then I'm totally, completely biased."

Forsyth, whose family home was near the Gandolfini residence at 251 Park Avenue, remembers him as an energetic, playful kid. "Jimmy and my brothers of the neighborhood gang, myself included, dug a hole on the side of my mom's property that could have probably gotten us to China. It was that deep. And the guys, they had all these little army men that they played [with] for hours and hours and hours in there." The Gandolfinis were a "very traditional Italian household," one of many in the neighborhood, she said. "We would play in the backyard while his dad mowed the lawn, and his dad gardened a lot. I always remember his dad being out in the yard tooling around. . . . We didn't play inside a lot in those days. So I didn't have a lot of interaction with his mom, but we had a lot of interaction with his dad because his dad was always outside."

Before Tony Soprano, the town was best known as the home of Mittag & Volger, the world's largest producer of carbon paper and typewriter ribbons. In 2002, after *The Sopranos* had made a star of Park Ridge's favorite son, the *New York Times* sent community reporter Patricia Winters Lauro to report on his Jersey roots. "Not that much has changed in Park Ridge since Mr. Gandolfini's youth," she wrote. "When he was growing up in the 1970s, the misspent youths of most teenagers here unfolded at Pop's Sweet Shop, the local hangout, next to the high school at the end of Park Avenue. Today, they still hang out there, but Pop's is now Marc's Pizza."

"Were you a well-behaved kid?" James Lipton asked Gandolfini in 2004.

"Up to a point," he said, shrugging. And what point was that? "High school," Gandolfini replied, with a smirk.

That smirk became one of his defining features at Park Ridge High. "When you're all in a room together and stuff's going down, he was always the quiet one in the corner," Forsyth explains, "but he got it. You know what I mean? You could look around and he'd have that smirk on his face. He got it and he was just gonna watch it. . . . I don't think Jimmy's

Young "Fini," as seen in the Park Ridge High yearbook, circa 1979.
(Courtesy Ann Camarto.)

personality changed at all. I remember Jimmy as being a very even-toned person. I don't ever really remember him getting mad, or being involved in any of the drama. Or actually even being involved in any of the trouble."

Teacher Ann Comarato agrees: "He had a great group of friends, a lovely family, hardworking parents." But school was sometimes a struggle. "Jim definitely had an issue with his attention span," says his longtime friend Tom Richardson. "Being able to focus on things might not have been his strong suit. But he definitely was a very good student at Rutgers and a very good student in high school. So whatever abilities he had to mask it, he did a good job as far as I was concerned—I always found him to be superintelligent. But could he be ADHD, had he been born in 1990 instead of born in 1961? Yeah."

Jimmy was less interested in academics than athletics—tall and graceful, and still slender, he kept a busy extracurricular schedule as a freshman, playing basketball, football, and baseball. "At Park Ridge he could play, and do well," recalled assistant football coach Tom Bauer. "He was an all-round athlete, but not really a standout." He would eventually get more realistic about the demands on his free time, dropping baseball after freshman year, and then football, so that he could focus on basketball, his strongest sport.

Chris Schneider and Jim Gandolfini on the defensive.*

Left to Right. First Row: Coach Livathares, J. Zderko, M. Santoro, J. De Lorenzo. Second Row: D. Morgan, C. Schneider, C. Grande, B. Brill. Third Row: J. Zuber, J. Gandolfini, C. Schneider, J. Solarino.

The young sportsman. (Courtesy Ann Camarto.)

A 1979 senior yearbook photo captures Jim—or "Fini," as he had been nicknamed by then, a shortening of his surname—in action, caught in a midair leap while playing defense. Wearing number 45 for the Park Ridge Owls, long arms extended, his face a picture of focused intensity, the lanky senior looks every inch the high school jock. Elsewhere in the yearbook, he's frequently seen with female classmates, and he's one of two students awarded "Class Flirt." He looks the part: His long brown hair, feathered in the distinctive late '70s style, recalls the coiffure that Tony Manero (Gandolfini's future co-star John Travolta) defends so zealously in *Saturday Night Fever.*

But whatever success he found with the ladies, he didn't let it go to his head. "He wasn't a showboat," Duffy notes. "He wasn't a ham in high school, ever. That's not a part of his DNA. . . . I would say, as he matured from the boy to the man he carried with him, I think, our small-town ethics." There were, however, ample opportunities to ham and showboat: In addition to his athletics and flirting, Jim had started acting.

HE'D ALWAYS LIKED GOING TO the movies. "John Wayne," he said, simply, to the *Newark Star-Ledger*'s Matt Zoller Seitz. "You can't go wrong with John Wayne." He told James Lipton, "The first thing I remember seeing and registering was *West Side Story* as a kid. For some reason, when I saw that, I went, *wow.*"

As he grew older, his tastes grew more expansive. "*Mean Streets* is one of the things that I saw ten times, like in a row, I just sat there," he recalled. "I just thought it was great. Everything about it. That was the first movie—that, and movies that affected me seem to have something to do with Robert Redford. *Jeremiah Johnson*, I thought, was an incredible movie. *Ordinary People.* Those movies I remember when I was young."

At Park Ridge High, "we had a small theater with a great theater program," Duffy recalls. Jimmy had done plays as a kid, mostly on a lark, nothing serious. But in the spring of his junior year, he auditioned for the school's production of the musical *Can-Can.* "A couple of his friends were auditioning, and they'd been in the theater program since freshman year," says drama teacher Ann Comarato. "*It's a lot of fun rehearsals*, et cetera, et cetera. So I think he thought, *OK, I'll give this a try.* Terrific. Thank God for us he did. . . . My student director and I looked at one another and said, *Where has he been?*" He played a small role in that production, and enjoyed himself enough to go out for *Arsenic and Old Lace* in the fall of his senior year.

"Most of the kids held their script in their hand," Comarato says of that audition. "He came in and had it all memorized. His delivery, voice, body, movement—he just nailed it. And it was like he wasn't doing anything but having real-life conversation." Comarato cast him in the supporting role of Jonathan, the evil brother, "kind of a prelude to *Sopranos*. But he was great. Oh my God, he just blew us away. And he fell in love with it."

"He had a natural knack," says classmate Susan Coughlin, who says his work onstage increased his confidence elsewhere. "He was already a good athlete and everything," she says, "but interpersonally, I think he expanded in those years."

Near the end of his senior year, Jimmy was cast in the school's spring musical, *Kiss Me, Kate*. "Once again, he nailed his audition," Comarato says. "He could do drama, he could do comedy, his delivery was so natural." He landed the show's male lead, a dual role, playing both Fred Graham, the director-producer-star of a production of Shakespeare's *The Taming of the Shrew*, and Graham acting as Petruchio in the show-within-the-show. The character dances, sings Cole Porter songs, and recites pages of dialogue, more than Jim had ever done.

Young Jimmy's first forays into the spotlight.
(Courtesy Ann Camarto.)

The memorization became a problem. He would struggle through rehearsals, groping for his lines, berating himself, an act of self-laceration that would linger throughout his career. "It was almost as if, *I'm gonna do this, I'm gonna do it the best way possible*," Comarato explains, "and then if he wasn't happy with that, he would just keep doing it and changing it until it's all right. And that's kind of hard to do sometimes, when you're just starting out, to know *this is what counts*. With filming, you can always do separate takes, but when he was onstage it was a one-shot deal. And that was it. Had to be perfect."

Two weeks out, and he still wasn't off book. In frustration, he would bark profanities when he couldn't recall his lines. ("I think he got detention once for saying the f-word during rehearsal," Comarato says, laughing. "Then when he got *Sopranos*, we were at a bar talking and he said, 'I'm doing this new show, I want to count how many times I say the f-word. And then I'm gonna tell you what they're paying me.'") The show's musical director threatened to call off the production entirely if the young star couldn't get his lines and songs memorized. Faced with a hard deadline (and afraid of letting down his friends and colleagues), he reported to rehearsal the next day with his lines down cold. This, too, would become a recurring pattern in his life as an actor.

Once he got over his nerves and learned the lines, the show was a smashing success. His friends were supportive of his theatrical endeavors—no matter what it took. The school drama department would mount special performances at the town's senior center, "so my friend and I got dressed up in gray wigs, and we got walkers, and we dressed up to get in," Duffy recalls. "We felt that we were *seniors*, we could probably pull this off. And we absolutely got in, and I just remember sitting there with Debbie Marone, two seventeen-year-olds dressed up to try and look like we were in our eighties. And we drew varicose veins on our legs with blue markers. I just remember him having a laugh."

His adventures in theater were the highlight of Jim's senior year, and he said as much in his inscription to Comarato in the 1979 Park Ridge High yearbook. "Thanks," he wrote. "That just about sums it all up. You've helped me through many bad times, and with me that takes a lot of doing. I'm a pain in the ass and I need someone to keep my butt in line. Thanks for the good times and the help. When I'm a rich actor (*sure*), I'll come visit you. Thanks. Love, Fini."

CHAPTER 2

BUCKY

AS MUCH AS JIM ENJOYED himself onstage, he treated acting purely as a hobby, a high school distraction. Show business, he wryly explained, "wasn't something my family generally did." While he received one of the 162 diplomas handed out at the Park Ridge High School graduation on June 20, 1979, and won an "outstanding achievement award" at the school's Senior Award Program a few nights earlier, he deemed his academic performance at Park Ridge High "not great." But that didn't matter much in terms of where he was going next.

"I basically went to college because I was the first male Italian born in America" in his family, he recalled, so "I was *going* to college." Santa was especially insistent on this point, pushing him to apply to Rutgers, where his sisters, Johanna and Leta, had matriculated. "My mother . . . beat it into me that *I was going, I was going, I was going*," he explained, "and I got into Rutgers, and the first night they had a five-keg party there. And I said, 'What was I fighting about? The *school* put out a five-keg party.' I was like, you've got to be kidding me."

He enrolled as a communications major—"Whatever that is, I had no idea what I was doing"—and soon realized that free beer wasn't the only virtue of the sprawling flagship campus in New Brunswick. "I got there, and I thought, *Jeez, fifty thousand eighteen-year-olds in one place—what the hell was I complaining about? This is great.* I was around a lot of fun people and I had a ball. I had more fun than somebody probably should have and I learned a lot, although I don't think I remember anything from Communications." (As if to prove the point, asked for his major in an interview shortly before *The Sopranos* debuted, he replied, "I don't remember.") Jim settled into college life, and several of the friends he made at Rutgers would remain close for life (including Tom Richardson, later project manager for Jim's production company, Attaboy Films). With them, he took on yet another identity; at Rutgers, he was known as "Buck"—or, on more affectionate occasions, "Bucky."

He received his first bit of university press coverage as a freshman, in a searing exposé in the *Rutgers Daily Targum* on a broken plate glass window. "Rutgers College freshman James Gandolfini, a resident of Tinsley, was in the area when the slingshot was fired," reported the *Targum*'s Paul Savage. "'It seemed the whole thing started out as a joke,' he said, 'and no harm was intended.'" After freshman year, Buck moved out of Tinsley Hall and into his first real, adult digs: the Birchwood Terrace Apartments on Hamilton Street, still close to campus but offering some separation and privacy to party with his guys. "They were crazy," recalls college friend and future journalist T. J. Foderaro. "There was always a bag of pot laying out on the coffee table." But what was most striking to Foderaro was the bond that was already in place between Bucky and his longtime compadres. "He was an excellent friend," Foderaro says. "And he was loyal to the people that were loyal to him. Extremely loyal."

In the meantime, he'd taken up with his first serious college girlfriend. Lynn Marie Jacobson was a waitress at a campus bar where he'd bounced and bartended, and they'd become friendly there, though she was a couple of years older. She began spending more and more time at Jim's place; they dated through his sophomore and junior years. "She was a smart, lovely girl who worked two jobs to get her way through college and to help her family," Jim said. After Lynn graduated in 1981, she worked days in Manhattan. But she earned extra money working nights at the Manor, a catering hall and restaurant in West Orange, New Jersey.

Lynn was driving back to her family home in Caldwell after one of those late shifts, just blocks from their house on Bloomfield Avenue, when her 1971 Mustang crossed the center line and hit a utility pole. The impact cut the car in two, killing Lynn instantly. She was twenty-two.

"I went to college, and then this girl I knew died," Gandolfini said, almost offhandedly, in a 2004 interview, quickly adding, "Let's not make a big deal out of that." But it was certainly a big deal to him at the time. Foderaro first met him not long after Lynn passed, when they were both hired as bartenders at Ryan's, one of New Brunswick's newer and fancier restaurants and bars. "That hugely affected the color of his life for at least a few years," Foderaro says. "We frequently would leave Ryan's at one or two in the morning, and then we would have some beer or smoke some pot and hang out, party with his friends—or just the two of us." Once he was in private, and had relaxed with the help of a beer or a joint, Buck would open up. "One hundred percent, he was depressed," according to Foderaro. "He'd take a hit of a bong and sit there kind of hulking over and look up at me with these eyes, these eyes that basically said, *this is all so fucked up*, you know, *the meaning of life is just so fucked up*. You can just tell, as an artist, how sensitive he is as a person. He's so intensely sensitive. And yeah, he really took that hard."

Behind the bar at Ryan's, however, Buck put on a different mask. "We were the bartenders, and the bar was at the center of this vast room," Foderaro explains. "We were kind of onstage every night. And Jim has *always* had such a magnetism. Like, it was completely clear to me, when I looked down the bar, that all the women were looking at Jim, not at me." Foderaro was impressed with Gandolfini's skill at slinging drinks—"He was very quick with his hands, very quick on his feet, could cover a bar quickly, could make drinks quickly"—but more at his ability to connect with this audience of customers. "If he handed somebody a drink, he'd look them in the eye," Foderaro says. "And with his gleam in his eye, he would invariably elicit a smile—especially if it was a pretty young woman. Very magnetic. Just kind of oozed."

"He was always interested in people and always interested in what they had to say, and their point of view," confirms Tom Richardson. "If he was at the bar and somebody was there and they wanted to talk, he would talk—find out what they were up to, just asking questions and listening. He had that kind of a gaze. When he fixed that gaze on you, you felt like you're the only person in the world and you could open up to him."

After hours, Gandolfini and Foderaro bonded over more refined pursuits. The latter was "a kind of a literature/philosophy major," he recalls, and was thus the first of Buck's group of friends with whom he could discuss these big ideas. "Most of his other friends were business majors and, you know, hardcore burnouts," Foderaro says, with a laugh. "We ended up talking a lot, about poetry, history, philosophy, literature." One night, Foderaro brought in a copy of Allen Ginsberg's *Howl*: "I thought he would appreciate the whole Beat aesthetic." As Ryan's was closing for the night, the friends began reading passages from the book to each other, turning a staircase near the bar into a makeshift stage. "We ended up taking turns, and maybe a few others, standing up in the staircase and reading *Howl* to the other people who were still left in the bar," Foderaro says. "He loved that kind of thing. Because that's not something he was doing regularly at the time."

But that was about to change. "At the time I met him," Foderaro says, "he was already thinking, *Why the hell am I studying marketing or communications, because what I really want to do is act*." The bug had not left him; he had merely put it aside, presumably to fulfill his parents' wishes for his time at Rutgers, gaining a general education and working toward a degree in a marketable skill. But Lynn's death shuffled his priorities. "That changed me a lot," Gandolfini confessed, in 2004. "Before that I don't know what I would have done."

He'd said as much the first time he spoke publicly about her passing. A year earlier, when he won his third Emmy, he told the audience, "I'd like to dedicate this to the memory of a girl I knew a long time ago who basically, inadvert— . . . I can't say that word. She made me want to be an actor. Her name was Lynn Jacobson, and I miss her very much."

She made me want to be an actor.

Jim hadn't acted at Rutgers, which was odd, as he had time on his hands, and the university boasted a robust theater program. "I dabbled a little bit in acting in high school, and then I forgot about it completely," he would later explain, which feels . . . oversimplified. He still talked about acting; "Even then, Jim Gandolfini wanted to be an actor and made sure everybody knew it," his friend Mark Di Ionno wrote. But he didn't audition for any school productions. He took, as far as anyone could tell, a single, solitary shot at acting during his four years as an undergrad, an audition for a summer stock company at the University of North Carolina at Chapel Hill, several hours' drive from New Brunswick. "And he failed. He failed miserably," according to Di Ionno. "I remember driving home, he was angry with himself. He felt he'd been unprepared, that he'd given the thing no thought about what he might be asked to do, or something. And he was just very upset that he'd done that." Years later, Di Ionno wrote, he reminded Gandolfini of that day while visiting him on the set of *The Sopranos*. "I didn't know what I was doing then," Jim told his old friend. "Not that I know what I'm doing now."

She made me want to be an actor.

"I do think that the death of his girlfriend set him off and back," Foderaro surmises. "And he definitely, for a couple of years there, he kind of oozed, you know, *life is full of shit, life sucks, people are full of shit*. And I don't think he really felt like participating in *anything*, other than getting high and hanging out and dropping out a little bit. So I think that was part of it."

She made me want to be an actor.

"It didn't make much sense," Jim said of her death, that one time he opened up about it. "It made me very angry." And that anger changed him—his perspective on who he was, what he was doing, what he wanted his life to be. "I think I was studying advertising or something before that, and after that I changed a little bit," he reflected. "I think I might not have done what I've done. I don't know what I'd have done. I think it definitely pushed me in this direction. I don't know why. Just as a way to get out some of those feelings. I don't know."

He certainly didn't understand it at the time. "In a way, I'm only realizing now how much it affected me," he said. "I think I'm calming down now from the anger and being able to look back at it. It still affects me." In that interview, Jim hesitated to make her death about him: "I don't want this to come across as 'poor me' or anything. The tragedy of it is her—what a lovely, lovely person she was—not how it affected me. I just need to say that." But the idea of doing something safe (be it communications or marketing or journalism, the degree on his final transcript) now seemed unthinkable. "If anything, it was, 'Why plan for the future? Fuck it,'" he explained. "It was like, 'Fuck this.'"

And with that, he knew, even if he couldn't admit it to himself (and certainly not to his family) just yet. He was going to finish his degree, sure. But then he would move to New York, and become an actor. Time to stop fucking around.

CHAPTER 3

MITCH

IT TOOK FOUR YEARS FROM his move to New York for James Gandolfini to make it into the paper of record, the *New York Times*—though he first appeared not in the pages of the arts section, but in a column about real estate trends. THE APARTMENT GYPSIES OF MANHATTAN ran on May 29, 1988, detailing how young, starry-eyed New Yorkers were engaging in apartment-sharing, sublets, unconventional roommate arrangements, and the like in order to afford living in the City on a limited budget. Some complain, but "Jim Gandolfini," wrote Lisa W. Foderaro, "seems to thrive on the apartment-hopping life. Since moving to New York City four years ago, Mr. Gandolfini, 26 years old, has never had his name on a lease, never paid more than $400 a month in rent and never lived in one place more than 10 months. His wanderer's existence has given him sojourns, some as brief as two months, in Hoboken, N.J.; Astoria, Queens; Clinton and the Upper West Side of Manhattan, and Park Slope and Flatbush in Brooklyn."

Foderaro—whom Jim had briefly dated, following an introduction from her brother, his fellow Ryan's bartender and Rutgers pal T. J.—quoted Jim about his transient lifestyle: "'Moving, to me, is no big deal,' said Mr. Gandolfini, whose calling is the theater but whose living comes mostly from bartending and construction. 'I have a system down. I throw everything in plastic garbage bags and can be situated in my new place in minutes. Without my name on a lease, I'm in and out. I have no responsibilities.'"

Those two paragraphs paint a concise but accurate picture of Jim's early days as a nomadic New York actor. He continued to pay the bills by working in hospitality; his first job in the city was at a fancy wine bar on the Upper East Side (one of the city's few, at that time). T. J. Foderaro had set it up for him—he was vacating the position to manage a restaurant back in Jersey, so his boss had asked him to recommend a replacement.

"He didn't know a lot about wine going in," Foderaro says, "but he quickly learned, and everybody loved him." From there, he answered an ad for a job at Private Eyes, a nightclub over on West 21st Street between Fifth and Sixth Avenues. It opened in the summer of 1984 and quickly became a hotspot, known not only for its upscale clientele and pumping dance music but for the bank of thirty-four video monitors that *New York* magazine described as "like a department store television section, except that at Private Eyes you can have a beer and you can't change the channel."

"It was the first nightclub that had videos," Jim recalled. "The Cars. Duran Duran." Five months after the club opened, Madonna held her *Like a Virgin* album release party at Private Eyes, with Andy Warhol and Jean-Michel Basquiat among the guest list; Jim wasn't yet famous, but he was rubbing elbows with people who were. Foderaro remembers that Gandolfini was originally hired as a bartender ("he might have literally been running ice or something") but, in a comically short time, was managing the entire club. "That speaks volumes about who he was, and the influence he had on people," Foderaro notes. "The way this kid, who'd been in the city a matter of months . . . in very short order, is running the place. I remember going in there, and people were just all over him. Jim was an excellent manager, in terms of just his interpersonal skills, always treating people with respect, but just . . . he was in charge."

Being "in charge" of a club like Private Eyes could mean any number of things, from dealing with employee schedules to procuring a few toots of Colombian Dancing Dust for VIPs. "I was way too young," Jim said, laughing, "but I tried to act like I knew what I was doing, and I had no fucking clue." He faked it till he could make it, sometimes with laughable results; he panicked while placing orders for his first weekend and ordered enough beer for six months. "I was pretty miserable at it." He laughed. "But I was learning a lot and experiencing a lot."

He would come to reflect on his time at Private Eyes as vital to his future endeavors. "I got a lot of great research stored up here from those years managing a nightclub," he told James Lipton. "The club was straight two nights a week, gay two nights a week, and kind of everything else two nights a week. So I spent a few years just watching people, just in amazement. And saw a lot of interesting things that I stored up for later."

At the moment, though, he was mostly just having a good time. "I got drunk, I got laid, I had fun," he said. "I saw a lot of stuff and didn't have to wake up at six-thirty in the morning." Foderaro concurs. "When I visited him, there were a number of nights where large amounts of cocaine were going on everywhere," he says. "Jim and I were participating in that, for sure. A lot of drinking, very late nights, they might have stayed open till three in the morning, and Jim would be there till four or five in the morning. But even then, I never felt that he was doing anything more than everybody was doing in the early '80s."

Jim tried to keep his eye on the ball—he'd come to New York to be an actor, after all, not a nightclub manager. Back at Rutgers, Foderaro had introduced Jim to Roger Bart, who was studying acting in the university's Mason Gross School of the Arts. "I looked at him, and I talked to him, and I thought, 'He's such a great type,'" Bart recalled years later. "He was this interesting, deep, funny, sweet, and gentle giant. Even when I met him, at twenty-three, he was sort of twenty-three going on forty-five." After Jim had been in New York for a couple of years, he and Bart reconnected; the actor recommended that Jim try working with a teacher he'd studied under at Rutgers who was now running a conservatory program in Manhattan. Her name was Kathryn Gately.

Bart had his work cut out for him. Gandolfini was reluctant—"I'd talked about taking acting classes, but it wasn't really something anyone in my family ever did," he explained, "and he kept pestering me to go to this class"—and Gately did not typically work with actors as inexperienced as Jim. After all, at that point, his entire résumé consisted of three high school plays and a blown summer stock audition. Bart pleaded with his teacher to at least meet him, and gave Jim her number to set it up. "He asked what no other student before or since has ever asked," Gately said. "He said he wanted to do the interview, but he wanted to do it over a good meal. So I trooped uptown to this restaurant that had white tablecloths and met this well-dressed young man, so tall, towering, I thought. And he conducted that interview. And the food was great. It really was. . . . It was like a presentation; he told me about everything, it was so Italian. He seemed to have so much dignity." She invited Jim to attend one of her classes.

"I went in," Jim recalled, "and I was scared to death. I was *shaking*." The work that day consisted of a simple physical action, miming the threading of a needle, but Jim's sudden case of the shakes made that task impossible. "I was so angry, and so nervous at the same time. And she kept making me go back up and try it." His natural inclination was to push back, or to get mad and walk away. But Gately knew how to push his buttons—"not *just* push buttons, but push buttons in a good way"—to take him new places, even if they were scary to him. "It really made me very nervous," he would later explain, "and I was shocked by that, really. So I ended up staying two years."

Initially, he struggled in Gately's class. "I had such anger back then," he recalled. "I guess, you know, when you're young, a lot of people do. Everybody does. You're pissed. And you're not sure why. . . . Because you want to express something, you don't know what it is." Because of that anger, and his own self-consciousness, he could never let himself go the way he needed to; he couldn't "make a fool of yourself, basically," so one day, in a two-person exercise, Gately encouraged Gandolfini's scene partner to push him.

"And I *destroyed* the place," he said. "Just all that crap they have onstage." By the end of his breakdown, his scene partner had fled, and he was alone on the stage, his hands bleeding. Gately broke the heavy silence by assuring him that it was OK. "See, everybody's fine," he remembered her telling him. "Nobody's hurt. This is what you have to do. This is what people pay for." Audiences weren't there to see "the guy next door," she explained; they wanted to see rage, heartache, tragedy, intensity, big emotions. He was capable of displaying those emotions; he just had to be able to control them. *That* was the key.

Gately had studied under, among others, the legendary acting teacher Sanford Meisner; she taught his version of "the Method," which he'd developed in his time at the Group Theatre alongside such other early Method practitioners as Stella Adler, Harold Clurman, and Lee Strasberg. Gandolfini was immediately taken by the tenets of the Meisner Method, and its emphasis on "listening and paying attention and looking at somebody and when they go, just going with them," he explained, tentatively. "If somebody you're working with is having difficulty? Say they have to get mad. I mean, I guess you've seen this before. Instead of using the line, say something else to them. You know, 'You piece of shit, you fuckin' piece of shit,' and they just go, and they get mad. You can use it sometimes, and then they'll react and it'll go from there. That's what I use a lot of the Meisner stuff for. I'll try to do different things and see what we can get."

Acting wasn't paying the bills yet, so Gandolfini bided his time between auditions, rehearsals, and performances with a series of odd jobs. The full-time, all-night gig at Private Eyes was incompatible with the life of an actor, so he picked up whatever he could make fit. "Waiter, bartender, bouncer, nightclub manager, street bookseller—all kinds of stuff," he recalled. "I planted trees. I delivered seltzer for a business that was owned by a Hasidic Jew I loved." Its name? "Gimme Seltzer," he said, laughing.

He spent those years doing "all kinds of crap, just get enough money to go out and fart around." He didn't want to take on anything serious, in case a steady acting gig came in. And then, finally, one did.

The American Drama Group Europe was formed in 1978 by Ohio native Grantly Marshall, based out of Munich, with a lofty goal: "to perform high quality theatre in as many countries in the world as possible." They cast actors out of New York, London, and Paris; after a successful tour of *One Flew over the Cuckoo's Nest* in 1986, the group was planning to tour Tennessee Williams's classic *A Streetcar Named Desire* in Scandinavia and Europe.

"We met on Theatre Row," recalls Robert Funaro, who would play Stanley Kowalski, the rough-edged leading role originated by Marlon Brando. "And he was like, standing in the doorway of the theater, and he's sweating. He's got a white shirt on, and I said, this has *got* to be Mitch."

"He originally auditioned for Stanley in *Streetcar*," explains Joanna Mulkern, who played Stella in the production. When director Judith Joseph proposed that Gandolfini read Mitch, "He was like, *I knew that was gonna happen*. I think he knew that he had this vulnerability, this softness, that even though he didn't look it, he gave it off." Mitch, Stanley's neighbor and friend, was played by Karl Malden in Elia Kazan's film version, and it was an ideal role for Gandolfini—a working-class, salt-of-the-earth type whose sensitivity and vulnerability are slowly revealed by the dramatic events of the narrative. Jim got the part.

"It really was my first professional job, as well as, I think, James's," Funaro says. "We got paid in deutsche marks." It would also be Jim's first trip abroad.

After a couple of weeks of rehearsal in New York, the company set off on the three-month tour, debuting on September 15, 1987, in Motala, Sweden. They were "a caravan of New York actors, weirdly doing Tennessee Williams in a very frigid climate in Scandinavia," Mulkern recalls. "Here we are doing, like, Tennessee Williams in Lapland. You can't get much further from New Orleans." The tour was something of a ramshackle affair, with a collapsible (and, eventually, deteriorating) set that the cast would take down and reassemble at each new venue. "We were like gypsy actors," Mulkern says. "It was an adventure!"

Indeed it was. *Streetcar* played more than thirty venues in Norway, Finland, and Sweden before the tour wrapped up on December 2, with the

James Gandolfini with co-star Robert Funaro on the Scandinavian *Streetcar* tour. (Courtesy Robert Funaro.)

actors often performing the lengthy and emotionally exhausting play twice a day, one matinee and one evening performance. It was a long way from Broadway—in both the showbiz hierarchy and a literal, geographic sense—but they had a blast. "I remember us having a break," Funaro recalls. "So we went to Denmark to Elsinore Castle, the castle of *Hamlet*. And to make a long story short, we go down, descend into one of the dungeons—we're taking the tour, and the tour guide leads us into one of these torture chamber dungeons." The guide explained the specifics of the chamber, which became a slowly shrinking space, trapping the subject in the corner.

Gandolfini looked in and nudged Funaro. "Well, Bob, come on, let's go," he insisted. "Let's go to the corner."

"Are you crazy?" Funaro replied. "The sign says don't cross the line!"

"Come on, what's going to happen?" And with that, Jim was over the ropes.

"We went to the very, very last little corner of that, and we experienced it, and then we left," Funaro says. "That's the best way I can describe him, in his work. . . . I think this is why James is such a great actor. People could tell you not to do something, and you don't do it. But he was one that wanted to experience it first, and *then* tell you if the fire was gonna burn your hand."

The *Streetcar* tour may have been small-time, but "we took it really seriously," Funaro notes. "I remember James being very, very unhappy with his performance, especially on tour. And it kind of seesawed until I remember one night, he finally 'got it' as Mitch, and he was so brilliant."

"He never lapsed in his effort to perfect his role," Mulkern confirms. "If he felt like he didn't do a great job, you could tell afterward. He was not in a great, great mood, no. He was incredibly instinctive, dedicated, and hard on himself, *really* hard on himself, if he didn't feel like he rose to the occasion of what Williams wrote."

Of course, some nights, the quality of the performance was out of even Jim's keen control. "He fell off the stage once," Mulkern says. "It was on his date with Blanche, when he's walking along the stage—these are always different stages, and the lights are dim, because it's coming home from a date."

"There was a ten-foot drop into the orchestra pit," Jim recalled. "When the lights went out, you were supposed to walk offstage. Well, I was on the end, and I walked straight off the edge of the stage into about twenty metal chairs. The noise was unbelievable." The rest of the cast heard the tumble, and a gasp from the audience, on the backstage intercoms; Jim came through

Jim on the Scandinavian *Streetcar* tour. (Courtesy Joanna Mulkern.)

the backstage area from the orchestra pit to make his way back onstage. "He was laughing," she says. "He thought it was funny. He thankfully didn't hurt himself too badly—I think he had a bruise or two."

His resilience wasn't all that impressed his co-stars. "He had, even at that young age, just this innate sense of people," Mulkern explains. "He could just *see* people, and that's, I think, why he evolved into such a great actor, was his instinct. But he worked really hard at it, as easy as it looked."

HIS CONFIDENCE IN HIS ABILITIES *somewhat* lifted, Gandolfini embarked on the bleakest ritual of the struggling New York actor: audition after audition, one after another, going up for roles he was never going to get, for directors who were never going to hire him. For a novice, it can be soul-crushing. Luckily, in 1988, Jim met a fellow actor who would become a trusted friend and collaborator for the rest of his life.

Susan Aston hailed from Texas, and retains her soft Southern accent to this day. Like Jim, she was a young actor looking for work and opportunities, but also doing her best to create both for herself. "I had a girlfriend that was casting a play at Theater for the New City," she recalls, "and Eric Roberts was in it, and she was in it, and she was looking for the third character. I was looking for somebody to be in this play called *Big El's Best Friend* that this theater company I was involved in was doing. And so I asked her if I could tag along to her auditions, and she said sure—she was staying at my apartment for free, so she couldn't much deny me. And so James came out and auditioned."

Aston was immediately taken by not only his talent but his taste. "He did a monologue from a play that I had just done in Dallas. I had just been in this Romulus Linney play called *Holy Ghosts*, and he came out and did a piece from it. And it's kind of kismet, that I love that play, and he came out and did it. He did a really good job on it, and he was a huge presence." Aston asked her friend if she wanted to cast him, "and she said no, he was all wrong for the part she was casting, which . . . I wouldn't agree with that now. When he left, I went out down the hall and introduced myself and gave him the script."

Jim summarized the one-act play *Big El's Best Friend* thus: "There's a woman who thinks she's in love with Elvis. So this impersonator comes in to tell her how horrible Elvis really was, to get her to fall out of love with him." He would play the Elvis impersonator, Aston was the woman obsessed with him, and Melissa Gilbert (late of *Little House on the Prairie*) was, in

Aston's words, "the other woman, the normal woman. . . . We did it a few weeks, you know, a Village thing." But Aston and Gandolfini had "real chemistry with each other," so they started looking for something else to work on together.

Tarantulas Dancing was, in his words, "about two people from the Lower East Side that are just—both of them are out of their minds. And I return to her apartment for an iron, and high jinks ensue from there." The play was something of a work in progress, developed, written, expanded, and performed for over two years, the actors collaborating with director Michael MacKenzie Wills and playwright Larry Myers, "a writer who saw us and, you know, latched on to the two actors in a tumultuous relationship," Aston explains. A November 1988 ad in *Back Stage* includes a photo of the playful stars, promoting the show's paired performances with another Myers-penned one-act, *Sexual Gravity*, at the Trocadero Theater Downstairs on Bleecker, with shows Tuesday to Thursday nights through mid-December. Tickets were $7 ($5 for students), with a one-drink minimum. "Sells Out!" warns the ad.

That might not have been entirely true—Aston notes that the drink minimum often meant that even their less cash-flush friends couldn't come to their shows—but at this point, that didn't matter much to Gandolfini. He was finally living the New York actor's life, and wasn't worried about audiences, or money, or much of anything else. "I think he got used to nice things," Aston says, "but he was happy in a very modest apartment with, you know, the same old brown leather jacket and jeans and T-shirts."

With time on their hands and enthusiasm to burn, Jim and Susan developed a process for character research and scene study that they would use for years to come. "We both were very much invested in our character's bios, writing them out. We did journaling," she explains. "You do research on the character. Of course, the first place you look to is the script, anything that's in the script, and then in terms of backstory, anything that would support that, that would strengthen your choices, that's what you do. Because what you're hoping is when you let go of all that, and walk out onto the stage . . . you'll have character thoughts instead of actor thoughts, when you're in the moment up there. And so the more seeds you planted, the more likely something is to sprout. We both were very much into that."

They also, like many young actors, spent a fair amount of time passionately discussing and analyzing their craft. "Neither of us were fundamentalist in the way we approached acting," she says. "It's whatever works that's not hurting you or somebody else. You don't want to be hurting yourself or risking hurting anybody else—and this goofy stuff people are doing today and calling it the Method just makes me want to puke, you know? My God." They were drawn to the Meisner Method specifically because of the "exercises that Meisner had created to help people *really* listen, to really be in contact, to have a strong need, to be able to isolate, and build obstacles into what they were doing, and to stay in the moment. And those are all really at the heart of any good acting."

Jim kept working, kept auditioning, and kept performing and expanding *Tarantulas Dancing* with Aston. "This is just, like, what people did in the late '80s, to be seen," she explains. "You had to do plays to get seen. I mean, we love plays. That's what we were both trained in, theater. But you know, they weren't anything that I'm sure anybody remembers." Jim took pains to keep himself grounded. Aston would recall their working together in one of those Village basement theaters in the '80s, on opposite sides of the stage during the preshow, waiting to go on, nervous. "I was trying to sequester myself," Aston recalls, "doing my acting thing, and he yelled over to me while the preshow music was blaring: 'Aston! What's the worst that can happen? We suck?!'"

This became one of her most cherished memories of that period. "You know, we're not doing brain surgery," she says with a laugh. "And we would remind each other of that a lot. On the set you can get so, *Oh man, we've got to get this right*, you know, *this is happening*, or some drama's going on. . . . And then we have to remember, we're not saving lives here. We're doing a fucking TV show. You have to remind yourself of that, because you're not allowed to fail in this country. You're not allowed to make a mess of things, but you *have to*, in the creative arts—you have to be able to make a mess.

"So, that's one of my favorite stories. 'What's the worst that can happen? We suck.'"

IN THE SUMMER OF 1989, Jim landed a role in a new play called *Doogan's*, written and directed by playwright Heather Holmberg. Set entirely in a bar over a single weekend, the play deals in the slice-of-life dramas of the establishment's staff and regulars. Gandolfini was cast as a cop who moonlights as a bouncer, and whose gruff exterior masks (shades of things to come) a soft center. The show ran for a month at the Walker St. Theatre (now the home of the SoHo Rep); in a review for *Back Stage*, critic David Sheward singled out "Jim Gandolfini" as "particularly good."

Jim was starting to form ideas about the kind of actor he wanted to be, and the sort of persona he could imagine as a movie star. "In the eighties, Mickey Rourke was the shit," he told Matt Zoller Seitz in 1999. "If you were a young guy who loved movies and wanted to be an actor and [were] seeing a lot of movies in the eighties, there was nobody better than Mickey Rourke. De Niro, Pacino, Dustin Hoffman, they were all great, don't get me wrong. But Mickey Rourke was the man. I wanted to be Mickey Rourke."

Seitz replied, "You wanted to be like Mickey Rourke?"

"No! I mean actually wanted to be Mickey Rourke," he clarified. "Like, steal his soul, like in *Angel Heart*, and actually *be* Mickey Rourke!"

He still worried, consistently, about what the Gandolfinis of Park Ridge would think of these endeavors. "I don't think anybody in my family thought it was an intelligent choice," he said. "I don't think anybody thought I'd succeed, which is understandable. I think they were just happy that I was doing something." Visiting his parents and sisters, he mentioned that he was considering taking on a stage name. "I said, 'If I get famous, it could be a pain in the ass,'" he told them. "'If I make it in any way as an actor, people will know, and if I do something stupid, people will know.'" His family listened carefully and thoughtfully to his suggestion. "I got up to go to the bathroom or something, and my sister and my mother were hysterically laughing. They were saying, 'Who the hell does he think he is? He thinks he's going to have to change his name.'" He shrugged. "Now they are bothered all the time about *their* names. So I got the last laugh."

Nevertheless, out of respect for his family, Jim had one hard-and-fast rule about the roles he sought out. "He didn't want to play a mob guy," Aston says. "He wanted to play a professional, a doctor or a lawyer or something, because he felt like his mom and dad had both worked too hard making sure their kids got a good education to end up playing, you know, somebody that was not representing Italians very well.

"So in the early days, he did not want to play a mobster. Ever."

WHEN THEY WERE ON TOUR with *Streetcar*, Robert Funaro could tell that Gandolfini wasn't just meant for the stage. "There was something about James, you said, *Wow, this guy is cinematic.* There's something about him that stands out. He has that *it*, that thing, you know?"

It took a while to get the "cinematic" element of his career going, however. Gandolfini made his very first film appearance in 1987, in a microbudget horror picture called *Shock! Shock! Shock!*, but don't bother tracking it down for his cameo as a hospital orderly; he appears only in shadow, and his voice has clearly been dubbed by another actor. Much more substantial was his role in *Eddy*, a $10,000 New York University (NYU) student film directed by David Matalon in 1989. Jim played Mike, pimp to working girl Madge, who attempts to run away with the title character, prompting Mike to turn violent.

Jim was one of fifteen actors to audition for the nonpaying role, Matalon told CNN in 2013, and "none of them were very convincing and threatening, and then he just had it. . . . He was really intense and always prepared on set. He was really focused. And he really loved acting. You can see he was a guy that was very conscious of the work."

But if Gandolfini was going to get real, paying work in real, honest-to-God movies, he was going to have to get some kind of representation. His first manager came to him, unsurprisingly, via Kathryn Gately. "She called me up, she knew I had gone from being an actor to being a manager," says Michael Greene. "And she said, 'I have this actor that's very special that I want you to meet.' And I said, 'Of course I'll meet him.' So he came in and did monologues for me in my office. And I was like, *Oh my God, this guy is a thug with a heart of gold*. . . . I thought he was going to be a huge star from the second I met him." Greene started scouring casting notices and sending Jim out on auditions for films.

His first big one, however, was "kind of more like extra work," according to Greene. *The Last Boy Scout* made industry headlines at the time as, according to *Variety*, "the most lucrative script deal ever made in Hollywood": $1.75 million to screenwriter Shane Black, who'd made his name perfecting the buddy-cop formula with *Lethal Weapon* for producer Joel Silver. Black and Silver were reteaming for *Boy Scout*, in which a burned-out private eye (Bruce Willis) and a washed-up football player (Damon Wayans) team up to solve a murder; the director was Tony Scott, the British filmmaker who had honed a sleek, distinctive aesthetic on television commercials and music videos that he translated into such feature films as *The Hunger*, *Top Gun*, and *Beverly Hills Cop II*.

The Last Boy Scout went in front of cameras in January 1991, shooting in and around Los Angeles for seventy days. Jim flew in to play a role so small, his name doesn't even appear in the end credits. He shows up about an hour in, as one of three goons who approach Wayans on the street, beat him up, and throw him over a railing. He turns up again in the picture's climax to hold a gun on Wayans, punch him in the face, and threaten both of the movie's stars. Gandolfini doesn't have a single line of dialogue; he's used for his tough-guy glower and imposing presence. But clearly director Scott saw something in Jim—something he would remember when it came time to cast his next picture.

GREENE WAS PERUSING THE CASTING notices in mid-1991 when he spotted a role that sounded like a good fit for Jim. "So he went in and pre-read," Greene recalls. "And then they called me up and said, 'Wow, this guy's amazing. We want to bring him to the director.' And then I remember Sidney Lumet calling me and going, 'This guy's got a major career ahead of him.'" Lumet's new picture was called *Close to Eden*, starring Melanie Griffith; before its release in the summer of 1992, that title would change to *A Stranger Among Us*.

"*Stranger Among Us* was different because it was shot here, and Lumet was one of those great directors that loved actors, and loved the process," Susan Aston explains. "Lumet rented a big warehouse and said, 'Those of you that will come rehearse, let's rehearse,' and he'd rehearse it like a play. And James loved that."

The young actor, playing his first speaking role in a major movie, needed all the help he could get. "I really didn't have a clue," he said. "Because they generally don't teach you a lot of things about hitting your marks, and unless you've been on a set, I didn't have a clue. So that's basically it, it was basically just trying to figure it out as I went on." But Lumet, the legendary director of such contemporary classics as *Dog Day Afternoon*, *Serpico*, and *The Pawnbroker*, was a patient guide. "He's wonderful," Gandolfini beamed. "He says, 'I know which, I know what I need. Don't worry.'"

Jim was immediately struck by the stark differences between the stage work he'd been doing and the meticulous processes of feature filmmaking. "Stage acting is about two hours of concentration, and the concentration is intense," he explained. "Film acting is concentration in little snippets all throughout the day. After a day of film, you're exhausted; at the end of two hours on stage, you're energized from the interaction with the audience. That is why 95 percent of the time after a play, everyone goes out to eat or do something. After a film, everybody goes home because they're exhausted."

Stranger is a loose riff on Peter Weir's *Witness*, a critical and commercial success a few years earlier, which concerns a police detective going undercover in an Amish community to solve a murder. Lumet's film stars

Melanie Griffith as a tough New York cop who goes undercover in the city's Diamond District, and in the Hasidic Jewish community that populates it. Jim, who was billed in the opening credits for the first time (listed second to last, but still!), was cast as Anthony Baldessari, a low-level hood from Bay Ridge. Strolling into a Hasidic jewelry store alongside his brother Christopher (Chris Collins), and sporting a gray suit with a wide-open collar, a gold chain, and a big ol' roll of cash, he does much of the talking as the pair attempts to make the store a client for their "private security company."

The tough-guy posture is familiar, though the dialect he adopts isn't quite the full-on gangster sound he would become famous for. Here, his voice is deeper, yet softer, as he assures Griffith's undercover cop, "Nobody fools around with us, nobody. And we take care of our own." The brothers return for a second scene later in the film, as Griffith baits them by accepting the offer ("Congratulations," he says, "you just bought yourself peace of mind") and then arresting them ("And you just bought yourself a cage," she retorts). They make a run for it, prompting a shoot-out and car chase in the Diamond District that ends with Jim's Anthony Baldessari dying in a cab. "Oh God, oh Jesus save me," he prays aloud. "I'm scared. I'm so scared." His acting is so deeply felt, it's almost jarring—a moment of uncommon and unexpected genuineness, an oasis in the desert of this formula cop movie.

A Stranger Among Us began shooting in late September 1991 and landed in theaters the following July. It was not well received, and Jim's fine work went unnoticed. But by then, he was in the midst of the most exciting chapter of his career yet.

CHAPTER 4

STEVE

WHEN GREGORY MOSHER, THE DIRECTOR best known for his brisk staging of David Mamet plays, approached Alec Baldwin about starring in a Broadway revival of *A Streetcar Named Desire*, the actor didn't hesitate. "He never asked about money," Mosher told the *New York Times*, "or who else was going to be in it. With Alec, it's grab the moment." Their production would run at the Ethel Barrymore Theatre, the same stage where Elia Kazan's original 1948 production debuted. Baldwin would play Stanley to Jessica Lange's Blanche; Timothy Carhart, an actor best known for his television and film work (he'd just appeared in *Thelma and Louise*) was cast as Mitch.

Manager Michael Greene got auditions for both Jim and Susan, who was also a client. Gandolfini was cast as Steve Hubbell, one of Stanley's neighbors and card-playing buddies, in addition to understudying the Mitch role—"the part he *should* have played," Aston says. "I should have played Stella, but they had movie stars doing it." (She was cast as "A Woman.") "He played the upstairs neighbor, Steve, which wasn't a huge, emotional arch. He didn't have to go in early and do heavy prep, you know. But he loved it." Even better, he would have four opportunities during the show's six-month run to step up and fill the Mitch role in Carhart's absence.

"We were both just tickled to death to be in it," Aston says, not only for the career affirmation of a Broadway credit, but for more practical reasons: Thanks to the movie star leads and the accordant demand for tickets, "we knew going in, it was going to be a six-month run." Six months of steady work was a very big deal for a New York actor.

Baldwin was a particularly hot property at the moment. He'd famously tossed away the opportunity to follow up his star-making role in *The Hunt for Red October* because production for the sequel, *Patriot Games*, would overlap with *Streetcar*. Paramount forced him to choose; he chose the play. (Harrison Ford took over the Ryan role.) Industry observers said it was a career-ending move, but it was exactly the kind of Hollywood-immune bullshit that a working-class actor like Jim admired. He and Baldwin became friendly on the production, and a few years later, they'd co-star in the thriller film *The Juror.*

Jim met another future collaborator on the show as well. "He played my husband," Aida Turturro wrote in 2013, "and the first day he walked in late to the rehearsal wearing his bike chain around him . . . I was like, 'Oh no, here comes trouble.'" She would describe him as "very open and great, but he's got a lot of power and I'm just like, *Oh, no, another fucking actor. This guy*. But you know, attractive and charismatic. So I go to therapy that day, I'm like, 'Oh my God, that guy I gotta work with, I gotta stay a *million miles away from him.*'" She and Gandolfini would co-star in two films and several seasons of *The Sopranos.*

A Streetcar Named Desire began previews on March 17, 1992, and opened on April 12. Baldwin got raves ("His Stanley is the first I've seen that doesn't leave one longing for Mr. Brando," wrote the *New York Times*' Frank Rich, "even as his performance inevitably overlaps his predecessor's"), but reviews were generally mixed. There are no remnants from which to judge Jim's performance—when Baldwin and Lange made a TV-movie adaptation three years later, the rest of the roles were recast—but *Newsday* praised his

Jim, center, in a publicity photo for the 1992 Broadway production of *A Streetcar Named Desire.* (Courtesy Photofest.)

work in a show otherwise dismissed as "lethargic and bland," noting, "In smaller roles, James Gandolfini and Lazaro Perez are aptly raucous as Stanley's poker buddies."

Among that opening night crowd was Mary Collins, an agent for the boutique agency Harter Manning Woo; one of its clients was understudying Stella for Amy Madigan. "In the first act, there's a card game being played," Collins says. "And it's Stanley and his pal, Mitch. And then the two upstairs neighbors come down, Steve and Eunice. So James Gandolfini and Aida Turturro come down a circular staircase, and they were so alive and so funny. And so real, both of them." She introduced herself to Jim at the opening night party, and asked if he'd meet with her about representation. "He came to the office, we had a little conference room with no windows," she says, laughing. "He wore a suit and tie. He was very correct. Very, very nice manners. A little shy, a little nervous. And I just knew in my heart that he was talented—obviously, he was on Broadway and he didn't have an agent."

He signed with Harter Manning Woo. "I really began to care about him and care for him," Collins says. "He reminded me of my older brothers. His warmth, his charm, his sense of humor. He had a mischievous quality, a twinkle in his eye, even though he was a tough guy."

"He knew nothing about the business," says Patty Woo, who co-owned the agency. "He didn't know anything. So he had no expectations, but also no limitations."

A STRANGER AMONG US HAD already completed its brief theatrical run when *Streetcar* closed on August 19, 1992, but the exposure of the show and the hard work of his new team had helped him line up several more small but memorable film roles. *Money for Nothing*, co-written and directed by Ramón Menéndez (*Stand and Deliver*), was based on the true story of Joey Coyle, a twenty-eight-year-old ne'er-do-well whose fortunes changed, ever so briefly, when he grabbed $1.2 million that fell off a truck in South Philly in 1981. John Cusack played a version of Coyle more befitting a film released by the Disney-owned Hollywood Pictures (several of his rougher edges, including a meth addiction, were sanded off); casting director Victoria Thomas surrounded Cusack with a who's who of up-and-coming '90s actors, including Michael Madsen, Benicio Del Toro, "Philip S. Hoffman," Debi Mazar, and Gandolfini's future *True Romance* co-star Michael Rapaport.

Jim plays Billy Coyle, Joey's big brother, who hands out jobs on the docks but refuses to give his brother special treatment over the other longshoremen. "Billy's always gotta prove to everybody that he's fair, all the time. It's like . . . acute integrity," Joey explains, a description that would prove apt to both the character and the actor playing him. Billy Coyle is a middle-class family man who follows the rules and does what's right, and wants nothing to do with the money his brother has stolen: "You don't take somethin' if it's not yours," he insists, convincingly. "You just don't." They eventually come to blows, with Billy kicking Joey out of the house they share unless he returns the money—though he also steps in, later in the story, to save his brother from a violent bookmaker (Del Toro). It's a character who lives by a code, one of complex morality, which would become the actor's trademark.

Money for Nothing is a decent little programmer. The cast is tip-top, the humor is admirably cockeyed, and it feels properly lived-in; by the picture's end, you feel like you know this neighborhood, who knows who, who hates who, and who you'd stay away from. But its release was stifled, at the eleventh hour, by a real-life tragedy. On August 15, 1993, less than a month before the film's release date, the real Joey Coyle was found dead in his home, having hanged himself with an electrical extension cord. The forty-year-old had lived a troubled life since the events of the film, continuing to battle drug addiction and various crimes connected with it, including an upcoming sentencing that some neighbors and friends felt had influenced his decision to take his own life.

Out of respect for its subject, Disney scaled down the film's planned wide release and marketing considerably, tacking a dedication onto the film and releasing it in fewer than five hundred theaters on September 10. The reviews were decent enough, though Carrie Rickey, writing in Coyle's hometown *Philadelphia Inquirer*, correctly noted, "This tragic event has the unfortunate effect of making our laughter seem disrespectful, however sympathetic Menendez and co-writer Tom Musca are to their subject's lapses of judgment." *Variety*'s Brian Lowry cattily complained that Cusack had been surrounded "with various unattractive characters," but the *Dallas Morning News*' Philip Wuntch singled one out for appreciation in an otherwise mixed review, writing that "there are some special moments from James Gandolfini as Joey's priggish brother." Whatever its flaws and virtues, *Money for Nothing* couldn't get out from under the shadow of Coyle's passing, grossing barely $1 million in theaters—or, put another way, less than Joey Coyle stole from that truck.

Jim had a much smaller role in Anthony Minghella's *Mr. Wonderful*, as a potential suitor for the ex-wife of co-worker Gus (Matt Dillon), who is attempting to marry her off so he can stop paying alimony. As Mike, Jim is shy and reserved, a nervous wreck when he shows up for his lunch date with hard hat in hand ("I never had a date at 11 A.M. before, so . . ."), scaring her off immediately with a too-soon mention of marriage. It's a short, slight little scene, but it shows a softer side of the actor (his managers would show it to potential directors as proof of his capacity for vulnerability)—and he shares it with Annabella Sciorra, with whom he would explore a much different on-screen dynamic several years later.

Similarly unspectacular notices ("Well cast and convincingly played," the *New York Times*' Janet Maslin wrote, "but its actors are hamstrung by the cute excesses of the story") and box office returns (just over $3 million domestic) greeted *Mr. Wonderful* on its October release. But by that time, Jim had another movie in theaters. And it was a game changer.

CHAPTER 5

VIRGIL

QUENTIN TARANTINO HAD ORIGINALLY ENVISIONED *True Romance* not as James Gandolfini's breakthrough, but his own. Written (with some uncredited help from his eventual *Pulp Fiction* co-writer, Roger Avary) during the future filmmaker's fabled education jockeying VHS tapes at Video Archives in Manhattan Beach, California, Tarantino planned this talky action-comedy—a tale of lovers on the run from Detroit to Hollywood with a suitcase full of the mob's cocaine—to be his feature directorial debut. But after three years of failing to raise sufficient funds, he sold it as a spec screenplay for the Writers Guild of America minimum of $50,000. He planned to use that fee as the seed money for a much simpler indie debut, but his *Reservoir Dogs* script was such a stick of dynamite that he ended up attracting a cast of name actors and a much more sizable budget.

While *Reservoir Dogs* was working the festival circuit in 1992, the *True Romance* script made its way to Tony Scott, who decided to set it up as his next feature, and the considerable buzz around *Dogs* attracted a hotter-than-average cast to *Romance*: Christian Slater and Patricia Arquette would play Clarence and Alabama, the young lovers, while Dennis Hopper, Christopher Walken, Gary Oldman, Brad Pitt, Val Kilmer, Chris Penn, and (very briefly) Samuel L. Jackson would turn up in support.

One of the trickiest roles for Scott to cast, however, was Virgil, a ruthless (but, this being a Tarantino script, chatty) mob enforcer. "I had read the script," recalls manager Michael Greene. "I saw the scenes. And I thought, *This guy is like an angel, but he's a demon—he's got all these demons in him. Oh my God, James is perfect for this.* So I fought and fought and we got him in and Tony Scott fell in love with him."

"When James came in, and I cast him for this role, I thought . . . every cast member of this movie has got a real sweetness, a real charm, and yet a real danger," Scott explained. "And Gandolfini is loaded on the dangerous side, yeah? James is the dangerest motherfucker on two legs. But he's charming, and he's funny. He came in and read for me, and after the first reading, I turned to my casting director and said, 'It's his, he's got it. This guy's great.'"

Jim knew he had to go to a dark place to portray a character with such a capacity for brutality. "Someone I knew was . . . was a very interesting man," he explained, enigmatically. "And he reminded me a lot of the character in *True Romance*. I had been hanging out with him occasionally, and I just said, 'Listen, will you help me?' And he told me some stories about . . . how do I put this? I just knew him, I knew him for a long time. And he told me some stories about, in his youth, what had happened to him . . . and that helped me get into this guy's skin a little bit." According to Scott, Gandolfini immersed himself in the sleazy character during the shoot: "He lived in a shitty motel off Highland whilst he was playing this character in the movie. We could never find him, because he's living in this hotel. He didn't have a phone in his room. . . . He didn't wash his hair, he didn't change his underwear, in order to stay in character."

Jim is first seen in one of the film's most notorious scenes, a tête-à-tête in which Walken, as a Mafia boss, matter-of-factly tortures Hopper, who plays Slater's father, to find out the whereabouts of the couple. Gandolfini stands over Hopper's shoulder, waiting for cues from the boss; when he gets the nod, he cheerfully inflicts pain and suffering, then waits, with a little smile, for his next go-ahead. He has no lines in the scene, but he skillfully establishes Virgil as an out-and-out sadist; it's not what he does but how he does it, the sheer glee with which he punches, pummels, and slices their helpless victim.

After a brief and funny encounter with Brad Pitt—with whom Jim would appear in two more films several years later—comes the picture's most violent and disturbing scene. Virgil has tracked Clarence and Alabama to their motel, but Clarence has dropped his wife off while he runs for burgers. Virgil is waiting there for her; small talk and giggling ensue, as Scott builds out the dread of what's coming. When Alabama refuses to tell Virgil where either Clarence or the suitcase of cocaine is, he tries to beat the information out of her.

Tarantino would call this "the most romantic scene in the movie," because Alabama "keeps her mouth shut, she takes the beating and, you know, faces death for him." Virgil taunts the petite young woman, pacing and smoking and glaring, warning her, "You're a very pretty girl, Alabama, but you ain't gonna be very pretty for very long," before throwing her around the room. The physicality of the sequence is horrifying; it's not just that he's beating her so mercilessly, but he's taking such pleasure in it, with a twinkle in his eye and a little "I wish you would" smirk curled around

Patricia Arquette and Gandolfini, before the fireworks start, in *True Romance*. (Courtesy Warner Bros./Photofest.)

his lips. And as she bleeds on the floor, Tarantino gives Virgil a short but bluntly effective monologue, a moment of quiet in the midst of the chaos, reflecting on what it's like to kill someone for the first (or second, or whatever) time. "Now I do it just to watch their fuckin' expression change," he says with a shrug, chillingly—something Jim was told by that "very interesting man" he talked to while doing research, and was allowed to add to the monologue. (According to Scott, Gandolfini also suggested the gooseflesh-raising moment when Virgil instructs Alabama to turn around so he can look at her, then punches her in the face as she completes the twirl.)

"He is so perfect for this Virgil character," Scott said, "in terms of the sweetness and the darkness of who his character is and was. And everyone loves Patricia in this scene, because, you know, she fights to the death."

Jim would remember taking five days to shoot the fight scene. "It was like a dance," he said. "We kind of made it up as we went along." Scott recalled Arquette insisting, "Get James to really bash me around, get James to do his thing," while Arquette found herself flummoxed by the complexity of the sequence. "Even though sometimes we would get the shots," she recalled, "and it looked like he hit me, the acting wouldn't be great. Tony would just have us keep doing it and keep doing it. So it wasn't enough for just the choreography to be right. . . . We had to get the emotion."

In his quest to make the scene convincing, Jim went to extremes. Alabama strikes her first real blow by slamming a nearby corkscrew into the top of Virgil's foot, and Jim wanted her to do it for real, so his agonized response would be authentic. "That's how much he was getting into the character, into the role," Scott recalled, "and Patricia said, 'I'm not doing it, this guy's fuckin' off his head.'" Jim modified his request, asking Scott to drive a pencil into the top of his foot; finally, according to Scott, "one of the second ADs got a compass and slammed it down at the top of his foot. You know, that was just for the reaction on his face."

Though it's since become a cult favorite, *True Romance* was met with a mixed reception when it hit theaters in September 1993. The *Wall Street Journal*'s Julie Salamon dismissed it as "a vile, soulless fairy tale, constructed as a hip homage to junky pop culture," and while *Variety* granted it "provides some amazing encounters, bravura acting and gruesome carnage," the trade ultimately ruled that "it doesn't add up to enough." But the *New York Times*' Janet Maslin called it "a vibrant, grisly, gleefully amoral road movie," praising its "malevolently funny bad-boy posturing."

Oddly, none of the mainstream reviews, good or bad, mentioned Gandolfini's memorable and terrifying work. Even Jim's own feelings about the performance were complicated; he called Susan Aston back in New York and asked her not to go see the movie. "He said he wasn't proud of it, and he didn't want me to see it," she says. "I think he felt he did a good job in the role, but that maybe he shouldn't have done it. Because it was so brutal." Susan honored his wishes—she's still never seen *True Romance*.

Luckily, others did. After its release, Michael Greene remembers, "Everybody was calling me: 'Who the fuck is this guy?'" Audiences may have rejected the picture (it topped out at $13 million worldwide, barely more than its budget), but other filmmakers and casting directors saw Gandolfini's turn, and more film offers began to present themselves. "He was just getting great little character parts and the right directors were responding to him," says Mark Armstrong, who joined Jim's management team shortly thereafter. "The *True Romance* thing really changed everything."

Between *True Romance*'s shoot in the fall of 1992 and its release the next year, Gandolfini played a supporting role in a low-budget New York indie, eventually released as *Italian Movie*; it was written and directed by Roberto Monticello, who met Jim while he was managing a bar in the Meatpacking District called the Gaslight. Jim wanted the work but was resistant to the character Monticello had in mind, a low-level neighborhood gangster. Monticello offered him a deal: He had another script, a comedy with a "good guy" lead; if he'd play this bad guy first, they'd make that film together next.

Gandolfini's "Angelo" is a gambler who is, as he notes, "lucky in cards" but not in love, so he makes a practice of taking out men's debts by seducing their wives. He's not the focus of *Italian Movie* (despite the box art when it was re-released during the run of *The Sopranos*); the story concerns a pizzeria owner who has to resort to working as a gigolo to pay off his gambling debts before Angelo starts busting heads and/or seducing his wife. It's an uneven picture, but Jim is genuinely menacing, especially when he meets the spouse in question and starts turning on the charm.

The shoot "was really like a three-ring circus," recalls co-star Michael Harney. "Our dressing rooms consisted of sheets and clotheslines in a church." That's where he first met Gandolfini: "I stumbled into him in those dressing rooms, as we were trying to figure out how we were going to get dressed and undressed."

Monticello found Jim to be naturally inquisitive about his character. "How bad am I?" he asked his director, who replied, "You are as bad as you need to be to survive," which became Jim's mantra on the shoot: "I'm just as bad as I need to be." Mostly, Monticello remembers him as hardworking. "He was very concerned with doing his best," the director says. "He kept asking me, 'Am I doing OK? Am I overdoing it?' He was a little concerned with that."

Watching the film now, it's clear—especially in a role with so many similarities to the one that made him famous—that Jim was locking into his abilities as a screen actor. "He was truthful," Harney says. "He was open and honest." Monticello agrees. "You can see the guy had something," the director notes. "I'm not gonna take credit for seeing the future because I auditioned about twenty-five people for that role. But he had a way of, what's the word? Being *true*. Not every scene or every take, but he had moments where he was very true, very true. You could see the pain in him. You could see the *I'll do anything if I have to* type of thing."

COMING OFF THOSE ROLES, GANDOLFINI had a clear vision of what to do next. "He wanted to play quality roles and wanted to be a chameleon, and wanted to do different kinds of roles each time," Michael Greene says. "He said, 'If you ever have me play a gangster again, I will fucking kill you.'"

Greene obliged. That April, Jim landed a leading role in the screen adaptation of Avra Wing's novel *Angie, I Says*—later shortened to simply *Angie*—a seriocomic drama from director Martha Coolidge, originally developed for Madonna but reworked for Geena Davis. Production began on June 1, 1993, in New York, with a supporting cast that included Stephen Rea, Philip Bosco, Jim's *Streetcar* co-star Aida Turturro, and their future *Sopranos* colleague Michael Rispoli. Davis plays the title character, a working-class girl from Bensonhurst; Jim is Vinnie, her boyfriend (but not husband) since ninth grade, a simple but likable plumber, "a nice guy, he's got a good heart," according to the dialogue.

Jim was originally cast in Rispoli's role, a friend to the main couple; Vinnie was to be played by Vincent D'Onofrio (who had also appeared in *Mr. Wonderful*). When D'Onofrio fell out of the production, Jim's team did some savvy bargaining, using his outstanding offers for supporting roles in *The Shawshank Redemption* and *Natural Born Killers* to not only get him into the Vinnie role, but at a significantly higher rate, and higher billing, than Hollywood Pictures head Joe Roth wanted to give.

It was worth the effort. Vinnie is a solid, juicy role for Jim; he gets to play the character's kindness and temper in equal doses, and when he discovers that Angie's been having an affair, Coolidge holds on the shock and hurt on his face, allowing the emotional truths of the scene to wash over him. If anything, he's *too* good—so likable and charming that we're not entirely on board with Angie's affair, and when he mostly disappears in the third act, he's badly missed.

"In *Angie*, I got the best of both worlds," Coolidge said, after Gandolfini became a star. "I wanted a guy who was very real but who also had leading man qualities to play opposite Geena. James is a real man, so he can be tough and sexy, but he also can be vulnerable and sensitive. He was ideal for that kind of part." The experience also provided an early example of the actorly generosity for which he would become known.

"We worked like the devil to get him third billing, even though he had no credits," Patty Woo says. "We killed ourselves to get him third billing, single card." But after Jim saw the film, he reached out to his agent. "Jim called and said, 'I need you to switch my billing,'" she says. "'Aida would really like it, give her my billing and give me the shared card behind her.' I said, 'No one has ever asked me to reduce their billing.' And I will say that thirty years have gone by since then, and *still* no one has asked me to reduce their billing below another actor."

"He had all this heat, and he was the male lead, so that wasn't going to happen," Mark Armstrong says. "But it's just an example, of many that I could give, of how he thought of himself, and wanted things to be fair, and treated his fellow actors."

Once again, the film didn't make much of an impression on audiences or critics (*Variety* deemed it "a skin-deep feel-good movie"), but the latter were finally starting to take note of Jim. Most notably, in the *New York Times*, Janet Maslin wrote that Vinnie "is saved from condescension by James Gandolfini's affable performance."

By *Angie*'s release in the spring of 1994, the acting work was getting steady enough for Jim to go bicoastal, spending the next five years paying two rents, while traveling wherever the job might take him. He was a working actor now, with a clear understanding of exactly what that meant: "It's just a matter of showing up every day, even when you don't feel like it, even when you don't want to be there, and doing what you're supposed to do," he explained.

That spring, he was showing up in and around Tucson, Arizona, for a Charlie Sheen skydiving picture called *Terminal Velocity.* "It was a rough shoot," Patty Woo says. "He wasn't loving it. But he did it." It's junk, but it's not hard to see what drew Gandolfini: He's third-billed in a studio action movie, and for the first time, it's a major role that's (initially) not some sort of Italian-American tough guy. As Deputy District Attorney Ben Pinkwater, he's a bit of a nerd, wearing an oversized suit and thick glasses, and using the crisp diction of his normal, off-screen speaking voice. A few scenes later, however, the character is revealed as a Russian spy, so Gandolfini sheds the character and goes into villain mode—a silly flip, but he's convincing enough to pull it off. He ends up punching the female lead (which was becoming an unfortunate trademark) and gleefully killing her in front of our hero, resulting in a rough-and-tumble climactic fight against Sheen, as well as a first-rate death scene, in which his parachute is deployed and pulled into a windmill blade.

Critics were surprisingly kind to *Terminal Velocity*—the *Los Angeles Times*' unpredictable Kevin Thomas called it "a rousing, good-looking action-adventure," while *Variety* praised it as "a snappy, thrill-packed political espionage/heist picture"—but audiences stayed away, with its $37 million return on a $55 million budget making it one of 1994's louder flops.

Jim's next couple of pictures were quieter affairs. Susan Aston was down in North Carolina shooting a feature called *Aberdeen*, written and directed by Kathy Fehl and Ian Teal—"a really low-budget thing that we did with some friends," Aston says. But there was one scene that was set in New York, "and then Kathy was like, 'Could you get James,' because we had done a play together."

James obliged. His cameo comes late in this strange but fascinating film, a single scene as "Mr. G," the landlord to protagonist Deirdre (Angelica Page), whom he's thrown out on the stoop while he ransacks her luggage for valuables, as her rent is six weeks overdue. "Maybe tonight you go to a bar, find yourself a nice man, and go home with him," he taunts, until she's finally riled up enough to slap him, prompting his reply of "Little bitch," and that's the scene.

The filmmakers spent the next couple of years scraping together funds and finishing the film, which would screen at the IFP Film Market in 1998 but never found a buyer. It finally hit screens more than a decade later, playing festivals in 2010 under the title *Mint Julep*, where ticket buyers drawn by the presence of James Gandolfini were shocked to see an actor thinner and markedly younger than the man they knew by then as Tony Soprano.

Jim spent the summer of 1994 in France, shooting the period drama *Le Nouveau Monde*. Based on Pascal Quignard's novel *American Occupation*, it's a memory play, set mostly in 1959 in a French village where American GIs are still stationed after World War II. Jim is Will Caberra, first seen roaring around in a loud car with Buddy Holly playing on the radio; a Hawaiian-shirt- and blue-jean-clad good-time Charlie making the best of his deployment, Will ends up taking protagonist Patrick (Nicolas Chatel) under his wing, taking the kid to hear jazz, getting into bar fights, teaching him how to do a proper handshake, and encouraging him to follow his dream of becoming a drummer.

But Will is no role model; he's also an abusive racist, tortured by his wife leaving him for a Korean. "So now I got nothin'," he says, "and now I got nobody, and that's the way I want it to stay." His characterization has more depth and complexity and danger than this messy coming-of-age movie knows what to do with; as with *Angie*, he's gone by the home stretch, and our interest goes with him. *Le Nouveau Monde* was retitled *New World* for its eventual direct-to-video release in the United States a couple of years later.

THE *NOUVEAU MONDE* SHOOT STRETCHED into the start of Gandolfini's next gig, but luckily, his director wanted him badly enough to adjust the schedule to accommodate the actor. He was working with Tony Scott once again, this time on a naval submarine adventure called *Crimson Tide*, something of a cross between *The Hunt for Red October* and *The Caine Mutiny*. It was a big-ticket summer blockbuster, from Disney's Touchstone Pictures division via super-producers Don Simpson and Jerry Bruckheimer (who'd produced Scott's *Top Gun* and *Days of Thunder*); the script by Michael Schiffer was rewritten by Quentin Tarantino, with scene doctoring by Robert Towne. The role of Lieutenant Bobby Dougherty wasn't as juicy as Virgil—there were no showcase scenes or searching monologues this time around—but it was Jim's biggest movie yet, and the ensemble cast was loaded with other up-and-coming actors, including Viggo Mortensen, Steve Zahn, Danny Nucci, future *Sopranos* co-star Lillo Brancato Jr., and Rocky Carroll. Most importantly, Denzel Washington and Gene Hackman were facing off in the leading roles.

"We were all sort of in awe," Carroll recalls. "Two of the biggest names in Hollywood at the time, two Academy Award–winning actors, Gene Hackman and Denzel Washington, and the rest of us, we were all working actors. But we were the ensemble, we were the accompanists to Hackman and Washington. So just being in that space, we were all just so grooved to be there."

Principal photography began on August 15, 1994, at Culver Studios, with the production taking over two giant soundstages for fifteen weeks. Jim and his director fell right back into a comfortable collaboration, a shorthand they had developed on *True Romance*. "To me, he was Hollywood of another era," Carroll says of Scott. "He had a cigar—unlit cigar—pink shorts. He was a man's man, but he wore pink shorts and this pink baseball hat. He could pull it off because he was this bigger-than-life character. And I'll never forget, he wore that outfit, that was sort of his signature outfit, he wore it every day. Cigar, the pink shorts . . . he looked like he was on vacation in the Bahamas when he was directing."

Scott had to use all his skills at defusing, diverting, and repackaging tension during the lengthy and difficult shoot. Because of the mutiny at the center of the story, the U.S. Navy had refused to assist the production as it had on the team's earlier *Top Gun*. To replicate the movements of the submarine, the cast spent days on a stomach-churning hydraulic gimbal (or moving platform), reportedly the largest such device ever built at that time. Further, Denzel Washington exchanged tense words at the craft services table with a visiting Tarantino, reprimanding him for the racial slurs in his *Pulp Fiction* screenplay.

The visiting screenwriter wasn't the only target of Washington's wrath. Ari Posner, covering the shoot for *Premiere* magazine, observed the scene where Hackman's minions removed Washington from the sub's command and wrote, "James Gandolfini, the actor playing Washington's escort, appears to surprise his colleague on the first take by grabbing him a lot harder than he had in rehearsal; Washington shoves back in kind. Within seconds the two actors are shoving each other with what might be deemed excessive force." Scott let the confrontation play out before calling cut. "Washington storms over to Scott," Posner reported. "*I'm not going to work with this guy* (or words to that effect). *Where does he get off . . .* ? Scott calms his star, assuring him that he's worked with Gandolfini before and all will be fine. But when the scene is resumed after a lunch break, the two are at each other's throats yet again."

"It got really heated really fast," says Carroll. "And Jimmy was just like, 'I'm doing my job, my job is to remove you, why would I handle you with kid gloves?' And I thought for the first time, this is the movie star, and this is the actor, you know? The actor's saying, *If neither one of us had an Academy Award, you wouldn't have a problem with this. . . . I'm doing what's written in the script for me to do, I'm not trying to one-up you. But my job is to come in here and physically remove you from this spot.*"

"Because he arrived late, they never got a chance to really know each other," Mark Armstrong explains. "Jim did get a little aggressive, more aggressive than I think Denzel was ready for. And there was friction."

When the day was done, a worried Jim put in a call to Patty Woo. "Hey, I'm calling you to say I'm getting fired," she recalls him telling her. "I might have hit Denzel. I mean, we were doing the scene, you know, we were fighting, and I might have made contact. And we might have had some words. And so I'm gonna get fired. So here's what I want you to do: I have a friend who's really right for this role, I'll give you his number. I want you to call them and tell them, you have a replacement for me. And here's his name and number. . . ."

"Jim," she explained, patiently, "it does not work that way, where if my client gets fired, I give them a sub."

"No, no, no, I mean, he's a really good actor," he replied. "I get it. But still, I want you to do this for me."

Luckily, Jim was not fired. Posner's *Premiere* piece concludes with a callback to the conflict. "'What the fuck are you doing?' Washington yells at James Gandolfini as the two actors scuffle vigorously once again. They fall out of camera range. Behind the monitors, Scott sits frozen in fear. Before he can get up and separate the battling actors, Washington and Gandolfini, unable to contain themselves any longer, burst into laughter. Cackles Washington, 'We fooled everybody.'"

"I almost feel like there was a respect from Denzel that happened," Armstrong surmises. "Jim ultimately apologized. But it's literally immediately after that, they started a great friendship. And Jim had a ton of respect for him." They'd adroitly turned down the temperature on a genuinely heated situation—the kind of conflict that was not uncommon on the tense, testosterone-heavy set.

"I felt like I was in an NFL locker room," Carroll says. "It's tough; you're being spritzed with this combination of water and sunscreen to give you that sense that you're sweating, between each take. You're literally nose to nose with the people in the thing. . . . And you're in the set, and we're playing up the elements, the heat, the intensity, the anger, the threat of death, and all that stuff. So after twelve hours of doing that, every day, the last thing you want to do is be like *Hey, let's go hang out*. Everybody just wanted to get home." But there was one exception to that general rule. "Hackman was a huge fight fan," Carroll explains. "One day we wrapped early, and Gene Hackman just turned us and said, 'You guys want to go see the fights?' And we were like, *Gene Hackman just invited us to go to the fights. Yeah, sure*!"

As luck would have it, Gandolfini and Hackman would work together again, on their very next film. But the big boost for Jim in *Get Shorty* was the chance to work with one of his longtime heroes: John Travolta, then white-hot off the career-reviving *Pulp Fiction*. "John is actually responsible for the chaos that has become my life," Jim would explain, at a tribute to the *Saturday Night Fever* star in 2004. "We grew up fifteen minutes away from each other in New Jersey, and his father used to own a tire store and my father would buy tires from his father. There was a picture of John in that white suit, and I thought, 'If this man can do this, then so can I.' So that's how it got started, this madness."

Based on a book by Elmore Leonard (which was inspired by the author's own Hollywood misadventures, particularly an extended period courting Dustin Hoffman for a film adaptation of his novel *LaBrava*), *Get Shorty* cast Travolta as Chili Palmer, a Miami loan shark who ventures to Hollywood to track down a debtor and finds his particular skills make him a potential power player in the movie industry. Hackman co-stars as a disreputable B-movie director, while Delroy Lindo and Jim are the criminals he's in business with—a study in contrasts: Lindo's Bo Catlett is a well-groomed smooth talker in a clean, crisp suit, while Gandolfini's Bear sports an untucked Hawaiian shirt, messy beard, and ponytail.

He's playing a thug again, but one markedly different from his previous films. Bear speaks not in the Italian tough-guy dialect that had become Jim's go-to, but with a soft, approachable Southern drawl. In 2004, he pinpointed Bear as the role he was most nervous about, "because I didn't know what to do with the character, and at the time, I didn't have any experience to be able to fix it. When I opened my mouth, a Southern accent came out. To this day, I don't know why."

"Jim had built an entire character for Bear that he came out of the South," Patty Woo says, laughing. "None of this was ever discussed. None of this was in the plot. But for Jim, it was important. And *then* he had to work on his Southern accent, and it became an issue—he got himself a coach, because Jim, from New Jersey, does not have access to an authentic Southern accent. And now he's killing himself to be authentic to it! So that was Jim's commitment to the authenticity of his roles, even when he's picking

Jim and Delroy Lindo in *Get Shorty*. (Courtesy MGM/Photofest.)

it. Which was, as a representative, a pain in my ass. *Take the very nice check, shove John Travolta and go down the stairs. And then you'll have $150,000!*"

Whatever the trouble, the accent gives the character a palpable, and necessary, softness. He's a big guy, intimidating (a former stuntman, we're told), but he's not effective in confrontations, because his heart's not in it. Virgil in *True Romance* takes actual pleasure in inflicting pain, but Bear only brightens up when he's with his little daughter, or when movie-crazy Chili Palmer, who's just laid him out flat, asks him about the films he's worked on.

That quiet, marvelous scene marked the beginning of a lasting friendship and collaboration between Gandolfini and Travolta, who would appear in three more films together. Jim took careful note of Travolta's technique on that shoot, telling his acting coach Harold Guskin that "the first time he acted opposite John Travolta in *Get Shorty*, he couldn't see him acting at all—even from a few feet away. Travolta seemed not to be doing anything. But when Jim saw the film, there was plenty going on. And the camera had caught it all."

These two big 1995 releases were successes both at the box office and among critics, and while few reviews singled him out among their large ensembles, having two hits on his résumé was an unalloyed good. "The response from film people was so immediate," says agent Mary Collins. "Always. It was so strong. Because everybody who met him wanted to work with him, if they could—you know, he wasn't right for *everything*. And if they worked with him, they wanted to work with him again."

He was becoming all he wanted to be: a frequently employed and well-respected character actor. "I like when you go to a movie or turn on a TV show that has people who, in one way or another, look like you, act like you, and feel some of the things you feel," he said. "I like stories about regular guys, not the cool guys. Cool makes me want to vomit."

His future co-star Steven Van Zandt concurs. "He liked being the character actor, and he was so good at it," Van Zandt explains. "Every movie he ever did, he was terrific—whether the movie was good or not, he was always great."

"Sometimes your character's got four or five scenes," Jim explained. "He's there for a reason. So you've got to figure it out. 'Okay, what's this guy's life like?' It's not in the script. You've got to work ten times harder, cause it's not there. Tony Soprano is easy to play because it's there. I don't have to fill in the blanks. Every time I turn around, they're filled in. Sometimes it's harder to be the guy who comes in and is just there, has a few lines, and doesn't really have anything pushing him along."

Nearly as impressive as the work he was doing on-screen was his success rate in the audition room. "There was rarely one that he didn't get," says Diana Doussant, who began working as one of Jim's agents at Harter Manning Woo around this time. Sure, there were occasional near-misses; he went in several times for the role of Clare Quilty in Adrian Lyne's controversial adaptation of *Lolita* (Frank Langella booked it), and he was asked to audition for the 1995 comedy *To Wong Foo, Thanks for Everything! Julie Newmar.*

"They wanted James to audition to be a drag queen," Mary Collins says with a laugh. "And he was like *Uh, me?* But the casting director wanted to bring him in whenever she could. So he and I went down on 14th Street at Ninth Avenue—there is a triangular little building, and on the second floor, a shop that catered to drag queens because that Meatpacking District of Manhattan was still a scene. So I went with him, and he got these huge shoes, high heels, feather boas, and makeup and everything, and he eventually made himself up and took some photos. Well, needless to say he did not book that one."

But it was the exception to the rule. "This will sound crazy, but he almost got everything he went up for," says his then manager, Michael Greene. "When he would go in, he would impress the directors so much that they would just call, it was almost automatic." Doussant concurs, while adding, "It wasn't like he was going out fifteen times a day. He was very specific, and he was very busy."

And there was one hard rule to cut down on those auditions, according to Collins: "He definitely didn't want to do TV. We never sent him out on a TV audition." Part of the logic was avoiding the stigma attached to television acting at the time ("TV didn't exist the way we understand TV to exist now," Doussant stresses); also, as a New York actor, there weren't nearly as many television opportunities—*The Equalizer*, maybe, or *The Cosby Show*. Even the mighty *Law & Order* had only begun its decades-long mission of providing steady paychecks to Gotham stage players. For the time being, he would keep doing what he was doing. "He kept making his mark," Collins said. "He kept being noticed. People would hire him; he did his job. And he made them look good."

Yet as he became more established, and as more offers came in, his always-shaky sense of self-confidence did not improve—if anything, the pressures of performing alongside Oscar winners and screen superstars increased his doubts about his own abilities. Most of the time, Armstrong and the rest of Jim's expanding team would talk him down. "I think he didn't feel he belonged in the company that he belonged in," Doussant surmises. "I think that he was almost surprised that the requests would come and the offers would come, and he always struggled about walking into a room to meet or audition. He always wanted to talk himself out of it. 'I'm not right for this. There are other people that are righter. . . .'"

Whatever doubts he'd harbored, they would soon be exacerbated by his most humiliating professional rejection to date.

CHAPTER 6

CHARLEY

GET SHORTY WRAPPED ON April 18, 1995, but Jim's scenes were long in the can—he'd headed back to New York for his presumably triumphant return to Broadway, in another property made famous by Marlon Brando. Budd Schulberg had adapted his original screenplay for the classic 1954 Elia Kazan film *On the Waterfront* into a Broadway play, first in 1984, then (somewhat revised) in the spring of 1995. Ron Eldard was cast in the leading role of Terry Malloy, with Penelope Ann Miller, Kevin Conway, and David Morse (who'd just shot a few scenes for *Aberdeen/Mint Julep*) in support. Jim was cast as Terry's brother Charley Malloy, the key role originated by Rod Steiger in the film.

On paper, it all sounded promising. But "it was just a disaster from beginning to end," Diana Doussant says. "The hardest thing is when an actor wakes up one morning and goes, *I'm not doing this*. And the commitment's been made, the contract's been signed, rehearsals have begun, and you come to the realization that it is a terrible fit. *I don't want to be here and what I've got they don't want, what they've got I don't want* . . . He was just drowning."

It wasn't just Jim. Several of the cast members were concerned about the show—problems in the script, inconsistencies in the direction, and so on—and were "really trying to make this thing work," according to Amy Appleyard, the show's associate lighting designer. "Everybody was passionate about the script. Everybody was passionate about the entire production. And I think he sort of became this voice for, *Hey, I'm gonna go talk to the producers—like this doesn't make any sense. Like, why are we doing this? Why are we doing that?*" In doing so, he made himself a target for the producers' and directors' frustration.

"Jim Gandolfini was a very strong personality and a strong man," Patty Woo notes. "A very good guy, but you could not fuck with him—or if he perceived being fucked with, you could not do that. Again, he would take a swing at Denzel if he felt Denzel was taking a swing at him. He didn't have any of that savvy of, *this could hurt me, this isn't the right place for that*. He had no edit function for that."

"The thing that I remember most was that he got into a huge contretemps about the fact that he wanted to use real money onstage," Doussant explains. "Because there's a scene where Charley is counting up money or whatever, and he was just balls to the wall. *Why am I not using real money? Why am I using paper?* That I remember. It was almost like, *I can't do this, I can't.*"

"I think he had just an artistic suggestion or something," Susan Aston says. "I think he overstepped his bounds." Gandolfini would only talk about it once, in an interview pegged to his return to the Great White Way fourteen years later; all he would say is that five minutes after "a lovely discussion" with one of the producers, "I got a call telling me I was fired for being too mouthy."

Previews began on April 12, 1995, and by the time the show opened on May 1, Jim had been replaced by his *Italian Movie* co-star Michael Harney. After the change was decided but before Gandolfini was dismissed, Harney went to watch him in previews. "I brought Jimmy a bottle of Johnnie Walker Black," Harney recalls. "Handed it to him and wished him well. It was a very brief encounter, but again, we knew each other from the movie." It wasn't the only change to what *Variety* called "the rockiest tryout in recent memory": The original director, Gordon Edelstein, was replaced by Adrian Hall less than two weeks out, and Morse had similarly taken over the role of Father Barry, after Edelstein's departure, from Terry Kinney.

In some ways, Jim dodged a bullet. *On the Waterfront* was poorly reviewed and closed after only eight performances, barely putting a dent in its $2.6 million budget, and earning the dubious distinction of being, according to *Variety*, "the costliest nonmusical flop in history." But it still stung. "He was really surprised that he had been fired," Aston says. "And it really hurt his feelings, you know, because he was very sensitive. Very sensitive."

Luckily, there was more work waiting. On May 1, the very day of *On the Waterfront*'s opening, production began on *The Juror*, a John Grisham-esque thriller starring Demi Moore as a woman pressured to sway her fellow jurors to acquit a crime boss, and Jim's *Streetcar* co-star Alec Baldwin as "the Teacher," the mob contractor who must persuade her to do so. Jim would play Eddie, the Teacher's right-hand man, who becomes sympathetic to the single mother and tries (and ultimately fails) to play both sides of the fence.

It's a fine performance—nuanced, sympathetic, smiling but intimidating, forceful when he has to be—in an undeniably silly film. The reviews

Jim with Demi Moore *The Juror*. (Courtesy Columbia Pictures/Photofest.)

primarily focused on the latter point, but several took note of the knotty work by this increasingly ubiquitous character actor. The *New York Daily News*' Dave Kehr praised the "number of fine actors who turn up along the way, including . . . James Gandolfini as a sympathetic mob functionary," while the *New York Times*' Janet Maslin name-checked him again among the picture's "strong supporting cast." Most notably, for the first time, Roger Ebert singled Jim out, devoting the entire closing paragraph of his *Chicago Sun-Times* review of *The Juror* to singing the actor's praises:

> A performance that caught my eye is by James Gandolfini, as Eddie, the Teacher's sidekick. He has a very tricky role, as a Mafia soldier who is about as sympathetic as a man can be who would, after all, kill you. His line readings during a couple of complicated scenes are right on the money (watch the careful way he learns from the Teacher about the death of Annie's friend). If the movie had been pitched at the level of sophistication and complexity that his character represents, it would have been a lot better. Of course, it would have been a different movie, too. I could have lived with that.

The good reviews couldn't lift Jim's foul mood about the film. "He hated that, too. That was shitty," Diana Doussant says. "I had surgery, and he was calling me and just beating the shit out of me because he was so unhappy about how the schedule was, and what the scripts were looking like and that his scenes are weird, it just . . . That was an unhappy experience. He did it, he did exactly what he was supposed to do. But it was not a thrilling time."

It was about to get worse. In 1995, HBO was going into production on one of its biggest original movies to date, *Gotti*, dramatizing the life and times of the notorious New York gangster. Armand Assante had been cast in the leading role of John Gotti. Jim was offered the second lead, as Gotti's underboss turned informant, Sammy "the Bull" Gravano. "We got the offer, we were doing it," recalls Patty Woo. "He didn't love it. He was like, 'I have to stop playing these roles. I have to stop playing Mafia guys.' But we had accepted, with his begrudging permission, and negotiated a fantastic contract. It was all set. And right before he was supposed to start, he told us we had to pull him, that he wouldn't do it, and that he would never do a Mafia role again. Never."

The timing couldn't have been worse. "He pulled out on the way to the airport!" Diana Doussant says, still shuddering at the memory. "He was determined, he was so clear. 'I am not doing this movie.' Couldn't be talked out of it." By dropping out mere days before his first scenes were to be shot, Gandolfini had put the cable network in a huge bind. Executive producer Gary Lucchesi scrambled, and quickly cast William Forsythe to fill the role. (Also among the cast were such soon-to-be-familiar faces as Tony Sirico, Vincent Pastore, Dominic Chianese, and Frank Vincent.) Lucchesi also gave Gandolfini's agents an earful. He would blackball Jim Gandolfini, he promised. Their client would never work in the film industry again. And he'd *certainly* never work for HBO.

THERE WAS ONE POSITIVE OUTCOME from the *On the Waterfront* imbroglio. "There was a pool table in the rehearsal hall; I do like to play pool," recalls associate lighting designer Amy Appleyard. "And at one of the breaks, I was just kind of knocking around the balls. Jim was also there. I had no idea that he was even a smidgen famous at all; I just thought he was the big guy playing Charley. And he was a flirt, and we just sort of started to have conversations." They would date, on and off, for about a year and a half—never exclusively, as they were both traveling for their work and seeing other people, but steadily.

"The thing about dating Jim is that he was exciting, smart, raw, emotional, and tough all at the same time," she explains. "Being with him felt dangerous, but he also made you feel safe. He could get you to do things you wouldn't normally do, knowing it would be a wild ride but that somehow everything would work out just fine. . . . I imagine this feeling was also the appeal of acting opposite him."

As she got to know him, she was surprised by the subtler aspects of his personality. "I do remember being really surprised at how much he enjoyed reading," she says. "I'm a big reader. And he was like, *Yeah, my idea of a great vacation is to just throw a bunch of books in a suitcase and drive up to Vermont to go find a little cabin in the mountains.* I was like, *Let's go!*" But he also enjoyed more physical pursuits. "He could dance," she says, still charmed by the memory. "I don't know if anybody knows that. The guy could *dance*—not dance-on-the-dance-floor dance, like real dancing with steps and moves and things like that. That was sometimes a thing. Because there was never any furniture [in his apartment], just the bed. We'd put on some music and just dance around.

"He was just so intense," she continues. "When he would just lock eyes with you, you really felt like, *This guy knows me. He knows what I want. He understands.* And I think he was able to do that with everybody. When he connected with somebody, it was deep, right? It got him out of speeding tickets! We were pulled over one time, and I remember thinking, *I'm glad I'm not driving*, right? Anybody would have been probably asked to do breathalyzer tests. But he rolls the window down, starts talking to the guy, and within minutes, we were driving off. Just us. Somehow, he connected enough that the person was like, *You're going home, right?* He was like, *Yep, we're going home.* And we were let go. I mean, he could just charm *anybody*."

They had some of their most enjoyable times together the following summer, Appleyard recalls. "He rented a house at the Jersey Shore—on the bay side, not on the ocean side," she says. "And he had Jet Skis, three or four Jet Skis. . . . Everybody came. His dad came, his sister was there, college friends, people would come up in boats, just come and hang out, and we would go grocery shopping and cooking and playing cards and reading. It was so chill and comfortable and happy—nobody was asking him for anything. I think that was just a really peaceful time."

THINGS WEREN'T QUITE SO PEACEFUL on the business side. Jim's manager Michael Greene had shepherded him from a struggling unknown into an established film actor, but Greene's own personal tragedies sent him into a tailspin of substance abuse; Greene was, by his own hyperbolic admission, "the biggest crackhead in the world and in the business." Jim was using cocaine as well, he says, and "it was the same reason, personally, I was doing it: because I just wanted to cover the pain. And there was a lot of pain in this man. There was a lot of vulnerability and pain and he wanted to . . . to numb it."

But by 1995, Greene was out of control, and his client came to his office to tell him so. "Michael, I'll never leave you," Jim told his manager. "But until you are sober, and people in the business recognize you as being sober, I can't be with you right now."

Greene, furious, threw a can of Coca-Cola at Gandolfini, who merely stood in the doorway, looked at Greene, and repeated himself. "I will never leave you, Michael Greene. But get yourself together, because I can't be seen as a drug addict. I can't be seen that way. And if you're representing me, and you're seen as a drug addict, it's going to have repercussions on me. So we have to keep it quiet." And with that, he left. ("I went bankrupt, I lost everything, all my clients left me," Greene continues, but that was not the end of his relationship with Jim. "I needed money, because I was basically homeless at that point. And he sent me $5,000 or $10,000 in the mail.")

Now under the guidance of Gold Bouchard Management, Jim got back to work. Whatever the fallout from the twin fiascos of *On the Waterfront* and *Gotti*, it was short-lived. Susan Aston was a member of the esteemed Actors Studio in New York, and as Jim explained it, "Susan got me in. I think she talked to Arthur Penn and maybe showed him some work. I wanted to get in. I wanted to come to the Studio a lot." His finances were secure enough to make his first home purchase in 1996, an apartment in the West Village, and to hire an assistant. She was Marcy Wudarski, a pretty, blonde Florida native and military brat six years his junior. "He was nobody when we met," she would later tell the *New York Post*. "I was between jobs, working for a movie company, and a friend suggested I be a part-time helper, do some piddling things for 'this actor you never heard of who's made a couple of nothing movies.'" Before long, they were dating.

"She was very helpful to him," says Amy Appleyard. "He needed somebody to help him—especially, I imagine, as his career got more and more intense." Appleyard had also started a relationship with someone else that grew serious, so the timing was right for her and Jim to taper off. "I believe that there was love there," Appleyard says of Jim and Marcy. "I'm certain that they had to have been really in love."

Now that Jim was building a name and reputation, he was often getting straight offers, without the requirement of auditions. "But Jim would always ask to read with the director, even if they were willing to offer," Armstrong says. "When he got even more famous, he would still ask to read sometimes, at least just for the director—because he wanted to make sure his take on the character is what they wanted."

His primary concern, with every potential project, was the same: "The writing, the writing, the writing, the writing, the writing, the writing, the writing. . . . I need to find, and I think this is important with acting, you need to have a point of view. I think good actors have a point of view about things, they have a point of view about who they are and what they want, and what they want to say in a character." He'd also developed clear ideas about how to best interact with his directors. "You should have your own idea," he said. "You should try to surprise the guy a little bit." What did he *not* want from a director? "To bug me too much. Especially in the beginning, if we're rehearsing."

Luckily, one of his favorite directors was casting again. "Sidney Lumet called me," he recalled. "Said, *I want you to do this*. He gave me my first job, so I said yes." It was for *Night Falls on Manhattan*, which Lumet not only directed but co-wrote, in the tradition of his great films about corruption in New York City's law enforcement apparatus (following *Serpico*, *Prince of the City*, and *Q&A*). As usual, Lumet rehearsed extensively in advance. "He knows what it's going to look like," Jim explained. "And he puts the tape on the floor, and you rehearse. I mean, you rehearse the scenes; he likes to get it on the first two or three takes. So you know your lines, you show up, and you better be ready, because you're gonna get two takes, maybe three." Production began in October 1995 and continued through the end of the year.

Jim turns in one of the best of his early performances as Joey Allegretto, a police detective and longtime partner to Liam Casey (Ian Holm). The pair are responsible for the bust of a high-profile criminal, whom Casey's son Sean (Andy Garcia), new to the DA's office, successfully prosecutes—only to discover that the bust might've been bad. Gandolfini gets to display a full range of emotions in the role: tearily calling in the "officer down" report when Liam gets shot, talking without saying anything when Sean's subsequent investigation starts to point in his direction, unable to look Sean in the eye when he asks about his dad. The scene where he finally comes clean is a virtuoso bit of acting, veering from offhand folksiness ("Got caught with my hand in the cookie jar"), hard yet hesitant when pressed for specifics, hurt and angry when Sean lets him have it, then deploying one of the deadliest weapons in Gandolfini's arsenal: the inappropriate and menacing smirk, the look that says *I could do something, but I won't.*

Jim turned up at the film's premiere in New York on May 12, 1997, which the mayor's office officially proclaimed "Sidney Lumet Day" in honor of the director. Critics were mostly kind (*Variety* praised the film's "complexity and artistry"), and Gandolfini was frequently singled out among the roll call of "stellar supporting actors." Even better, he met a key later collaborator during this project. "I remember we had a reading and this big guy comes in at the very last minute, apologizes, and sits down," recalled Dominic Chianese, who plays a trial judge. "When we finished the movie, I said, *That guy's a good actor.* So I knew who he was and he knew who I was."

AS HE MADE THE TRANSITION from part-time actor with day jobs to a full-time professional, Jim's preparation and technique grew more refined. Tom Richardson, still a close friend from the Rutgers days, explains:

> Whenever he would agree to a script, he would start researching. We would spend hours and hours—if it was a prison thing, visiting prisoners and finding out how they lived and what they did, whatever it happened to be. . . . He could just sit on a park bench and watch people walk by in a neighborhood, just to get a feel for that place. He'd immerse himself in books and do tons of research, just read and become part of that time. He'd people-watch, and see how people react, people's facial expressions. He would take thousands and thousands of photographs. This is before the iPhone; he would just take his camera with his telephoto lens, and he would just scan and take pictures, print them out, and put them up on a wall—he'd have like, an eight-by-ten-foot-high by twenty-foot-long wall just covered with pictures and photographs, just to develop his character.

Gandolfini's next movie, *She's So Lovely*, had a backstory as fascinating as anything that made it onto the screen. The groundbreaking indie filmmaker John Cassavetes wrote it late in his life, then developed it for over a year with Sean Penn, who was set to star. But Cassavetes's untimely death in 1989 ended that iteration of the project. When Penn moved to the other side of the camera a few years later, he optioned the script to direct himself, but was unable to make it happen. Shortly thereafter, John's son, Nick Cassavetes, made his directorial debut with *Unhook the Stars*, a showcase for his mother (and his father's frequent collaborator), Gena Rowlands. That film was well received, and Nick reread *She's So Lovely* and connected with Sean Penn about resuming the leading role. "I realized that perhaps my first movie was for my mom and my second would be for my dad," he said at the time. Penn's then wife, Robin Wright, was cast in the female lead, and John Travolta was plugged in as the third point in the love triangle at the story's center.

"I knew Nick Cassavetes," Jim mused. "I think that's how I got the part." In this case, "the part" was the small but pivotal role of Kiefer, a neighborhood scumbag who's always up to something (and it's nothing good). Taking advantage of the tension between Wright's Maureen and her ever-absent boyfriend (Penn), Kiefer lays on his charm; in a harrowing montage, Kiefer and Maureen engage in a spirited bout of day drinking that he escalates into a brutal physical assault.

"I find them difficult," he said of these scenes of violence against women. "I find they take a bit of a toll. . . . You know, you go home . . . feeling rotten, just absolutely rotten. It takes a while. For me."

The character's villainy is undeniable; he's not only unapologetic for what he's done, but amused by it, proud of himself even. ("I'm sorry but . . . you're the one that wanted it," he tells her.) Yet what's so remarkable about the performance is how well it showcases his duality—how, in his best roles, he was such a combustible combination of ill-fitting, incompatible elements. He could pivot, seemingly effortlessly, from warmth to menace, from folksiness to danger, on a dime. This character is laughing and smiling, but he's using his strength to force her to dance with him, and it gets very rough, very fast.

Jim shot his scenes for *She's So Lovely* in the summer of 1996, then spent that fall working on two more films. *Perdita Durango* (or, as it was sometimes known in the States, *Dance with the Devil*) is an all-but-unclassifiable cult item, situated somewhere between erotic thriller, action movie, and comedy/drama. It stars Rosie Perez, a pre-fame Javier Bardem, "Y JAMES GANDOLFINI como Woody Duras" (per the opening credits). Woody is a mostly comic role, finding Gandolfini in a bad suit, walrus mustache, big cigar, and deep (if slightly inconsistent) Texas accent as a DEA agent "from up there in Dallas" whose poor judgment and proximity to accidents make him a spectacularly ineffective law enforcement officer. The picture's odd stew of bank robberies, border politics, vampires, raunchy sex, and Herb Alpert make it a bit of a jarring ride (other indie crime movies of the mid-'90s aped *Pulp Fiction*; this one feels like it's knocking off *From Dusk Till Dawn*). Jim's performance is enjoyably unhinged, however, and at the very least, it was a welcome variation from the intimidating tough guys he'd been playing.

Fallen was a much more conventional effort, a combination of police procedural and supernatural thriller, reuniting Jim with Denzel Washington (and, in a smaller role, Aida Turturro) as cops pursuing a serial killer whose demonic spirit is passing from one person to another. Their characters don't get along, allowing the actors to further explore their maybe-real-maybe-not tension from the *Crimson Tide* set, but the script is such a haunted house contraption that it allows neither actor much in the way of character moments. Jim's best scene comes late in the picture, when he freaks Washington out by singing the Rolling Stones' "Time Is on My Side"—the killer's calling card—then claims no memory of the event. "I wasn't singin' it," he insists. "I hated the fuckin' sixties."

CHAPTER 7

AL

THE *RECORD* (NORTH JERSEY) RAN the obituary on January 11, 1997: "SANTA PENNA GANDOLFINI, 74, of Hillside died Thursday. Before retiring in 1995, she was a cafeteria manager at Holy Angels Parochial School, Demarest, where she worked for 20 years. She was a parishioner of Our Lady of Mercy R.C. Church, Park Ridge. Arrangements: Robert Spearing Funeral Home, Park Ridge."

Jim never spoke publicly about his mother's passing; it was certainly not a door this already private man was eager to open, at the time or after. But it was a difficult start to what would prove an especially tricky year for him, personally if not professionally. He again threw himself into work, and an especially busy spring. He appeared on an episode of the Robert Altman–produced *Gun*, an ABC anthology series with an ingenious central conceit: The show would follow a single handgun from one owner to another, with each episode detailing the trouble it caused or solved (mostly caused) in their hands.

The premise also allowed for actors like Jim, who normally wouldn't appear on television, to take a crack at it. "A lot of actors don't want to do TV, because they have to commit for such a long time, but they don't mind doing an anthology," Altman explained. "They don't have to come back every week and play second fiddle to the star." *Gun*'s cast included Martin Sheen, Carrie Fisher, Daryl Hannah, Jennifer Tilly, and, alongside Jim in the third aired episode, "Columbus Day," Rosanna Arquette and Peter Horton. As the title suggests, Gandolfini plays a proud Italian ("Anything that tastes good, or looks good, we invented"); Arquette is his wife, who he doesn't realize is having an affair with their handsome novelist neighbor.

"He has those very compassionate, empathetic eyes," Arquette recalls. "When you connect with somebody's eyes, you know, as an actor, and you can really connect in that way immediately? Our initial meeting led us to be able to truly do that, and bring that to the set, and be in our characters." Between setups, they talked about children; things were getting serious with Marcy, so Jim was considering starting a family, and Arquette's daughter was on set with her. "I was still breastfeeding too, which he thought was really funny," she says with a laugh. "I breastfed her until like two or something, two and a half maybe. . . . He thought it was a little too long. And I said, 'What can I tell you? I'm a hippie kid, you know?' He got a kick out of that.

"I loved him. He was just a pleasure, a wonderful, sweet human being to work with. Very, very connected as an actor." *Gun* didn't fare as well; reviews were bad, and the show proved too ambitious for the few audience members who tuned in to the Saturday night slot where ABC buried it. This would not be the television show that would make James Gandolfini a star.

Nor would ABC's next attempt to woo the actor. *Cracker* premiered on Britain's ITV in 1993, starring Robbie Coltrane as Dr. Edward "Fitz" Fitzgerald, a hard-drinking, chain-smoking, overweight, antisocial, but brilliant criminal psychologist who works as a consultant for the Manchester Police. It was a big hit in the U.K., running three seasons over three consecutive years, and like many a British television hit, it was targeted for adaptation by American networks.

ABC landed the project and offered the leading role to Gandolfini. "I think it was because he did the *Gun* series," says manager Mark Armstrong. It was a big deal, first on the call sheet for an hour-long network show, and they didn't even ask him to audition; it was a straight-up offer, and an enthusiastic one. "They were offering to jump on planes," Armstrong says. "He was renting a house in Mount Olympus [in the Hollywood Hills], and I was up there. This huge package arrived, and we started cracking up. And it was all the things that Cracker would have liked—there was like, bottles of different kinds of alcohol, and condoms, all these different funny things."

Ultimately, though, Jim turned it down. (The role went to Robert Pastorelli, a co-star on *Murphy Brown*.) "I just don't see myself hanging off the ABC sign," Armstrong says Jim told him, envisioning the corny promotional spots and similar obligations of network television stardom. For now, he wanted to focus on his movie career.

However, his next project was also for the small screen, albeit with a more impressive pedigree. *12 Angry Men* was first presented in 1954 as a live television play, part of the anthology series *Studio One*. In 1957, it was adapted for the big screen—the first feature directorial credit for the aforementioned Sidney Lumet. Forty years later, the story came full circle, shot as a TV movie for the cable network Showtime. Oscar winner William

Friedkin directed, his cast an even mixture of legends (Jack Lemmon, George C. Scott, Ossie Davis, Hume Cronyn), established character actors (Edward James Olmos, Armin Mueller-Stahl, William Petersen, Tony Danza), and up-and-comers (Mykelti Williamson, Dorian Harewood, Courtney B. Vance, and Jim). Gandolfini was somewhat intimidated by the heavy hitters around him, but he kept his head down and did the work. "I think he felt like he was invited to the party," Armstrong says.

Friedkin, who thought up the remake at the height of the O. J. Simpson trial, contemplated going all the way back to the script's roots and mounting it as a live broadcast. Instead, he rehearsed the cast for eight days and then shot the entire film in less than two weeks—in sequence, rare for a feature film, but possible for this one, as it was set in a single location that no one could leave.

"I'd seen his work," Mykelti Williamson says of Gandolfini. "But we get to the stage at Paramount and he's just the coolest, down-to-earth, East Coast, New Jersey, New York–type personality, you know? And he was just a sweetheart of a guy—but you could tell that there's a sharp edge on the other end of that thing, too. I mean, don't ever assume he's a pushover.

"We had a good time on the show," Williamson continues. "We really did. We worked our butts off, you know, and everybody there was fantastic."

Tony Danza agrees. "First of all, Jack Lemmon. Being in a movie with Jack Lemmon—you know what Jack Lemmon did every time, before the director called action? They'd do last looks, and then everybody'd get ready, and he'd say, 'It's magic time.' And then *action*. It was, it was unbelievable!" If Jim was intimidated by the legends in their midst, Danza couldn't tell. "I watched him work with Jack. And you know, you're working with *Jack Lemmon*, for Chrissakes, you've got to—first of all, it makes you better, because you know he's *so good*, but at some point . . . I look at everything like a fight for some reason, I guess because of my background, and he was holding his own."

That was easier said than done. *12 Angry Men* is a work of high drama, with stakes of life and death, and Jim's character, the blue-collar Juror #6, doesn't get any of the big dramatic beats or show-stopping monologues. He's initially standoffish, shy even, but is pushed by the bullies in the room to speak up for those who are reluctant to. He makes a meal of the character's complicated morality, and when he makes the turn from "guilty" to "not guilty," it's a firm one—a moment Friedkin lets him take his time with, indulging in a slight pause, and shifting his eyes, before he says those two words. In fact, his best acting moment in the film is one free of dialogue: He gets a good, lengthy close-up as Williamson stands next to him, spouting bigotry, while his own face hardens in anger, ready to snap.

"The guy was really, really good," Danza says, shrugging. "He had a different look than anybody else. He wasn't what you expected for an Italian leading man. And he had a real . . . I'm telling you, I'm just always trying to learn as much as I could, but he had such an ease of delivery."

The film was the first deal made on Gandolfini's behalf by his new team. Jim was looking for a change in management when he met with Nancy Sanders, a former agent who had started a boutique firm in 1990. "I gave him a really great meeting," Sanders recalls, and at its conclusion, Gandolfini said, "I want to sign with you, and I want you to have vodka in the refrigerator in your office for whenever I'm in town."

"OK, great," Sanders replied. "I'll buy a bottle of vodka." But Jim liked and trusted Mark Armstrong, who had stayed with him through these transitions, and wanted to make sure Armstrong was part of the deal as well. "I said, 'Mark, I'm gonna bring you over, too, and we'll do this together,'" Sanders recalls. "So we did it together." They would manage Jim for the rest of his career.

Often, that relationship was as much about personal support and emotional encouragement as it was about making deals. Sanders remembers getting many early morning phone calls from Gandolfini during *12 Angry Men*. "He had reverence for Jack Lemmon and a lot of those guys, and he still was just a hometown boy," she recalls. "Just a little anxiety. He had a tendency to be a little unsettled, you know, always striving for a kind of perfection—maybe he wasn't happy with the day before. He would never call if he was thrilled with the day. He was rarely thrilled with *anything*."

Once *12 Angry Men* wrapped in February 1997, Jim hustled off to shoot a supporting role in director Peter Chelsom's adaptation of Rodman Philbrick's best-selling young adult novel *Freak the Mighty*, shortened by Miramax to simply *The Mighty*. The bulk of the picture concerns the friendship between a disabled twelve-year-old boy (Kieran Culkin) and a fourteen-year-old outcast (Elden Henson) traumatized by his now-imprisoned father (Gandolfini). Though billed above the title, Jim's appearance is relatively brief, his unexpected parole and abduction of his son the inciting event for the film's climax, his reveal painstakingly prepared in dialogue and flashbacks.

Gandolfini's character looks and sounds different from the norm; his hair is close-cropped, he flashes a silver tooth, and he speaks in a good ol' boy accent that, along with his frequent chuckles, is both down-home and horrifying. He may just be a plot device, but Jim invests him with a real sense of humanity, and his mixture of evil and faux regret is chillingly effective. "He wanted to go up and spend a little time bonding with Elden before the shoot, and I think Elden was scared shitless," Armstrong says, laughing. When the film was completed, Armstrong and Sanders joined Gandolfini and director Chelsom for a private screening on the Sony lot. "In the middle of it, he got up and walked out," Armstrong recalls. "I found him at a bus stop on Washington Boulevard. Not because he hated the film, but he just wished he—he was not used to watching himself. It made him very uncomfortable."

THE FALL OF 1997 BROUGHT a new challenge for Jim: his Los Angeles stage debut. He and Sean Penn had become friendly during the production of *She's So Lovely*, and Penn brought him an opportunity. He was producing (along with Helicon Theatre Company) a West Coast staging of *Remembrance* by the Irish playwright Graham Reid, with his parents, Eileen Ryan and Leo Penn, in the leading roles. The younger Penn wanted Gandolfini to play the third lead. Jim accepted, and immediately panicked.

Susan Aston recalls these years of Jim's bicoastal living and working:

> He called me a couple of times, "Oh, I'm struggling with this part. Help me, I can't figure it out, I can't get to the heart of it." And so we'd go through all the steps that actors go through, all around the given circumstances, really trying to get to what the person needs, clarifying the obstacles. And he would call me after the next rehearsal and go, "OK, I got it, I got it." . . . You just need somebody to talk to you sometimes, you know, a collaborator. And so he continued to do that when he was in LA, just as friends. He was working on a play with Sean Penn's parents, and called me and said, "Oh, you know, I'm so fucked on this, I don't want to suck." I helped him with that, just on the phone, long distance.

He and Susan would soon formalize this relationship, with her providing coaching and scene study guidance throughout the years that followed.

In the meantime, opening night for *Remembrance* loomed. He was nervous about performing live, in front of a Hollywood crowd, particularly the boldfaced names that might be drawn by the Penn family's involvement. Perhaps he was still mourning his mother, and thinking of her because of the play's themes of aging parents and adult children. Or maybe he just needed to blow off some steam. Whatever the reason, on September 26, 1997, the night before *Remembrance*'s opening, Jim was arrested in Beverly Hills for driving under the influence.

"I was racing someone and I was over the limit," he told the *National Enquirer*, when the story returned to haunt him five years later. "Let me say it was the best French toast I ever had when they woke me up in the Beverly Hills jail!"

In the same interview, he said of his drug and alcohol abuse, "When I was 20 or 18 it started. And it progressed through the years." He had smoked weed as an undergrad at Rutgers; he'd certainly indulged in more expensive substances while running Private Eyes and working at other New York nightspots in the '80s. But as he got more successful, and attained more access to those substances, his partying increased.

"I'm sorry to say we probably witnessed his entry into that," Patty Woo says. "He might have been a drinker when we met him, but it was not a part of our representation of him. He didn't miss appointments, or show up drunk or anything. When we started with him, he was all on the straight and narrow. And actually, I will say during our whole time with him, I don't recall getting complaints from set, that he was not ready to work. That was not part of his MO. But he was a hard partier in our last several years together. Hard." He managed to evade serious consequences for the DUI, but his "demons," as those who knew him would take to calling them, would return.

In the meantime, *Remembrance* opened to warm notices from the Los Angeles critics; *Variety*'s Charles Isherwood wrote, "Gandolfini's loutishness gives off a charge of deep woundedness." And this recent run of roles was allowing him to show off a bit more of his range, though he was still mostly playing "the roles you'd expect a guy who looks like me to get," and was frustrated by the feeling that he was being typecast as murderers and palookas, rarely given the chance to play regular guys.

"My parents worked hard, were honest, were good people," he explained. "As I've said before, I'm standing on their shoulders here because they worked so hard and enabled me to go to college, and these are the kinds of people that I love. And these are the kind of people that I want to show in movies because I think they're getting screwed and that is where I think . . . if I have any power as an actor, that's where it comes from."

When *Remembrance* finished its run in November 1997, Jim finally got the chance to play an honest-to-goodness working-class hero. "James Gandolfini is in final negotiations to join the cast of Steve Zaillian's *A Civil Action*, for Touchstone Pictures," *Variety* reported that fall. An adaptation of Jonathan Harr's best-selling nonfiction book, it concerned a lawyer (John Travolta) taking on two giant corporations whose toxic dumping may be responsible for the leukemia deaths of several children in a small Massachusetts community. Gandolfini was cast as Al Love, an employee of W. R. Grace who becomes a key whistleblower in the case.

"He was thrilled, and he loved John Travolta as a person," Nancy Sanders says. "That was a wonderful experience." It was also one of the best performances of Gandolfini's career, a portrait of quiet anguish; he knows what he *should* do, but is fully aware of the implications therein. Much of his work is purely reactive, registering paranoia in the workplace and worry at home, attempting to show support to his neighbor (Kathleen Quinlan), who is the primary plaintiff, and public pariah, in the case against his employer. When they finally sit to talk, he tells her, softly and sincerely, "I'm very sorry about your son," and it just breaks your heart in two.

"I do remember sitting at that table with him, and he was so shy and so quiet," Quinlan recalls, of shooting that scene. "But obviously he was very occupied with the scene and what we were going to do. I just remember he had this very . . . he just had this incredible ability to make it all very real in that moment. And that really struck me because, you know, sometimes as actors we can see the actors working the words. And I couldn't really see that."

Something else about the scene stuck with her as well. "I remember him getting really mad—at himself. Because he didn't like what he did. And so the first time I didn't say anything; I didn't really know him that well. And then the second time I said, 'Hey, what's the matter? That was really wonderful.'" But Jim refused to settle for what he deemed a subpar showing. "He really cared, and he wanted to keep getting better and honing his work as an actor so, you know, I get it," Quinlan says. "But I also understand that when you're really in it, you can't see it."

Jim's performance was well received when the film hit theaters in the winter of 1998. The *Los Angeles Times* placed him among the "effective"

In *A Civil Action* with Kathleen Quinlan, who remembers him as "so shy and so quiet." (Courtesy Buena Vista/Photofest.)

co-stars; the *New York Times* name-checked his as one of the "shrewd, first-rate performances." But his most important, and unforgiving, critic was especially satisfied. "I was very proud of the film," Jim said. "It was a true story that had an actual hero, and I got to meet him and play him. You know, as you're playing so many dark characters, to play a character like that, it really . . . It felt like I could breathe a little bit again. It was really nice."

The respite was short-lived. In the spring of 1998, he reported to the set of *8MM*, a pitch-black thriller from screenwriter Andrew Kevin Walker (*Se7en*) and director Joel Schumacher. Nicolas Cage stars as a private detective hired by a rich man's widow to track down the source of a snuff film in his vault; Jim appears as Eddie Poole, a sleazy talent scout who may connect the world of legitimate pornography with the illegal underbelly. "A dark, dark film," Jim said, with characteristic understatement.

"He loved Schumacher," Armstrong says, "but I think the world was a little disturbing for him. Surprisingly." For Schumacher, coming off the debacle of *Batman & Robin*, *8MM* was an attempt at an edgy, gritty comeback. But it's all desperately overwrought, a *Reefer Madness* for porn;

Gandolfini in *8MM*, his last film before the role that changed everything. (Courtesy Columbia Pictures/Photofest.)

bereft of any humanity or complexity on the page, Gandolfini was left to simply seize on externals, tacky silk shirts and ornate facial hair. "I remember they wanted to book him into a regular hotel, as an actor who would get first-class accommodations," Sanders says. "And he's like, *No, I want to stay at some seedy place in Hollywood*, you know, very Method-y. I think, actually, when we saw the screening of *The Mighty*, he was shooting *8MM*, and he had to go back to that really seedy motel. . . . He needed to do whatever he needed to do, whether it meant sleeping in a bedbug bed, or not shower, he needed to surround himself for that to get into character." He finds his moments, flashes of genuine danger and menace, but ultimately, it's just another scumbag role, and after the high-water mark of craft and characterization of *A Civil Action*, just another scumbag role was depressing.

"Once *A Civil Action* was edited and we were doing some looping, I asked James what he was doing next," Steven Zaillian recalled. "He said, 'Another gangster thing,' like, *What else is new.*

"That turned out to be *The Sopranos.*"

CHAPTER 8

TONY

DAVID CHASE DIDN'T WANT TO work in television. David Chase didn't even *like* television. He had as a child; christened David DeCesare, he was born in Mount Vernon, New York, in 1945, right around the same time as the birth of the medium. He watched *Howdy Doody* ("It was funny, it was surreal, it was kind of violent," he recalled, a description that could also fit his own work), and *The Twilight Zone*, and Jackie Gleason and Sid Caesar's comedy/variety shows. But the most popular program in the DeCesare household was *The Untouchables*, which centered on the Prohibition-era FBI taking down mobsters, mostly of Italian descent.

"I'm Italian-American," Chase explained, "and my parents were somewhat defensive of the organized-crime aspects of the Italian-American culture. And so when my father would sit there with me, and watch these guys like Frankie Yale and Frank Nitti and those people, I felt encouraged, and I felt closer to him—my father. And I felt we were all part of the same . . . ethnicity."

His father owned a hardware store, and his mother was a proofreader for the telephone book. They were no-nonsense people, practical, so neither of them approved of his dream, in those halcyon days of the mid-1960s, of rock stardom playing drums and bass guitar. Eventually, his attention shifted from music to movies; he studied film at NYU and as a graduate student at Stanford, gorging on cinema, developing a particular affinity for the offbeat stylings of the French New Wave. One of his Stanford professors put his feature screenplay into the hands of the television producer Roy Huggins, who hired Chase to write a spec script for the series *The Lawyers*. It aired in 1971, and the following year, he co-wrote his only produced pre-*Sopranos* film, an exploitation cheapie called *Grave of the Vampire*. More film offers were not forthcoming.

But TV work was. Chase had a gift for cranking out quality teleplays, even while feeling a failure for making his living writing for the idiot box instead of the big screen. He spent the 1970s accumulating credits on shows beloved (*The Rockford Files*; *Kolchak: The Night Stalker*) and forgotten (*The Magician*; *Switch*), which led to producing in the following decade. He created his first show, *Almost Grown*, in 1988, but it lasted only thirteen episodes. He was executive producer on the acclaimed *I'll Fly Away*, but it was canceled after two seasons for low ratings, and he joined *Fly Away* creators Joshua Brand and John Falsey's previous series, *Northern Exposure*, as an EP for its final two years, until it met a similar fate. By the mid-1990s, in what must have felt like a stinging step backward, he was writing and producing episodes of NBC's *Rockford Files* revival.

In June 1995, Chase signed a development deal with the management-production company Brillstein-Grey Entertainment. Chase's entertainment lawyer, Lloyd Braun, had joined the firm and brokered the arrangement, and he gave Chase a suggestion: an hour-long series about organized crime, kind of a *Godfather* for TV. "That was the last thing I wanted to hear," Chase said, "because I wanted to be in motion pictures." But Braun's suggestion became a piece of flypaper in his brain, attracting stray thoughts that had been rattling around in there for years. Back in the '80s, he'd had an idea for a feature film, a comedy about a mobster who goes into therapy to work through his difficult relationship with his prickly mother; it was inspired by Chase's own time in treatment, and his own touchy matriarchal relationship. His agents at UTA didn't even bother shopping it around. Mob movies were out, they told him.

"Then I was driving home that night," Chase said, "and I started thinking about the fact that the guy had a wife and a son and a daughter, and the shrink could be a woman, and that network TV drama was very female-oriented, so I thought, 'Maybe that feature idea could work as a TV series.' It had home life in it, it had . . . women's points of view, kids, all of that." He got home and opened a new file on his computer, tapping out a quick note: "Mafia Mother and Son—The father dies. Junior is in charge. His only rival is his mom. The old victim becomes the ballbuster/killer she always was. She must kill him or vice versa. (Or maybe he should put her in a nursing home.)"

Brillstein-Grey got him into a room with execs from Fox, who bought his pitch, and a commitment to do six episodes, for $300,000. It seemed too easy, and it was; he turned in the pilot script in December 1995, and Fox got cold feet. (Chase recalled an exec telling him, "'I'm not getting the feeling we may do this for a certainty. But I want to tell you as one human being to another, I really liked what you did.' So I knew I was dead.") They took the pitch to CBS, where Chase said head honcho Les Moonves objected, "I don't really have a problem with the robbing and murdering and all that, but does he have to be seeing a shrink? Does he have to be on Prozac?" Fox came back around a year after its initial offer, nearly green-lighting with Anthony LaPaglia in the lead, before passing again. Chase, who had all but given up on the show, was on the verge of signing a deal for something else at Fox when Braun told him to hold off. "Listen," he said. "We sent the script over to HBO. There've been some changes over there and they may have some needs in this department."

HBO was still best known as a premium movie channel. It had enjoyed some success with original shows—including Brillstein-Grey's *The Larry Sanders Show*—though those had all been comedies. But it had an intense, hour-long drama called *Oz* in the can, slated to debut in July 1997, and the powers that be at the network thought there might be room for more. (Ironically enough, they also thought there might be an audience for the show because of the huge ratings drawn by the *Gotti* TV movie that Jim had so unceremoniously exited.) Chris Albrecht, president of HBO Original Programming, gave Chase a soft go-ahead: HBO would finance a pilot episode, and would then decide if it wanted the show to go to series. *The Sopranos* was off and running.

WHILE THE PILOT SCRIPT WAS knocking around from one network to another, Chase had been up for a job on a CBS series for Marg Helgenberger, centered on the Witness Protection Program. He used the *Sopranos* pilot script as a writing sample, which was how it got in front of Gandolfini's managers, Mark Armstrong and Nancy Sanders—Helgenberger was also their client. CBS passed on the Helgenberger pilot, but when word got around about the HBO deal for *The Sopranos*, Sanders saw an opening for Jim. "I read it again," she recalls, "and I went, *Oh my God, I think I have Tony Soprano.*"

She called Chase at home and told him as much. He was enjoying a Sunday night dinner and bottle of wine with his wife. "He sounds familiar," Chase said. "I'm totally into having this conversation with you, but I may not remember it. Call me tomorrow morning and send me the VHS." The following morning, a messenger delivered Jim's reel to Chase; he called Sanders back at 11 A.M. "All right, here's the deal," he told her. "I think he's brilliant. I have one concern, and that is, is he threatening enough?"

"David, if your only concern is, is he threatening enough . . . ," she said, laughing. "If you said to me, he's a little chubby, or he's losing his hair, I could understand. But he's *threatening* enough. This is your guy."

"In the movie version of *The Sopranos*, I thought about Robert De Niro," Chase said. "There was never anyone after that, seriously, who I thought could be Tony Soprano." He'd hired casting directors Georgianne Walken and Sheila Jaffe, based on their work on the Steve Buscemi film *Trees Lounge*. "We didn't know anything," Jaffe said. "Georgianne and I had been doing independent movies; we'd never done television." In 1996, they'd helped writer-director Melissa Painter cast a project she was workshopping at the Sundance Labs (it became her 1999 feature, *Wildflowers*), about a father and daughter. Painter suggested Gandolfini, whom she knew personally.

"We had only seen Jim Gandolfini play heavies," Jaffe said, "and this father was this hippie who was very different, but I thought he was a good actor. I'd seen him in *A Streetcar Named Desire* with Aida. I always thought he was really good, interesting, but I had never seen him do this kind of thing. But it was a lab and it was like, 'Why not?' He did it, and it was great. So I knew this other side of him that I don't think the general public had seen yet, which made me know he was capable of so much, because he was a really great guy."

With Sanders pushing for him, and Walken and Jaffe in his corner, Gandolfini was thrilled with Chase's *Sopranos* script. "I think my exact words were, 'I could kick this guy right in the ass, but I'll never get cast,'" he recalled. "'They'll hire some fucking pretty boy.' I thought they'd hire, you know, one of these Irish-looking guys who are all over TV now." What's more, Gandolfini wasn't the only one up for Tony (although, Walken noted, "everybody had to be Italian—that list was long, but it wasn't *that* long"), and everyone had to audition, first for Chase and then for the suits at HBO. "We said, 'No, you should know who he is,'" Mark Armstrong says. "Who is HBO to ask him to read when ABC, which was the big deal then, is offering him the lead of a show? So we said, 'No, but we will have him meet David,'" and they arranged a breakfast.

"At the time I was younger," Gandolfini recalled, "and I stayed out late a lot, and I was like, *Oh, for fuck's sake. This guy wants to eat breakfast? This guy's going to be a pain in the ass.* So we met and we spent most of the time laughing about our mothers and our families."

Next Gandolfini met with the powers that be at HBO, "and then he offered to read," Armstrong says with a laugh. "After all of us teeing it up and telling him he didn't have to." As Jim put it, "I was born to play Tony. . . . I wanted it so much I agreed to audition for it."

Walken and Jaffe rented an audition room on 72nd Street, a table and a couple of chairs, and set up a camera. Jim came in, chatted with Chase a bit, and started to read. "He was very good," Chase said. But Jim had barely made a dent in it when he stopped reading, and started apologizing. "I'm not doing this right," he insisted. "I didn't prepare for this right. I'm not doing it right. And I don't want to do it anymore. I want to come back and do it for you again."

He offered to come back the following Friday, Chase recalled, "and then Friday came along and he couldn't come in. I swear this is what we were told: his mother had died." It was purely a delaying tactic; Santa had passed months earlier.

By the time Jim finally felt ready to return, Chase was back in Los Angeles. But Walken and Jaffe were pushing hard for him—"He was really our favorite idea from the beginning," the latter confessed—so they flew him out to Los Angeles to put him on tape. "David ran the camera, and I read," Jaffe said. "And it was VHS tapes. That's how long ago it was. And David and I ran back to his house, watched it, and we both got really excited."

"When he finally settled down and really did a reading, it was just obvious," Chase said. "There was just not any question about it. He was the guy." But Chase had to be certain. "It was audition after audition—a lot of people went up for that role," he said. "As a matter of fact, they don't like you to bring in one person—they want to have some input. So three people were brought to HBO for the role of Tony, and Jim was one of them."

"There were three people testing for Tony," according to Michael Imperioli, who was also at the network test, for another role. "Jim Gandolfini, who I didn't know; Mike Rispoli, who I was good friends with, who went on to play Giacomo Michael 'Jackie' Aprile Sr.; and one guy who looked familiar but I couldn't figure out who he was. The casting director pulled me aside and said, 'That's Little Steven Van Zandt wearing a wig.'"

There was not an immediate consensus in the room. To Susie Fitzgerald, who was there on behalf of Brillstein-Grey, "the minute he walked in the room, I was like, *Oh, that's totally him.*" But Chase "took some convincing," according to Fitzgerald. "He loved Stevie Van Zandt." Fitzgerald pushed hard for Gandolfini; she recalled Chase worrying, "He's a pain in the ass on set."

"I don't care about that," she replied. "Is it him?"

According to Albrecht, "Rispoli was great. He was funnier than Jimmy, just because of the normal rhythms that he had. And we talked about it, and David said, 'It's a very different show if you put Rispoli in it or Jimmy in it, but the show I envisioned is the show that's got Jimmy in it. It's a much darker show with Jimmy in it.' I think we sat with that for a moment. 'Dark' is not really a word you ever want to go for in television, but the other one was 'more real.' So we cast Jimmy."

No one was more surprised than the actor himself. "This was an incredible leap of faith," he admitted. "I mean, it wasn't four pretty women in Manhattan [as in *Sex and the City*]. This was a bunch of fat guys from Jersey." Privately, he wasn't so sure about the show, or the role. Nancy Sanders remembers sitting with Jim and his agent David Brownstein in the Century Plaza Hotel restaurant near HBO's headquarters, pressing him to sign the contract and dealing with an eleventh-hour bout of second-guessing.

"Why am I doing this?" he asked her. "I came to you to do fucking movies. And now I'm doing an HBO series? I don't even know what the network is!"

"Jim, listen to me," she replied. "This is the best piece of writing I've ever read, whether it be TV, film, or theater. I promise you, this is worth doing. It's not going to change the world, but it's going to change TV."

"Fine," he sighed. "Fuck it." He signed the papers. When he broke the news to *Italian Movie* director Roberto Monticello, Gandolfini despaired, "Oh my God, Roberto, I'm gonna be unemployed in less than a year. Who the hell is going to see a television show about Mafiosos in Jersey?"

WITH HIS TONY SOPRANO IN PLACE, Chase set about filling out the cast. He initially approached Lorraine Bracco about playing Tony's wife, Carmela, but she demurred; the role was too similar to her Oscar-nominated turn as a mob wife in *Goodfellas*, so she asked to take a crack at Dr. Jennifer Melfi, Tony's psychiatrist, instead. "The first time I saw Mr. Gandolfini was when he was on Broadway," Bracco says, "in *Streetcar Named Desire*. That's the first time I saw him. And I remember going to the *Playbill* to see who that person was. I was like, *Who is this guy?* And I looked it up, and I said, *Oh, James Gan-Doll-Fee-Nee*. Nice Italian boy."

For Carmela, Chase cast New York stage actress Edie Falco, who was currently appearing on *Oz*. "I had been told that he got the part. I didn't really know who he was, as I'm sure he didn't know who I was," Falco says. "But they said he had been in a Quentin Tarantino movie." When she watched *True Romance*, she was somewhat taken aback, "because he beats the hell out of a woman or some horrible thing to watch. And I thought, listen, I'm grateful for the job, we'll just see how it all works out!

"And when I met him, it was just sort of easy-going. He seemed like a New York actor. And not—his personality betrayed his physical presence, you know what I mean?"

Imperioli landed his role as well, as Tony's nephew and possible successor, Christopher Moltisanti, while Chase collaborated with Steven Van Zandt to create the character of Silvio Dante as something of a consolation prize. Filling out Tony's crew were Vincent Pastore—like Gandolfini, he was a nightclub manager turned actor, and had appeared in small roles in *Italian Movie* and *Night Falls on Manhattan*—and Tony Sirico, who had turned to acting as a way out of his early life of crime, frequently appearing as underworld types in Woody Allen movies. "I loved Tony Sirico since the '80s," Pastore says. "We were running clubs together. Michael, when he was a kid, he used to come in my nightclub. We all knew each other, you know?" (Imperioli, Pastore, and Sirico had also all appeared alongside Bracco in Martin Scorsese's *Goodfellas*, which was Chase's key inspirational text.) As Tony's manipulative mother, Livia, Chase cast Nancy Marchand, a stage and television veteran then best known for her Emmy-winning work as a newspaper publisher on *Lou Grant*.

"I knew who all the different people were that they were auditioning," says Drea de Matteo, who went from a day player in the pilot to the supporting role of Christopher's girlfriend Adriana. "I was like, *They're going with people that nobody really knows. That's so interesting, that they're letting the show create itself, instead of the famous actors creating the show.*"

HBO was somewhat reluctant to grant Chase his wish to not only write but direct the pilot episode, as his directorial experience was somewhat limited. But he sold the powers that be on his sheer enthusiasm ("David committed his life to that show," Albrecht said, pinpointing Chase as "a guy who didn't have a whole lot of fun doing other things"), his knowledge of the milieu, and what he saw as the show's primary aesthetic mission: to look and sound less like television and more like cinema. "David Chase, even though his background is all steeped in television from *The Rockford Files* on, is an incredible cinephile," explains Phil Abraham, who was cinematographer for roughly half of the show's episodes (and camera operator for much of the first season). "Every reference that he made was never to another television show. Never, never. And I think he sort of said, *Look*, *you know, they're giving me a chance to do this, no one wanted to do it* . . . and this should be like a movie, a new movie every week."

Jim got to work on the character. "I had no interest in doing the dapper don kind of deal in *The Sopranos*," he later explained. "I know that's a part of the Mafia thing and I think a lot of those gentlemen are like that, but human frailty and confusion are what interest me. The more sensitive the character and the more he's in touch with things, the more confusion there is. People who just bludgeon everything as they go along, that's easy to do."

Since the show would shoot on the East Coast, he started working one-on-one with Susan Aston, doing intensive character prep and scene work. "We didn't know what it was gonna be, it was just a chance at something," she says. "And I helped him with that, you know, behind the scenes, no money. Because who knew?" He drew on his own experiences and connections to build the character: "I met a few mob guys over the years," he said at the time. "Living in New York and New Jersey, you kind of do." As time passed, he would downplay the work he had to put into the character. "It wasn't that hard," he insists in HBO's official companion book. "I grew up ten minutes from where this show took place. I'm an Italian kid from Jersey. My family—while there's nobody in it like Livia Soprano—is a dark group. I'm from this world."

He seized on the key visual and thematic motif of the pilot episode, in which Tony becomes enchanted by a family of ducks inhabiting his backyard pool, then depressed by their seasonal departure. "Once you identify for the actor, that it's that loss of control, *your family's flying away*, then he can start to personalize that in his own way—which he was able to do," Aston explains. "And that remained. So many of the scenes in *Sopranos* are still, continually, about trying to get his ducks in a row: trying to get the crew in control, trying to get his family in control, trying to get his mind in line."

Jim shot the pilot episode over two weeks in August 1997, right around *12 Angry Men*'s debut on Showtime. The process began with a full-cast table read, and though it was his first television series, and his first leading role, Gandolfini wasn't the only one nervous that day. "I was concerned, because I was coming into a whole new craft as an outsider," says Steven Van Zandt, who was then known only as a member of Bruce Springsteen's E Street Band. "On a set like that, the star really does set the mood and set the attitude, and Jimmy was just totally respectful from day one. He appreciated what I accomplished in my other world, and respected me jumping into this new profession, this new craft, with the seriousness that I did—I was always quite serious about it and quite dedicated to it. So Jimmy was very respectful, right from day one, and that respect spread through the entire cast."

This was the beginning of a pattern that would continue through the show's run. "The whole thing about Jimmy is, we were family on and off the camera," Pastore says. "And it started from the first table read." Jim was humble, even now that he was the first name on the call sheet. "I think we bonded right away, based on the fact that he was a character actor in his heart," Van Zandt says. "And so am I, you know, I prefer being a sideman, I prefer being the guy behind the guy. I'm not crazy about the spotlight in my life, and I think neither was he. So he was always very surprised. I mean, he would literally grab me and drag me in front of a mirror and he'd say, 'Look at this face, look at my face. You believe they cast me as the lead of this fucking show?' And he was totally sincere about it, he just was shocked at becoming the leading man."

Jim's manager Mark Armstrong got a taste of that shock when he visited the set a few days in. His client pulled him aside, in a semi-panic, insisting, "I can't do this. I'm not the number one. I'm not the lead of a show. I want you to go talk to David, and see if this is working or not working."

Armstrong obliged, approaching Chase and asking, "Hey, how's it going? Jim seems, you know, he doesn't feel secure, that he's the number one." Chase invited Armstrong to sit with him for a few minutes and watch Gandolfini interact with his co-workers. "And so we sat back," Armstrong says, "and he said hello to every grip that walked by. Knew everybody's name from above and below the line. And David said, *That's the number one of a show.* And that was our discussion about that."

Chase was already convinced that he'd made the right call. "The first day we were shooting," Chase said, "there was a scene in which Christopher told Tony that he was going to write a movie script and go to Hollywood. And in the dialogue, Tony said, 'What are you, crazy?' and he gives him a love tap. That's what I pictured. And we came to do it, and Jim pulled him out of his chair, shook him by the collar and was like 'Are you fucking crazy?' And I thought: That's Tony Soprano. He just felt like a real gangster."

Yet Chase was also struck by the duality Jim brought to the character. "I had questions myself about Jim Gandolfini," he said. "I've always asked myself, he's such a big guy, and yet he's such a sweetie-pie. But he could really be nasty and unpleasant if he had to be. I've always asked myself, is Jim such a sweetie-pie because there's a tendency there to be a bully, and the ability to be one, because he's so big? Does he overcompensate and be this nice guy everyone loves so he won't come off like a bully? I never got an answer."

Imperioli remembered:

> My first day on the set, I have to drive Jim. That's Christopher Moltisanti's job. Problem was, I didn't know how to drive. I hadn't told anybody because I wanted the job, you know? I had to back down the sidewalk with him next to me, doing dialogue with him, and extras running out of the way. I managed to do it several times, and then the director said, *Do it again twice as fast.* I smashed the rear end of that Lexus into this tree really bad. The airbags went off and our heads snapped back. It was a fucking mess. I'm sitting there going, *They're gonna fucking fire me. This guy must think I'm an asshole.* I turned to look at Jim and he's cracking up.

Gandolfini quickly proved adept at maintaining the right, light mood on set. "The first thing I remember is he had to do a thing where he had a panic attack and collapses," says Robert Iler, the young actor cast as Tony's teenage son, Anthony Jr. "I remember he fell over and then we all are supposed to rush over, like, *Oh my God, are you OK?* And then we rolled him over, and he had a raw hot dog in his mouth. Everybody just started cracking up."

Jim and Falco proved a good match, both in their on-screen repartee and the professionalism they exhibited to their castmates, many of whom were not as experienced. "Jimmy and Edie made everybody better," Chase explained. "Both of them were extraordinary. And two totally different styles of working. Jimmy would argue about everything: *I don't know, this doesn't work, why is he saying that, I don't want to.* Edie came in, had it all memorized. Never any discussion, just did it. And yet, look at, look at how well matched they seem. . . . They came to work and they did their job."

The hour of television they created was strikingly unique, a perfectly executed little sixty-minute film. The structure of the episode was unlike the rest of the series, with Tony visiting Dr. Melfi for his first sessions,

Jim with young Robert Iler, during production of *The Sopranos'* first season. (Courtesy HBO/Photofest.)

narrating and explaining his life to her, over cutaways and flashbacks to the events he describes. Some television actors take a few episodes to find the right notes for a character, but not Gandolfini; the shadings of Tony Soprano would grow more nuanced over the series' run, but the foundations are firmly in place, specifically his danger (how he flips from giggling and cackling as he chases a debtor down to the fury and rage of the beating he administers) and his vulnerability (the tears he sheds over the loss of his ducks). Yet some of his most quietly powerful work is in the duet scenes with Bracco, as he carefully chooses what he will talk about, and what he will not.

But proof-of-concept pilots like *The Sopranos'* are ultimately like another audition; a network can still, for any reason, choose not to take the show to series. This was news to relative newcomer Iler, whose family had been abuzz about the gig: "This is it, you're gonna be famous, this is gonna be massive and huge." When he said something to that effect in earshot of Tony Sirico, the older actor grabbed him and said, "Kid, do you know how many of these fucking things we do?"

"What do you mean?" Iler asked, confused.

"We're never gonna see each other again," Sirico informed him. "So have fun while you're here, and we'll all hang out and it'll be nice, but don't expect to ever see any of us ever again." ("So then I had to go break that to my family," Iler says.)

Sirico wasn't the only one. "Nobody knew it was going to become such a behemoth," says Alik Sakharov, cinematographer for the pilot and roughly half of the shows that followed. "But I do remember very distinctly, David and I used to share an office. And he would come into the office, and he would have this million-mile stare looking out the window, very quiet, so contemplatively being in his own world. One day I just asked him, 'David, what's up?' He said, 'I have no idea who the fuck is gonna watch this show.'"

That question loomed larger after Chase turned in the pilot to HBO in October 1997, and days turned to weeks while waiting for the response, which the network executives had to deliver by December 20. They weren't just being coy; test screenings had gone poorly enough that many of the initial concerns about the show (its lack of stars, its cost, its antihero, its adult subject matter), and even its title (execs worried that it sounded like a show about opera singers) lingered. As his impatience grew—"David," Susie Fitzgerald deadpanned, "is not a good waiter"—Chase developed a backup plan: If they rejected the pilot, maybe he could get them to put up enough extra money to turn it into the feature film he'd originally imagined, or even buy the pilot back from them and scrape the rest of the budget together himself.

The cast went about their work; Jim went out to Los Angeles for the *Remembrance* run (and his night in the Beverly Hills jail), then to Massachusetts to shoot *A Civil Action*. "I remember us sitting down with him after we saw it," Armstrong says of the pilot. "And we said, *This will be the best work you've ever done that probably a lot of people won't see.* Because we thought, it's not any of these network shows. Even if it gets picked up, a lot of people aren't gonna be watching HBO. So he wasn't sitting there waiting on pins and needles to hear if it was going. At all." If anything, he was regretting taking the role to begin with. "He had concerns because his father, who was probably just jabbing him, said, *I don't think this is any good*," says Sanders. "And then he wanted to get out of it. Obviously he didn't, because I'm sure he loved it. But he had a personality that always could come up with a better actor for a role, that typical thing, *Maybe I shouldn't be doing this*—a lot of second-guessing of himself."

Finally, on the day before the deadline, the network gave the order. "It was like a big Christmas present," Imperioli said. The announcement hit *Variety* on January 12, 1998: "HBO has committed to its second-ever episodic drama series, 'The Sopranos,' a Mob-themed hour for which the Time-Warner cabler has purchased 12 episodes, plus the completed pilot, for a total of 13 installments."

CHAPTER 9

BOSS

THERE WAS MUCH WORK TO do before Chase and company would go back in front of the cameras. "We had to figure out what the permanent sets would be, how to do it economically, who had worked out really well in the pilot," Chase said. "Almost everyone in it was pretty good." And there were twelve more episodes to write. Chase staffed up, hiring several experienced TV writers as well as consultants from both sides of the law. After mapping out the season and writing the first four episodes in Santa Monica, the crew went east, to settle into the show's production home at Silvercup Studios in Queens.

To stay within its initial, slender budgets, first-season episodes of *The Sopranos* were shot in eight days. "In the beginning, it was ridiculous," Jim said. "We were shooting sixteen- or seventeen-hour days and then I had to go home and memorize five or six more pages of dialogue," a stretch for an actor who'd always had trouble learning lines. "And it was brutal stuff," he explained, "mothers trying to kill you and therapy scenes where you're talking for four pages with the camera right on your face. It was no joke."

Luckily, he had some help. Susan Aston officially came on board at episode 3, credited as "dialogue coach," and continued working closely with Jim on character development (he was still filling journals with notes and thoughts on his characters' backgrounds and inner lives) and scene preparation. "David was very specific about a lot of things, and then, you know, he gave me a lot of leeway after a while," he said. "But there's a million things written into the show—like Tony taking the ham and dipping it into the mayonnaise. Or just opening the refrigerator and standing there, staring through it, you know? A lot of those physical things were written in there."

The show's writers and directors quickly learned that Gandolfini did not need them to flatter him—if anything, he delighted in looking physically out of sorts. He hits the wall throughout the series, never more so in the first season than in episode 12, "Isabella," a tour de force in which Tony is home, sick, depressed, and sweaty, the weight of his entire world on his shoulders, a dead man walking, literally and metaphorically. "Those were

Gandolfini as Tony Soprano, in a season 1 publicity photo.
(Courtesy HBO/Photofest.)

his choices, to look that bad and disheveled and all that. I think a lot of great actors don't care about that," Aston says. "As long as he's in character, I think he kind of thought that was fun."

He delighted in playing the character's softer side, and those are some of the most affecting moments of the season: the glimmer in his eye as he comes in and sees his daughter singing, a smile dancing around the corners of his mouth; how misty-eyed he gets packing away the family photos in his mother's now-empty house; the push in to a tight close-up as he throws dirt on Jackie's coffin; his candid confession of a wildly inappropriate crush on Dr. Melfi; the hurt he displays when his neighbor reveals that he can't get Tony into his WASP country club; the little master class in reactive anger after Junior insults him—bruised feelings, then fury, then bloodlust. He does much of his best acting with his eyes, carefully choosing when to bore them into a potential enemy, when to lower the hoods of his eyelids to shield his real feelings, and when to let them pierce one of his underlings so they know he means business.

But of course, the moments that made the firmest impression on the show's initial viewers were those in which Jim conveyed the character's rage, menace, and danger. He ends the show's second episode with a terrifying act of physical violence, clobbering the Bada Bing strip club's lunkheaded bartender with a telephone, then stalking away carrying a face that mixes anger and confusion in equal proportion. He perfected his signature move, which he'd been practicing on and off since *True Romance*, in which he smiles jovially while seething and/or threatening. And the most memorable moment comes in the season's final episode, when a simple smile from his mother causes Tony to become absolutely *unhinged*.

The most controversial episode of the first season, at least for HBO executives, was the fifth. In "College," Tony takes his teenage daughter, Meadow (Jamie-Lynn Sigler), on a road trip to visit the campuses of potential colleges in Maine, spots a one-time associate who testified and went into witness protection, and murders the "rat" coldly and efficiently. Until this point in the show, Tony Soprano had only roughed guys up; he had not killed anyone, or even directly ordered a murder. In "College," Tony doesn't just kill—he takes pleasure in the act, temporarily staving off his own depression and restlessness, or perhaps taking it out on a man who's given him an excuse for violence.

"The network didn't start complaining about that episode until after we'd shot it, and it was because that murder was really great," Chase said. "I don't think a lot of TV actors would've done that, or given their all for that, the way Jim did. He had spit coming out of his mouth.

Tony Soprano commits his first, controversial on-screen murder in the season 1 *Sopranos* episode "College." (Courtesy HBO/Photofest.)

When HBO read the script, they didn't see any of that. Once they saw it and he was schvitzing and everything like that, that's when Chris Albrecht called."

"David, you can't do this," Albrecht insisted. "He can't kill this guy. You haven't earned it yet. The audience is going to hate him. It's the fifth episode. Wait 'til the end of the season."

"If Tony Soprano were to find this guy and doesn't kill him, he's full of shit," Chase reasoned, "and therefore the show's full of shit."

Albrecht considered this. "Okay, that's a good point," he granted. The scene stayed in.

Luckily, that first year, there was no critical or popular consensus to consider. HBO didn't have a regular season with hard fall debut dates to deal with, and since no one there really knew what *The Sopranos* was going to be, or how they were going to market it, Chase was able to shoot, cut, and complete all twelve of the additional episodes before any of them had aired. They were working in a bubble, that summer and fall of 1998, with no one to satisfy but themselves. When they finished shooting, Chase said, "Jim, Edie, all of us were like, 'This was fun. It was an interesting challenge. We enjoyed ourselves.' Which of course meant that we weren't going to be able to continue, because TV is never about enjoying yourself."

And Jim did enjoy himself, that first season—he liked his co-stars and collaborators, and he felt comfortable with the character as he'd played it. Part of that came from identification. "The character is a good fit," he said at the time. "Obviously, I'm not a mobster, and there's other aspects of the guy I'm not familiar with, like how comfortable he is with violence. But in most of the ways that count, I have to say, yeah—the guy is me." He also found that much of the character's inner life mirrored his own. "It's a man in struggle," he said. "He doesn't have a religion, he doesn't believe in the government. He doesn't believe in anything except his code of honor, and his code of honor is all going to shit. So he has nothing left. He's got nothing left. And he's looking around . . . it was that searching that I think a lot of America does, half the time. You know, you can go buy things, you can do whatever. But it was that he had no center left. And I really identified with that."

AS THE SHOW'S DEBUT CREPT closer, HBO was still giving Chase grief about the title. "They went to an ad agency who submitted a thousand alternate titles," Chase said, "but they wanted *Family Man*"—a title that even made it into a *Variety* roundup of the network's original programming that October ("'Arliss,' 'Oz' and 'Sex & the City' will be joined on HBO early next year by 'Family Man,' the previously announced hour-long drama laced with black humor from Brillstein-Grey Entertainment"). "By that time, we were in production and the cast was very upset," Chase recalled. "Then *Family Guy* came on, luckily, and we called it *The Sopranos*."

The premiere was set to air on January 10, 1999, a low-profile date that betrayed the modest expectations of the network—and, frankly, of everyone involved. "We had no idea," cinematographer Phil Abraham says with a laugh. For the season 1 premiere party, HBO rented out the four-hundred-seat basement theater at the Virgin Megastore in Times Square, "and then we had a wrap party at John's Pizza. Then you cut to a couple years later, and we've got the whole skating rink in Rockefeller Center, and we bought out every restaurant, and the premiere's at Radio City. So yeah, we were humble." But not for long; Bruce Springsteen attended, sitting next to Steven Van Zandt as the first two episodes were screened. And in spite of Jim's concerns about staying away from gangster roles so he wouldn't embarrass his family, as well as his father's initial hesitancy, James Gandolfini Sr. attended and was "just very proud of him," according to Susan Aston. "His family was proud of him."

They had every reason to be. "Out of the hard work came something transcendent," Chase said. "It doesn't look like hard work. It looks like magic."

The critics agreed. The initial reviews were raves: The *Village Voice*'s Tom Carson called it "audacious—Mario Puzo rewritten by John Cheever," *TV Guide*'s Matt Roush deemed it "subtle, droll, and utterly original," and in the *Los Angeles Times*, Howard Rosenberg wrote, "Hands down, it's the series of the season." By the time that season was over, the reviews were borderline hyperbolic; the *New York Times*' notoriously finicky film critic Vincent Canby wrote an appreciation in which he appraised *The Sopranos* as a "magnificent megamovie" and compared it to *Berlin Alexanderplatz*, *The Singing Detective*, Erich von Stroheim's *Greed*, and the works of Charles Dickens.

Critics were just as overwhelmed by Gandolfini's sterling work at the show's center. The *New York Daily News*' David Bianculli praised his "brilliantly subtle, always surprising portrayal." In *Variety*, Phil Gallo wrote, "Gandolfini does a lot with body language, and his mood is nicely limned in virtually every scene; it can be summed up as a midlife crisis, yet it feels like so much more." In the *New York Post*, Michele Greppi raved, "Gandolfini joins the club of character actors who become sought-after leading men with his subtle, Emmy-worthy portrait of Tony." But no one was more rightfully rhapsodic than Matt Zoller Seitz, TV critic for Tony Soprano's driveway newspaper, the *Newark Star-Ledger*; he wrote, "In an era when television and movies prefer to fill leading roles with known quantities, it is a real thrill to watch a star being born. That star is James Gandolfini. . . . His is the kind of excellence that doesn't announce itself. In scene after scene and episode after episode, he keeps sneaking up on you, pulling small miracles out of his hip pockets."

Audiences were just as taken with the show when it unspooled on HBO that Sunday night in January, as a snowstorm crept up the Eastern Seaboard. Not everyone was on board immediately; there were some objections to the show's characterizations of Italian-Americans, including a *Los Angeles Times* op-ed accusing *The Sopranos*' "negative, cartoonish images" as being "culturally respectable prejudice being passed off as satire." Chase and his writers had deftly predicted and preemptively responded to this discourse in the season's eighth episode, "The Legend of Tennessee Moltisanti," where both Tony and Dr. Melfi engage in spirited dinner table conversations about the damage mob stereotypes have done to the public image of Italian-Americans. Gandolfini would say of this controversy, which recurred through the run, "Come on, you can't poke fun at yourselves?"

But for the most part, *The Sopranos* was an unqualified, and overnight, success. By the middle of the season, the show was topping ten million viewers per episode—the highest for a drama in HBO's history, and topping anything else on cable at the moment. "We didn't know if the show was going to be a big deal," Robert Iler explains, "and then there was a billboard in Times Square, and then, for every day for the rest of my life, the show was huge."

"I think having to go to the airport and have escorts at the airport, that kind of blew my mind," Drea de Matteo says. "I know that sounds really stupid, but I was like, *We need a golf cart to get us to the—isn't that for people that can't walk?* But they were like, *We need to get you guys through the airport quickly, and we don't want to stop the whole time*, and I was like, *Stop for what?* And 'stop for everyone' was what they meant. Especially when we were with Jim. All of them! They were so recognizable."

"The fuss started probably middle of the first year," Gandolfini recalled. HBO was known for its big boxing events, so executives invited him to one at Madison Square Garden; he brought Armstrong and Sanders as his guests. They were enjoying a pre-bout party when five security guards approached Jim. "You ready to go in?" one asked.

"We went down through the kitchen," Armstrong recalls (shades of *Goodfellas*), "and came out of these elevators, and then we went through the lobby to the tunnel. And I felt everyone getting tighter, crowds noticing him, security pushing us all together. And we went through the tunnel, and a spotlight came on."

"LADIES AND GENTLEMEN," boomed the announcer, "JAMES GANDOLFINI! TONY SOPRANO!" And the crowd was on its feet. "It was this crazy, loud, 'TONY, TONY, TONY,'" Sanders recalls. "It was like the Beatles had arrived." On their way to their ringside seats, Gandolfini put his arms around his managers and said, amused but accusingly, "Look what you did to my life."

"So that was like, O.K., it's pretty big," Jim granted. Ever modest, he was embarrassed by all the attention. "I feel like I'm being singled out for praise when it's an ensemble thing," he said in an early interview. "It's not fair to the other actors on the show—Edie, Michael, Lorraine, and all the rest. And David Chase, who is, let's face it, brilliant. Without the mind of David Chase behind this thing, we actors might as well just go home." He quickly developed an aversion to doing press, not only to preserve the enigma of the character, but because, in his words, "Who cares what an actor has to say about anything?"

"If there's one thing I hate, it's an actor getting up on a soapbox," he told Matt Zoller Seitz, before chuckling and miming a "scratch that" motion. "Hey, forget I said that. If you print me saying that, it's me getting up on a soapbox."

The HBO powers that be, knowing a good thing when they had it, quickly picked up *The Sopranos* for several additional seasons; CEO Jeff Bewkes explained, "We looked at each other and said, 'Let's pick it up not for one year, let's pick it up for four years. Let's sign everybody before they become hard to get.' And we did." (It proved a sound investment, becoming the first TV series to generate over $1 billion in combined revenues for syndication, DVD sales, video games, and other ancillaries.)

Accolades kept rolling in. The *New York Times*' Bill Carter reported, "network executives are trying to figure out how they can copy the breakthrough style of the HBO miniseries [*sic*] and perhaps make up for the mistake several of them made in passing up the show in the first place."

The *Times* also claimed that, thanks to the cool factor bestowed by *The Sopranos*, New Jersey was "no longer the punch-line state." New York City mayor, former mob prosecutor, and future accused criminal Rudy Giuliani told reporters, "It's a great show and I enjoy it very much." And FBI surveillance tapes revealed that even real wise guys were obsessed with the show ("What characters . . . great acting," raved alleged DeCavalcante family capo Anthony Rotundo).

And then the real awards began. When the Emmy nominations were announced in June, *The Sopranos* netted the first best drama nomination for a cable series, and more total nominations (sixteen) than any other series on broadcast or cable—among them, Gandolfini's first Emmy nomination for best actor. The awards themselves, handed out in September, were a disappointment; the show lost best drama to David E. Kelley's *The Practice*, set in a Boston law firm, and (according to the *New York Times*) an "obviously unhappy" Jim lost the best actor trophy to *NYPD Blue*'s Dennis Franz. The show won awards for writing, casting, editing, and a best actress prize for Edie Falco, but, still, the *New York Post*'s Austin Smith proclaimed that the show "wuz robbed" by a "clubby L.A.-based TV industry" that didn't want to reward a "New York show."

It would perform better at the following winter's Golden Globes, winning prizes for best drama, best actress for Falco, and best supporting actress for Nancy Marchand, as well as Jim's first Globe for best actor (he dedicated the prize to Marchand, unable to attend due to health woes, saying, "She couldn't be here tonight, and I'm standing here 'cause of her"), and at the Screen Actors Guild (SAG) Awards, where they repeated the best drama/actor/actress hat trick. "I don't think any of us expected that many people would watch a show about a bunch of lunatics from New Jersey," Gandolfini said in his acceptance speech.

BECAUSE SO MUCH OF WHAT was new and exciting and unusual about *The Sopranos* has become the norms (or even the clichés) of "prestige TV," it can be hard to explain the sheer blunt force impact of those initial episodes, of what made it a hinge point for how people both made and watched contemporary serialized drama. The antihero protagonist, for example, may as well be the current default setting; Tony Soprano was followed by Vic Mackey, Al Swearengen, Don Draper, Walter White, Frank Underwood. But once upon a time, television executives *and* creators were terrified of unlikable leading characters turning away audiences and sponsors. HBO's schematics weren't that cut-and-dried, and it was willing to take a chance by hanging an hour on a lying, cheating, killing criminal.

The miracle that Chase and Gandolfini managed to accomplish with Tony Soprano was not only to center such a character, but to make him sympathetic, even likable, in spite of those qualities. Traditional, terrestrial television, all the way back to Chase's beloved *The Untouchables*, trafficked in black and white; Tony Soprano, and the (predominantly) men who followed him, operated in shades of gray.

Jim's take on all of this was unsurprisingly nuanced. "I think the interesting thing is, David wrote not just from his darkness, but he wrote so honestly from himself," he said. "These weren't terrible people. They were people adrift. I once knew a guy that had been in this life for probably 15 years, and he said to me, 'I'd love to leave, but most of the stuff I have is in other people's names. I've never had a job. What legitimate job am I going to be able to get?' I mean, that was an old-school guy."

His thoughts on his own character, and the presentation of him, were similarly thoughtful:

> I think you cared about Tony because David was smart enough to write the Greek chorus, through Dr. Melfi. So you sat there and you got to see his motives, what he was thinking, what he was trying to do, what he was trying to fix, what he was trying to become. And then you saw it didn't really work out the way he wanted it to. If you took the Melfi scenes away, you wouldn't care about this man as much, or care about anything that was happening to him. With Dr. Melfi, he got to say that he cared about his son now, or cared about his wife—and then he'd go out and fuck everything up. I think you see that Tony's not the happiest guy, and that makes you feel a little for him, that he's trying to make himself better. If he was the happy mobster killing people, I don't think anybody would give a shit about him.

Matthew Weiner, who went from writing on *The Sopranos* to creating *Mad Men*, pinpointed the character's appeal succinctly. "The casting of Gandolfini is very important," he said, "because he allows us, because of his natural charisma, to enjoy all those fantasies of power that we wish we had. We love Tony because he has all of our animal appetites. Everyone would love to walk into a room and pick the biggest sandwich and take the best chair and have sex with the best-looking women. But at home he has the same life that we do. You can't get any respect at home! That's just the way it is."

Jim also understood Tony's appeal from this perspective: "I think a lot of people feel powerless sometimes. And Tony's powerless a lot. Here's this guy with all this power. And you know, his wife and his mother can cut him down to size in about three seconds." He put it in another, slightly lighter way in a dual interview with Bracco, laughing, "Tony just sits there and is completely abused by women. It's very much like my life."

But Jim also keenly understood the character's relationship to his specific time and place—it was a key piece of timing and serendipity, beyond the control of anyone who made the show, that it would debut in January 1999, as the notion of the end of the millennium was alternately gripping and thrilling the world around them. There are occasional textual references (Christopher announces, in the second episode, "I'm talking 'bout the year 2000! The Millennium! Where do we go from here?"; during the season finale, Father Phil notes, "I realized this morning I can set one of the dials to the millennial countdown!"), but the subtext is more potent. In the very first episode, one of the first things Tony wants to discuss with Dr. Melfi is his feeling of malaise for the end of an era: "It's good to be in something from the ground floor. I came too late for that, I know. But lately, I'm getting the feeling that I came in at the end. The best is over."

Jim expanded on this explicitly in interviews at the time: "I see the show as being about the pressure of being the first. Tony is the first guy to really rise high in his profession, to get out, to move into a nice suburban neighborhood, to have a shot at fitting in. But there's this conflict between that and what you might call the Old World way of doing things." He was more analytical toward the end of the run:

> What you see in Tony is that a life of materialism, of constantly feeding on the world, leads to nothing but emptiness. Someone like Paulie Walnuts has his way of life and he is what he is. He can be happy. But Tony is smart enough to know that there should be more, a bigger picture. He sees through all the bullshit around him. So he's empty. That's what eats at him: Why can't I be happy? Even when things are going well, I'm

> not happy. And there's too much history, too much baggage, for anything to ever really change. There's no way out. He's not really that different from anybody else.

Including, presumably, James Gandolfini himself.

Chase knew exactly why the character was received as he was. "For whatever reason," he surmised, "Tony Soprano was very available and recognizable to a great number of people who had never gone near a mobster, who'd never eaten a meatball sandwich. They related to that guy; they saw who he was. Part of it has to be because of James Gandolfini, and the magic that he worked. His eyes are very expressive. There's something about him that's very caring, which you see in him no matter what he's doing. There's a sadness there." He put it more bluntly in another interview: "He was extremely emotional. He couldn't shut off his emotions."

Jim never apologized for this quality about himself. "It's like showing emotion has become a bad thing," he said in 1999, as the show was launching. "Like there's something wrong with you and you're really in love or really angry and you show it. Like if you feel those powerful emotions and you express them, instead of keeping them inside or expressing yourself politely, then you must be someone who needs therapy, or Prozac. That's the world we're in right now."

When *that* aspect of the actor and the character merged, it defined both of them. "There is something sad about Tony Soprano," Chase said. "For one thing, there's something sad about Jim, a big guy with those eyes. I think in real life, there was something sad going on there. I think that's maybe why people liked him so much—he was like a big child or a big puppy dog, in a way. There was something sad about him, period, and something sad about Tony Soprano because you knew he was a gangster, and an efficient gangster, and yet he wasn't happy. In fact, he was very unhappy. He was depressed. Of course it would be sad."

What's fascinating about this explanation is that, by the end, it's unclear if Chase intends "he" to be Tony Soprano or James Gandolfini, or both. But by the end of production for season 1, even at this moment of professional victory, trouble in his personal life was making Jim unhappy. He had been seeing Marcy Wudarski since 1997; she had moved into Jim's West Village apartment the following year. One day on the set, Christine Gee—the script supervisor for that and every season through the show's run—noticed that Jim seemed down. "You can tell when something's weighing on somebody," she says. "And I remember him just kind of sitting off by himself, and he seemed distracted. So I just went and I sat to talk to him, like, *What's going on?* And he's like, *I don't know what to do*. I'm like, *About what?* And he said, *Marcy is pregnant*. Before he was married.

"He's like, *Marcy is pregnant*. And he's trying to decide, do I marry her or not. And he was torn . . . this was not a planned thing. But again, trying to do the right thing, you know. And so he made the choice to get married, to do the right thing. But I think he knew, from the beginning: it was not gonna work."

CHAPTER 10

PATRIARCH

JAMES GANDOLFINI AND MARCY WUDARSKI were married in March 1999, in a small, intimate ceremony; she gave birth to their son, Michael, on May 10, barely a month after *The Sopranos* aired its first-season finale. It was a whirlwind five months for Jim, who could've booked a lucrative movie role or two in the hiatus between *Sopranos* seasons (*8MM* slithered in theaters midway through the season, looking all the worse for so egregiously underusing the now star). He instead chose to take some much-needed time off, devoting his attention to his new wife and his new baby, and to prepare for what was shaping up to be a high-pressure return to his already iconic creation.

"When I sat down to start the second season I did have the feeling, now what am I going to do?" David Chase told the *New York Times*. "And you're aware there's a thing called a sophomore slump." He started meeting with his writers that February, not long after HBO gave him the go-ahead for a second season, but the stakes were already higher; this lark of a show, this experiment in expanding what both the television network and television drama was and what it could do, had boosted HBO's ratings and profile immeasurably, even prompting the broadcast networks that had passed on the show to launch their own pale (and short-lived) imitations.

Jim had been paid $55,000 per episode for season 1—a nice, healthy paycheck, but nothing like the hundreds of thousands (or even millions) per episode paid to the stars of hits like *Friends*, *Frasier*, and *Home Improvement*. When HBO and Brillstein-Grey Entertainment renewed Chase's contract, boosting his salary and budgets for season 2, they also gave Jim a bump. "Reps for HBO and Brillstein-Grey declined to comment on money matters," *Variety* reported, "but Gandolfini's fee is said to have been hiked into the low-six-figure per seg [episode] range." The overall boost to the (already high, by television standards) budgets of $2 million per episode was also left unreported, but the increase was enough for Chase to plan a location shoot in Naples, Italy, double the backbreaking one-week shooting schedules, and expand the cast.

The most significant addition to the Sopranos family was reported by the *New York Post* on May 11, the day after Michael Gandolfini joined the Gandolfini family. "A hand-delivered 'breakdown' alerted talent agents on both coasts yesterday that 'The Sopranos' is looking for Janice Soprano Parvati, described as 'Tony Soprano's older sister mid-to-late 40s. . . . Self-educated ex-hippie. Still a free spirit. In point of fact, she is Livia's daughter. Trouble.'" The new character was a quiet narrative insurance policy; that September, the *Post* reported that Marchand had been diagnosed with lung cancer. The reporting was new, but the diagnosis was not. "She was coughing when she came in for the initial reading," Chase recalled. "Coming up the stairs. We were on the second or third floor of this little building on 79th Street or something, and she was coughing then. She was very straight up about it."

"I've known I've had cancer for five years," Marchand said. "It was explained to [HBO] by my agent and they went on anyway," as Chase "had no belief this thing was going to go anywhere but the pilot." Per the *Post*'s source, "Her attitude is, 'Whatever happens, use it on the show,' and I think that's the way they'll go."

Whatever happened, lining up a secondary familial antagonist for Tony wasn't a bad idea, so Jim reached out to his old *Streetcar*, *Angie*, and *Fallen* castmate Aida Turturro. "I worked with her a lot," he said, "so when they did the auditions for my sister I made sure that she came in. She and I were like brother and sister. We've always had a love/antagonistic relationship. So it worked out well."

Gandolfini did what he could for Aida, offering to run the audition scenes, whatever might help her land the gig. "Listen, Jimmy, of course, I want this, but what are you going to do?" she told him. "If it's meant to be, it's going to be. I just have to say, if I don't get it, you have to lend me my rent money." In July, the trades announced that Turturro had booked the job.

Production on the second season began on July 6, 1999. In sharp contrast to the first year, created in a vacuum before anyone had seen a single frame, season 2 was shot under a microscope. Visiting a location shoot at a basketball court in Lower Manhattan, the *Newark Star-Ledger*'s Matt Zoller Seitz noted "the non-stop click-click of camera shutters: newspaper photographers, freelance paparazzi, amateurs with Polaroids and camcorders," as well as onlookers, autograph hounds, firefighters, and a woman

Aida Turturro and Gandolfini. (Courtesy HBO/Photofest.)

who "braves punishing Canal Street traffic to find out if 'The Sopranos' needs any extras. (It doesn't.)"

Most of the time, however, work was concentrated at Silvercup Studios in Queens, where the show had taken over most of two floors—four of the facility's stages downstairs (including the oversized Stage X, which housed the interiors of the Soprano home), and the production offices above. Among the latter was the writers' room, where Chase and his staff convened to work out the narratives and scripts. First they would determine what they called "tentpoles," the major events that would define the season arc, followed by the laborious task of breaking down the story for each episode one by one, determining major and minor plot lines. "A lot of this stuff was generated by writers' real experience and incidents," explains Steve Kornacki, who worked as both a production coordinator and writers' assistant. "David's big thing was truth—what's the truth of the character? What's the truth of the story?" As the run progressed, Chase developed a method of taping together eleven-by-seventeen-inch pieces of graph paper, running left to right and divided into episodes, to create a "map" of the season.

From their conversations in the writers' room (sometimes brainstorming scenes, often just swapping stories and chitchat), Chase would draft an outline with short, succinct scene descriptions. "But these guys had talked it through so much that they knew instinctively what to do," Kornacki says. "They didn't need a detailed network outline, which can end up being twenty pages, and by the time you see the script, it seems so stale, because everybody's had input, the network notes are in it, and it's just piece-of-shit television by that point." That outline went to the writer who'd been assigned to that episode; when they finished, Chase would lead the room in a session of notes, which the writer would incorporate into subsequent drafts before Chase took over for his final tweaks, which he could continue to make into the episode's production.

Once the scripts were close to completion, the episode's director would meet with key members of the creative team—Chase, executive producer Ilene Landress, the assistant director, the cinematographer, the unit production manager, any number of writer-producers, and members of the Los Angeles–based postproduction staff—for a "tone meeting" to discuss their execution of the episode. (The show began with a large rotation of for-hire directors, though during the run, Chase would winnow that down to a handful who were particularly adept and tuned-in to his specific aesthetic, and bring them back with increasing frequency.) Next would come production meetings with department heads, to coordinate costumes, props, locations, sets, makeup, and so on; the regular cinematographers, Alik Sakharov and Phil Abraham, would start working on their shot lists.

And then the scripts would make their way to the cast. Of the large ensemble, only Jim, Edie Falco, Michael Imperioli, and Lorraine Bracco would receive full teleplays. Everyone else would get only their own scenes in advance of the full-cast read-through—which made that event vastly more entertaining, as the supporting players realized how their scenes fit into the overall picture, or reacted to other threads fresh, as viewers would. Read-throughs were typically held during the lunch break of the previous episode's final shooting day; Chase might make a few more tweaks, based on how the script sounded out loud. "Then it was just off to the races with shooting," Kornacki says, "and then it started all over again for the next episode."

"You'll start Monday morning, usually 5:30, 6:00, even earlier," Gandolfini explained. "You'll go fourteen hours. And then, because the actors have a twelve-hour turnaround, you go to 8, and you start at 8:00 the next day, then you'll work till 10. Then you start at 10 the next day, you'll work till 12, and they can work you later on a Friday night. So Friday, usually

Jim and Edie Falco, on the set for season 2. (Courtesy HBO/Photofest.)

they're until 2 to 3 in the morning. Sometimes we've seen the sun come up on Saturday."

"We would call that Fraterdays," script supervisor Christine Gee says, laughing. "We were working Fraterdays: You would go in on a Friday and not leave until Saturday."

WITH THE FIRST SEASON AS a testing ground (and an extended round of getting-to-know-you), many of *The Sopranos*' logistics and conventions solidified in season 2. The cast saw its first noteworthy departure near the end of the year: Vinny Pastore's "Big Pussy" Bonpensiero, whacked by Tony and the crew upon his discovery (suggested by a food poisoning–induced fever dream) that his trusted associate and friend turned "rat" for the FBI. The cast had already become close, and they took Pastore's exodus hard, launching what would become a regular tradition of taking the departing actor out for a send-off dinner immediately after shooting their final scene.

Season 2 also began a pattern of "villains du jour," new characters who would appear for a year or two, antagonize Tony (often in a manner so vile and repugnant that he couldn't help but seem sympathetic in comparison), and threaten his power before their eventual dismissal. Character actor David Proval, best known for his work in Martin Scorsese's breakthrough film *Mean Streets*, served this function in the second season as the loathsome Richie Aprile, older brother of Michael Rispoli's late Jackie Senior and newly released from prison.

"The first day of shooting—the first day I worked with James Gandolfini—we drive up to his trailer," Proval said. "We're parked in Jersey in a mall, so you had to go over to his trailer to pick him up. Guy gets out of the van, knocks on the door, comes back in the van, and we're waiting five, ten minutes. Guy goes out again, knocks on the door, Jimmy is not coming out. And I'm biting at the bit. I was up all night. I can't sleep. You know that one, you're going to work the next day, you can't sleep. I'm sitting there and then he comes out and screams, 'Can't anybody take a shit anymore in the morning?' He screamed at everybody. I said, 'Okay, right. This is perfect.'"

Proval and Aida Turturro were not the only new additions to the cast. Las Vegas–based actor Steve Schirripa was still fairly new to the business when he was cast as Bobby Baccalieri, originally conceived as more or less a one-off role. His first scene was with Jim, "and he's trying to scare me, and when you worked with Jim, you didn't have to act scared, you know what I mean?" Yet Schirripa recalls feeling immediately at home. "He knew that I was a little green. And once the scene was over, it was like I knew all of them, Jim included, I knew everybody for twenty years. It was like, *OK, we did the scene, you're one of the guys.*"

That warmth extended through the rest of that first day for Schirripa, who was outside the studio waiting for his ride when Gandolfini's car was pulling out. Jim, riding in the back seat, had his window down, so Schirripa offered up a friendly, "I'll see you, Jim." Gandolfini had the driver stop the car and back up, so he could get out and tell Schirripa, warmly but firmly, "I'll see you again."

"Jim is the star," Schirripa says, still moved. "If Jim is a prick my first day on the set, he could just fucking destroy me. I'm outta the box. . . . But I thought that was pretty nice, the star of the show, this huge star, coming back. I was a nobody. I was a day player."

Diva antics wouldn't fly. *The Sopranos* may have been the hottest show in the country, James Gandolfini an "overnight" sensation at age thirty-nine, but he refused to take himself too seriously. "We do this long walk-and-talk," Proval said. "It's my first fucking day. I'm standing there in the clothes, Members Only, and I'm wearing the pants high. I look down at myself and the people walking by who are going shopping."

"Do you feel a little silly right now?" Proval asked Gandolfini. "Silly like we're going to go pretend something right now?"

"Always," Jim replied, immediately. "I always feel very dumb doing this."

"And then the guy says, 'Action,'" Proval said, "and we spilled into it."

The inescapable nature of the show's popularity would become clear over the course of that season—never more so than when they headed to Naples in late October. "We get to the island, and we get off the boat and get on the what do you call it, the train up the mountain," Tony Sirico said. "And so Vincent [Pastore] and I are there in the car, we're just sitting there, and there's like fifteen tourists from Ireland in the car, and we hear them start saying, 'Hey, it's Paulie, that's Pussy!' Like, they know us. Tourists from fucking Ireland know the show! That's when it hit me. This thing was a really big deal."

PERHAPS THE TRICKIEST DYNAMIC ON the *Sopranos* set, and one that evolved (and not always in positive directions) throughout the run, was the relationship between Jim and David Chase. Chase directed the pilot episode and would not do that job again until the series finale, even though directing had always been his ultimate goal. But the director is, to a great extent, merely a hired hand in television. Power is held by the showrunner, and the fact that Chase was not calling "action" and "cut" did not mean he was ceding control—quite the opposite, in fact. From his office above the stages of Silvercup, there was not one element, not a single detail, of *The Sopranos* that he did not touch, approve, or reject. "He was always upstairs in the offices, he didn't come to set all that often," Christine Gee says. "So he was sort of this godlike figure in our minds." Frequent director Tim Van Patten nicknamed him "the master cylinder."

"Some new actors would come in, and they would paraphrase the lines," Gandolfini said. "When you paraphrase, it's easier, so you don't work as hard. But if you respect the writer and you say the lines the way they're written, you discover things. So one guy said, 'My character wouldn't say this,' and David Chase said, 'Well, it's not your character. It's mine.'"

But Jim had never responded well to authority, and the more Chase became the Great and Powerful Oz, the more Gandolfini pushed back. "Look, they had a great relationship," explains Phil Abraham. "However, that kind of relationship is fraught by its very nature. They're both, to some extent, creators of the show in that sense." The more time Jim spent in Tony's skin, the more he felt that he knew what the character would and wouldn't do, say, or tolerate. And the more time Jim spent on the set, the more entitled he felt to speak up, often sharply, when scenes or beats weren't working for him.

Yet even here, the back-and-forth wasn't simple—Chase was not a "my way or the highway" type. He not only took feedback, but welcomed it. "What's good about David and his way of working is that he was always inspiring a debate," says Alik Sakharov. "Argument as a philosophical discourse. So what's interesting about David was that if you didn't agree with him on something, or didn't like something, he wouldn't recoil. . . . He would be more like, *Well, what do you mean by that?*"

Complicating matters further were Jim's own insecurities and uncertainties. "People would probably never say this," he confessed, "but I think the character of Tony, David Chase, and myself all have a sense of self-loathing that we share in common. I think he can write it, I can play it, and Tony has it. It all kind of works out in the end." It did, but their debates were often spirited. Gandolfini pushed back "all the time," Chase said, mostly to the character's brutality, "because it was so dissonant with his own values. I could say, 'Well, Jim was a big guy, an angry guy, and he was concerned about that. He didn't want to be taken for a bully or a thug, even before the show.' It was for the obvious reasons: he didn't like what the characters were doing and he didn't want to portray that."

Jim's resistance to the less savory aspects of the character was an ongoing source of frustration for Chase. "He said in front of a bunch of us, more than once, that he had to tell Jim, 'You have to say the line,'" says location manager Mark Kamine. "'That's the line, that's the right line,' and that's what he would do. He had to draw the line—say the line, draw the line. Like, we're not being good citizens here. We're doing a fictional show about a creepy guy, who's also very appealing, obviously."

"It was rare that I didn't understand what David was trying to say or where the character was going," Gandolfini said. "I can count on my hands the times I went up to him and I said, 'Tony wouldn't do this, or say that,' but I don't think there was any time that I ever said, 'No fucking way.'" Nancy Sanders confirms this: "He never, ever laid a heavy hand on material. David was the man and there was respect for him. He wasn't pushing his weight around."

"We'd go around and around, I'd say this and he'd say that," Chase said. "It depended on the case. In the end, he'd always do it." But with each passing season, no matter how hard Jim worked to distance and compartmentalize, he could feel the darkness of Tony Soprano seeping into his own soul.

The intensity of his process, and the sheer, overwhelming volume of the work, certainly contributed to the fusion of the actor and the character. Jim had taken pains, especially when playing sleazier characters in *True Romance* or *8MM*, to place himself in a character's world and circumstance, but he was also reluctant to cross the line into Method madness, "becoming the character" and staying in it for days on end—mostly due to his ongoing, working-class cynicism about the job itself. Co-star Robert Iler defines Jim's approach as "take the acting seriously, but don't take yourself so seriously, because you're just fucking acting. When you're doing it, it's important to take it serious. But when we're done here, don't go thinking you're fucking special, because you pretended to do something that someone wrote for you."

To that end, he would sometimes minimize the extent of his preparation and the degree to which he intellectualized the work. "Jim had a mantra, and I adopted it," Vincent Curatola says. "Jim's thing was, if I had my head on my hands on the table ready to begin the scene, and they're still lighting, getting ready, whatever, he would say, 'What are you doing?' 'Nothing.' 'You're thinking right now.' 'Jimmy, I'm not thinking.' 'What do I tell you, all the time. Don't fucking think!' He was right. And I tell my students, stop thinking, no thinking, you will fuck it up. Just open your mouth, react, talk, whatever is in the script."

But the Gandolfini Method was not a casual one. "I've heard him talk sometimes, he just learned his lines and tries not to bump into furniture, the Spencer Tracy thing," Susan Aston says. "But that wasn't true. That was a big fat lie. You know? Because he worked really hard."

As had always been the case, much of the work for Jim was simply learning, and remembering, the dialogue. "It's rote. You memorize it by rote," Aston says. "You don't learn it with feeling, right? Because don't you want that, to be able to be in the moment? You just memorized the lines." But

Tony Soprano had voluminous dialogue. "It was really hard for him, I think, to retain," co-star and sometime director Steve Buscemi said. "He had *so* many lines, you know, and the character was so dark. He really struggled."

Jim's memorization method, which he'd used for years, was to write his lines out in longhand on one side of an index card ("it was just that kind of sensory thing," Christine Gee says), and then to write the other actor's cue line on the reverse side. Then he could stack them up, like a kid using flash cards, read the cue line, and recite his response. (He taught this technique to Vinny Pastore, who still uses it to this day and teaches it to his own acting students.)

Breaking down and analyzing the scripts got more complicated. Jim's preference was always to work through the text in sequence—especially for films, which were never *shot* in sequence. "It's kind of like when you do a play," he explained, "and you rehearse scenes three, four, and five, and six, seven, and eight, but you don't really know the character until you do a run-through of the whole thing. And then you go, Oh! And something happens—the guy starts to come to life and you get the whole thing. . . . I'll know I can do a role, but it doesn't take shape sometimes until I talk it out."

He didn't always have that luxury on *The Sopranos*, with its quick turnarounds and ongoing script tweaks. "You would be in the middle of shooting the end of an episode, go read the next script at the lunch break, and then start shooting it the next day," Susan Aston says. "But I could do the prep for him, which is what I did. We would meet together, and I would have all the questions laid out and all the priors clear for him."

"Susan is as much a part of all of this *Soprano* thing as me," Jim confirmed. "It's fifty-fifty. We will work twelve to fourteen hours, shooting scene after scene after scene, and then you're gonna come home. And you got another day of it. Seven, eight pages. Four, five scenes. This is every day. So you got to go home, and you got to memorize all the stuff for the next day." After a typical shooting day, he would go home and shower, and Susan would meet him at his apartment at midnight to work the next day's scenes. They'd work the lines until he was most of the way there, then put the scenes on their feet.

"A lot of times, she's given me great insight into things that I never would have thought about," he said. "A lot of times, we argue, and a lot of times, she tells me to calm down and stop being such an idiot or something." These arguments were not uncommon, Aston says, but they were healthy. "We both were highly intelligent, opinionated people," she notes. "We each said anything to the other. We were not precious with each other. If we had a different point of view about something, we might argue." Once they had the next day's scenes down, or once Jim was too exhausted to work—whichever came first—he would go to bed for a couple of hours before the car came to pick him up for the next day. "I mean, we were just madmen," Aston says. "Nobody slept. It was crazy." ("There's where your 'gravity' comes from," he would joke. "Pure fucking fatigue.")

"Jim was very serious about his work," Steve Schirripa says. "Very, very, very, very serious. He thought things out." But he worked that hard to achieve a kind of freedom. "I don't want to give the impression that his work was *studied*," Aston emphasizes, with some urgency. "We would rehearse. But part of the rehearsal process is using your intellect to ask the right questions—and then allowing the heart to rise up and answer them. Then when your camera would actually start rolling, *then* you let all that prep go, all those things, and you have this trust. He would allow himself to go very much into what I call 'the abyss of the unknown,' working without a net, and just being with that other person, and allowing this thing to happen in the moment."

On set, he would use more direct methods to get into the right mood for a scene. He developed what he dubbed "the Breathing Thing," an exercise involving taking and holding a quick breath, vibrating it within the diaphragm, shaking the solar plexus, and letting the mind wander, "picking up whatever memories, images, or thoughts come to you in relation to the scene you're playing and the emotion you're exploring," according to coach Harold Guskin. "It throws everything off," Gandolfini explained. "When you do it, you can go a lot of places really quick. It helped me because when I'm doing *The Sopranos*, sometimes I literally only have time to change clothes before I have to go to a scene where I have to get angry."

Other times, he would explore external and physical motivations to get where he needed to go emotionally. "Lack of sleep will piss you off to no end," he told James Lipton. "Sleep two, three hours a night for two nights before you have a really violent scene, every single thing that anyone does will piss you off." His son, Michael, who would become an actor himself, questioned the validity of this method. "I've always wondered about the sleep thing," he told *Esquire*. "I've heard that before, but I also feel like my dad had the worst sleep apnea and he was like, 'I'll tell people I do that.'"

"I'll do a lot of weird things," Jim said. "Do whatever you need to do. You can put a rock in your shoe, a very pointy rock, walk around with that all day. I mean, it's silly, but it works." In a later season, when Tony was lying in a hospital bed in excruciating pain, he had a crew member put several nails through a block of wood. "He tucked it under his side, as he's laying in the bed, in order to make himself really feel pain," Christine Gee recalls. "So that it would be legit. He didn't want to fake it."

Michael Imperioli remembered that "he wasn't a smoker, but sometimes, to get into his scene, he'd asked for unfiltered Lucky Strikes, and he'd smoke one. Jim's father used to smoke those. So I don't know what connection he was making or how that got him into it, but sometimes he'd smoke one, not on camera." Crew members would often hear him grunting or cursing in his trailer to work himself up for scenes; he'd often use music as well, Sinatra or Skynyrd or AC/DC, depending on the vibe of what they were shooting. "Especially in the morning if I have to be pissed off, I'll put on a little AC/DC," he said. "Bang my head against things."

"I saw nothing but the good side of him," Steven Van Zandt says, "but on the *Sopranos* set . . . he would not *one hundred percent* be that guy all the time? But it was definitely present. Tony Soprano was *definitely* there, quite a bit at a time." Jim took to wearing Tony's heavy bathrobe between scenes, even under the blazing lights, even during shoots in the summer, because it helped him stay in the character. "He'd be walking through the hallways, arriving to set, and the robe is blowing behind him," Iler says with a laugh. "You were like, *Oh, shit's about to go down*, you know. *Tony's coming.*"

ONCE "TONY" ARRIVED, THE ACTORS and their director would begin reading and staging the scenes while the cinematographer and his team finalized placement and worked out lighting. When it came time to roll cameras, Jim would often focus himself with sounds, grunts, curses, or even animal noises. The latter came from an old acting class, where he'd learned that sharp noises can release tension. "It's almost like, you are about to make a fool of yourself, so you might as well make a fool of yourself right away," he explained, "and then making a fool of yourself on camera is a little easier."

After the director called "cut," Jim would often confer with Aston, who was on set as well. As the show became more popular and he grew more famous, he relied on her more and more to keep his work honest. "When you get to a certain level in your career," she explains, "people are just so excited to be working with 'Tony Soprano,' they don't even see him as a person—and they're sure as heck not gonna give him a major adjustment if he's coming in from the wrong direction. I didn't have anything at all to lose by telling James my, for what it was worth, absolute point of view. That's why he wanted me there."

But Jim was also open to adjustments requested by the directors, even if they modified his entire approach to a scene. "I remember going to him and saying, *this line* or *this beat*, and I talked about it," recalled frequent director Alan Taylor. "And he said, *Oh, OK*. We did the next take, and the entire performance of the whole scene shifted. And in the shifting, he hit that moment the way I wanted him to, but it wasn't like he just nailed that little beat for me. It was like he said, *OK, I get what you're saying*, and did the work that put the character there, so that that beat would play that way."

Abraham remembered this incident as well. "To me," he says, "that's very telling of an actor who fully understands what the director is telling him and what the character needs to do to get there." Cinematographer Alik Sakharov was often struck, while marking the points on the floor where the camera would move for coverage, that Gandolfini was "clocking it all, he's working it out. And he was basing his performance toward the anchor points. Very clever. Very smart. Very, very advanced, *thinking* actor."

"I worked with him first as a director," Buscemi said. "And so I would ofttimes not see, you know, I didn't understand what he was doing. He'd take his time. And I'd be, *What the fuck is he doing? Say the line!* And then I'd watch it in editing, and you just go, *Oh my god*. Like, you could see the process, you can see him thinking." Once the camera was rolling, he kept working, modifying, fine-tuning. "He was willing to do as many takes as it took to get what they needed," Aston says. "And sometimes he would be the one asking to go again—*There's something I didn't get. I just want to do it one more time*."

Yet he would do whatever it took to keep a scene fresh. "There's a corny saying, where it's like, *acting is doing*, and that's what I would see with him," Iler says. Sometimes that was an understatement. In one of their scenes together, in the Soprano kitchen, Tony gets angry about a phone call and yanks the telephone right out of the wall. Before the take, Gandolfini warned Iler to stand still. "I winged the thing this close to his head," Jim recalled. "I'm so glad it didn't hit him. It ended up in the dishwasher. That was all a surprise. It's the best thing that happens."

It's the best thing that happens. As the grind of the job set in—as it always does, even when you're making the best show on television—Jim looked for those little moments, those sparks of electricity that brought scenes to life. "Jamie-Lynn Sigler told me an incredible story," Schirripa says. "They were working, and it was early on, and they were in the car together. It was the college episode. And, she was a little nervous, and Jim said, 'Just look me in the eyes, and talk to me. Just look me in the eyes and talk to me.'" Those interactions, those connections, were what it was all about. Because he had done all that intense, analytical homework with Aston, "he's free to be in the moment," she says. "Because he's not saying, *Oh, what the fuck does that mean*? Or *Why am I saying this*? Or *How long has it been since I saw this person last?* When you do your work, you can be grounded in that reality, and be instinctual. You're free. If you do your work, you're free."

That freedom could be both intimidating and inspiring to Jim's colleagues. "He didn't let himself get bossed around by a lot of the things that I let walk me around," Edie Falco explains. "Like, this good student mentality I always had, *get the lines just right and do the blocking exactly the same every time*. He was following something . . . bigger and deeper, you know? If he had an impulse to say something a little different, or to change the blocking, he just did it. And I was jealous that he had somehow gotten permission from himself, to do that kind of thing."

"He did that all the time," Imperioli said. "And he made you do it. Made you *want* to do it."

"You've got to be present," Falco continues. "You can't do it the way you rehearsed it in your bathroom. You've got to show up and just be in the room with him—and what could possibly be more fun than that, from a performance point of view?"

"He was a great Ping-Pong player when it came to acting," Lorraine Bracco says, a metaphor that Annabella Sciorra echoed: "It doesn't matter what you throw, you know, you're constantly throwing and it's coming back and throwing and it's coming back. . . . He's just *there*, constantly in the moment." His presence, his commitment, was sometimes intimidating to his fellow actors. "It's almost as if his energy was so intense that I could talk to Tony Soprano, without actually *looking* at Tony Soprano, because that's how immense his character was," Vincent Curatola says. "And that's how layered his portrayal was."

Yet he was also sensitive to his co-stars, and instinctively picked up on how they wanted to work. "We kind of stayed out of each other's ways when we weren't shooting, if we had a break, or if they were changing the camera angle," Falco says. "There was no chitchat, and there wasn't like, *What do you need me to do? Should I leave?* There was no discussion about it. There was an intrinsic understanding." But other actors wanted that chitchat, and he treated them accordingly. "Once you would hear *cut*, boom, we're back to Jimmy, we're back to Vince," Curatola says. They even had a go-to topic of conversation: "We both love Turner Classic Movies. He would go nuts on them. We would go through movie after movie after movie."

He extended his generosity to his fellow actors in other ways. Vinny Pastore came to see Gandolfini as something of a mentor. "Listen, I didn't start acting till I was forty-two years old," he says. "I was in the nightclub business for years, after I got out of the service. Guys like Jimmy were doing it from the minute they get out of college, and they went into theater. I didn't start until years later. So I was like a new kid on the block, and I was trying to learn as I worked." Leading actors, in film and television, frequently slip out once their coverage is complete, retreating to their trailers to relax or prepare for the next scene, rather than performing more takes, off camera or over the phone, for another actor's close-ups. Jim didn't work that way.

"He was always there for the other person's coverage, even a person that might just come in for the day," Aston says. "I've seen him even ask if they wanted to go first or second, because he wanted people to feel comfortable and do a good job. He was a very generous actor." Phil Abraham concurs—"Typically, number one gets to go first, and he just didn't want to be part of that kind of thing"—while noting that this emphasis on accommodation sometimes worked to his own detriment: "Oftentimes, when it was Jim's turn to go, he would lose what he had, when he was doing what he was doing off camera."

He would also use his power as "number one" to ensure his fellow actors were satisfied with their work. "He would say to you, *You want another take? You're OK with that? You're good?* He would ask that you were OK," recalls Schirripa. Pastore had the same experience. "I said I dunno, and he turned around to one of the guys behind the camera and says, 'Give him another take.' And David didn't say nothing, and Alan didn't say nothing, because they knew that Jimmy had that power."

With Lorraine Bracco, however, all rules were off. As the show's regular routine developed, Jim began asking to make Tony's scenes with Dr. Melfi the last that were shot, since they typically had the most (and longest stretches of) dialogue for him to memorize. "We had very long scenes," Bracco explains. "He always wanted to shoot it in one long conversation, so he would tell the camera crew to make sure that they had enough film, that he didn't have to stop. So that was important for him. And yes, we definitely went up on our lines. But he always had to tell the story."

"We would end up doing these things Friday at like three in the morning," Jim said. "They're long scenes and she would be wonderful. She calmed me down. She'd sit you down and we would work together. She would really bring me along, much like the relationship that was there. And I think she does that innately because she's a good actress. You know, as time went on, we became friends. She's a wonderful lady." Because these were often her only scenes, he said, "she would always come in with a fresh spirit 'cause she wasn't in a lot of the week. I would be—*Thank God, 'cause I don't know how I'm going to get through this*, and she would take me through it."

Jim often struggled with the lines for these long scenes, keeping his "sides" (pocket-sized script pages for easy reference) close at hand, stuffing them into his chair at the last possible second before they'd call action. When the show ended, Christine Gee recalls, set dresser Jeffrey M. Marchetti "reached into the back of the seat because he saw a piece of paper sticking out. They were all the sides, from all these seasons, stuck down in between the cushion and the back of the seat." They even found one from the pilot; Gee showed it to Jim and asked if he still remembered the lines. He shot her a look and deadpanned, "I don't even remember *last* week's lines."

The Melfi duets became some of the most memorable scenes to shoot, though not always because of the first-rate acting on display. "It was late some nights and you know, a lot of weird shit comes up," Gandolfini said with a shrug. Bracco is more pointed: "He was a pain in my ass," she says, laughing. "What happened was, he would do his sides first because he was the precursor of the story. And then when he was finished, he was relaxed and done with it. He didn't care, it was over for him, except we had to turn around and do my part! He would dance, he was crazy!"

Jim made specific requests for his coverage, asking the crew to set up black screens behind Bracco so he wouldn't have anything in his eyeline to break his concentration during the long monologues. Then they'd move the screens to his side when it was time for her coverage, and he would try to break her up. Sometimes he would do his "hula dance" (asked by James Lipton what kind of dance it was, Gandolfini replied, "One you're not going to see, my friend"). And sometimes, he would stick his bare ass between the screens.

"Mooning occurred," she confirms. "He had an ass the size of Staten Island!"

Joking aside, Bracco understood the pressure Gandolfini was under, and the steam he was letting off on those late Friday nights. "I think it would take a toll on anyone," she says. "Tony Soprano was not an easy character to play. In spite of everything, he was a mobster, he was a killer. He went home and worried about what kind of orange juice he was gonna get, but he was still a mobster. Not easy."

"I used to call David in the middle of the night and scream at him: 'You're fucking killing me! I'll give the money back, just make it stop!'" Jim said. "Obviously, they didn't cast me in this part because I'm such a normal, well-balanced human being."

As the pressures of the show piled up, his castmates would marvel at his work ethic. "Doing a show like that, do you know how much work it is for him?" Turturro said. "For a lead on any of these shows, these people *work*, they're in it, all the time. And I never saw anyone work so hard at each scene, analyzing it, working on it." Tony Sirico agreed. "He worked so hard, that Jimmy. I did the 'Pine Barrens,' I was in thirty scenes—thirty scenes! I lost like ten pounds. And Jimmy did that every week."

"For nine months, basically, he would work," Schirripa explains. "You're working until two, three, four in the morning on a Friday. You sleep half the day Saturday, you have Saturday night to go out to dinner and see your family. Sunday, you've got to go to bed early, because you've got to be back at work at seven in the morning on Monday. So it's not much of a life, you know?"

As the shows, and seasons, and years stretched on, it began to feel less like a dream job than a life sentence. "What I witnessed was, at the end of every day, we'd sit—sometimes in a bar, sometimes just during the lunch breaks," Van Zandt says. "And he basically quit the show, like, every day. He's like, *I can't do this, I just can't do this*, you know. Literally every other day." But what always brought him back from the brink, and kept him re-upping for each new season, was the realization that there was now a giant machine of writers, technicians, and actors whose livelihoods depended on him. He couldn't let them down.

The feeling was mutual. "Naturally you hear from actors, because he was so giving to the other actors," says Don Scardino, who was also working at Silvercup at the time (as a writer-producer on *30 Rock*) and would later direct Jim in *The Incredible Burt Wonderstone*. "But you also hear from all the crew guys, *everybody* worked on that show. Not a person was forgotten in Jimmy's orbit. And I think it's one of the things that gave this show such integrity—obviously the writing and everybody's contribution, but because the fish stinks from the head. When the guy at the center is a guy like that, everybody comes to do their best work. Nobody wants to let him down."

Reports of his personal kindness and camaraderie circulated during the run of the show; Jim was typically modest when it came up in a rare interview. "Well, that whole group of actors is just a good group of people," he said, "a little embarrassed," according to the reporter. "I mean, I think we all watch out for each other a little bit. . . . I've worked with a lot of people, and I just don't see a lot of this nonsense you read about people refusing to get out of their trailers. Everybody I know just works really hard and does their job."

"There were no stars," director Tim Van Patten said. "There's Jim and Edie setting the tone, and they carried such a huge burden on that show in terms of just physical labor." The other oft-repeated characterization—perhaps an easy one because of the nature of the character he played—was that Jim was the patriarch of *The Sopranos*, both on- and off-screen. Sometimes the characterization was quite literal; Jamie-Lynn Sigler told *Rolling Stone*, "I think of him as my second father," and said he would get on the phone with her boyfriend and remind him to treat her right. But as usual, it wasn't something he sought out. "I think he was the patriarch because we *made* him the patriarch," Iler says. "I don't think he came in and was like, *I'm going to be the patriarch of this, I'm going to do that*. I think he obviously stepped up whenever it was necessary. But I really think he just wanted to be one of the guys."

And not everyone experienced that kind of closeness. "I really didn't have much of a relationship with Jim outside of our shooting relationship," Falco says. "He was a very gregarious person, but we didn't socialize. We didn't have the same group of friends. So it was certainly cordial and professional, but we didn't hang out—and it was not on purpose, it was just the way it was. And I don't know how all this stuff is done, I don't know how the whole acting thing *works*. I don't understand it. If I try to get in there and figure it out, it just confuses me. But I'm thinking part of me really just loved the very full, dimensional relationship I had with him as Tony. And I think maybe I only wanted that."

Frequent director Allen Coulter also found it hard to connect. "Jim, as we know, was not easy," he said, granting that he was "a great actor" but "a very complex man. . . . Being around Jim was like being around someone who's flailing around. And every once in a while, you get an elbow in your eye. But, you know, it wasn't aimed at you. That was kind of what it was like to direct him."

Director and producer Chiemi Karasawa first met Jim as a fill-in script supervisor on the show, taking on the job when Christine Gee was out, and was struck by his memory and attentiveness to detail. "I'm the messenger they kill when everything goes wrong," she says, laughing. "So I would always end up in these weird situations with Jim where he'd be like, 'No, that wasn't it. It was supposed to be in the afternoon' when the scene happened, 'it was supposed to be over here.' He was really good-natured about it." It was a give-and-take; he would rely on the crew himself, and entrust them, in similar ways. "We were working on an episode," Abraham says, "and he actually pulled me aside, and we walked behind the set. And he said, 'Listen, I don't know about this guy—the director—because I just tanked that last take and he said, print.' So he goes, 'You gotta watch, you gotta keep your eyes open.'"

As a general rule, Jim was "not in his trailer, none of that bullshit," according to Sakharov, even when he should've left to rest. He soon found a solution for that: Tony's recliner on the set of the Soprano house. "The crew would try and get dibs on whatever lounging equipment they could get their hands on for lunchtime, so they could take a nap or whatever," Christine Gee says. "But Jim would often be in there in the recliner, Tony Soprano's recliner, napping—because he had sleep apnea, and he didn't always get a good night's rest. There were days where he was just exhausted, and you could see the rings under his eyes and makeup trying to cover it. So he would very often go sleep in the Soprano living room." But, Gee stresses, "Anybody would give it up to Jim. And, for sure, he would never toss anybody out of it."

He would also offer to take whatever bullets might come the crew's way. As the budgets increased, so did the pressure to make their days, exerted by producers and network suits alike, who would sometimes come on the set to push things along. Phil Abraham remembers Gandolfini coming over to him when this happened once, early in the run, and quietly conspiring. "Listen, anytime that you're getting the bum's rush," he told the cinematographer, "and you feel you need more time, just give me [a signal] and I'll walk off set. I'll go. I'll just walk off set and then let them worry about that."

It was all a result of, as Iler puts it, "the working-class thing." Though Jim was now well regarded, and well paid, he was keenly aware that many of those around him were not. Some actors prepared for stardom by reciting Oscar acceptance speeches in the bathroom mirror; his old pal T. J. Foderaro believes Jim learned how to treat his colleagues during his years managing clubs like Private Eyes—"just the way he related to and connected with people quickly and naturally, effortlessly, in a way that everybody just felt comfortable and good around him."

Beyond personal respect, he gained a reputation for his financial generosity. "Always getting presents for people, doing nice things, taking care of people, families," Falco says. "He was a tremendously generous soul." Not long into the show, he began a tradition that continued through the run, providing food for the crew on those long Friday nights—eventually regular, weekly meals from the hot, Tribeca-based sushi restaurant Nobu. "There would be a spread, whether Jimmy was there or not, that would be paid for," Sakharov says. "It was his way of thanking the crew."

When he wanted to give a jokier gift, Gandolfini also had a go-to, from his favorite Jersey deli. "A huge box that had two big mozzarella balls," recalls Mark Armstrong. "I mean *big*, on the bottom. And then, you can use your imagination, a long salami in the middle."

"I NEVER SAW HIM BE anything but great to any other actors, for sure," Iler says. "Just super kind and sweet." As ever, his anger and impatience only pointed inward. "If he messed up a line or said something wrong, he would be *so hard* on himself," Iler says. It would manifest itself in many ways, some verbal—he'd reprimand himself, or shout profanities, as he had since *Kiss Me, Kate* at Park Ridge High—and some physical. He'd slap or even punch himself. He'd bang his fists in frustration. "I mean, he punched holes through walls," Gee says, nonchalantly. "He busted up his camper. More than once."

"Yeah, he definitely would lose his temper with himself," says Drea de Matteo. "Which was, you know . . . you don't want to be in that space with him as much, I would say?" Phil Abraham recalls, "I remember once, he was messing something up, and I saw him pounding a brick wall. Like literally, *pounding a brick wall*, cutting his knuckles up, and like, What the fuck, Jim, stop! Is this the tool you need, to find what you're not getting? I don't think it's working, you know?"

"He would punch the walls," Schirripa grants. "He punched the walls if he blew a line. But listen, he had all the pressure on him. Michael, Dominic, Edie, Lorraine, they all had stuff to do, Jim was not carrying *all* the weight, but certainly a lot of it. He had a lot of work to do!"

"I did witness this at times," Falco says. "There are many ways that kind of energy could have gone, but for him, it seemed to go inward. This is for a therapist to say and not me, why he has so little sense of his own value, as a person and as an actor. People behave in the strangest way toward themselves. You can't *believe* the way people talk about themselves sometimes."

Vince Curatola has a theory. "He's a perfectionist, and anybody of this caliber of talent is going to be a perfectionist," he says. "You've got a lot of people relying upon you, you're the star of a major juggernaut of a series. And time is money on set, and you just want to be perfect. And he was the kind of guy, he never fluffed it off. . . . I never saw him punch a wall. I never saw him break anything. But I've seen that redness in the face. And that's when you turn around and go smoke a cigarette. Come back later, you know!"

Gandolfini's habits would prove infectious—often comically so. Robert Iler recalls his first post-*Sopranos* acting gig. "On the second day," he says, "we were filming something and I messed up a line. And I was like 'Motherfucker, fuck!' I'm yelling and cursing and they're like, 'OK, cut,' and the director's like, 'Can we take five?' And the director comes over to me like, 'Is everything OK? You seem really angry, is everything all right?' And putting it together after, I was like, *oh, that's what Jim would do.* I learned from watching Jim."

Yet for all his focus, exhaustion, and self-flagellation, there was plenty of fun on the set, at least in those early years. "He was gentle, and self-deprecating, and funny and playful as hell," Falco says. Vincent Curatola had his own experience with Jim's playfulness. "For some strange reason, all those years, I was the target of him throwing ice cubes at me," he says with a laugh. "Because my resting face looks like I'm pissed off and depressed, but I'm not. And if there was any ice around, in a bucket, he would just throw it at me. This went on for years! This was like, I knew he was in a good mood when he put his hand in an ice bucket."

The omnipresence of food props on the set—between the many dinner scenes and the subplots concerning Vesuvio's restaurant—made for some memorable moments as well. "One time they had to make quail," Christine Gee recalls. "So they just cooked it enough to make it look nice on the outside. It wasn't really cooked. And I remember going to Jim's camper for something, I think it was a dialogue change, and he's sitting there eating the raw quail. He's like, *What you talking about, it's just a piece of meat!*"

A man of prodigious appetites, Jim frequently found the food props hard to resist. Gee remembers a shooting day that began with a scene in the Bada Bing's VIP lounge. "They were having steak and lobster," she says, "and they were eating it *during rehearsal.*" But there was a problem: "They hadn't cooked enough of them. The actors went and ate all the food during rehearsals, so we had to hold off shooting until they could thaw out and cook the steaks. It was ridiculous, but nobody stopped them from eating it in rehearsal. And I'm like, *Who the hell eats surf and turf at seven in the morning*?"

Edie Falco recalls a Tony-Carmela dialogue scene where Tony eats ice cream. "We did it, and we had to do it again," she says. "And we had to do it again. And every time, even when they said cut, he continued to eat the ice cream. And they put more in, and they put more in, and eventually he would kind of look at me to say his line . . . and he wasn't home. He was in a full-blown sugar coma. He looked like a giant toddler. And he kind of looked at me and I realized, holy crap, *he doesn't remember his lines.* So we had to wrap the scene and reshoot it another day because he had too much ice cream!"

CHAPTER 11

STAR

"I REMEMBER AT THE END of season 2, he sent me this picture of the two of us with a note behind it saying, *We did it*," Phil Abraham says. "Because season 2 was this ball-busting season; we went to Italy, we were shooting crazy hours. . . . It was all-encompassing, and I remember that. *We did it*, you know, we did it together. We all did this, we should be proud."

Indeed, they should have—Jim especially should have. The intensity and complexity of his portrayal of Tony Soprano in the second season somehow surpassed the brilliance of the first. The addition of Janice, and of Aida Turturro's marvelously prickly characterization, opened up a new source of tension for Gandolfini; their relationship is one of the show's most fascinating, the warmth on the surface a thin veneer for the deep suspicion and resentment between them. He may have severed ties with Livia, but Janice gets him going the way no one can but their mother, though Richie Aprile, a marvelous foil, comes close. Perhaps Gandolfini's best single acting moment of the season is his knottily complex response when he looks over at his crying sister and sees that she's shot his sworn enemy, though his reaction to the news that he's off the hook for a murder (alone in his bathroom, in the dark, smiling and giggling in relief as tears form in his eyes) is a strong contender.

He plays the moments of darkness with equal aplomb: the guilt of murdering Big Pussy and Matt Bevilaqua (particularly the latter's final cry of "Mommy!"), his proclamation that "everything's black" in a season finale haunted by nightmares of suicide and death, an especially raw and ugly fight with Carmela (which gets momentarily and scarily physical) that shows Chase and Gandolfini were already taking pains to keep Tony Soprano from being *too* likable or sympathetic.

HBO set a January 16, 2000, debut date for season 2—the first and last time that a season of the show would debut, in the norms of the industry, a year after its predecessor. The ad campaign for season 1 had been sharp and accurate but cautious; there was no such modesty this time around, as HBO spent a fortune on magazine and newspaper ads, TV spots, subway billboards, and branded buses. The campaign was the biggest in the network's history to that point.

The big season premiere and party left the humble environs of the Virgin Megastore basement and John's Pizza far in the rearview; the first two episodes would screen at the legendary Ziegfeld Theatre in Midtown, which typically premiered major Hollywood movies, with the after-party at the similarly beloved Roseland Ballroom, where vegetable lasagna and ziti with meat sauce were served. The guest list included Spike Lee, Jerry Seinfeld, Sarah Jessica Parker and Matthew Broderick, Aida's cousin John Turturro, and Christopher Walken, Jim's old *True Romance* co-star (and husband of *Sopranos* casting director Georgianne Walken).

Jim attended but kept as low a profile as he could, keeping his comments to the attending press brief, with one exception. "At that point, I was working for HBO," says Jim's Park Ridge High School classmate Karen Duffy. "My job was the entertainment host. So I would have to go to all the HBO productions and do that excruciating job of interviewing celebrities on the red carpet." When HBO found out that she had an existing relationship with their notoriously press-shy star, they would push her to get a sound bite or two from him. "I would never, like, embarrass him or bring anything up," she says, but no matter the event, he would always pause his hustle down the red carpet for his old friend, announcing, "I have to do Duff."

It wasn't only a reunion for Duffy and Gandolfini. "At every one of those events, he brought our high school collection of mugs," she says, affectionately. "The knuckleheads that we grew up with were now grown men, but he had his high school best friends, they were the ones that he had walk on the red carpet with him and attend the parties. I just love that. That shows you who he is."

"The evolution of Jimmy Gandolfini was not shocking to any of us," says classmate Elizabeth Forsyth. "It was just, you know, *Hey, Jimmy's in a movie.* Or, *Hey, did you hear that Jimmy's doing well?* One of the things that I always was proud of was when Duff interviewed him. It was just a cool moment for Park Ridge, two people that really made it."

Anticipation for season 2 was breathless—the *New York Times* called it "the most talked-about show of this year and the most anticipated of the next"—but the reviews were, if anything, more enthusiastic this time around. "As startling and unpredictable as the first season" (*TV Guide*); "'The Sopranos' is perhaps even savvier and more wicked than last season"

(*Newsday*); "'The Sopranos' remains a showcase for ferociously distinctive writing, inventive direction and brilliant portrayals of surprisingly, even disturbingly sympathetic characters by a perfectly cast group of actors who hold back nothing" (*New York Daily News*).

Chief among them, of course, was Jim, whose notices were similarly ecstatic. *Variety*'s Phil Gallo: "James Gandolfini continues to expertly play the most compelling character on series television." The *New York Times*' Caryn James: "How magically James Gandolfini embodies this likable, despicable character. . . . he is the greatest of the series' many wicked delights." The *Los Angeles Times*' Howard Rosenberg: "James Gandolfini's brutal but complex Mafia chieftain, Tony Soprano, is as gloriously coarse and seductive as ever."

The raves didn't stop there. The fever pitch of coverage continued, particularly in publications around the tristate area, with check-ins (Vincent Pastore got two write-ups in the *Times*, in two months, after Big Pussy was whacked), weekly recaps, mid-season reviews, and post-finale postmortems. There were takes from real-life wise guys, real-life psychiatrists, and feminists. The controversy over Italian-American representation returned. ("We'd get accused, back then, of glamorizing mobsters, but we were all half miserable, you know," Jim said.)

At the beginning of the season, the *New York Times* ran an opinion piece titled, "Why America Loves 'The Sopranos.'" On NPR's *Fresh Air*, David Chase had the answer: "Without Jim Gandolfini, there is no *Sopranos*," he told Terry Gross. "People always ask me, why do people like the show so much? Why the furor? And it's because of him. That's why the whole thing, I think, is so identifiable to so many people, because he just is so human, and people respond to him. Their hearts and their heads go out to him, despite the heinous things he's doing on screen."

The ratings continued to soar in season 2, up 60 percent from the freshman year. HBO reported adding over a million new subscribers, and re-upped Chase's deal. The show again got the shaft at the September 2000 Emmys, with its voluminous nominations resulting in only one major win—but it was for Jim, his first trophy for best actor.

The ceaseless attention was anathema to Jim. Everything related to the show was somehow deemed newsworthy. There was no topic the New York tabloids wouldn't spill ink on, interviewing extras, reporting on the rap sheets of day players, profiling (per one *Daily News* headline) THE BRAINS BEHIND THE TALKING FISH, and that "everything is news" philosophy extended to the show's star; a 2000 *New York Times* piece on a Manhattan company that specialized in exotic car rentals, for example, took pains to mention Jim's patronage. ("'He was a very down-to-earth guy,' Melena Montana, the manager, said. 'But I doubt he'd come by himself now to pick up a car. He's too important.'")

"He was married to Marcy," says manager Nancy Sanders. "And then Michael was born—very important to do that shielding of the kid. But he didn't go out and there wasn't social media. So this was not a party guy. I mean, he still was best friends with his high school friends and his college friends. Like, he wasn't cool. He *wasn't cool.*" Nevertheless, the tabs gobbled up crumbs. The lead item in a 2000 "Rush & Molloy" *New York Daily News* gossip column stalked a "boys night out" with Jim (who was, they wrote, "apparently up for a break from family life") and a group of friends, from a Ford agency party at Lot 61 introducing a new supermodel ("Gandolfini appeared to enjoy the surroundings") to an inadvertent stop-in at a gay nightclub before landing at Privilege, "the new gentlemen's club on W. 23rd Street that feature 40 topless beauties. It may not have compared to the Bada Bing Club on 'The Sopranos.' But the Gandolfini crew liked what they saw. They emerged around 2 a.m."

The tabloids weren't just thirsting for salacious stories of strip club visits. Near the end of the first season, the *New York Post* reported on a dispute with his co-op board; the item, trivial on its face, also inaccurately claims the altercation was over moving his mother into his apartment (Santa had passed two years earlier). In 2001, when a real estate deal between Gandolfini and then-married Ethan Hawke and Uma Thurman went south—he was in contract to buy their West Village brownstone—the *Post* gave the non-story a full-page spread, headlined "MOB" CONTRACT WAR and featuring an insert image of Jim as Tony Soprano, scowling in the direction of a photo of the smiling celebrity couple.

This was par for the course for the tabs, whose art choices favored threatening Tony stills, and whose headlines frequently featured variations on "mob," "godfather," or "goodfella." When they weren't connecting him to the criminal life of his character, the headlines and text went at his weight, deeming him "burly" or "beefy" or worse. The *New York Observer* awkwardly shoehorned him into a 2001 article about acid reflux, headlined ACID REFLUX, CHIC GASTRIC AILMENT, REPLACES THE ULCER—ASK GANDOLFINI. More repulsive was an *Observer* article the following year headlined EAT! IT'S TUBBY TOWN, in which writer Alexandra Wolfe insisted, "Take a look around: New York is fat as a house, and enjoying it. The city's new layer of fat is not the apologetic fat of yore; it's a fat that pronounces itself. It's the fuck-you fat of James Gandolfini and Rosie O'Donnell and Alec Baldwin."

"He hated it," Susan Aston says, sadly. "He *hated* it. And it hurt his feelings. He's a sensitive guy. And it's like, why do they just want to be so mean? Why do they just want to ruin your life? Why can't they just be happy that you're making something in the city that's giving a lot of people jobs, and they just want to make your life miserable?"

"He definitely tried to ignore it, because nobody would send it to him," Sanders says. "If he *had* seen it, he didn't really talk about it. If something pissed him off, he'd want to right a wrong. But for the most part, he hung his head low, and just got through his rapidly changing life and popularity."

Conversely, he was also put off by a strain of coverage, not only restricted to tabloids, proclaiming him a sex symbol. As the first season concluded, the *New York Daily News* devoted two pages to the reasons that "Gandolfini's goodfella stirs up plenty of heat with NYC women": "He's strong. He's rich. He's armed. And he's sexy. Dead sexy."

It wasn't that the notion was off base, particularly among those who knew and worked with him. "We all had crushes on him," Drea de Matteo says. "My friend Ginger, who was a PA on the show at the time, we used to walk around and make like, the sound of a faucet going? Meaning like we need a cold shower, every time we walked by Jim. Who knew that we would have crushes on this big, hulking, balding, middle-aged man? Like, I was obsessed with Axl Rose when I was a kid."

Jim's modesty and cynicism prevented him from embracing the idea, at least publicly. Sometimes he'd respond analytically. "It's true that Tony's a very passionate guy—he's passionate in everything he does—and I think that's what his appeal is," he said in 2001. "I think his passions are one of the things that people find sexy about him. . . . He lives by his passions. Of course, they also f- him up." A few years later, he theorized "that happened when I started wearing my underwear and let all my fat rolls hang out. And all of a sudden it's like, *Oh, he's sexy*. But he's sexy because he likes to fuck on the show. I think that's what's sexy about him." He was willing to admit, "It's flattering that anybody could—at a certain age and a certain paunch and a certain baldness—the fact that anyone would suppose their attention on you is extremely flattering."

But there was always an edge to that talk, typically couched in the language and construction of *Hey, isn't it wild that I/we/these women think THIS GUY is hot*? (A typical passage from that *New York Daily News* piece: "And that couch-potato body . . . well, let's not even go there.") In private, he took a highly cynical view of the entire thing. While they were out at a restaurant, director Rod Lurie took note of "women that were hitting on him, *really* dramatically. Just being really, really overt with him."

"Do you look at yourself as a sexy guy?" Lurie asked.

"I'm a fat slob, not a sexy guy," Gandolfini replied. He pointed at a nearby television and added, "That's what makes me sexy."

That same thinking was at the root of his discomfort with fame. "I don't think he ever really wanted to be famous," says manager Mark Armstrong. "He loved getting opportunities for good parts, but I think he would have loved staying a character actor under the radar if he could." He resisted it as long as possible. Steven Van Zandt remembers the planning of one of the early premiere parties. "I said, you really need a VIP section," he recalls. "And he was like, *Oh, I don't want a VIP section*. I said, Jimmy, trust me on this, OK? It's gonna be a thousand people there. If you want to actually

Gandolfini with his longtime manager, Mark Armstrong, circa 2000. (Courtesy Mark Armstrong.)

have a calm drink or something to eat or just a conversation with anybody, you gotta separate from the pack a little bit, or else it's one big meet and greet, it's no fun. You won't have one single conversation of any meaning. And he's like, *Nah, no, no, no, no.*

"So, you know, we put the VIP section up anyway, and the first thing, he wouldn't go in there. And of course he got attacked by a thousand people. About an hour into the thing, he stumbles into the VIP section saying, *OK, OK, I get it now! I give up!*"

Even other celebrities were dazzled by the intensity of his connection with fans. In 2001, Armstrong and Sanders were trying to put Jim and Meryl Streep together for a project, so they all met at a hotel for a script reading. Gandolfini had driven in, so afterward, he offered to drop Streep at her home. "No, no, no, I'll just hop in a cab," she demurred.

"That's crazy," he insisted. "I've got my car here. Let me take you home." So as they stood on 55th Street near Fifth Avenue in Midtown Manhattan, waiting for the valet to bring his car out, everyone who passed hollered out to him: "Jim!" "Tony!" "Love the show!" "Hey, Jim, you know my sister . . ." and so on.

"How do you do it?" Streep finally asked.

"What are you talking about?" he replied, incredulously. "You're *Meryl Streep.*"

She smiled. "Do you see one person saying anything to me?"

HIS RESISTANCE TO SUCCESS IMMEDIATELY became part of his persona (and enigma), and theories abound as to what was at the root of it. "I think there was a certain amount that Jim possibly didn't think he deserved it, for some reason," Steve Schirripa opines. "I think he was very confident in his work and acting. But I also think he struggled for years—he started late, and then he was a character actor, and then he becomes this huge, worldwide star." Jim admitted as much himself: "I'm under no delusions about what all this is about. Well, I'm sure I have some delusions. But you know, basically it's a job. You work hard, and you get tired a little bit, but that's all it is."

"I think, given how he grew up and who his parents were, very working class, he was facing a world that he never expected to enter," says his former agent Diana Doussant. "I think he thought he was going to be a janitor like his father, or like a bartender or something, and live down the shore."

"He was just a regular guy, and that's all he wanted to be," says his *12 Angry Men* co-star Mykelti Williamson, who remembers bumping into Jim during the height of *Sopranos* mania at a New York nightclub. "We were having drinks, and cigars, and someone came over to the table and said their friend wanted to know if they could take a picture. And I just remember the look Jimmy had," Williamson says. "He took pictures with them, and he took pictures with somebody else, and then, after a couple of minutes, we all left. He just didn't like that. He was cool until somebody approached him and singled him out. He figured he's a target tonight, so let's break it up."

"I know that he missed his privacy," Susan Aston says. "On more than one occasion, he would introduce me as his wife and say that we hadn't seen each other all weekend, to please go away so that we could get caught up. Just so people don't bother him while we're trying to have a bite to eat or something." He would eventually have to resort to even grander gestures. "I remember being out with him once," says filmmaker Robert Pulcini, "and I was like, *I can't believe we're just at a restaurant and nobody's freaking out.* And then when we got up to leave, I realized they pulled back this huge divider and there were just people standing there just waiting to get a glimpse of him, on the other side of the room. They had been standing there during the whole meal."

"Jim Gandolfini was just part of that system, and it fucked him up," says Patty Woo. "Listen, when people tell you you're the Godfather and the best thing since sliced bread for twelve years, you're not going to walk away from that thinking, *I'm just Jim Gandolfini from New Jersey*. It doesn't work that way. . . . He had such strong emotions, but was really a neophyte in the business. He didn't have any defenses."

Jim's general discomfort with fame and wealth, coupled with the tone and tenor of the tabloid coverage, locked in his existing resistance to media interactions. Interviews were even less frequent in the later seasons of *The Sopranos*; during a rare on-set report, *Rolling Stone*'s Chris Heath wrote, "For the first two days I'm on the *Sopranos* set, James Gandolfini does not say hello to me, though one time he catches my eyes across a crowded soundstage and raises his eyes as if to say, "Yeah, I know you're there." In time, he gets friendlier. One morning he walks in and stretches out his hand. 'Hello, Satan,' he says to me, in the sweetest of ways."

He had firm feelings about what too much Jim Gandolfini would do to his audience's perception of Tony Soprano. "He was adamant about it,"

Armstrong explains. "He said, *When I'm in people's living rooms every Sunday night, I don't want them to think of Jim Gandolfini.*" Later in the run, Gandolfini expanded on this. "I'm saying that I do my job," he said. "When I'm playing Tony Soprano, they think I'm like that, and when I'm playing someone else, they should think that character's like that. It's not me." And as far as he was concerned, he was doing them all a favor: "When people want to ask you to dinner sometimes and they don't know you, they want Tony Soprano to come to dinner. They don't want Jim Gandolfini to come to dinner. I would bore the fucking tits off them."

It's a good excuse, but the most likely explanation is the simplest: He didn't enjoy giving interviews. "It's just not comfortable," Aston says. "You're afraid you're going to say something wrong or something that will get twisted around; if things are working the way they are, why risk mucking them up? I have a career, why do I need to talk about it?"

"I actually learned that it was OK not to play the celebrity game from him," Drea de Matteo says. "Because he didn't like to do press. I didn't like to do press. And I was getting forced into doing tons of it, lots of talk shows, and I did not feel comfortable doing it. So I did learn that if he doesn't want to deal with them, why the fuck do I have to do it? But then my PR would be like, *Because he's James Gandolfini, and you're just Dre.*"

One aspect of the job they both participated in, and at least enjoyed to some extent, was the events HBO arranged to help promote the show—the premieres and parties, as well as fan events and meet and greets at nearby casinos and hotspots. "We had so many awesome celebrations together, and he was our leader," de Matteo says. "We were not a Hollywood bunch of people. And Jim was our ringleader for that, because we were a bunch of New York actors. So it was just kind of a different vibe."

"When we went to do the meet and greets, that's how the public wanted to see us," Vinny Pastore says. "Jimmy would get upset when people called him Tony. I didn't, I kind of took it in. I said, *OK, that's what you want to call me? OK!*" That wasn't the only time the fans spooked Jim. According to Schirripa, "We were in West Virginia, and some guy took off his shirt and he had a tattoo of Jim's face on his back. He had a tattoo of Jim, and a tattoo of Scarface, Al Pacino. And he went, 'That really freaks me out, man! That guy's got my face on his back!'"

"We'd be in the bathroom and he'd be like, at the urinal," co-star John Ventimiglia recalled, "and people were coming up to him at the urinal wanting to shake his hand. Honestly!" He did occasionally appreciate the spoils of celebrity—he could always get restaurant reservations, and if someone he knew was sick, he could pull strings to get them the best care. "God love him, he would help," his old friend Tom Richardson explains. "He had a lot of ability to help. He had a lot of wisdom, and he had a lot of resources, and had a lot of friends." But ultimately, he saw fame and celebrity as fundamentally absurd, based less on his considerable talent (which had always been there) than luck, timing, and soon-to-be-passing fads.

"When it came down to it, none of us were stars, and none of us behaved like that," Falco explains. "We were just actors who couldn't believe our good fortune, that we got a show that's actually up and running. It was a tremendously exciting time for us." As time passed, for Jim, the excitement did as well. "I would call Jimmy on the phone and I would say, *Jimmy, man, I'm so happy for you,*" Alec Baldwin said. "And he would always say to me, *I can't fucking believe I gotta get up at four o'clock in the morning, get in this fucking van, and drive over. This is the biggest pain in the ass! This show is the biggest pain in my ass! You have no idea what a pain in the ass this thing is!* I mean, he was such a whiner."

The pressures—of the fame, of the show, of family life—were getting to him. In 2004, on *Inside the Actors Studio,* host James Lipton pressed Jim on his own experiences in therapy. "I've been in some of those rooms," he said. "I don't think when I started the series I did."

"Was it research or was it real?" Lipton asked.

"No, it was—it was real," Jim replied.

"It was real," Lipton confirmed.

And then Jim pulled back. "It was a cry for help," he replied, mockingly. He was laughing. But the real cry for help wasn't far behind.

CHAPTER 12

LEROY

IS TONY GETTING TOO BIG FOR TV? asked the headline of a 2001 *New York Post* article—typical for the tabloid, in both its conflation of Jim with his character and its winking reference to his physicality. But the question posed by writer Don Kaplan was a legitimate one: "While Gandolfini, 39, enjoys his immense popularity and rising stock in Hollywood, some within the entertainment trade are beginning to wonder out loud whether he has become too hot a property to remain on the HBO mob opera." There was certainly more money to be made in films, and the temptation was to strike while the career iron was hot, though there were also dangers; Kaplan quoted *TV Guide* columnist Matt Roush, who warned, "If the idea is that he's become too big for his britches and decides to turn his back on HBO—where everyone in the world is clamoring to work—then he falls into David Caruso-land." (Caruso was the white-hot lead of *NYPD Blue* who'd left that show in 1995, barely a season into its run, to pursue a film career that immediately fizzled.)

To avoid that fate, Jim had to choose his film roles carefully, from the offers available during the show's hiatuses between seasons. He hadn't worked in the months between the shooting of seasons 1 and 2, mostly to focus on Marcy and Michael; he couldn't afford to do the same after season 2 wrapped, especially since Chase (in what would become a tradition, and an expanding one, in subsequent years) was taking a longer break to prepare season 3.

His primary concern with his initial film roles, all of which landed in theaters during the calendar year of 2001, was to show his versatility. Since he gave so few interviews, people were always surprised that he not only didn't act like Tony Soprano, but didn't even *sound* like him. "Jim's natural vernacular was really a very well standardized English," says Vince Curatola. "Jimmy sounded like he could have taught at Harvard. He was a very educated man, loved to read."

"He played tough guys so compellingly that I think people would be astonished by his intellect," says Geoffrey Fletcher, who would direct Jim a few years later. "At dinner before a screening at the Savannah Film

Festival, he spoke about the diminishing size of the crabs in parts of New Jersey and its greater implications, while sounding like a marine biologist and climatologist."

He flirted with a few close calls during this period. He was attached, for a time, to appear opposite Leonardo DiCaprio in *Catch Me If You Can*, at the time a Gore Verbinksi picture, slated to shoot in early 2001 before schedule overruns on *Gangs of New York* (co-starring DiCaprio) delayed it out of Jim's *Sopranos* hiatus window; Tom Hanks would eventually take over the role for director Steven Spielberg. He "looked likely," according to *Variety*, to co-star with Will Smith in the comedy *I Now Pronounce You Chuck and Larry* for director Tom Shadyac, before that package fell apart; it was retooled several years later as an Adam Sandler project, with Kevin James in the role Jim was to play. When he heard Paramount was planning a big-screen version of *The Honeymooners*, his team made his interest in the role of Ralph Kramden clear; it was released in 2005 with an all-Black cast, with Cedric the Entertainer as Kramden. Most tantalizing was *Scared Guys*, a comedy from director Dean Parisot (*Galaxy Quest*) that would've cast Jim opposite Robert De Niro, who had stumbled into a new career as a comedy star after the success of *Analyze This*, released two months into *The Sopranos'* first season and working off a similar logline, with De Niro as a mob boss who seeks the help of a therapist. *Scared Guys* died when De Niro (who was also a producer) walked away for a career-best $20 million payday for the sequel, *Analyze That*.

Gandolfini realized that at this key inflection point, where he was famous but only famous as one character, he would have to blow up expectations or he'd be stuck in that character forever. "He wanted to diversify," says Vincent Pastore. "We get locked into these roles. Like Telly Savalas—he was a wonderful, diversified actor, and then when he stopped playing Kojak, he was Kojak for the rest of his life. Same thing with Peter Falk, with Columbo. Jimmy didn't want to end up being Tony Soprano for the rest of his life."

But he also didn't want to stray *so* far from the character that he ended up neutralizing his gifts—the pieces of himself, as a person and an actor, that made that character so affecting. "He was always worried about just being Tony," Susan Aston says. "And I was like, you can't worry about that. If you're going to accept a role where you're playing an Italian guy, you can't worry about people thinking about Tony, or you're just going to shoot yourself in the foot. You have to just do your job."

He was firm on one point, though. "I couldn't play another thug," he insisted in 1999. "Not to sound like a pretentious ass, but if you don't do something different, you don't grow. If you don't challenge yourself, then you don't find anything interesting." Yet the genius of his first major post-*Sopranos* film role was that he took on a character who seemed, at first, quite a bit like Tony Soprano—and then turned him upside down.

THE MEXICAN, THE STORY OF a nice girl who leaves her criminal boyfriend when he won't change his ways, was first announced as a reunion of star Brad Pitt with his *Fight Club* director, David Fincher. When Fincher left the picture, Pitt cooled on it as well, only to return when Julia Roberts signed on. And she had a suggestion for the third lead, a hit man sent by the mob to kidnap the girl and ensure the boyfriend completes his assignment. "It's so amazing what James does with Tony Soprano," Roberts said. "Here he is, a cold-blooded killer. And we love him! That's quite an achievement."

"He loved Brad Pitt, because of *True Romance* and some other things, and Brad Pitt loved him," says manager Nancy Sanders. "And it was Julia Roberts, it was basically the three of them. It was a no-brainer."

Julia Roberts and Jim in *The Mexican*. The co-stars remained friends for the rest of his life. (Courtesy DreamWorks/Photofest.)

"Julia wanted me to do it," Jim said, "and I didn't want to do anything that was completely different from Tony Soprano as I didn't have a lot of time to do any research. It was a little bit different, but it seemed to fit with me, so I figured, what the hell?" The salary—reportedly in the neighborhood of $2 million—presumably didn't hurt, either.

On the surface, he was right. The character of Leroy wasn't all that different from Tony Soprano; he would again play a criminal (a "thug") and speak in the Jersey dialect. But Leroy is also gay, which entered into the calculus of playing the role without actually changing *how* he played the role. "I don't think the fact he is gay is an important aspect of his character," he said. "I didn't play him as gay—I don't think there is any way to play a gay man. Gay men come in all different shapes and sizes." He did his usual research ("I read some books and things"), and selected the character's facial hair based on "some pictures in a magazine for gay men or something."

Though he made the admirable (and frankly progressive) decision not to overdo the character's sexuality, it was the focus of much of the picture's advance press. (*Daily News* columnist Mitchell Fink giggled, "Talk about not wanting to be typecast.") The tabloids also noted that he'd lost twenty-five pounds for the role ("Basically, I worked out a lot and slept. That's how I lost the weight"), though that didn't last long. "I started to slim down to play Leroy," he explained. "Then halfway through the film, I had a different idea about him and realized I didn't have to lose weight, so I started eating again. I think Tony Soprano is funnier when he's fatter, so that was my excuse."

That wasn't the only thing he changed his mind about on *The Mexican*. In this phase of his career, according to manager Mark Armstrong, "He usually called us or the director—day before, two days before, five days before—to give a list of three to five other actors that could play this part better than him, and he wants to make sure the director considered them before. It was like clockwork. I'm not exaggerating, it was probably at least five or more projects that he did that on." Armstrong attributes this pattern of eleventh-hour jitters to a combination of nerves and low self-confidence. "It wasn't really that he was trying to leave the production," he emphasizes (*Gotti* notwithstanding). "I want to make sure that's clear, he wasn't going to put them in a bind. It was just, *Are you sure you have the right guy?*"

The picture started production in May 2000; three days in, Jim felt his fears had been warranted. "I didn't think it was going well," he said. "Some scripts, you do this much backstory; some scripts, to support things, you need to do *this* much backstory to get everything in. But you need it. And the times I don't do it, and I think I don't need it, are the times when I get on there and the camera goes on—I'm standing there and I feel like I don't got any pants on. Because I didn't do my work."

He brought Susan Aston in to help him work through the character's backstory and motivation. "It was nowhere in the writing," she says. "Because all there was on the page was *gay hit man, isn't that funny, hahaha*, you know? And he just turned it into a very complex, deep human that, to me, wasn't there just reading the script. In anybody else's hands you wouldn't have had that movie."

Julia Roberts would dispute Jim's assessment of his struggles early on. "He's a liar," she told the *Daily News*. "He was genius from the moment he arrived. He's very self-deprecating." Though the picture was marketed as a Pitt-Roberts romantic romp, the stars shared only a handful of scenes; the bulk of Roberts's screen time was spent in scenes with Gandolfini, and they developed something of a mutual admiration society. "This is a smart lady, who knows what she needs, who knows what she's doing," he said of Roberts. "I think she's a smart, capable woman who's had a lot thrown at her and walked around with her head held high and has taken it and given her right back. I admire her." They would remain friends, with Jim speaking at a Museum of the Moving Image tribute to the actress shortly after *The Mexican*'s release ("She's one of the good ones," he said), the pair often popping up at each other's premieres in the years to follow.

Gandolfini shows up about twenty-five minutes into *The Mexican*, wielding a gun and threatening Roberts, hardcore and scary—immediately using his *Sopranos* persona and baggage in his favor. He softens up a bit when she insists that she broke up with his target, displaying a delightful little grin and assuring her, with sincerity, "You seem like a very nice girl. But it's a fact, that in these life-threatening situations, people do lie." Their scenes really take flight when they start comparing their love woes, and when he opens up about his sexuality; there's something heartbreaking about the halting way he tells her, "Unfortunately I seem to be unable to keep relationships together."

The film is as matter-of-fact about Leroy's queerness as Jim was, portraying the character's one-nighter with Frank, a kind postal worker, with neither a nudge nor a leer. "No one in the movie theater I went to seemed to bat an eyelid at this icon of Italian masculinity being gay," noted columnist Andrew Sullivan in the *New York Times*. Gandolfini (and therefore the film around him) takes the character and his heartache seriously, and when he and Roberts meet up for a quiet, contemplative morning-after breakfast, he displays the kind of vulnerability even Tony Soprano typically kept at bay (but all while still speaking in Tony's voice). He shares his fears about the new man in his life—"What happens when he finds out what I do? And who I am and what I've done? Who're we kiddin', let's get serious"—but also his hope. "He said, the past doesn't matter," he says, tears rolling down his cheeks. "The future's what counts." He mines similarly rich emotional soil in a soulful monologue to Roberts late in the film, about the dilemma of "sending people off" who have been loved. "I see that from time to time and I am awed by it," he tells her, before taking a beat and adding, "I don't think I'd be telling you any of this if it weren't for Frank."

He steals the movie, and it's a role designed to do that. Critics were mixed on the film—"it wants ever so desperately to be successfully hip and offbeat, but it can't manage to make it happen," the *Los Angeles Times*' Kenneth Turan wrote in a typical review—but wild about Jim. "Gandolfini brings a dignity and depth to Leroy," Turan wrote, "a substance that keeps him from descending into the kind of shtick that hampers 'The Mexican' as it does so many modern screwball attempts." *Time Out New York*'s Mike D'Angelo attributed the film's "surprising depth of feeling" to "Gandolfini's towering performance."

"Thank god for James Gandolfini," raved the *San Francisco Chronicle*'s Bob Graham. "As a lovelorn hit man, Gandolfini and his melancholy puss raise the interest level of every scene they share in 'The Mexican.'" When it opened in March 2001, *The Mexican* topped the box office with a $20 million weekend, and Jim had proven he could more than hold his own in a major motion picture.

THE MEXICAN WRAPPED IN JULY 2000, and Jim rolled right into one more movie before *The Sopranos* returned from its hiatus—the back half of a bargain he'd made with his team. "He sort of was intrigued by the [*Mexican*] role," explains Mark Armstrong, "but he really was excited about the Coen Brothers film. They were right around the same time, and he said, 'I'll do one for you, if you let me do one for me'—meaning, I'll do one commercial one, if I could do this scale-plus-ten, black-and-white film. So that's what we did."

His turn in *The Man Who Wasn't There* seemed a conscious attempt to return to the kind of film work he specialized in before *The Sopranos*, a memorable but decidedly supporting role for a director of note, the consummate character actor making an impression and then (as had often been the case) expiring. The directors were Joel and Ethan Coen, the indie legends behind *Raising Arizona*, *Fargo*, and most recently, *O Brother, Where Art Thou?* "He was never gonna say no to the Coen Brothers," Nancy Sanders says. "He would have said yes to them without reading the script, almost like people did for Woody Allen at the time." Billy Bob Thornton was cast in the title role, a barber who says little and does less—until, in self-defense, he kills "Big Dave" Brewster, the boss of his wife (Frances McDormand), whom she's been sleeping with. Gandolfini played "Big Dave" as a cheerful, gregarious, literal backslapper whose chattiness is a stark, comic contrast to Thornton's stone-faced silence.

"The script was unlike anything I had ever read," he said. "I laughed a lot. And Big Dave was unlike anything I had ever done. He's kind of a big lug, a bit of a loudmouth." Jim is clearly having a great time in the role, playing a character with Tony's voice and carriage, but who is soft and wormy and weak underneath. His capacity for violence isn't in question—when he boasts that to get information, he "beat it out of the pansy," you don't doubt him—but there's a depressing quality to the way he ties brutality to masculinity, underscored by the clumsiness of his physical altercation with Thornton's Ed.

Jim enjoyed working with Thornton, whom he found "a very smart guy. He always gave me his lunch. Came over to my trailer to give me his lunch. And I found out later he went to the hospital because he was too skinny or something—and I felt quite bad about that because I was eating his lunch all those days. But he's a smart guy and the Coen Brothers are a joy."

"It was a worthwhile experience and a good credit," Sanders says. "It had to feel important enough to show up. We were no longer going to ever entertain something that didn't have, hopefully, value to it. We knew that this did, and it wasn't resting on his shoulders—and he didn't want shit to rest on his shoulders every single time, because he had enough on his shoulders with *The Sopranos*."

The Man Who Wasn't There premiered at the Cannes Film Festival in May 2001 before rolling out in theaters the following fall. Critics were mostly kind, and several singled out Jim's fine work ("terrific," per A. O. Scott in the *New York Times*; "a force of nature," noted *Rolling Stone*'s Peter Travers). But it was beaten to theaters by one more major movie, in which Jim would attempt his starkest departure yet from his signature character.

WHEN DREAMWORKS OFFERED GANDOLFINI A leading role in *The Castle* (later modified to *The Last Castle*), "he was really reluctant to do the film—or any film at all," recalls director Rod Lurie. The shoot fell during the hiatus between *The Sopranos*' third and fourth seasons, and he was again considering taking some time off; he'd been working basically nonstop for well over a year. But he met Lurie for lunch in the Meatpacking District to hear him out. Lurie's first pitch point was that Robert Redford was attached to star—one of Jim's favorite actors, so "he was really drawn to the idea of working with a guy who's going to be on the Mount Rushmore of cinema," Lurie says. "The way that I described it to him is, Redford is going to be this great military figure who was a natural-born leader, and you're going to be a guy who has the accoutrements of leadership, the rank and the power, but not necessarily the natural ability to lead."

Moving in for the kill, Lurie told him, "It's basically Salieri and Amadeus," smiled, and continued, "and you know who won the Oscar for that one?"

Jim grinned "that great grin," Lurie recalls, and replied, "You're gonna talk me into this, aren't you?"

"I sure hope so," Lurie said.

The deal was announced in the trades in January 2001. The turnaround would be quick; Jim would finish season 3 in February and start shooting *The Last Castle* in March. It was far and away the biggest payday of his career to date, a cool $5 million. But the money wasn't the deciding factor. As Colonel Winter, the warden of a military prison, Jim would play a character who was the polar opposite of Tony Soprano: a buttoned-up career military man, a meek intellectual who never raised his voice. "Tony's emotions just take him everywhere, and then he picks up the pieces later," he explained. "Everything Winter does is manipulative and controlling, and I'm not sure he would feel an honest emotion even if he had one. He sees human beings as being there to be experimented on, so he can see the results." In another interview, he explained, "Usually I play characters whose emotions are much more on their sleeve, so yeah, that was a change. But he's conflicted, too, and I'm always drawn to that. I play a lot of confused characters, actually. I like that," he added, laughing, "probably because I'm confused."

Production commenced at the Tennessee State Penitentiary near Nashville, which had closed in 1992. Jim was "ferocious in his commitment to the role," intellectually and physically, Lurie says; the director and his crew were at first thrown by the animal noises that Jim would make before a take, "like for a full minute, it's a really weird thing," Lurie says. "And then Delroy Lindo comes on, he's doing two or three days. And he does the same thing. The barking thing, right?" So the old *Get Shorty* co-stars would do a barking duet, and then Lurie would roll camera, and they'd do their scenes.

There were other light moments as well. "The other thing that was dichotomous about him," Lurie says, "was he also had—please quote this qualifier I'm putting with this now, OK?—he had a *wonderful* ego. He was proud that he was an athlete, right?" The wonderful ego reared its head in a scene where Winter was scripted to shoot, and miss, several baskets on an outdoor court.

"But I don't *miss* baskets," Jim said.

"Yeah, but Colonel Winter does," Lurie told him. Yet sure enough, when he called action, "I swear to you, he makes twenty baskets in a row."

Once he'd shown his true stripes, he told Lurie, "Okay, now I'll be Colonel Winter," and missed the baskets as scripted.

Gandolfini found other ways to show his prowess. He started playing chess during the shoot, inspired by a supporting player who used it to pass the time between setups; rather than going to his trailer, Jim would stay in Winter's office, playing against whoever would sit with him. "I play chess rather well, and I played chess on the set quite a bit," Lurie says. "And I would sometimes look over my shoulder and I would see him making real rookie mistakes and so on. But toward the end of the shoot, he said to me, 'Hey, hey, can we play a game?' And I sat down and I played him and he beat me. And I refused to play with him ever again after that.

"That was prototypical of what he was. He was just a gigantically competitive athlete, and he brought that athleticism also to chess. I found it absolutely fascinating."

Redford, however, didn't sit with Jim at the chess table—or anywhere else, much to his disappointment. The chance to work with one of his acting inspirations was a major factor in Jim's decision to sign on to *The*

Last Castle, but they didn't develop much of a relationship; Jim would strike up conversations with Redford, who was polite but closed off. They had dinner only once during the months-long shoot. "It's not Bob's style," Lurie says with a shrug. "And I think that genuinely saddened him. Redford told me how much he respected Jimmy—he hadn't seen *The Sopranos*, didn't know what it was, but he loved what he was getting from him, across from him." Being the kind of actor he was, Jim likely used this perceived rejection to enhance the performance; Colonel Winter is similarly enamored of Redford's General Irwin, and hurt when his admiration is not reciprocated.

There were other frustrations. "Often actors will find a certain scene or a certain speech they're going to give," Lurie says. "and that becomes their North Star, they can't wait for the day that they're going to do that scene. That's the scene that they're most prepared for." For Jim, it was what they called the "shadow of a soldier" speech, in which he explains to the military prison's inmates that they, and General Irwin specifically, are no longer soldiers but shadows of them. When the day came to deliver the speech, however, Jim had a cold, which amplified the already nasally quality of his speaking voice. He did the best he could, but Lurie knew they'd have to

Gandolfini and Robert Redford in *The Last Castle*. Jim idolized Redford but was unable to get close to him during the shoot. (Courtesy DreamWorks/Photofest.)

re-record it during the additional dialogue recording (ADR) phase of post-production. By that time, the scene had been shortened considerably—not because of the performance, but because the scene (and the film overall) was running too long. Lurie called Jim before his ADR session to warn him that the scene was shorter. "He was very hurt," Lurie says. "He thought that either he had fucked it up or that I was making the wrong decision. And he didn't speak to me for like a couple of months after that. He was very disappointed."

"I thought it was a very good script, when we first got it," Jim said later. "And to work with Robert Redford, man, I would have done anything. . . . Be very wary, when they give you a script, and they say, *Well, we're gonna make a few changes, if you just sign on.* Because then you get one later, and it's very different."

He and Lurie would eventually mend their fences, and the director has nothing but fond memories of their time together, including off the set. "There was no such thing as bringing a wallet to any restaurant you went with James Gandolfini to," Lurie says. "There have been very few actors who have pulled out their credit card at any meeting I've taken. When we first met, he paid for the meal. That's when we were *courting* him. And he was like, you know, *In case I don't do this. . . .*

"He was not hard to get to know at all," Lurie continues. "And look, there's stuff that it'd be inappropriate for me to discuss. Because, you know, I think that was about the time that things were getting rough in his private life."

GANDOLFINI IS QUITE GOOD IN *The Last Castle*, overcoming what a lesser actor would've played as a two-note character (first obsequious, then petty) by seeing in him a frustrated bureaucrat. He's first seen listening to classical music, polishing his weaponry, and cleaning a glass case of military paraphernalia; he's fastidious, by the book, his diction crisp and clean. (What a shock it must have been for the audience to hear this almost nasal sound, basically Jim's regular speaking voice, coming out of the man they knew as Tony Soprano.) He likely felt some connection to the character's necessity to role-play—everyone expects him to be this tough military man, and he collects the knickknacks and does the reading and learns the trivia, but it's not *him*. It was the same with Gandolfini and these thugs and gangsters he played so well, while considering himself, as he often said, a "260-pound Woody Allen."

Most importantly, he goes toe to toe with a screen legend, and even when the character deflates him handily, Gandolfini remains a formidable opponent for Redford. The latter's aloofness through the film (and on the set) is a sharp counterpoint to the vulnerability that Lurie allows Jim to display in the private moment when Winter overhears Irwin casually insult him; the camera slowly pushes in to reveal a man hurt and offended by this personal slight, which will fester, curdle, and motor the entire narrative.

Beyond the physical and aural contrasts, the most striking shift from his playing of Tony Soprano to Colonel Winter is the latter's lack of menace. We have to feel that his capacity for violence is minimal, no easy feat for an actor of Gandolfini's ferocity and physical presence, but he pulls it off. Winter is in a rage by the story's end, when the inmates take over the prison and firebomb his office, but it's an impotent rage, and he's on the defensive in a way his characters rarely are.

Critics certainly appreciated the contrast. In the *New York Press*, Matt Zoller Seitz called Winter "an about-face for an actor whose typecast specialty is animalistic rage," and wrote that Gandolfini has "been so good for so long that he's starting to enter Gene Hackman country." In the *New York Times*, Elvis Mitchell wrote, "Mr. Gandolfini shows us a big man deflated, and his sudden physical diminution is a shock to the movie's system. The actor's tics—the nervous smile, the slight lisp—become the tools of a man struggling to retain his dignity."

"Redford's chiseled nobility is no match for Gandolfini's sly underplaying," Jan Stuart wrote in *Newsday*. "Stoop-shouldered, nebbishy, spitting out sarcastic rejoinders with a *gotcha* smile, he is the personification of the banality of evil. It's a virtuoso characterization." And again, Roger Ebert raved, noting that Gandolfini "creates not simply a villain, but a portrait of a type that is so nuanced, so compelling, so instinctively right, that we are looking at the performance of a career. This actor, who can be so disarmingly genial (see his scene-stealing in 'The Mexican'), who can play bad guys we enjoy (see 'The Sopranos'), here transforms his face and posture to make himself into a middle-aged boy, a hulking schoolyard bully. He does a lot with his mouth, making the lips thin and hurt, as if he is getting back for a lifetime of wounds and disappointments."

Jim participated in much more promotional work this time around, reasoning that "there's been a lot of money spent, and they were good to me and I think you need to do something. I mean, Robert Redford's doing interviews for it, you know, so who am I to say no?" He also recognized that now that he was playing someone other than Tony Soprano, he needed audiences to not identify him purely as that character. "This is why it's very rare for TV stars with iconic characters to translate, especially when the show is still going on," Lurie explains. "He was two or three years into *Sopranos*, so he could still maybe get away with this."

But *The Last Castle* was a bust at the box office, opening in fifth place and topping out at $27 million worldwide against a reported $72 million budget. It was easy to read as a rejection of Jim's commercial viability; DreamWorks spent big to snag him, hoping that his presence would lure the audiences who watched his show. They stayed home, an early indicator of how TV would increasingly become the alternative to movies for adult viewers, not the complement. And the following summer, Sam Raimi's *Spider-Man* would begin a seemingly inexorable shift into a cinematic landscape that only had space for four-quadrant blockbusters.

No one really blamed Jim for the film's financial failure, in light of a much more obvious explanation: it was released on October 19, 2001, barely a month after the 9/11 attacks. "The first poster for the movie was an upside-down American flag on fire," Lurie says. "The trailer had two towers on fire with Redford in between them. It was an anti-authoritarian film at a time where people wanted to know that we had strength in our government. It just completely collapsed." Plenty of films were upended by the events of September 11, recut and/or delayed, while more traditionally "patriotic" pictures like *Behind Enemy Lines* and *We Were Soldiers* were boosted. DreamWorks needed to keep the film on the schedule for financial reasons but had to cover its ideological bases. The press kits included a disclaimer about the upside-down-flag image ("Please note that the CDs and CD covers which depict our teaser campaign for 'The Last Castle' were printed prior to the tragic events of Sept. 11. We apologize for any concern this may cause"), and the final campaign attempted to bury the picture's themes, to the dismay of many involved, including its star. "They tried to seize on September 11th," Redford fumed to Liz Smith. "Suddenly there's this big patriotic thing with flags waving. Then they put in a rap score. The director, Rod Lurie, just about jumped off a bridge."

Jim was in New York on 9/11, in the West Village apartment where he, Marcy, and Michael were joined by friends who couldn't get to their apartments farther downtown or didn't have power. Once the dust had settled and cleanup was underway, he and several of his *Sopranos* co-stars were asked to go down to Ground Zero to boost morale. "I was a little leery of it because a lot of people died there. It was an odd thing to be signing autographs," he said. "But it seemed to help people who had been [working] there for a long time."

"They loved him and he loved them," Lorraine Bracco said at the time. "You get him with the firefighters and police, and that's where Jimmy shines." Tony Sirico concurred. "The guys who were working there were so happy to see us," he said. "Any break from searching through that mess of wreckage, thinking you'd find a body. Only, they found out, there weren't many bodies. . . . You just had to do something. We all felt it." Jim would continue to "do something" for years, contributing to charity events, visiting troops in Afghanistan and Iraq, and eventually producing and participating in documentaries about the horrors of war.

One of his first contributions was more modest, but no less heartfelt. For the Helping Hands II: Handmade in America charity auction, held on December 12 at the new Folk Art Museum, Jim contributed a painting of a red, white, and blue apple that he'd made with Michael. "The Spirit of NYC" was emblazoned in red glitter; it was signed "James Gandolfini and Michael Gandolfini, age 2."

The project was indicative of the joy Jim was taking in fatherhood. "The baby has changed my life," he said that spring. "He's made me realize there are other things in life." Marcy brought Michael to Nashville to visit his dad on the set of *The Last Castle*, where Rod Lurie remembers, "I'm up in the warden's office, which we built, and looking down on the yard, and it's just this vast prison yard. And this giant man is walking across the yard with his two-year-old son. The kid can barely walk, and he's holding his hand. And it was just this beautiful image of him and his son. He very much loved his child."

Paparazzi frequently spotted Jim out and about with Michael—often with the younger Gandolfini sitting upon his father's shoulders—in downtown Manhattan, where they still spent most of their time, though Jim and Marcy had also purchased a historic four-bedroom farmhouse on five acres in Chester Township, New Jersey, for $1.14 million. "I just like the house," he told the *Star-Ledger*. "My two-year-old needs to run on grass a little bit." They were the public portrait of a happy family; Marcy even made the gossip columns when she pulled a clever fast one on Jim, throwing him a surprise fortieth-birthday party in July 2001—two months early, which she tricked him into attending by claiming it was a party to celebrate his sister's fiftieth.

But behind closed doors, the marriage was already in trouble, and it was beginning to affect the work. His self-confidence, which should have been at its zenith, was instead continuing to crater. "I think a lot of it was that a lot of people were depending on him," Susan Aston says. "And he was not sure, personally, that he wouldn't end up letting them down. I'm not talking about in terms of his acting—but that his personal life wasn't together enough to lead the show, or lead a film."

"I had it put this way to me by some spiritual teacher or something that I used to listen to," Edie Falco says. "The idea that he's a cup, right? And all of this stuff is being poured into it—this good fortune and money and fame and success in this industry—is being poured and poured and poured. And if the cup is not strong enough to hold all that stuff, it's going to break."

CHAPTER 13

AWOL

THE NO-SHOWS STARTED DURING SEASON 3. The stress of *The Sopranos* had weighed on Gandolfini from the beginning; Steven Van Zandt recalls spending "most of my time talking him into coming back the next day. . . . We'd have the same conversation at least once a month." Van Zandt would reaffirm how lucky they were to be on such an excellent show, how few comparable film roles there were out there, and then he'd deliver the clincher. "Come back and do us all a favor, because you're helping to employ, I don't know, sixty people here?" he'd remind him. "So think of them every time you want to quit. Think of the other fifty people that are trying to make a living, depending on you."

"So he would sometimes take a few days off, whatever," Van Zandt says. "But he always came back. He always came back, and he was the most generous guy in the world."

The reasons for his "days off" varied. Sometimes he was avoiding a difficult or embarrassing scene. Sometimes the difficulties of line memorization would send him into a tailspin. Sometimes he wanted to get an early start on a weekend of partying, which was increasingly his coping mechanism for his unhappiness at home; sometimes he hadn't quite recovered from one of those weekends. "He likes to have a good time," explains series-long script supervisor Christine Gee, "but sometimes, you know . . . some people don't know when to stop."

Whatever prompted it, the outcome was the same. The production office would get a call from the transportation department; the driver who had gone to Jim's apartment to pick him up reported that he was not answering his door or his phone. "So that could throw a day into a tizzy," says Steve Kornacki, then an assistant production coordinator, "because then you had to punt and you had to figure out what to do, until somebody got ahold of Jim." As updates were relayed from his driver to the Teamsters co-captain to executive producer Ilene Landress—he's up and around, he's in the shower, he's coming out to the car—the crew would do what they could: establishing shots, maybe, or coverage of his scene partners over his stand-in's shoulder, with Gee reading Jim's lines.

"Find something else to shoot or shoot what you can, as long as you hear he might be coming in," explains location manager Mark Kamine. "You pull up whatever work you can do without him until he gets in, or says he's not coming in. And then the Teamster tells the other Teamster who tells the producer who tells me, if I'm the one on set, he's not coming in. And then the first question is, what can you do instead? And if you can't do anything, it's like, OK, go home."

On the occasions when the driver could get him out of the apartment, albeit late and hung over, they would pour coffee into him to sober him up and get him camera ready, and take a shot at making their day (sometimes shooting his medium shots and close-ups simultaneously). "After the first time, there was a contingency plan," Kornacki notes. "And I don't think it happened a lot. But the producers were ready for it."

"Look, it was difficult on production, obviously," says cinematographer Phil Abraham. "I don't remember ever getting a phone call saying, *Don't come in to work. . . .* I remember specifically, Jim even giving them advanced warnings, like *I'm not coming in tomorrow.* And people would go, *Ha, yeah, right.* And he wouldn't come in tomorrow! It wasn't necessarily always like, he went out drinking that night and then disappeared. I mean, it *was* that a lot. But I know that playing this character was a huge burden on this guy. He was not this person. And yet he needed a release—it's almost like the noise in his head was probably too much. Now, whether or not that's the way one does it . . ."

The absences became cyclical over the next couple of seasons. "Time would pass, and the crew would all get kind of a sense of, *Oh, we're due for a day of absenteeism,*" Gee says. "You would just get a sense, *Wow, he's been pretty good. He's been showing up and he's been doing the right thing.* Next thing you know, boom—that would happen."

"It's a hard scheduling thing," according to Landress. "The guy was working so hard, so much of the time, they were like, *Okay, we'll give them a three-day weekend.* But I learned pretty quickly that he might go out on Thursday night. And so I'm not going to see him on Friday. So as much as I want to schedule to give them a break, you almost got to the point of not wanting to give them a break because you couldn't know what would happen."

"I can't say I've ever been on a show where something like that has gone on, but this was sort of a different beast," Abraham says. "At a certain point, HBO was fining him 250 grand a day. And he would say, *Fuck it. I can't come in to work.* So we knew then, it's not just him doing a lot of blow and drinking, and he's not getting up because he doesn't want to get up. No, it was deeper than that."

"I'm not sane at all when I'm doing the show," Gandolfini said. It was a question of pressure—the pressure of maintaining the quality of *The Sopranos* and his performance on it. Some of that pressure was external; much of it was not. "The guy was such a workaholic and put so much pressure on himself," Landress said. "Jimmy was never going to give you a B performance. He was always going to give you an A performance. And if he felt like he couldn't give an A performance, he was so hard on himself."

Unsurprisingly, a perfectionist like Chase was exhausted as well. "I was concerned, but I was also so sick of his bullshit," he recalled. "They flew me back from France and then back. It was crazy. He was sick of me, too. Let me just say that. It wasn't a one-way street. He could always find something humiliating and mortifying so he wouldn't have to show up for something." Edie Falco, meanwhile, had been diagnosed with breast cancer midway through the third season, and would frequently come to the set after a morning of chemotherapy only to discover that her co-star was MIA. "It was infuriating to her," Gee says. "I remember her getting just really irate, and saying how she's struggling so hard to do all the right things to save her life, while he's pissing his away."

"Someone like Edie, or one of the other actors, who's geared up and studied their lines, and maybe stayed up late to do that and gotten up early to go to hair and makeup," Kamine says, "that's not nice. And did he think about that? The night before when he was out partying? You know, but he couldn't help it, obviously."

"As I remember it, the feeling I had, overall, was empathy, that he's going through something," Falco says. "And if he could do better, and be on set, he would be. Nobody wants to be holding up a production, and nobody goes out hoping someday they can screw up a very complicated schedule. He's . . . the guy's in trouble. And coming from a place where there are quite a few of those people in my family, or there were, I have a great deal of empathy, sympathy, compassion. You wouldn't wish it on anybody."

When he'd blow a day, or come in late, he was overwhelmed with guilt; in fact, the famous Friday night food spreads were initially "sort of like an apology to the crew," Gee explains. "He knew we all traveled to get there, and that we're not getting paid for the day if we're not working." But she says

Falco and Gandolfini in a scene from *The Sopranos*' third season. (Courtesy HBO/Photofest.)

their resentments were outweighed by empathy. "The crew understood that this was an illness. It's not a light switch that you could just shut off."

He was grateful for the doors the show had opened for him, and the good work it allowed him to do, week after week. But by this point in the run, "there were regrets," manager Mark Armstrong says. "A 'be careful what you wish for' kind of thing—as much as he loved the writing, and he really did, and he knew he was on a great show with great people—I think he wished it wasn't as big as it was, and that people cared about him as much as they did."

The late days and absences continued through the run of *The Sopranos*, Gee says. "It kind of peaked and then it tapered off, but it never just went away completely." The more the pressures of the show and the darkness of the character were rattling around inside Gandolfini, the smaller the chasm between Jim and Tony became, the more he would require an escape hatch. "I just think, when you feel the weight of that much responsibility, or that the onus is on you for everything, then there's got to be a release," says collaborator and producer Chiemi Karasawa. "I feel like he must have sought relief and respite from that kind of pressure."

"Jim did not spend a lot of time, I don't think, attending to his own mental health," Falco says. "I had a conversation with him once. I said, 'Listen, no one's gonna say, *Jim's probably tired. Let's give him some time off.* This is your job, to say, *Guys, I need a month, we've got to shut down production for a month, I've got to take care of myself,* or whatever.' And he would never do that. The sense of obligation he felt, for a crew that would suddenly be out of work for a month? He was always looking at other people before himself, which I think he probably thought of as altruistic. But ultimately, it's a form of suicide, you know."

Or, as Steve Schirripa puts it: "Sweet guy. Listen, not perfect. Not perfect. By any means."

"HE WAS THE SUN OF the show, and we were just the other planets that circled him," says Joe Pantoliano, who joined the cast in season 3. "And years later now, I truly believe that *The Sopranos*' success was Jim Gandolfini. He was everything." The flip side of that kind (and accurate) summation is that Jim was an essential, irreplaceable piece of what had become a giant money-printing machine for HBO, and that complicated, quite considerably, its strategies and motivations for getting him the help that he needed. "It was a product, the show was a product to be put out," Gee explains. "And sadly, that's putting that product above the human being. Everybody loved Jim, but at the same time, you have a responsibility to the show, to HBO. So it was, I think, a tricky thing."

To its credit, HBO was making efforts to pay him what he was worth. TONY SOPRANO HITS JACKPOT, read a September 2000 *New York Post* headline, announcing that the network had renegotiated his multiyear contract to pay Jim $10 million for the next two seasons, "said to include future obligations as producer and actor in TV series and movies for 'Sopranos' partners HBO and Brad Grey Television," according to *Variety*.

The production piece of the puzzle may have been what was most compelling to Jim. "It wasn't really to find stuff for him to star in," says manager Mark Armstrong. "It was more that he was such a well-read guy, and he had really amazing taste. So I think he was just excited to find projects that maybe he wouldn't be cast in, but where he thought the world should hear these stories."

"Being an actor was great and very fulfilling for him," says his old Rutgers friend and roommate Tom Richardson. "But the real drivers are the producers and the people behind the camera, and he wanted to be one of those guys. When you act, you can pretty much do one thing at a time. When you produce, you can do a lot of things at one time." Jim would bring Richardson in to help run his production company, which he called Attaboy Films.

"It was a fun thing that we used to say in college to each other," Richardson explains, "like, *Attaboyeeeee*, whenever something good would happen. It's an old-fashioned saying, you know, *attaboy, good job, good job.* That would be our little thing, if things were going well, or somebody did something nice or fun or interesting. And it kind of stuck with him."

ON JUNE 18, 2000, AS JIM was finishing *The Mexican* and Chase and company were prepping season 3 of *The Sopranos*, Nancy Marchand died. One day shy of her seventy-second birthday, the character actress who had brought Livia Soprano to such vivid life succumbed to the emphysema and lung cancer that had plagued her for years. Gandolfini took her passing especially hard. "Jim loved the scenes with Nancy," Christine Gee recalls. "It was hard because when she was very sick, she had an oxygen tank with her and the cannula on, and she couldn't remember her lines. I'd have to feed her her lines, off-screen, one at a time, which impacted editing or whatever—but what are you gonna do?"

"If I die, it's not my problem," she had said in one of her last interviews. "It's David left holding the bag." That he was; they'd already plotted out and written sections of the season to include Livia, so those would have to be revised, and they would have to figure out how to incorporate her death into the show without a proper, planned send-off. (Recasting the role does not seem to have been seriously considered.) In an attempt to fill that void, the writers created a final scene for Livia, using snippets and outtakes from previous shows, a body double, and green-screened, computer-generated visual effects.

Gandolfini arrived on set, took one look at the setup, and blanched. "Oh my God," he said. "Oh, no." He walked out in a daze, insisting, "I can't do this. How am I going to do this scene?" The crew and Marchand's stand-in did their best to block it out, making markings on the monitor with grease pencils to ensure that eyelines matched. When Jim finally returned to set, he issued a dictum: "I'm having this put in my contract. Nobody ever does this. If I pass away, nobody's doing this to me."

"It really freaked him out," Gee says.

Additions to the cast that year, however, were a source of joy—and a chance for Jim to help old friends. He'd run into a pal of Robert Funaro, Stanley to Jim's Mitch in that Scandinavian touring production of *Streetcar* all those years ago. Funaro had all but quit acting, he was told, and was tending bar at Caroline's on Broadway, the Midtown stand-up comedy club. So Jim paid him an unannounced visit.

"Hi, James, how you doing?" Funaro asked, delighted. "What's going on? What are you doing here?"

Jim told Robert he had set him up with an audition for *The Sopranos.* "I can't get the job for you," he explained. "You'd have to audition with Georgianne (Walken), which is right across the street. But if you get in, you get in." Funaro got in; he would play Soprano family foot soldier Eugene Pontecorvo for four seasons.

"That's his generosity," Funaro says. "He knew how hard it was for people to get a job, to crack into the business, to get your foot in the door. He helped me get my foot in the door by his generosity."

Jim might have also wanted to have a few more familiar and supportive faces around. The psychological collateral of stepping back into Tony's skin, especially after the (comparatively) lighthearted work of *The Mexican* and *The Man Who Wasn't There*, was daunting. "Doing an hour-long drama—it's not like you're doing a movie for three months and you're out," he said at the time. "You're working a lot, and for a long time, six, seven, eight months. The amount of work and the subject matter, it can really get to you."

The subject matter was especially dark in season 3, grimmer and more violent than the previous years, as if Chase and his writers had sensed that their audience was becoming too comfortable, too cuddly, with Tony and his crew. They needed to be reminded of exactly how monstrous these men were, resulting in episodes like "University," in which Pantoliano's villain du jour, Ralph Cifaretto, bashes his pregnant girlfriend's head in, or the arc involving Tony's affair with Gloria Trillo (Annabella Sciorra), which veers into psychological and even physical abuse. "It was dark," says manager Nancy Sanders. "He didn't like the violence. For a big guy who could be intimidating, he was a teddy bear. Having to live in that place of violence every single time, it weighed on him. It colored everything for him."

A scene in which Gandolfini had to pick Sciorra up and throw her across the room was "an all-day sucker, to get him to do that," according to Chase.

"He didn't want to be seen that way, thought of that way—he probably didn't want to experience it, because he has to go there to do it. It has to be believable, and he actually has to be doing it. He didn't want to be thought of as a beast, you know?"

"We had been going at it for a long time," Sciorra said. "It was one of those long, long Friday nights. I really think it was like three or four in the morning. I was on the floor, and he was sort of coming toward me to pick me up off the floor. And kind of twists my arm and everything. He was like, *Do you want to just stop? Should you just pick us up on Monday*? And I was like, *No, no, I want to keep going.* But he was right.

"I never got hurt," she noted. "He was very good about being safe, and I learned a lot from him."

If anything, the conflict over that scene was indicative of the further strain in the relationship between the man who played Tony Soprano and the man who created him. "At the beginning, David came to the set a lot, but once it got bigger and it became this thing, you know, he was a little more standoffish," Gandolfini said. "You have to pull back and try to protect yourself in a way. I had to learn it, and I wasn't very good at it. But then it starts to take its toll. The first couple years, it was easier. It wasn't such a huge deal. I've said this to him, but maybe not so clearly. I got it. He had to be a little bit of the Great and Powerful Oz. There was no choice."

In Chase's absence, Jim would often step up. "We'd have a director come in that hadn't been working on the show, and they'd do the blocking," Chiemi Karasawa says. "And he'd always explain, really nicely, to the director, *Tony would never sit with his back to a window, that just doesn't happen. You've got to put me over there*, you know, he would direct through the director. And he knew everything inside and out, he was never condescending, he was always polite. He just took responsibility. For everything."

It wasn't all Sturm und Drang; there were high points and highlights in that third year. Pantoliano, with all his Hoboken authenticity and nervous energy, was one. "My first day on the job was a scene between him and me outside of a pizzeria in New Jersey," he recalls. "And we had our niceties and in between a take, he looked me in the eye, and he said, 'Listen, it's an honor and a pleasure to be working with you.' He had the ability, as the captain of the ship, to make people comfortable. And it's very hard for an actor coming into a show—a lot of actors are day players or they're on an episode with two scenes. But he always went out of his way to make sure that everybody was comfortable." (He was just as gracious with colleagues on their way out; when writer and producer Todd A. Kessler was let go during the third season, Gandolfini took him out to dinner that very night and told him, "You hold your head high and know that you did great work." Kessler went on to create the hit series *Damages*.)

The shooting of one of the most memorable episodes, "Pine Barrens," also led to one of the funniest behind-the-scenes moments of the series. The script required Bobby (Steve Schirripa) to show up in hunter's camouflage, prompting a huge laugh from Tony. Jim had already seen Schirripa in the costume the day before, so he warned his co-star, "You better know how to make me laugh tomorrow morning."

"So I told the prop guy, I said, *Listen, do you have any dildos?*" Schirripa recalled. "And he found me the biggest dildo, looked like an Italian bread. And when I come into that room, which is the scene you see, I'm off camera. And you see Jim practically fall out laughing on the counter, and you could almost catch Dominic cracking a smile. That was a funny scene. We had a lot of laughs that day."

"Once you got him laughing, he really couldn't recover," according to writer and producer Terence Winter. "I remember in a different episode, Uncle Junior had a CPAP mask for sleep apnea, and the line was, 'How many MiGs you shoot down last week?' Jim Gandolfini could not look at Dominic with that mask on and say that line. It was the night before Thanksgiving when we shot it, and all Jim had to do was come in and say the line, and like, eighteen times in a row, he broke down. It was two in the morning, everyone wanted to go home. I remember Tim Van Patten directing that and he was like, 'Jimmy, enough already, let's do it.' 'All right, all right.' And he came in, and ultimately, it had to be done in two separate shots. We had to send Dominic out of the room. It was the only time Jim could not physically do his job."

There were other laughs as well. "When Michael was very young, I think he was getting his first haircut," says Edie Falco. "And they cut his hair in the trailer, because we were shooting at the time. So Jim sat in the hair chair, he put his son on his lap, and then the hair person covered both Jim and his son with the cape. And Michael was *not very excited* about getting his hair cut. So he was wiggling and screaming, and Jim was cooing to him and holding hands. And you could see Jim was *drenched* in sweat because this kid was sitting on him. It was hot in the trailer. And he was just a dad of a young kid, getting one of his first haircuts, and didn't want to."

Family visits to the set were not uncommon, according to Christine Gee. "He had his dad come to set, and he had his sisters come to set, and he was so good with them—he never came across as blue or depressed or whatever. But obviously when you're drinking, that will come out, anything that you're repressing can come out. In trying to do the right thing, he deprived himself of his own happiness." Finally, he reached a breaking point. In February 2001, a couple of weeks before the third season was set to debut, Jim left the home he was sharing with Marcy, and didn't go back.

GANDOLFINI CONTINUED TO MINE NEW emotional depths of his already nuanced characterization in season 3. The death of Livia, while inconvenient to the logistics of the show, prompted some of his most complicated acting yet; his initial reaction to the death of this woman, and the end of this relationship that defined him, is a shattering combination of grief, regret, and relief. The relationship with the emotionally destructive Gloria allows for further reflection of the psychological toll his mother has taken on Tony—when Dr. Melfi asks if Gloria's chaotic behavior reminds him "of any other woman," Tony thinks, deeply, carefully, and then shakes his head. It's a truly potent example of Gandolfini's gift with nonverbal acting, saying everything by saying nothing.

His physicality is in full force throughout these episodes—he's like a tightly coiled snake from frame one, taut and ready to pounce, slamming doors, bulging eyes, breaking mini-fridges—but it's his emotional breakdowns that pack the biggest punch. The deterioration of Tony's relationship with his kids is an affecting through line, culminating in an extraordinary monologue in the season finale in which he breaks down over A. J.'s ongoing scholastic and disciplinary issues. He blames himself and his "rotten Soprano gene," a rare moment of articulating his overwhelming self-loathing, before choking back real tears and asking, in something resembling desperation, "How're we gonna save this kid?"

The nearly one year since the end of season 2 prompted an even more feverish sense of anticipation as the March 4, 2001, premiere loomed. There were now official *Sopranos*, cigars and humidors, T-shirts, and DVD box sets, so nonsubscribers could see what all the fuss was about (and fans could watch, and rewatch, and rewatch). On February 21, the first two episodes premiered at Radio City Music Hall for "a mob of 3,000 fans," per the *New York Post*; the cast rubbed elbows with the likes of Keith Richards and mayor Rudy Giuliani. The first two installments also played back-to-back on HBO that first night, perhaps to preemptively calm the concerns of fans who might have complained about episode 1, "Mr. Ruggerio's Neighborhood"—in which the focus was not Tony, his family, or his crew, but the FBI agents tracking him. It was a ballsy move for a show returning from a one-year hiatus at its apex of popularity, but at that point, it seemed Chase could get away with just about anything.

Critics not only reiterated but accelerated their praise; *Variety* raved, "'The Sopranos' retains the title of the most involving series on television and James Gandolfini continues to be a powerhouse of a performer," while the *New York Observer* ran a lengthy appreciation headlined, LIKE IBSEN OR DICKENS, SOPRANOS IS OUR PEAK. In a separate item, the paper noted that restaurants mentioned on the show were seeing bumps in business. Buses began popping up across New Jersey, giving guided tours of the show's locations and lore. And in an astonishing case of life imitating art, the *New York Daily News* reported that mob boss Joseph "Joey Flowers" Tangorra was undergoing psychiatric evaluation for panic attacks and depression.

The Italian-American representation controversy, however, not only wouldn't die, it grew teeth. U.S. Representative Marge Roukema (R-N.J.) introduced a resolution condemning the show, insisting, "If this kind of ethnic profiling were being directed at African-Americans and Hispanics, they would have been marching in the streets." (She alternately admitted she had not watched the show, or claimed to have seen it only "once or twice.") Under pressure from Italian-American groups and staff, several schools refused or rescinded permission to serve as stand-ins for scenes of Meadow Soprano at college. Officials in Essex County, New Jersey, banned the production from shooting on county property, though their counterparts in Union, Middlesex, and Passaic Counties made it clear that the show was more than welcome there. (In an amusing twist, James W. Treffinger, the Essex County official who led the charge against the show, was later sentenced to thirteen months in prison after pleading guilty to corruption charges.) Oddest of all, a group of Chicago lawyers that dubbed themselves the American Italian Defense Association (AIDA) filed suit in Cook County Circuit Court against HBO's parent company, Time Warner Entertainment Co., citing the "individual dignity" clause of the Illinois State Constitution. They sought not monetary or punitive damages, but affirmation from a jury that the show offended the dignity of Italian-Americans. (Judge Richard A. Siebel threw the suit out with prejudice.)

Other criticisms carried a bit more weight. It was unsurprising to see ultra-conservative commentator William F. Buckley condemn *The Sopranos*' "arrant exploitation of sex, exhibitionism, murder, sadism, cynicism, and hypocrisy," but even some fans in the press were taken aback by the graphic violence of the aforementioned "University" episode ("unusually sleazy and gratuitous," complained the *New York Post*), or "Employee of the Month," in which Dr. Melfi is brutally raped in a parking garage stairwell. Backlash is inevitable for a show this popular and praised, and it began to seep into weekly recaps midway through season 3—"the first three weeks were the equivalent of a domestic soap opera," whined the *Daily News*' Marvin Kitman—while the *Post*'s Austin Smith voiced a complaint about the season finale that would become louder among a certain segment of fans: "Just a lot of talking—and not nearly enough action."

The ratings, however, continued to climb. The season premiere earned the highest numbers in HBO's history, reaching 11.7 million viewers, and held close to that benchmark all year. When the Emmy nominations were announced that summer, *The Sopranos* dominated with twenty-two nods, including another best actor nod for Gandolfini; he won again, as did Falco for best actress, though the elusive best drama trophy again went to their chief rival, *The West Wing*. Jim would lose the best actor statuette to *West Wing*'s Martin Sheen at the following spring's SAG Awards, but he had a good time at the show's nominee dinner, where, as Michael Imperioli recalled, "he hit Richard Dreyfuss in the head with a piece of bread, and then Richard got up and started throwing shit back at Jim."

"They serve liquor, they serve wine and liquor and drinks, there's bars," Steve Schirripa said, laughing. "So Jim had a few and he was throwing dinner rolls at people."

CHAPTER 14

DEMONS

WHILE GANDOLFINI WAS OFF SHOOTING *The Last Castle*, David Chase took an even longer break between seasons 3 and 4. Steven Van Zandt took credit for this turn of events, noting that the showrunner looked "like a dead man" at the season 3 rap party. "David, this is supposed to be a celebration here," he joked.

"Yeah, sure, for you," Chase replied. "I got postproduction, I got another two fucking months of work, and then I get my two weeks off, and then I start again."

Van Zandt encouraged Chase to take more time. "What're they going to do, fire you?" he reasoned. "So what—we lose the twelve-month cycle? Who the fuck cares? We're solid right now. They'll wait fifteen months." And they did, "and that fucked up the whole universe," Van Zandt said, "because that's how we ended up doing seven seasons in ten years." Season 4 was targeted to debut in September 2002, nearly a year and a half after the March 2001 bow of season 3.

There had been discussions, during the previous year's deal-making, that the show would end after season 4, or that Chase would step back into a less hands-on role at that point. ("I'm just speaking for myself," Jim said at the time, "but I started it with him, and I'd like to finish it with him.") The two-year time frame shifted again after season 3, when HBO persuaded Chase to extend his contract into a fifth year. But he remained conscious of the need to conclude the show before it became a "numb parody" of itself.

Production commenced on season 4 of *The Sopranos* on October 15, 2001, delayed a month from its original start date by the events of 9/11. *New York Daily News* feature writer Stephen Battaglio visited Silvercup Studios, where he observed Jim walk off the set of the Bada Bing for a word with director Alan Taylor, requesting an alteration to one of his lines. "While Taylor calmly listens and nods his head," Battaglio wrote, "it's easy for a visitor to feel a bit intimidated to hear America's favorite TV mob boss and family man, Tony Soprano, make a request."

Those requests weren't always on his own behalf. Peter Riegert appeared in a recurring role, through seasons 3 and 4, as a corrupt state assemblyman whose arc culminated with an ugly scene in which he was beaten and humiliated by Tony—while nude, a discovery the actor made during the episode's table read. According to Riegert, Jim approached him after and asked, "How are you with this?"

"I'm not happy about this, man," he replied. "I don't think you have to humiliate an actor in order to humiliate a character, and I'm a little upset." Jim called Chase over, explaining and intervening on his colleague's behalf, and while Chase was noncommittal, Jim assured Riegert, "Whatever you decide to do, I promise you I will have your back."

"At that table read," Riegert later noted, "I didn't realize that Jim recognized, on my face, that there was an actor in trouble. And he made it so it was my choice. And I know this was not the only time that he did so."

AS PRODUCTION FOR SEASON 4 rolled into 2002, Jim's work stoppages had become a pattern. "There was probably a peak of it," Mark Kamine recalls, "like the fourth season. That season had the most peak audience for the show; I'm sure that's when he was most besieged by people, and probably when it was worst for him, because that was so contrary to his personality." Jim would claim to be sick, or not answer his door and his phone, or simply disappear, only to show up the following day overflowing with apologies and make-goods, a sushi chef at lunch or a masseuse for the day. "So first, you worry about, *Okay, where is he? Is he okay?*" Ilene Landress said. "And then the next part is, *What are we going to do while he's not here, and then not make it a big event when he does come back?* You lose a day, then there's the guilt of missing the day. And, *Oh, I let everybody down and everybody hates me.*"

It came to a head during "Eloise," the penultimate episode of the season. They were shooting one of the final scenes for Tony's body man, Furio Giunta (Federico Castelluccio)—a tense encounter while boarding a helicopter in which we think, for a fleeting moment, that Furio might attempt to kill his boss. A night shoot was set up at the Westchester County Airport; call was 6 P.M. It came and went with no Jim. One hour became two, and then three, and it was clear that Jim was MIA again. "It was an annoyance, but it wasn't cause for concern," according to Terence Winter, who was the writer-producer on set that night. "Nobody was particularly sad to go home at 9:30 on a Friday night."

But on Saturday, it became clear that Gandolfini was simply gone. "Nobody could find him," Christine Gee says. "He was really gone for, like, a couple of days. He had been on a tear with Abel Ferrara." Friends and colleagues worried; higher-ups on the show and the network began to panic, imagining the worst, calling all the hospitals. Winter recalled driving in to work and hearing a "sad news from Hollywood" report over the radio. "It was some drummer for a band," Winter said. "But I thought, 'Holy shit! He's dead.'"

They finally heard from him on day four. He'd wandered into a beauty salon in Brooklyn, without a wallet or any ID, and asked to use the phone. He called the only number he could remember, to the production office at Silvercup, and asked if someone could send a car to bring him home. "And we just said like, *Okay, thank God*," Landress said. "You just hope he's okay. And you keep going."

It's still difficult for those involved in Jim's life and work to discuss this period in his life. "He had real struggles in his personal life that got in the way of his work," Susan Aston says, diplomatically. Phil Abraham grapples with how much weight to give it: "I wouldn't want to make this, like, a scene. It's not a—it's not a focal point of who Jim was in any way. It's a sidebar, and yes, it's worth mentioning, because it happened. It's a thing, but we still made the show. And, you know, Jim did what he needed to do."

Drea de Matteo is crystal clear on the subject. "What I think is interesting is that if Jim were alive, these are not the stories anybody would even be talking about," she says. "It's like everyone wants to latch on to this party aspect, or this vice aspect of Jim, when he was so much more than that."

"He was a man with a golden heart, but who had his demons," Christine Gee says. "Did he like to drink too much? Yes. Did he do cocaine? Yes. And did he do these things to excess? Yes. He went to rehab, and he tried. But it's very hard, I think, because of the fact that you're in an industry that doesn't protect you from those kinds of things. When there's publicity parties and stuff like that, that you go to, it's just very difficult to stay clean." HBO would send the cast out often, especially in early years, throwing out first pitches at Yankees games, casino appearances in Atlantic City; booze would flow, and sometimes more. "You cannot protect them, once they start going to awards parties and stuff," says Patty Woo. "Even if you surround them completely with the best people, with the best intentions. You cannot shield an actor from having access to really tough stuff. And if they're inclined, if they have a weak spot? Very, very tough."

James Gandolfini as Tony Soprano, season 4. (Courtesy HBO/Photofest.)

Jim certainly wasn't alone in indulging on those trips, nor was he usually enjoying more than anyone else. "It didn't strike me as anybody completely out of control," says de Matteo. "I mean, then we were *all* fucking out of control, if that's the case. I drank more than everybody on that set. I hung with those men until six o'clock in the morning on those days—we were doing signings, we were filming until four o'clock in the morning, we were working like dogs. My perception was never, *Holy shit, this particular man's out of control.* It was more like, *Oh my God, we had a fun night, the other night,* all *of us.* So yeah, maybe there were a few fucking mishaps here and there. Oh well! You're under a fucking microscope all day! And you have to be at work every single day! We didn't have to be at work every single day, because we weren't Tony Soprano."

And Jimmy could be hard to resist. "He was fun," Kamine says. "He wasn't mean, he liked to joke around, he liked to tell dirty jokes. It was very charming and enjoyable and you wanted to participate and get involved. He was a great guy to go have drinks with—and I shouldn't talk like this, I did it twice or three times or something. But if that's how he behaved all the time, then I could see why people wanted to hang around with him, because it's really fun."

But it began to affect the work, and not just in terms of his ability to make it to the set. "Props would give him those red Solo cups," Gee says. "And there'd be Coke and Jack or whatever in it." No one made a big deal of it. "If there was drinking on the set, it was no different than eating on the set," Abraham says, noting they'd sometimes sub in the real thing for the props, usually at the end of the day. "If that scene were up front, they wouldn't be drinking. But if he had to have a drink in his hand and be talking about something, he'll have a drink in his hand."

"We were all having a blast during the filming of that show," de Matteo says. "And if you know any actors, the ones who aren't sober hang out and have drinks. If you're in the theater, you used to go to Elaine's or Sardi's after the theater and have a drink. We would go to Dick Manitoba's bar in the East Village. That was our hang."

"I didn't see him drunk on set or hungover on set very often," Mark Kamine says, but "that happened a few times. I didn't see drugs. I think at the end of the night, maybe? That seems to be when those things happen."

Sometimes, however, it got out of control. Abraham remembers shooting the disposal of Ralphie's body, a night scene at a giant quarry location, which required a long time to light for very few lines from Gandolfini and Michael Imperioli. "He and Michael, during that time, are hanging out, and they were probably having a few too many," he says. "So when they came to do the scene, it was clear that they were a little shaky—and they were also on the precipice of a big fall. And I remember we had to tie them both off."

More troubling was a scene with Edie Falco in the Soprano living room, in which a drunken Tony attempted to get his frustrated wife to dance with him. "Jim was drinking," Christine Gee recalls, "and Edie found out he was drinking, and Edie was upset." Beyond the breach of work etiquette, Gee says, Falco feared for her own safety. "She says, *He's drinking, and he's a big man, and I'm a small woman, and I'm afraid I'm gonna get hurt.* Because you have to remember in that living room, everything was marble, brass, glass, and he's supposed to be kind of swinging her all around. And she really was nervous."

"I was nervous. That's true," Falco says. "I remember also, little by little, the Teamsters started to kind of trickle into the room—it felt like they were there to make sure nothing got out of hand, kind of? I do remember that."

It was a rare point of contention between the two actors, who typically had a smooth working relationship; only their characters fought. Their on-screen conflict reached a fever pitch in the fourth-season finale, "Whitecaps," in which Carmela discovers her husband has been cheating yet again, and throws him out of the house. The result is a series of long-simmering, now-raging arguments, ferocious in their intensity and theatrical in their performance, two miserable people spewing all their bitterness and resentment at each other. This was some of the most forceful acting either of them had done on the show. It was also perhaps the most egregious example of why Jim gave the show's writers their nickname. "I used to call them the vampires, the writers," he said. "*Say, what have the vampires come up with this week? What blood are they sucking this week?*"

"I know Jim, at certain points, just felt like, *These fucking writers, they're mining my real lif*e," Abraham says. "I remember specifically, there was something in the tabloids about some real estate thing that Jim was gonna buy, and then, lo and behold, the next episode, some real estate shit shows up in the script. And Jim just goes fucking nuts."

Chase would insist, "Jim always said that, but I don't recall any instance where we took anything from Jim's real life. I could be wrong. It's been a long time." And Falco noted, with characteristic nuance, "In all of these serial television shows, the characters and the actors start to mirror each other—become one and the same. It must be the way the writers and the actors swim together through this journey."

But she also remembered Gandolfini fuming, "I'm not telling them another goddamned thing about my life because it always ends up in the script." And by the time they were shooting "Whitecaps" in mid-2002, he had filed for divorce from Marcy.

"TONY SOPRANO" WHACKS HIS MARRIAGE, bleated the *Post*, with characteristic sensitivity, on March 13, 2002. There was little in the way of facts—Gandolfini had initiated the split and had no comment, the couple had been married since 1999, etc.—so there was plenty of space for speculation. "No reasons were given for the failure of the marriage," wrote reporter Richard Johnson, "but Gandolfini, 40, has been known to display some similarities to his hard-living Tony Soprano character, sources told *The Post*." The *Daily News*' gossip columnists Rush & Molloy reported that friends said the couple "had trouble right from the start" but "tried to stay together for the sake of their toddler, Michael, now 3." Those friends further detailed a "tempestuous marriage," strained by Jim's long hours on the set and preference for unwinding at nearby watering holes after work.

Within a week, the *Post* gave the story a full-cover spread, boasting an exclusive (and extremely sympathetic) Cindy Adams interview with Marcy. Under a banner BADFELLA headline, the paper contrasted an unflattering paparazzi pic of Jim with a soft headshot of a despondent-looking Mrs. Gandolfini. Interviewed in a hotel room, where she was registered under an assumed name to avoid the paparazzi at their apartment, Marcy told Adams, "I still love my husband very much. I was in my marriage for a lifetime." The paper had reported on a rumored affair with a model turned actress who was introduced to "the beefy actor" by Michael Imperioli; the *National Enquirer* further investigated, with anonymous friends providing salacious details of the "wild sexual affair."

The *Post*'s notorious Page Six would subsequently report that Jim's steady extramarital squeeze was Lora Somoza, whom he had met during the 2000 shoot of *The Mexican*, where she was assistant to director Gore Verbinski. They were "together constantly during the filming of 'The Mexican,'" according to "a spy on the set"; "We were surprised because up until then everyone thought he was so happy with Marcy." In May, Page Six reported that Somoza had moved in with Jim.

But Mrs. Gandolfini was more general in her assessment of their failures. "My husband basically wants to be free and have not responsibilities to anyone," she said. "One day, he'll cuddle my face, next day he'll tell me I look terrible and I'm fat; a third day, he'll say, 'I know I'm a problem. Don't give up on me.'

"He's a man with problems," she continued. "Through the years, he's wandered away and come back. It's like a love-hate relationship . . . He makes you feel so loved, and then he abuses you psychologically. He tells the audience at the Emmys if not for his wife and child, he'd be nothing. Then he tells me, 'If I stay with you one more day, I'll die of unhappiness.'"

Marcy would get more specific in the divorce filing, which leaked to the *Enquirer* (and was then picked up by the *Daily News* and Page Six). The tabloids claimed that the divorce papers included accusations that "Jim would go on a drug binge every 10 to 14 days," that he often "woke up somewhere not knowing his whereabouts," and that Marcy discovered "he would do drugs with various bimbos and women and have sex with them."

They claimed that Marcy named fifty-two people who knew about Jim's drug problem, including Julia Roberts and Edie Falco, that both had tried to help him kick the habit, and that he "would get drunk and punch himself repeatedly in the head to see if he could get a reaction from Marcy during a quarrel." The tabloids also detailed his 1997 DUI arrest, as well as an alleged April 2000 stay at the New Directions drug rehabilitation facility, where Jim had reportedly checked out before completing the twenty-eight-day program. (Marcy's lawyer told the *Daily News* that some of the reporting of Marcy's allegations "was true," but "some parts are not," without specifying which was which.)

The Enquirer's sources also detailed Jim's claims in the divorce papers, including that Marcy was "emotionally unstable, with a volatile temper which makes her unsafe to live with," that she had "threatened several times to commit suicide" during their separation, and that she was "a risk to their son, having told a friend one month after his birth she was so angry at James she feared she might hurt her baby."

His allegations were serious, but hers were potentially career-ending, particularly as the *Enquirer* speculated, "If the divorce case goes to trial, Marcy could drag a whole set-load of 'Sopranos' cast members onto the witness stand, engulfing the show in a drug scandal as she tries to prove her claims that her husband did drugs with his fellow actors." Jim (and his lawyers) went into damage control mode, submitting to a humiliating "tell-all" interview with the *Enquirer.*

"God, I can't believe I'm doing this," he told the *Enquirer*'s Barry Levine. "I've watched celebrities do this. It's like a rite of passage." He claimed he had hit rock bottom in 1999. "It was a dark time for me," he said of the year when *The Sopranos* premiered, he and Marcy were married, and Michael was born. He insisted that his stay in rehab had taken ("'The Sopranos' had ended, I had needed a break, I needed to go off by myself") and that "I'm clean and sober now. I'm done with everything."

It was all spin, of course, but it cooled the headlines—and tempers. The papers had been filed in March; by October, when they hit the tabloids, the couple had determined to make it an amicable split, for Michael's sake. "We're getting along fine now," he told Page Six. "This is the mother of my child. She's a great mother. I love her very much, and I would never do anything hurtful to her."

Their divorce was completed, without a trial, on December 18, 2002, in what Jim's lawyer Robert Stephen Cohen called "almost record time."

Judge Judith Gische granted the divorce in favor of Marcy; grounds were not stated, but "they appeared to be abandonment," according to the Associated Press, citing Jim's permanent departure from their Greenwich Village home in February 2001. Leaving the courthouse, Jim joked, "Perp walk, perp walk" with the news photographers, before announcing, "It's over. Everyone loves each other very much."

Marcy would retain primary custody of Michael, as well as their adjoining condos in the West Village. Just three days before filing for the divorce, Jim had closed a $1.05 million deal to buy a condo nearby, at 99 Jane Street. The next month, Vines, a restaurant and bar in upstate Oneonta for which he was primary investor (alongside boyhood pal Clive Griffiths), threw its grand opening party; Jim showed up to pour drinks, just like the old days.

The new bachelor was frequently spotted out and about in downtown Manhattan, often perched atop his favorite mode of transportation, a small but speedy scooter. "I catch a lot of grief because of the scooter," he said. "A friend told me I look like Shrek . . . this huge thing on this little thing." That August, he introduced fellow Jersey boy Bruce Springsteen at the MTV Video Music Awards; in October, he appeared at a benefit for Denis Leary's fund for firefighters, sipping a bottle of water and telling the *Daily News* that the allegations of days-long binges were "highly exaggerated. I do too much work for those stories to be accurate."

The tabs also reported (and surmised) about his love life. The *Daily News* quoted confidential sources about trouble already brewing between Jim and main squeeze Lora Somoza ("They have some issues—she thinks he's been partying too hard"), while the *Post*'s sources said the couple was over ("He's hitting downtown spots saying he's free"). Neither was accurate; Gandolfini and Somoza would date through the following year, become engaged in December 2003, and though they never married, they stayed together until 2005. "He was always a smart ass, playing practical jokes and doing silly things to try to embarrass me," Somoza said. "He would sing silly songs and goof around."

He also made as much time as he could for Michael. He and Marcy split custody, with Jim seeing his son on Tuesdays, Thursdays, and for weekend sleepovers. Paparazzi caught them tooling around Tribeca or the Village, and sometimes Marcy even joined; mere days before the divorce hearing, all three were spotted at the premiere of *The Wild Thornberrys Movie* in Manhattan, and the family made an annual tradition of attending the

Dream Halloween event, a fundraiser for children affected by AIDS. They would always go together, often in costume.

This event was just one of Gandolfini's many charitable contributions. "He just was generous and caring and giving," his friend Tom Richardson says. "He worked very hard. And he was very talented, and he was very intelligent. You knew that, but he also felt he was incredibly lucky and incredibly fortunate, and he never took that for granted. He really was a 'there but for the grace of God go I' kind of person."

"One day I get a call," Tony Sirico recalled. "He says, 'What do you think about Iraq?' Three weeks later, we were saying hello to the troops." Gandolfini and Sirico did multiple USO tours, traveling into some of the hotter areas of the conflicts in Afghanistan and Iraq. "We went up to Mosul," Sirico said. "We were on top of a police department roof that had just been taken over by our guys and the mortars started to hit, down the block, boom, boom. And I looked at Jim, and he looked at me, and then we looked at these young kids—these were young soldiers on the roof, and all they did was look over the roof. And you know right away, they've been shot at before, they were real deal guys. We're very proud of these guys."

He also lent his voice to a series of radio spots for the "FDNY Is Worth It" campaign, supporting pay raises for New York City firefighters in the wake of 9/11. ("Everybody remembers what the FDNY did one day," he said in one spot. "Maybe one day they'll get paid like it.") Other charitable pursuits hit even closer to home. Elizabeth Parcell, one of Jim's Park Ridge High classmates, had died of breast cancer, so classmate Donna Mancinelli started the OctoberWoman Foundation for Breast Cancer Research, which included an annual fundraising dinner. "He came every year and brought cast members of *The Sopranos*," says teacher Ann Comarato. "He was a big draw for people to come and support this cause. It brought everybody out of the woodwork."

CAREER PURSUITS WEREN'T QUITE SO cut-and-dried. In June 2003, Gandolfini left his talent agency, Writers & Artists, over an internal dispute between its powers that be and Jim's agent, David Brownstein; he issued a statement reading, "David Brownstein's integrity is beyond question. He continues to be my agent and close friend." That fall, he would sign with United Talent Agency.

Several tantalizing feature film opportunities would present themselves in this period, though few came to fruition. In September 2002, *Variety*

Jim returned to Park Ridge every year for the OctoberWoman Foundation's breast cancer research fundraising dinner. (Courtesy Ann Camarto.)

reported that Jim would reunite with director Sidney Lumet for a remake of Robert Wise's classic film noir boxing drama *The Set-Up*, with Benjamin Bratt also attached and Halle Berry in talks to co-star. When that didn't happen, Jim was set to appear in a 2002 iteration of Lumet's *Before the Devil Knows You're Dead*; the director finally made that film (his last) in 2007, with Philip Seymour Hoffman in what would've been the Gandolfini role. When the Coen Brothers commissioned Glenn Ficarra and John Requa to pen the screenplay for *Bad Santa*, they were told to write it for Gandolfini, whom the siblings had so enjoyed working with on *The Man Who Wasn't There*. (It was subsequently directed by Terry Zwigoff with *Man* co-star Billy Bob Thornton in the role.)

And *Variety* announced Gandolfini as one of the celebrity voices in the mob-infused animated DreamWorks comedy *Sharkslayer*, which underwent a title change to *Shark Tale*. He ultimately passed on it, however; he didn't want to play another gangster, and he also had some problems with the script, which he shared with DreamWorks co-founder, and *Shrek* mastermind, Jeffrey Katzenberg. "I will respectfully take your pass," Katzenberg replied, "but I think I know a thing or two about making kids' films." (Robert De Niro would step into the role.) Jim was no stranger to family entertainment, however; in the spring of 2002, he appeared on a wonderful segment of *Sesame Street*, sharing strategies for overcoming fear with the Muppet Zoe, and dramatizing them as well, resulting in the memorable images of Jim clutching a teddy bear at bedtime and accepting a lollipop from his barber.

His oddest near miss was a 2002 opportunity to star in commercial spots as "a tough-speaking spokesman for the communications company Global Crossing," according to the *New York Times*. "But the plans were scrapped a few months later, as Global Crossing's financial problems were mounting, the advertising budget was cut and other executives at the company concluded that Mafia wiseguy imagery might not be the wisest course."

That imagery was best saved for *The Sopranos*. The season 4 premiere was approaching, with the now-customary elements in place: the roar of hype, this time exacerbated by the extended hiatus ("It's like we have to sort of apologize that we take the time and spend the money and the effort to do a really good job," Chase complained); the theorizing of fans (the *Post* ran an entire story about the conclusions they were drawing from Annie Leibovitz's now-traditional annual cast photo); an influx of new tie-ins (this year, a *Sopranos Family Cookbook*, framed as "compiled by Artie Bucco," that was a number one *New York Times* bestseller, and marinara sauce, creamy Caesar salad dressing, and dry ziti pasta branded with Artie Bucco and Nuovo Vesuvio); and the big premiere and party, again taking over Radio City Music Hall and the Rockefeller Center rink and concourse on September 5, 2002. Gandolfini brought Lora to the premiere; the *Daily News* reported that he was overheard telling a friend, "She's *everything*. It's 100% better. I'm so much fucking happier."

Tony Soprano was, again, first seen in the season padding down the driveway in the bathrobe for the *Star-Ledger*, the equivalent of a band opening up a concert with their most recognizable hit, but Chase and his writers were not content to keep nailing the same notes. Season 4 continued to take the show into darker directions, refusing to pull punches on the violence and ugliness of these men, while sprinkling in sly references to life in post-9/11 America (note the ubiquitous American flag pins on the lapels of corrupt authority figures).

Gandolfini spent the season working out deeper and knottier variations on Tony's pain, anger, and frustration. *He* wasn't going to do his greatest

Joe Pantoliano with Gandolfini. (Courtesy HBO/Photofest.)

hits, either. His warmth and joy with the ducks was one of the most endearing facets of the early episodes, but by now, it becomes clear that Tony only truly finds peace with animals. That manifests most memorably when he discovers that Ralphie killed their shared racehorse for the insurance money, so Tony murders Ralphie with his bare hands in retaliation. This is the most brutal we've ever seen him, this ugly and true-to-life brawl, which is certainly choreographed but doesn't *feel* that way. ("That was like a day's rehearsal with Tim Van Patten, and Jim and I and David and then a stunt coordinator," Pantoliano says. "They had to physically build the set, and then they had to decide where they were going to cut holes and put the cameras. That scene, I think, took three days to shoot.")

Jim does some of his best nonverbal acting in the seventh episode, "Watching Too Much Television," which includes that tricky scene of Jim beating and humiliating Peter Riegert. He's terrifying there—wild, brutal, borderline feral, literally foaming at the mouth—but his finest acting is in the scene that immediately precedes it. As "Oh Girl" by the Chi-Lites plays on Tony's car radio, we prepare for another amusing driving-and-singing scene, only to watch him listen to the lyrics and become overwhelmed with emotion.

But it felt as though everything he'd done with the character was leading up to "Whitecaps." It's a decathlon of emotion for Gandolfini and Falco, from the deep well of sadness in their poolside fight sequence, sifting through the ashes of this broken marriage together, to his metamorphosis (in a slowly expanding close-up) from smirking disbelief to pain and anger when Carmela tells him about her crush on Furio. The sequence goes and goes and goes, taking the episode a full fifteen minutes past the maximum running time to that point, stretching every minute to unsettle the viewer; that's how long the argument would go, and they're not going to let us out of it. We have to sit in this domestic hell alongside them.

Critics were still over the moon for the show—"as subtle, explosive, complex, ironic, sad, metaphorically potent and funny as ever," raved the *Chicago Tribune*'s Steve Johnson—and the fourth-season premiere was another record-breaker, the most-watched show in HBO's thirty-year history. But the quiet backlash that had started brewing the previous year returned in some of the less patient recaps and commentaries. By mid-season, the *Post* had declared it "monotonous, aimless, and deadly dull," *Newsday*'s Marvin Kitman was complaining that the show "basically has been vamping, repeating the story," and the *Wall Street Journal*'s Tunku Varadarajan proclaimed it "in a bit of a rut, plot wise," particularly if "one is beginning to tire—in the absence of any new, clever twists in the story—of Tony Soprano's relentless boorishness."

If awards-giving bodies shared those concerns, you couldn't tell. *The Sopranos* nabbed sixteen nominations at the 2003 Emmys, and though they *again* lost best drama to *The West Wing*, Jim and Edie took home their customary gold, along with trophies for best writing and a best supporting actor nod for Joe Pantoliano. Jim made a splash back home with what was on his lapel: Rather than a red ribbon or American flag pin, he wore a campaign button for Joe Renna, a mutual friend running for the office of freeholder of Union County, New Jersey. Renna had given Jim a handful of buttons when they'd met the previous summer, hoping one might make its way onto *The Sopranos*; Jim said, "I'll go one better—I'll wear it to the Emmys." So he did.

"I DID HAVE SOME CONVERSATIONS with him, just the two of us," Edie Falco recalls, "about how desperately he wanted out of the cycle of what he was trying to deal with, and different treatments he'd had. My brother was going through it at the same time. So he was telling me, you know, 'Your brother should try this thing, it's really good, they do the thing,' whatever the latest thing he tried was. He's offering me advice for this thing that he's just desperately wanted to be free from. It's a nightmare. It's a nightmare."

The separation between Jim and Tony, once such an impenetrable abyss, had become so negligible that he found himself living out events from the show. One of the most memorable scenes in season 4 comes in episode 10, "The Strong, Silent Type," in which the Soprano crew attempts an intervention for Christopher's drug problem, which turns into an all-out melee. That episode aired in November 2002; the following May, Jim's friends and family attempted the real thing, with similarly disastrous results. "We had an intervention with him in my apartment in New York," HBO's Chris Albrecht told author James Andrew Miller. "The intervention wasn't my idea. I think it was his family's idea because his sister was there. It was definitely a crisis situation."

According to Miller, Jim arrived at the elegant Museum Tower under the false belief that he was meeting the executive for a casual hangout. Instead, about a dozen people—friends, family, and David Chase among them—were waiting in Albrecht's apartment. They had spent two days conducting intervention "rehearsals," surmising his objections and reactions, and their possible responses to them. If all went well, they could move quickly; a private plane was standing by to transport him to a rehab facility.

All did not go well. Jim walked in, surveyed the room, realized what was happening, and immediately announced, "Oh, fuck this. Fuck all of you." He then glared at Albrecht and snapped, "Fire me."

And with that, he left.

CHAPTER 15

TOM

IN JANUARY 2003, JAMES GANDOLFINI ARRIVED in Chicago to take his next stab at crossing over to big screen stardom. *Surviving Christmas* sounded good on paper: a holiday comedy, which could mean not only a warm reception but ongoing residuals if it became a perennial (*Elf* and *Love, Actually* would hit theaters later that year); a return to DreamWorks, where he had done so well with *The Mexican*; a chance to share scenes with Catherine O'Hara, a comedy legend from her work on *SCTV* and in the improvised mockumentaries of Christopher Guest; and second billing only to straight-up movie star Ben Affleck, who personally made "the most passionate, heartfelt, ridiculous plea" to Jim to make the film, according to producer Jenno Topping. Affleck was so set on securing Gandolfini, in fact, that he pulled strings at HBO (where he was currently producing and appearing in the reality series *Project Greenlight*) to move that season's *Sopranos* start date to accommodate the film.

But *Surviving Christmas* was "kind of a disaster," says manager Nancy Sanders. "Jim was considering it. Mark and I were saying no, there's no reason to do this movie. This is not a good script." It was sold on the strength of its simple longline—a rich but vapid yuppie (Affleck) returns to his childhood home and pays the family who lives there now to celebrate Christmas with him—by its original writers, Deborah Kaplan and Harry Elfont, who were directors themselves. But another screenwriting team was brought on to rewrite the script, which was then handed over to director Mike Mitchell, whose sole feature directorial credit was the desperately unfunny *Deuce Bigalow: Male Gigolo.*

"It was a little chaotic because they kept doing rewrites," says Josh Zuckerman, who co-starred as Gandolfini and O'Hara's son. "They were doing so many rewrites, all the time. In fact, I think Affleck started rewriting some stuff at a certain point." Mitchell was "a nice guy, but it felt, in a way, that other people were directly felt or were pushing the shoot along. . . . Mike was certainly there, and he directed it, and he was great. But it was a little scattershot."

"Jim was well-paid for his appearance," Sanders says, "but he didn't need to do this movie. And he did it."

Not that the stress of the shoot seemed to affect Jim all that much. "I remember him smiling a lot," Zuckerman says. "He just seemed to be very happy to be there." Gandolfini's trailer was something like a playground, with the latest gaming system and other time killers, "and he was having a ball. I remember a big smile on his face when I came in the trailer, and he was playing, and he's like, *This is great*, you know? I thought it was so funny. He felt like a big kid who'd been to Toys R Us."

The production shot for two weeks in Chicago in order to get the properly snowy exteriors before heading to California's Mammoth Mountain ski resort for a tobogganing set piece, and then settling in Los Angeles to finish up on soundstages. Jim wore a full beard and a wardrobe of flannels and ugly holiday sweaters to play family patriarch Tom Valco, which combined to give him a new look (if not sound; he oddly retains his Tony/Jersey dialect to play the Midwestern family man). "It never felt like he was trying really hard," Zuckerman says. "He didn't seem to feel like he needed to assert his presence, or be the center of attention, or any of that. . . . It all

Ben Affleck, right, pulled every string he could to get Gandolfini for the comedy misfire *Surviving Christmas*. (Courtesy DreamWorks/Photofest.)

just felt very natural. There was no difference between how he conducted himself when the cameras are rolling or when they weren't."

Surviving Christmas is a mess; Affleck, a hot property just a couple of years earlier, had fallen out of public and industry favor after a series of turkeys, and he turns in an obnoxious, flop-sweat performance, trying desperately to be "funny" and coming off as anything but. Gandolfini plays it straight, and real, seeking out laughs in the deadpan impatience of this working-class guy, and he has a couple of good moments: the way he keeps muttering the amount of their payoff to himself when Affleck makes him put on a Santa hat to go Christmas tree shopping, or how he musters up all his malice when a mirthful snowball fight takes a turn. But the disparity of tones and styles in the acting is nearly as much a problem as the weak script; Affleck is so broad, so sitcom-y, that it seems like he and Gandolfini are in different movies.

Though it wrapped in the spring of 2003, the picture didn't land in theaters until October 2004 (at the premiere, co-writer Josh Sternin said it was "just ten months late from last Christmas"), and it's hard to decide if critics or moviegoers received it with more hostility. The *New York Post*'s Lou Lumenick gave it zero stars and proclaimed, "Nobody survives 'Surviving Christmas'—not even the supremely talented James Gandolfini," while the *New York Times*' Stephen Holden shrugged it off: "Mr. Gandolfini's Tom suggests a chastened Tony Soprano walking around in a daze." It opened in seventh place for the weekend, and in an apparent attempt to recoup some of its cost before the holidays, was rushed out on home video a mere eight weeks later. It was a less than noble ending for what *Variety* dubbed "an almost mirth-free, poorly conceived comedy," even with Gandolfini's "most Tony Soprano-like feature turn—but that may cause many to wish they were actually home watching the HBO show."

But not that even *that* was guaranteed.

IN LATE 2002, *SOPRANOS* CO-STARS Robert Iler, Tony Sirico, Drea de Matteo, and Jamie-Lynn Sigler had joined forces to demand a group raise of their per-episode rate, from the $20,000 to $30,000 range up to $100,000 a show in season 5. It was a collective bargaining tactic that had recently resulted in success for several members of the cast of *The Sopranos*' regular Emmy rival, *The West Wing*. "James Gandolfini is said to be waiting for the group to resolve their contracts before trying to snag a nice raise for himself," wrote the *Post*'s Michael Starr. "Gandolfini shouldn't have much of a problem since, without him, the show would lose its main attraction."

By late February, that quartet had successfully negotiated up to $60,000 per show (as had Michael Imperioli, who would now get $80,000 per episode). But new deals needed to be made for several of the show's leads—including Jim, whose $400,000 per episode was still markedly less than the record-breaking deal of $1 million per episode recently made by the stars of *Friends.* What's more, even $1 million per episode for Gandolfini wasn't truly commensurate with the comparative work. *Friends* was a half-hour sitcom, taped live in front of a studio audience at the end of a four-day work week that they'd made part of their deal. *Friends* also produced twenty-two episodes per year to *The Sopranos*' thirteen, but as an hour-long drama shot on sets and on location, each *Sopranos* episode took two to three weeks of fourteen-hour days (or more, by the show's conclusion). So he was working roughly the same calendar year, but only getting paid for about half as many episodes.

"He wasn't making that much," Susan Aston says. "And he was never a fucking producer on *The Sopranos*—and now, every little Netflix series, the main actor is a producer. He was never a producer. That's where the money was. I wouldn't have spit at his salary, don't get me wrong, but . . . he was, in my mind, underpaid to what other people were making, and the kind of hours he was putting in, and the kind of money that show was making."

"A lot of us came from parents that were blue-collar workers—I'd say everybody, tell you the truth," Jim said of the *Sopranos* cast. "If you go down the whole line of people, their parents, you know, were pretty blue-collar and pretty East Coast, not far removed from immigrants. I think there was a good work ethic. I think we all worked hard and there wasn't a lot of nonsense. It was a good group, you know, and nobody wanted to do anything less than they could possibly do." In exchange for that, a source told the *Post* in 2003, "he wants fair-market value," and that value had a number: $20 million a year. HBO wasn't willing to go that far, or to meet his team's follow-up offer of $16 million per year.

So Gandolfini took them to court. On March 6, 2003, less than three weeks before the scheduled March 24 start date for production on season 5, Jim filed suit in California Superior Court, seeking declaratory relief to release him from his contract with HBO, due to violations of said contract's duration by the network. "Our legal position is that there is no obligation for James Gandolfini to perform services for the coming season," said his attorney, Martin Singer. The network snapped back a few days later, with a $100 million countersuit. "We are exposing the frivolous nature of (Gandolfini's) claims in our answer and cross-complaint," said HBO's lawyer, Bert Fields. "If he doesn't show up by March 24, he's going to owe a huge amount of money."

It was an ugly turn of events, battled out in the tabloids and the trades—rather than behind closed doors, where salary negotiations were most fruitful. "It became a public fight between the two of us and I didn't handle the situation very well," HBO's Chris Albrecht would later admit. "I said something to the press that I shouldn't have said, called him a fat slob or something." The insult, attributed in the *Daily News* to a "network official," was "greedy pig."

"That just rocked his world," Armstrong said. "He was incredibly upset and hurt." Albrecht insisted that he "was really offended that one of his representatives wasn't operating with a lot of integrity," a sentiment echoed by his successor at HBO, Mike Lombardo. "Jim was a brilliant actor but a complicated guy to deal with," Lombardo told James Andrew Miller. "He had his own demons about success. And unfortunately, he was surrounded by representatives who took advantage of that."

Michael Imperioli, Jim, Tony Sirico, and Steven Van Zandt.
(Courtesy HBO/Photofest.)

Those demons, however, were part of why Jim was willing to take a hard line in the negotiations—because he'd reached a point where he wasn't sure if he even wanted *The Sopranos* to continue. The dark place he had to go to in order to play Tony convincingly, and the increasingly grim situations Chase and the writers were creating, was amplifying his considerable personal, psychological struggles. Walking away from *The Sopranos* might end his career. It could also save his life.

On March 12, *Variety* reported a stalemate. "Production on season five, scheduled to get under way March 24, remained in peril Wednesday, as HBO execs said negotiations with the series star James Gandolfini are dead." The network made a final offer of $11 million, part of it paid in profit participation; they would engage in no further negotiations until Gandolfini's suit was withdrawn. "Gandolfini's agents believe they're holding a gun to HBO's head to get them to pay this massive salary increase," Fields told the trade paper, "but it's really a water pistol—and doesn't even have any water in it."

But Jim and his team held firm. "He had a lot of people in his corner that were like, *No, no, no, no*," Nancy Sanders says. "*This is one of those moments where we own it. It's not TV, it's HBO. You're the cover page, we're gonna get it and God bless that you're in a position to get it.*" Five days later, *Variety* reported that production on the season had been postponed indefinitely, with cast and crew told not to report for work until further notice.

But there was more to the story than met the eye. Jim wasn't the only one whose salary was being negotiated that season; Lorraine Bracco, Edie Falco, and Steven Van Zandt, among others, were trying to get more money as well. "I remember at one point, money wise, we were in a negotiation, and it got a little ugly," Steve Schirripa recalled. "And Jim was, *Whatever you guys want to do*. He was in."

"In contract negotiations, he would come off looking like a bad guy, just so everybody else was taken care of," Robert Iler explains. "He didn't care that, from the outside people were like, *Oh, well, Jim's holding out*. There were times where he wanted to make sure everybody else got paid before he got paid, because he didn't want it to look like, *the only reason you're not getting the money you want is because I took so much*."

Finally, with the clock ticking, executive producer Brad Grey—whose company Brillstein-Grey (which held the original deal with David Chase that led to the show) was not named in Jim's suit—stepped in to play peacemaker. Meanwhile, Albrecht's decision to shut down production of the show, essentially laying off the entire staff and blaming it on the contract dispute, had played right into Jim's reliable concern for the financial well-being of his colleagues. On March 17, the *Post* reported, "Lawyers for the mob opera's star, James Gandolfini, and HBO talked into the small hours of yesterday morning"; two days later, the deal was done, with production scheduled to resume a week late, on March 31, and Jim insisting on back pay for the days everyone had missed. "I'm very happy that *The Sopranos* will be back," went his official statement. "It's a show that I love doing with people I love working with."

"I have nothing but respect for HBO," Jim told *Entertainment Weekly*. "I want to work there. I want to go back, and I'm sorry for all this nonsense." (The *Post*'s Austin Smith took all of this in and sneered, "His fat salary demands almost sank the entire show, but now, pot-bellied 'Sopranos' star James Gandolfini is apologizing to HBO.")

The deal they hammered out was less than the $16 million he wanted but more than the $11 million they'd offered; factoring in salary and advances against syndication, he would make around $13 million for the show's fifth year. "He got paid like the actors are getting paid now, like a Kevin Costner would get paid," Nancy Sanders says. "It was fucking great."

The deal also included—and this was a sticking point—profit participation points, not only going forward but retroactive to the beginning of the show. "The deals that were made for the cast back then on cable shows were shitty," Drea de Matteo says. "He got a great deal; of course David Chase got a great deal. But a lot of the cast just sort of got left out in the cold." The supporting players were uniquely bereft of leverage for salary renegotiations; any of them could be killed off at a moment's notice. But their salaries didn't reflect the show's cultural ubiquity, and their deals did not include future residuals for repeat airings or DVD sales.

Once his deal was finally sewn up, Jim did what he could to show his appreciation to his colleagues. "He pulled each and every one of us in his trailer during work one day, and gave us all a check," de Matteo says. "I remember, I think it was for $36,000." The sixteen series regulars each got one of those checks, with a simple explanation: "Thanks for sticking by me."

"That's all he said," Schirripa says. "He called you into the trailer, I went in, he gave me an envelope. And back then, that's like buying everybody an SUV."

De Matteo, for one, was in shock. "Jim, I'm not taking this check," she said. "Are you insane, dude?"

"Everyone's taking it, and if you don't take it, it's going in the garbage," he told her. "So you may as well take it."

And so she did. They all did. "He wrote checks to a lot of people that didn't have the power to get the raises," Joe Pantoliano says. "He was extraordinary in that way."

"Nobody knew at that time that he had always planned to divide it up among the regulars," Armstrong explains, "because they weren't getting it. And he knew that. And so that was right around the same time they called him a greedy pig, when we, as his team, knew that was his intention."

Something else about that interaction stuck with Robert Iler. "Especially in show business, when somebody does something like that for you, they want the reaction," he explains. "They want the like, *Oh my God, this guy's so good*. And he wanted none of that. He didn't even want to look up when he handed me the check. He didn't want you going, *Oh my God, thank you so much*. He's like, *Come on, come on, just get out of here*." And according to Armstrong, even though this was Jim's intention all through the public salary squabble, "that part we couldn't talk about. Because he wouldn't let us."

"He split it up amongst the cast," Van Zandt chuckles. "He's unbelievable. Unbelievable. I mean, I can guarantee you, no one ever, in history, did anything like that before."

"His generosity was unparalleled," de Matteo says. "I think he felt like he had hit the jackpot, and he just wanted to fuckin' share it with everybody. He was just a different breed. A completely different breed."

ROBERT FUNARO REMEMBERS SHOOTING A scene on a golf course; he was behind the wheel of a golf cart, and Jim was in the passenger seat next to him. Between takes, as they were waiting, Jim made him a proposition: "If you drive the golf cart into the lake, I'll give you $3,000. Come on, Bobby, drive it into the lake."

Funaro looked at him. "Are you crazy?"

"No, I'm serious. Drive it in there."

"Jimmy, I'm not driving in there," he insisted. Funaro still has a picture from that day, the two of them in the golf cart, Gandolfini looking miserable. "There are some days you don't feel like doing it," the actor says. "He was serious. He wanted me to drive."

There were other challenges, besides boredom, in season 5. Robert Loggia, the legendary character actor who'd previously played tough-guy gangsters in the likes of *Scarface* and *Lost Highway*, joined the cast for a brief arc. Schirripa explains:

> There was no ad-libbing at all, you had to be word-perfect. Some people kind of figured they could come in and just paraphrase, you know? And so we shot a scene—me, Jim, Dominic (Chianese), and Robert. It was supposed to be a four-hour scene that turned into an eight-hour scene. Robert had a tough time with his lines. He wound up having Alzheimer's or dementia—I don't know if this was the beginning of it, but he was having a tough time. Now, somebody else would have said, *Get rid of this fucking guy. What the fuck is going on here? I can't work like this.* Other actors might say that. You know what Jim did? Jim offered, and sent someone over to his hotel to run lines that night and work with him. He was as patient as patient can be.

Other additions were more comfortable. Steve Buscemi had directed an episode in each of the previous two seasons before joining the cast in season 5 as Tony Blundetto, aka "the other Tony," Tony Soprano's cousin and partner in crime who just completed a long prison stint. "When I was acting in a scene with him, I felt that it made me better, because I felt as though Jimmy *was* Tony Soprano," Buscemi said. "It put me on my toes a little bit more. Just knowing that he would give a thousand percent every take, and really be listening to you, and be looking at you. And not to take away anything from any of the other actors, because everybody has their own process. But Jimmy had this internal thing going on that just drew you into him. That was thrilling, to work with an actor like that, to feel like you're getting this attention from this other actor. And you better be giving it all right back."

Drea de Matteo was also feeling more of that intensity this year, as the machinations of the plot brought the characters of Adriana and Tony into closer proximity than before, with genuine affection that blurs into sexual tension between them. "I was nervous when I had to go do those scenes with him, because I was so used to working with Michael (Imperioli)," she says. "And now all of a sudden we have these romantic scenes together and I'm like, holy fuck, are you kidding me? I gotta do this with *the boss* right now?

"I wasn't used to his process and how he was," she continues, "whether he was going to be fun or serious on set. He was definitely serious."

His on-set no-shows were still frequent—enough so that the new HBO deal included a clause making him financially responsible for any costs incurred by his absences. "This doesn't put an end to it," Mark Kamine wrote in his memoir *On Locations.* "Word is HBO never charges him for a day." But it took other steps, according to Kamine, most notably dismissing "a crew member who steadily interacted with the actors and who considered himself invulnerable due to his close working relationship with Jim. Apart from an edgy attitude toward production and increasingly frequent substandard performance of his non-Jim-related tasks, there has been suspicion that he has been providing drink and drugs during working hours to the cast and crew interested in such things. His removal doesn't stop the drinking and drug-taking."

Some aspects of the job had become easier with the passing years. The memorization troubles that had dogged Jim were dissipating, for example. "It's like a muscle now," he said in 2004. "I was so used to doing two pages for film. I mean, in the first two weeks, I was in shock. Slowly you get into a groove with it, and you can't do anything else. During the week, I can't do anything because otherwise I'm not prepared. There are 200 people standing there the next day. If you're not prepared, you feel pretty stupid."

Whatever the process, the result was another season in which Gandolfini took one of the most complex characterizations in television history and continued to deepen it, finding the rage, regret, grief, and helplessness in a character who was only becoming more powerful and dangerous. The bitterness and resentment over the separation with Carmela were new notes to play, as was the melancholy, culminating in a dark night of the soul scene where Tony, disheveled, drunk, in his undershirt, hair a mess, incongruently puts a painting of the Rat Pack up on the wall of his sad bachelor pad.

Such moments of vulnerability were increasingly becoming the key to the character. He has one of his most emotionally open non-Melfi scenes when he presses Uncle Junior about his repeated mentions of young Tony's subpar athletic abilities. "Why's it gotta be something mean?" Tony asks. "Why can't you repeat something good? I mean, don't you love me?" And with that question hanging in the air, the episode slams to a conclusion.

We see a similar softness and tenderness, a real affection for his cousin (who is like a brother), which leads to his best single scene of the year, a breakdown in Melfi's office in which he opens up about the panic attack he had so many years ago, after a fight with his mother, that kept him off the criminal job that got cousin Tony sent away. "I'm just a fuckin' robot to my own pussy-ass weakness," he cries, and that guilt adds extra weight to the scenes in which he thinks, brews, and then, over the fresh body of Tony B, grieves.

The extra weight of his person was also contributing to the extra weight of the character. Over the previous year, his heavy breathing had become increasingly pronounced, in scenes of both dialogue and silence. By season 5, in which Tony spends so much time stewing and contemplating, the heavy breathing had fully become part of his actor's toolbox; when Carmela tells him she's drained the pool, he can reply *just* with the breathing. And it's scary.

By now, the dance of a new season of *The Sopranos* was all but set in stone: the wailing over the wait (fifteen months lapsed between the airings of the season 4 finale and the season 5 premiere, meaning no new episodes aired through the entire calendar year of 2003); the hype-stewing previews (*TV Guide* asked, "Can a hit series just flake out for 15 months, then come back and kill the competition?"); the new Annie Leibovitz cast photo for the superfans to analyze ("SOPRANOS" ACTORS SLEEP WITH THE FISHES IN PROMO PIC, shouted the *Post*); the star-studded premiere and party at Radio City Music Hall (Rudy Giuliani was again in attendance); the rave reviews, albeit some of them with qualifiers ("'The Sopranos' returns for a fifth season with all of its early verve and none of the torpor that weighed the show down last year," opined the *New York Times*' Alessandra Stanley). Not all of it was well received; a twenty-plus-minute dream sequence divided critics and fans sharply, with some finding it inventive and emotionally informative, and others complaining of nonsensical self-indulgence ("Wake me when it's over," complained the *Post*'s reliably grouchy Austin Smith). But the season premiere was yet another ratings record-breaker for HBO, and the numbers held steady over the run.

And there was another overdue victory in the wings. When the Primetime Emmys were handed out on September 19, 2004, Jim lost the best actor prize to *The Practice*'s James Spader—but *The Sopranos* finally won the award for best drama series, along with the first Emmys for Michael Imperioli (best supporting actor) and Drea de Matteo (best supporting actress). Before season 5 even hit the airwaves, HBO announced the show's renewal for a sixth (and, it would seem, final) season. It was time for Jim to start thinking about what his career—and his life—would look like without Tony Soprano.

CHAPTER 16

NICK

FOR THE FIRST FILM OF his lengthy hiatus between seasons 5 and 6 (a staggering twenty-one months would elapse between finale and premiere), Jim landed a lead role in a big risk. *Romance & Cigarettes* was written and directed by actor John Turturro, with a packed cast—including Susan Sarandon as his wife, Kate Winslet as his mistress, Mary Louise Parker, Christopher Walken, Elaine Stritch, and fellow *Sopranos* stars Steve Buscemi and Aida Turturro—and the Coen Brothers as executive producers. They suggested Jim to Turturro, after their pleasant experience with him on *The Man Who Wasn't There.* "He did a reading and he was great. After that I really wanted him for the part," Turturro said. "He liked the project, but he was a little nervous about it. We went back and forth for a while. I decided to wait for him and I am really glad I did."

"It was like, dude, you've got money," Nancy Sanders says, laughing. "I think he was paid scale for it. It was like one of those things like, *I can do that now and still send my kid to private school.*"

But the premise was tricky. Summarized by *Variety* as "'Pennies from Heaven' meets 'The Honeymooners,'" *Romance & Cigarettes* was a "working-class musical," in which the characters burst into song (mostly standards, accompanying old records), and musicals were, as ever, not exactly a safe bet. Plus, Jim had never sung or danced on-screen before.

Perhaps because of nerves, perhaps because of the extra pressure, or perhaps because it was just how he was used to working (and living), he brought over some bad habits from *The Sopranos* when *Romance & Cigarettes* began production in March 2004. Chiemi Karasawa, who'd been a substitute script supervisor on *The Sopranos*, was fully filling that role on *Romance.* "Jim was, you know, Jim," she says, "and everything that he is known for, happened." There were no-shows and there were late-shows. When he'd turn back up, he'd pull her aside: "Who's mad at me? How bad is it?"

"Pretty bad," she'd reply. "Susan Sarandon is back in the trailer, we had to reschedule all the scenes. Now we're doing this."

"Okay. How mad are you?" he'd ask.

"It was like talking to a little kid," she says. "He would always get himself really worked up and it was like, dude, you just need to show up. But as I think many people know, he was having substance problems, and, I think, a lot of emotional things going on. And it would sort of be like this Jekyll and Hyde behavior sometimes."

"There's something about James that's like a bad 8-year-old," Sarandon would say later. "He can get away with being so naughty, because he's so lovable, and so charming, and clearly loves women that you can't blame him."

On an independent film, his erratic behavior wasn't as costly as on an expensive HBO production—but there was far less money to cover those costs. When Dr. Jekyll returned to work, Karasawa says, "He would absorb the financial responsibility. If they went over, if he was a no-show, and it screwed up their day, he would front all the money to pay for it. . . . He felt like it was always his responsibility to make everything right. If he made anything wrong, he didn't want it to injure the production in any way."

The production, centered in Queens from mid-March through mid-May 2004, was chaotic. "We'd do these incredible musical numbers, and

Jim joins a kick-line of singing, dancing, working-class stiffs in *Romance & Cigarettes*. (Courtesy United Artists/Photofest.)

he'd be singing at the top of his lungs," Karasawa says. "And I'd come over to him, to ask him a question about continuity or something, and he's like, *This is never going to be in the movie, don't worry about it.* And I go, *What do you mean, this is a huge, huge number. Are you kidding?*

"*It'll never be in the movie. Doesn't work.* He would always say things like that. And you know, he was fucking right. . . . It didn't end up in the movie."

As certain as Jim was about his instincts, he still lacked self-confidence about himself as a person—specifically, about his physical appearance. He had only one concern about his casting: that a woman who looked like Kate Winslet wouldn't be attracted to a man who looked like him. He took his director aside and asked (demanded, really), "Why would her character want to be with someone like me?"

"What are you talking about?" Turturro replied, baffled.

"He just never saw himself as that guy," Karasawa says. "I think he thought he was fooling everybody."

So Turturro talked him through not only the dynamics of the character, but his attributes as a human being. "Jim, you know, you're funny, you're this guy, you're a caregiver, you have this presence."

Gandolfini remained unconvinced. "But that's his humility," Karasawa says. "He's very insecure about that kind of stuff."

His inescapable celebrity on location was another source of stress. "One of my former students was Michael's nanny at the time," Susan Aston says. "He had brought Michael for us to have lunch with. So the four of us were having lunch at this diner, and it comes time to leave, and it's like that scene from *The Birds*. You look out and there's birds everywhere, only it was people in the parking lot. You couldn't even see, it was a sea of people." The manager helped the quartet escape via the diner's back door, but "that was the only time I was afraid for him and Michael."

Romance & Cigarettes is a strange, sometimes strained, yet occasionally wonderful picture, featuring some of Jim's most delectable screen acting. Sporting a neat little mustache, he's a true working-class hero; he looks and sounds like Tony, but he spouts poetry and holds his kids dear and has the heart of a romantic. There's an innocence to this character (even though he's an adulterer) that is a lovely new note in his acting arsenal, and when he insists, "I have love to give," there's a choke in his voice, and enough desperation and emotion in his eyes, that you believe him. His singing is pure and guileless, blasting a pleasing tenor voice with warmth and conviction.

The film's road to theaters was a tricky one, covered in the potholes of Hollywood financing and niche distribution. United Artists, then a subsidiary of MGM, was slated to release it in the fall of 2005, after screening (to enthusiastic audiences and critics) at the Venice and Toronto film festivals. But when Sony bought out MGM, much of its slate was left in the lurch—including *Romance*, which didn't exactly look like a box office home run. It lingered in limbo for two full years, finally premiering in New York in September 2007. Turturro spent that interval pleading with Sony to release the film, which it wouldn't; to back down from its asking price of $3 million so he could sell the film to a smaller distributor, which it also wouldn't; and finally, thanks in part to the intervention of Sony star Adam Sandler (with whom Turturro had acted occasionally), to allow Turturro to self-distribute the picture, which it did.

The reviews were off the charts. "There is more raw vitality pumping through 'Romance & Cigarettes,' John Turturro's passionate ode to the sensual pulse of life in a working-class neighborhood of Queens, than in a dozen perky high school musicals," raved the *New York Times*' Stephen Holden. *Salon*'s Andrew O'Hehir called it "the most original picture by an American director I've seen this year, and also the most delightful." And Roger Ebert deemed it "the real thing, a film that breaks out of Hollywood jail with audacious originality, startling sexuality, heartfelt emotions and an anarchic liberty. The actors toss their heads and run their mouths like prisoners let loose to race free."

Most importantly, Jim was happy. "It's one of the things he ended up being most proud of," Mark Armstrong says. "He just thought it was the most unique film, and loved John's direction." But in spite of Turturro's best efforts, and respectable numbers in its art house run, *Romance & Cigarettes*—and one of Gandolfini's best performances—never broke through to a wider audience.

JIM TOOK SOME MUCH-NEEDED TIME off in the summer of 2004. He'd taken to renting a house on the Jersey Shore in the summer months, inviting a variety of family, friends, and co-workers out for days on end. "He liked to gather his friends around him all the time," says filmmaker Jon Alpert. "I don't think that you could say he was a loner; he liked the people that he liked, and he wanted them to be with him, so he would rent a house at the Jersey Shore for a couple of weeks every year. I guess he could have bought a house, but I don't know why—he just always rented, and he always rented the same house."

He restricted work to charity appearances. That June, he appeared (along with Edie Falco and Dominic Chianese) at the Alzheimer's Association benefit and silent auction at the Pierre Hotel, at the urging of then fiancée Lora Somoza. "My grandmother has Alzheimer's, so Jim knows that this has been a very passionate cause for me for quite some time," she told the *Times*. "And he also shares the belief that we have to do as much as we can to raise funds and awareness." He also appeared—alongside Marcy and Michael—at that summer's Pediatric AIDS Foundation Kids for Kids Celebrity Carnival, and returned to Park Ridge that fall for another October-Woman Foundation fundraiser, bringing five *Sopranos* co-stars along. He was spotted hanging out with Bill Clinton at the Central Park Zoo, not long before joining labor leaders at a rally held during the Republican National Convention to protest president George W. Bush's anti-worker and anti-union policies.

He named a flower for the African Rainforest Conservancy's dinner and auction, and participated in a roast of a Rutgers pal, celebrity chef Mario Batali, benefiting the Food Bank for New York City. He and Batali were also inducted into the Rutgers Hall of Distinguished Alumni in 2004. "So the two of us were inducted after a microbiologist, someone who invented the patch for nicotine," Jim said, laughing, "ten of these people, and then it was us, so I was like, 'Well, here's Heckle and Jeckle at the end.' It was nice, you know. I said, 'To be honest, I haven't a clue how I graduated from here, but thank you—I met a lot of intelligent people that are still my friends, and I had a ball.'"

He spent much of the hiatus doing charitable career acts as well. In 2004, Jim submitted to a rare, extended, on-camera interview, walking through his career and his process on Bravo's *Inside the Actors Studio* with host James Lipton. Susan Aston was working as a teacher at the Actors Studio and was key in putting the show together. "Lipton did ask me to ask him," Aston says. "Because that's where I worked. And he said, *Well, is it going to help you? Are they going to give you a raise?* I said, no, they're not going to give me shit. So don't do it for me!

"I did emphasize to him that it should be craft-based. That was the whole point of it, was to give the Actors Studio drama school students a seminar, a craft seminar; it wasn't going to be, like, an interview with

People magazine. . . . I think he also was proud of being a member of the Actors Studio. So he wanted to maybe share some of that with the students."

He also appeared in the inaugural episode of Sirius Satellite Radio's *The Wiseguy Show*, executive produced by Steven Van Zandt and hosted by Vincent "Big Pussy" Pastore. He popped up, as a kind of spectral, Jiminy Cricket-ish presence, in the short film *Club Soda* alongside first season co-star Michael Rispoli (it was inserted into the 2010 anthology film *Stories USA*, released on video as *American Breakdown*). And he did a favor for his *12 Angry Men* co-star Tony Danza, appearing in the first episode of Danza's eponymous daytime chat show in a sketch as the booker, barking Tony Soprano–style threats and demands to potential guests.

"He tells the guy, at one point, 'Not only are you gonna be there, but you're gonna bring Mr. Danza a gift!'" Danza laughs. "It was funny as hell. That's how we launched my show! . . . I basically put the arm on him and he did me a favor. The thing that always touched me was that he was so giving. Once you were his friend, you know, you were his friend."

But he was still having trouble finding the right kind of roles, ones that would play to his strengths while still showing his range. "On one level, I am typecast, because this show is so popular, so in-everybody's-face," he said in 2004. "So am I typecast? In a way, well, yeah. I'm 260 pounds and look a certain way. I'm not going to play Tinkerbell."

In another interview that year, he admitted that he was modifying his self-description as a "260-pound Woody Allen," because "it's 270 now." Within a couple of years, he'd upped it again: "I used to say I was a 260-pound Woody Allen. You can make that 295-pound now. . . . I should exercise, but I'm too old for that shit."

He managed to find a couple of projects that were worth his time. He was developing one himself, the first green light of his production deal with HBO, a made-for-cable movie in which he would play Ernest Hemingway; it would focus on the novelist's romance with war correspondent Martha Gellhorn, who *Variety* reported could be played by Jim's *She's So Lovely* co-star Robin Wright Penn. While that script was being written, he was cast in *All the King's Men*, an all-star adaptation of Robert Penn Warren's Pulitzer Prize–winning novel (and its earlier 1949 film version). There were reunions all around on the picture; it was written and directed by *A Civil Action*'s Steven Zaillian, and would also feature his *other She's So Lovely* co-star, Sean Penn; *Romance & Cigarette*'s Kate Winslet; and *The Last Castle*'s Mark Ruffalo.

The high-profile production was shot in Louisiana in late 2004 and early 2005. Jim was cast as "Tiny" Duffy, an affable but evil political power broker; Penn would play the leading role of the Huey Long–inspired Willie Stark, who goes from idealist to demagogue over the course of the narrative—and the film's basic, unavoidable error is that Penn is wildly miscast in a role that Jim would have crushed. Though he gets a couple of juicy moments early on, and sports a convincingly gravelly Bayou accent ("People are sayin' that God himself had a haaan in this schoolhouse bidness"), Duffy is a big nothingburger of a role, hanging around for much of the (rather bloated) running time with little to do beyond providing reaction shots and exposition.

Once he wrapped his scenes for *All the King's Men*, Jim headed off to Jacksonville, Florida, where his next picture, *Lonely Hearts*, was slated to begin principal photography in March 2005. This would mark another welcome reunion: his third pairing with John Travolta. "That was a mistake," Nancy Sanders says. "I don't even remember what that was about. But that was again a loyalty thing; he loved Travolta." This time they would have equally meaty roles—the duo would play the '40s-era homicide detectives tasked with tracking down Martha Beck and Raymond Martinez Fernandez, the real-life "honeymoon killers" who used personal ads to find lonely, wealthy women to kill. Jared Leto, Salma Hayek, and Laura Dern co-starred; the writer and director was Todd Robinson, whose grandfather Elmer was the basis of Travolta's character.

There was much more for Jim to do in this one. He narrates the story, which begins in Sing Sing in 1951 as the killers await execution, and provides the buddy half of the buddy-cop equation for the police procedural sections, which take up about half of the running time. It's a good performance of quietly stinging moments: the dread and fear on his face as he explores the shed out back, where the bodies are buried; the weight with which he removes his hat from his head; his bleary-eyed, wrecked expression after he witnesses the execution. His final piece of voice-over narration applied to the character, but also to the job from which Jim was moonlighting: "It started to hit me what the job had become for him. And for me too."

GANDOLFINI WAS BACK IN NEW York by May 2005, when *The Sopranos* began shooting its sixth season. That June, Jim received the Joe DiMaggio

Award at a fundraiser for Brooklyn's Xaverian High School and the Loyola School in Manhattan. He almost had to miss it; his father, James Sr., was in the hospital. While visiting that day, Jim asked the old man if he remembered anything about "Joltin' Joe."

"I saw him hit a beautiful centerfield drive once," the elder Gandolfini replied.

"The grin on his face reminded me of my father before he was ill," Jim said that night. "So I thank Mr. DiMaggio for letting me see that again."

James Gandolfini Sr. died that September. He was eighty-four. "Of course we went to the wake, my wife and I, we all did," says Vincent Curatola. After the funeral, Jim invited Curatola to join him at a relative's house for the repast, but his co-star didn't know his way around Park Ridge.

"Get in your car, I'll get in mine, now follow me," Gandolfini told him.

"No problem," Curatola recalls. "We come to a red light, some guy comes around the corner in a car, making a right-hand turn, who does he see? Tony Soprano, driving a car at a red light, and Johnny Sack driving his car right behind him. The guy had a fucking heart attack. These are the fuckin' moments of the show, what can I tell you? This guy went home, probably told the story, and everybody's goin', *Yeah, right. Yeah, we believe that.*"

Jim's father's death wasn't the only big change in his life that year. In February, the gossip columns reported that he and fiancée Lora Somoza had split. Just as his dad's health was worsening, Somoza's grandmother's Alzheimer's was escalating. "They are still friends, but he will be working for the next year straight and she needs to move to Los Angeles to care for her grandmother," Mark Armstrong confirmed to the *Daily News*.

"Sometimes love does not conquer all," she said in 2013. "Sometimes you really want something but life gets in the way and it doesn't happen. There was no animosity, no acrimony. In fact my grandmother eventually died from Alzheimer's and Jim knew how much the Alzheimer's Association meant to me and he lent his name, and face, to the Forget Me Not ball–a big fundraiser. We split but never stopped loving each other. We stayed in touch."

This split would not prompt the flurry of out-on-the-town reports that his divorce had, and while Jim would eventually find love again, he had another, higher priority now: "My son. And realizing that going around swearing and acting like an idiot is not good for anyone involved. As you get older, you realize that all that wind signifying nothing is silly sometimes." He especially valued the time he and his son, now entering grade school, spent together at the rental house on the Jersey Shore. "We spent a lot of time on the beach doing nothing," he said. "We dig holes and get our feet wet."

He was recognizing a need to change his lifestyle in general. "I ran my body pretty hard for a long time," he said, "and I'm wondering if all of a sudden I'm going to get nailed in the next couple of years, so I want to take care of myself a wee bit better." He had, as they say in recovery circles, hit rock bottom the previous year, when he was slated to reunite with Patricia Arquette to present an award at the Golden Globes. But as curtain time approached at the Beverly Hilton, Jim was nowhere to be found. His co-stars quietly dispersed to track him down, finally discovering him drunk on the hotel lawn, making snow angels—an unfortunate position even if there had been snow, which there was not. Michael Imperioli was hastily dispatched to replace him.

"I told Patricia backstage about it and said, 'I should get Jim's gift bag for doing this,'" Imperioli said, "and later said to him, 'I covered for you. I ought to get that gift basket.' And this is the really funny thing. Patricia didn't tell me, but she sends her gift box to me, and Jim sent me his as well. I got two for doing that one job."

Whatever hopes Gandolfini had pinned on *All the King's Men* and *Lonely Hearts* shifting his on-screen persona were for naught; both sat on their respective shelves for at least a year, and made nary a ripple when they were released. *King's Men*, originally slated for Christmas 2005, didn't come out until September 2006. Sony originally said the delay was to avoid a too-short postproduction period, but Zaillian later revealed that test audiences were confused by his initial cut, which he set about rebuilding from the ground up. Based on the reception when it was finally released, he needn't have bothered. "Overstuffed and fatally miscast, 'All the King's Men' never comes to life," wrote *Variety*'s Todd McCarthy, while the *New Yorker*'s David Denby opined that "it's portentous and vague at the same time." Without critical support, audiences stayed away; the $55 million movie opened in seventh place, with a measly $3.8 million in receipts its opening weekend.

Lonely Hearts fared even worse. It premiered quietly at the Tribeca Film Festival in April 2006, but didn't see a domestic release until a full year later. The reviews were good—the *New Yorker* called it "superb," the *Times* deemed his performance "formidable," and *Variety* noted, "Gandolfini, in classic character actor mode, lends an effective 1940s presence to the film"—but they didn't matter. Neophyte distributor Millennium Films fumbled the ball, putting *Lonely Hearts* on twenty-three screens with barely any advertising, grossing a miserable $188,000 in its entire, brief theatrical run. It increasingly seemed that, at least while the show was on the air, all James Gandolfini's audience wanted to see him play was Tony Soprano.

CHAPTER 17

KEVIN

NOTHING ABOUT *THE SOPRANOS* HAD ever been simple, and the execution of its conclusion was no exception. First there had been talk of calling it at four seasons; then all seemed to agree that season 5 was its natural ending. Then, in the summer of 2003, Chase agreed to an abbreviated sixth season, only ten episodes, with a tentative debut date of March 2004. That target came and went; in July 2004, HBO Chairman and CEO Chris Albrecht announced that season 6 would consist of the customary thirteen episodes—but they wouldn't air until 2006. Then, over a year later, the network announced that the season's duration had been extended yet again, to a total of twenty episodes, split into a first part of season 6, with eleven episodes, that would start in March 2006, followed by a nine-episode wrap-up "part two" that would debut in January 2007. Those episodes would ultimately begin airing in April of that year.

The protracted back-and-forth over exactly when and how the show would come to an end is indicative of not only its importance to the network, but its impact on popular culture in general. By the time season 6 was in production, television was in the midst of a renaissance—"While the 1950s may be referred to as the Golden Age of drama, the gold standard is back in a big way," wrote *Variety*'s Stuart Levine—and there was no doubt that *The Sopranos* was its starter pistol. Chase and company had reimagined and redefined serialized drama, and shows like *Six Feet Under*, *Deadwood*, and *The Wire* were following its lead. In the years to come, the *Sopranos* template of adult-oriented drama, with a mature approach to language and sexuality, uncompromising fealty to reality over dramatic tropes, and self-reflective genre exploration, frequently filtered through the prism of a complex male antihero (played, more often than not, by a hardworking but not-yet-famous character actor), would reappear in the form of *The Shield*, *Dexter*, *Breaking Bad*, *Sons of Anarchy*, and (from former *Sopranos* writers) *Mad Men* and *Boardwalk Empire*.

Most imperatively and immediately, however, *The Sopranos* remained a tremendous moneymaker for HBO. Beyond the spikes in subscribers that would greet new seasons, the deluxe DVD box sets were money lying on the ground for the network, and it found another revenue stream in 2005, when A&E made a record-breaking deal to air syndicated (and sanitized) episodes of the show, reportedly at a price of $2.5 million a pop. The season 6 agreement created enough episodes for such a syndication deal to happen—short of the customary one-hundred-show minimum, but close enough for a phenomenon like *The Sopranos*. And Chase, who always considered himself a filmmaker first, had occasionally dropped breadcrumbs about following the show up with a feature film of some kind, though the details were unclear; when the extended sixth season was announced, he put the kibosh on the idea, at least for the time being. "We used to talk about it. We don't anymore," he said in 2006. "I think what we're going to be doing over the next year and a half is what would have been that movie." ("I remember once the idea was floated, of a prequel with us younger," Michael Imperioli recalled. "Jim said, 'What are we going to wear, wigs and girdles? It'll be like 'Star Trek.'")

For once, Gandolfini was itching to get back into character. "Honestly, the last break affected me detrimentally," he admitted after wrapping the first batch of shows. "It was long. I think your brain starts to eke out other places. I don't think I was horribly affected—I hope not. But it was long." It was all so complicated, less a matter of missing Tony Soprano than being eager to shed his skin once and for all.

"Some days you wish you could just kind of get it over with," he told *GQ*'s Chris Heath. "Just get in there and get it done. . . . I'm ready to go, I think. I've done this now from probably the age of 34 to 43. And that's enough." Heath asked what, exactly, he'd had enough of. "I think some of (Tony's) flaws are my flaws. And so you try to get away from them, and then you kind of get pulled in a little bit by playing them. . . . It's a hard head to get into sometimes. I have a lot of fun at work, too, don't get me wrong. I love the people I work with. But there are some days when you get to work and you're not angry enough, and you have to kind of get angrier, and that's a little . . ." He trailed off. "When I was younger, it was . . . much more accessible."

He expanded on this idea to *60 Minutes*' Bob Simon. "I have a little bit of a temper, but it's . . . a useless temper. It doesn't accomplish anything, generally. It's just a lot of ranting and raving and nothing, so David probably saw that and put it into the character."

As had become a custom, the new season saw the addition of a high-caliber cast member: Julianna Margulies, making her return to series television after departing *ER* in 2000, for a brief arc as a real estate agent whose affections become a bone of contention between Tony and Christopher. She and Jim went way back; they were struggling actors in New York at the same time, crossing paths at many of the same staged readings and workshops, and she had dated Ron Eldard while he and (briefly) Jim were doing *On the Waterfront*.

"The truth is, it's like tennis," she says. "When you play with a better player, your game improves. It's just how it is, you just play better. You don't have to hit the ball very hard because they're hitting it so hard—all you have to do is put your racket out."

In their scenes together, Margulies observed Jim ding himself for blowing a line or flubbing a scene. "I actually really understood why he would get pissed off at himself, because it ruined the flow," she says. "When you're in a moment, and then you're not, and then the scene's not the scene that you wanted it to be. That can be infuriating." But she couldn't resist teasing him a bit about it. "Dude, you guys do ten a year," she said, laughing. "You have time to mess up a scene. When you're talking to me about doing twenty-two a year, *then* you can get mad because you're wasting time. Take the time, OK?"

The Margulies arc created one of Gandolfini's and Chase's most heated conflicts. In one of her episodes, Tony, sexually frustrated following an encounter with Margulies, was to pull off the road on his drive home, go into a gas station bathroom, and masturbate. "He really didn't want to do that," Chase said.

"I don't think it was that he didn't want to masturbate," Steve Kornacki, then an assistant to the writers, says. To Gandolfini, the scene didn't make sense; as scripted, he then goes home and has an argument, about not much of anything, with Carmela. Jim's position, Kornacki recalls, was, "I don't think he should masturbate and then come home and have an argument. That doesn't track for the character. Because then, his repression in his anger has been released—whereas if he's still sexually frustrated, then the argument makes sense.

"And I thought that was like, knowing the character. Inside and out," Kornacki says. The scene was ultimately cut. "He never said, *You never even used that show*," Chase said. "*You never even used that scene, after all I went through*. He never took it up with me or blamed me or anything."

"He was a big mush ball," Margulies says. "He was very tall, he could be imposing, but his character was supposed to be imposing; that's the point of that character. But really, inside, I think he was just a softy and a sweetheart." She had an opportunity, early on, to observe his sensitivity to the needs of his fellow actors. Her character was dressed in high heels, and in one of her first scenes, showing Tony a potential space, required several trips up and down a flight of stairs. Jim watched all this, and then approached her.

"Your feet are killing you, aren't they?" he asked.

"Shhhh, it's really painful!" she replied.

"C'mere," he insisted. "I'm really good at this."

"And he massaged my feet on set, and was so sweet and kind about it—not in a perverted way," she notes. "It was just actor to actor, like, *I do not know how you women do this*, you know. Just warm and welcoming and sweet."

She got another look at that sweetness during an extended night shoot. "I was thirty-eight at the time, and I was single and very happy," she said. Jim looked at her and asked, simply, "No kids for you?"

"No, I don't think I'm into kids," she said.

"They're the biggest joy of my life," he told her. "Have a kid."

He got "small and sweet and vulnerable" talking about being a father, she says. "It was just beautiful."

"Julianna, I'm telling you, it will enrich your life," he assured her. "You'll become a better actor, you'll become a better human being."

"And of all the people I've worked with, he truly was the last person I thought I'd hear that from," she says now. "I'm not sure the fans understand how important family was to him. And it definitely made me think about it. Look at me all these years later, with a kid."

She learned something else during that run that stuck with her for the rest of her career, particularly when she landed her next series lead, on *The Good Wife*. "I was often asked, who do you emulate, in terms of setting the tone?" she says. "Because when you're number one on the call sheet, it matters. And I learned everything I know from George Clooney and James Gandolfini. They are my North Star, in terms of how you treat people. And I think it's because they both were struggling, they both did menial jobs, they understand that this is a moment fleeting, possibly longer. We're all human beings. Let's treat each other respectfully."

WHEN CHASE AND HIS CAST and crew were shooting the first season of *The Sopranos*, in their little bubble, making their pay-cable drama that no one had heard of or had any expectations for, they had to bang out each episode in roughly a week. As the show's budgets grew with its popularity, so did its schedules; by season 6, they were spending nearly a month shooting each hour-long show, using more locations and creating more complicated sequences (and also, occasionally, taking a day off due to their absent star).

Vincent Curatola's Johnny Sack was the focus of a key episode, centered on his daughter's wedding. "We were two days in a gorgeous church in Brooklyn," he said. "I believe that they had scouted a Catholic church, who said, *Sopranos? No way, you're not coming in here.* So they scouted a Presbyterian church that looks a lot like a Catholic church. But it was extremely hot, and Jimmy hired an ice cream guy with a cart for two days to stand by, and everyone got ices."

Jim's unannounced absences hadn't ended entirely, but they were far more sporadic, and the looser schedules could accommodate them better by season 6. And sometimes he would ask for delays or rescheduling with more benevolent aims. Robert Funaro's character, Gene Pontecorvo, was the focus of the season 6 premiere—a tragic episode in which he attempts to leave Tony's crew, and finds the only way to do so is by taking his own life. "He said, work with Susan on your episode," Funaro recalls. "So I worked with Susan, and she's great." Much of their scene work centered on a pivotal duet between Gene and Tony, initially placed early in the schedule. "He kept delaying it, and we said to ourselves, why is he delaying it?" Funaro says. "James was so giving that he wanted me to really get a momentum, as opposed to doing it right up top." Ultimately, after several requests for postponement by Jim, they shot the scene near the end of the episode's production. "TV isn't chronological—you don't really do it like a play," Funaro says. "So by that time, it was right. And it really came out well."

Jim made a similar gesture to Robert Iler, who had to shoot one of his toughest scenes to date, a heartfelt duet between Tony and A. J. outside a police station. They got to the New Jersey location, only to scuttle the shoot due to rain. Jim, sensing Iler's nervousness, made him an offer: "I'll pick you up to go to Jersey next time we do it, so we can run the lines over and over and make sure that we've got it."

Iler agreed immediately, and the next night, Jim's driver picked him up to take them to the location. "I knew all my lines, and I was ready. And we talked for like, five or ten minutes. And then the next thing I know, somebody was waking me up."

Iller, stunned and embarrassed, immediately began chastising himself: "Oh my God, I'm such a fucking idiot. I fell asleep. We didn't get to run the lines."

Gandolfini's driver looked at him, and grinned. "Don't worry, you both fell asleep," he said. "Ten minutes into the ride, you guys passed out."

SEASON 6 ALSO GAVE JIM one of his biggest acting challenges on *The Sopranos* to date: playing someone other than Tony Soprano. The season premiere ended with Uncle Junior, addled by dementia and believing Tony to be a long-dead associate, shooting his nephew in the stomach. Tony, in a coma, descends into an extended, two-episode fantasy in which he imagines himself as "Kevin Finnerty," a mild-mannered precision optics salesman. He speaks with Gandolfini's everyday voice, and is played in a totally different, poignant key—a frazzled businessman who has lost his wallet and briefcase, leaving him helpless and abandoned on a business trip, and *then* discovers that he's been diagnosed with Alzheimer's. "It gave us a whole

Gandolfini as Tony's coma-induced alter ego Kevin Finnerty in season 6 of *The Sopranos*. (Courtesy HBO/Photofest.)

other look at Tony," Chase said, "and a whole bunch of different stories that we never would've had."

But the coma subplot provides more for Gandolfini than an opportunity to show his versatility. The turns of the characterization after his brush with death are a feast for an actor of his depth and skill. "Supposed to be dead," he says. "Now I'm alive. I'm the luckiest guy in the whole world. Listen, after this, from now on, every day is a gift." It feels like he means it; perhaps he will genuinely turn a corner, becoming a better husband, a better father, a better man. But Tony Soprano's manhood is inextricably bound to retrograde notions of brutality and physical strength, so when he sweats and struggles, losing his balance and bearing at the Sacrimoni girl's wedding (a devastating bit of physical acting, seeing this strong man so weak), he must reassert his masculinity by pummeling his tough new bodyguard—only to puke his guts out, in private, mere moments later.

He tries to be patient and tender with A. J. ("You're a nice guy, and that's a *good* thing"), only to end up physically assaulting the boy. He cannot resist the temptation of a fling with the Margulies character, even as his own wife is buttoning up his shirt as he heads out for a possible assignation. "My handsome man," Carmela beams, as pangs of both affection and regret pass across his face. He is what he is, and his new lease on life is short-lived.

This was one of the key themes Chase hoped to explore in the show's wind-down. Despite years of therapy, with the unlocking of painful childhood memories and realizations of how he not only was affected by familial trauma but was passing said trauma on to his own offspring, Tony had not become a better person. Despite opportunities for change or even escape from a life of danger and moral compromise, Tony always returned to the comforts of crime, and ruthlessly sought and acquired more power, even if it required more bloodshed. This middle-aged man was not going to fix himself, and no one was going to fix him. "Tony's lack of forward progress wasn't a case of a TV show refusing to change because it would disrupt a successful formula," wrote critic Alan Sepinwall, "but an expression of what seemed to be the show's deeply cynical take on humanity."

For Jim to continue to find unexplored aspects of that personality—for him to hold his audience's interest, and even sympathy, while playing a deeply flawed character who was fundamentally incapable of change—was miraculous. "The Tony Soprano that emerges from the shambles created by the calamitous events of the first four episodes borrows less from 'Goodfellas' than 'King Lear,'" wrote the *New York Sun*'s David Blum. "He is a tragic figure who has faced his demons at last, but too late to undo their damage."

The setting for the season 6 premiere party on March 7, 2006, was not Radio City but the Metropolitan Museum of Art, one more crystal-clear indicator of the series' cultural cachet. The show returned to HBO five days later, and critics had not yet run out of superlatives to describe it. "The best series on television are those in which two opposite things are true at the same time, and 'The Sopranos' is a perfect example: it has exhausted the material and remains amazingly fresh," wrote the *New York Times*' Alessandra Stanley. "It's very funny, except that it is also dead serious. This season is a lot like the others, except that it's different, and may be the most creative and richly imagined one yet: it begins by going over old ground and yet something new and totally surprising happens." But the show's twenty-one-month hiatus had clearly taken something of a toll on viewership; the season premiere drew 9.5 million viewers, a steep decline from the 12.1 million of season 5's inaugural outing—in fact, the smallest audience of a *Sopranos* season premiere since year two. Maybe they were getting out just in time.

CHAPTER 18

GOODBYE, TONY

HBO'S BREAKING AND BRANDING OF the final season into two parts—a strategy subsequently aped by *Mad Men* and *Breaking Bad*, among others—was deeply cynical in nature. These were, for all intents and purposes, two seasons, a sixth and seventh, written, produced, and released separately, just shorter than usual, and with a briefer hiatus between them. According to Chase, it was purely a contractual and thus financial decision, an attempt to avoid yet another round of salary renegotiations, for "the actors, specifically," he said. To that end, it failed; before production commenced in July 2006, Tony Sirico and Steven Van Zandt indicated that they would walk away from the final season unless their salaries were raised for the last nine episodes, while Lorraine Bracco, Jamie-Lynn Sigler, Robert Iler, and Steven Schirripa similarly took the opportunity to renegotiate their deals. Jim, with his contract for $1 million per episode locked into place, quietly helped his castmates get their raises. (Chase logically refers to the final nine episodes as season 7, and we will follow his lead.)

Gandolfini approached his own work with something less than a full heart; no doubt thanks to the extended shoots of season 6 and the shorter-than-usual hiatus following them, he was suffering from a bit of burnout. "By the end, I had a lot of anger over things, and I think it was just from being tired, and what in God's name would I have to be angry about?" he later reflected. "[Chase] gave me such a gift in terms of life experience, in terms of acting experience, in terms of money too."

"Toward the end of 'The Sopranos' he was tired of it and he was tired of me," Chase said in 2019. "And I was tired of his foibles. That's all."

"I can't see myself doing a show like that again," Gandolfini said, a few years later. "It takes too much. When it ended, it was time—more than time. It had been a long run and as much as I loved the people I had to move on. And hell, half of 'em were dead anyway."

There would be one more snag in the home stretch, however. Shortly after production was scheduled to begin in July 2006, Albrecht announced that the show was pausing in order to allow Jim time to deal with an old knee injury that would require surgery. It would only halt production for a few weeks, but it pushed the season 7 premiere to April 2007, to prevent the show from competing with the Super Bowl, the Oscars, and other Sunday events early in the year.

His surgery also required some slight reconfiguration of the shooting schedule. The season premiere, "Soprano Home Movies," in which Tony and Carmela visit Bobby and Janice at their lake house, was shot on location, but the climactic brawl between the two men was too dangerous to stage that close to Gandolfini's procedure; "I can't do this," Jim said. "I can't do it the right way." Months later, when the physicality was less of an issue, the interior was re-created at Silvercup Studios. "We shot for a day and a half, and Jim and I said, 'Let's make this as real as we possibly can,'" Schirripa said. "So the stuntmen choreographed it, but aside from Jim at the end falling into the table, that's all us. It's all me and Jim." The result was a rough, ugly, clumsily realistic fight, two big dudes that have hit their limit with each other. "It was two fat, sweaty polar bears fighting," Schirripa said, with a laugh. "That's how a real fight is."

This would not be the most harrowing physical action of the season, however. In the third-to-last episode, "The Second Coming," Tony barely saves A. J. from a drowning death by suicide, leaping into their backyard pool (which had once housed his beloved ducks) to heave his son back from the brink. He initially berates the boy before giving in to empathy, cradling him as if he's a baby again, and crying with him. It's a powerful scene, and some of the most wrenching acting of the entire series. "It was a lot easier because we were miserable," Iler says. "It was December in New Jersey, and we were jumping into a pool and then getting out of the pool and laying on the freezing cold cement. . . . It wasn't one of those things like, we were in LA and I'm jumping into this nice pool and it's sunny out and there's music. Like, it was it was fucking *weird*."

Jim took the opportunity to blow off some steam during a shoot in Miami. Location manager Mark Kamine recalls going back to the company's hotel after a day of shooting to find everyone, from the star to the production assistants, partying at the hotel pool; Jim greeted him by handing over a bottle of cognac. The party got rowdy and a few other guests complained, so the group moved to a nearby beach, drinking beers in the sand and contemplating a midnight swim. "The waves sound pretty big," Karmine told Jim. "I mean, there might be a rip current or something."

"What, you're gonna save me, Mark?" Jim asked with a smirk, before running in.

"He just wanted to keep going," Kamine says. "He was inclusive, you know? He wasn't snobby, there wasn't like, *Those people can't be here, because they're below the line or they're not producers or actors.* It was just, *Whatever. You want to party? You're in.* It was nice."

Chase chose to direct "Made in America," the series finale—his first time in the director's chair since the pilot episode. Perhaps as it was his preferred setting, the last table read was held in the writers' room. When it was done, "there was pin-drop silence," Kornacki says. "Everyone just sat around that table. Usually people get up, you know, *Hey, OK, great. Yeah, see you on set*, laughing, joking, *haven't seen you in a couple of weeks* or whatever. But everyone was planted in that seat, pin-drop silence. And you could hear sobbing, like this subtle sobbing from people. . . . There was just this very dramatic sense of like, *It's over. What are we going to do next?* And it was just incredibly sad."

Production on the episode was similarly heightened. "It was very emotional," Chase recalled, "and I remember Silvio didn't die of course, but he was comatose in bed, and I remember when we called a wrap on Stevie, Jim came to me and said, 'Well, that's the end of you and me working with a rock 'n' roll star.'" He laughed at this memory, but it was a bittersweet one. "I felt it then, and I felt it about Jim, because I also felt, 'That's the end of you and me working together.'"

On March 22, 2007, the cast and crew assembled at Holsten's Brookdale Confectionery in Bloomfield, New Jersey, to shoot what would be the final scene of the final episode. Word had leaked, so dozens of onlookers assembled outside of the old-fashioned ice cream parlor; one enterprising soul was even selling shirts, at $20 a pop, with an image of the establishment and the words "The Final Episode." (It almost hadn't come to pass; Chase had written the scene with Holsten's specified, but just a week before its scheduled shoot date, the Bloomfield Town Council barred the show from shooting there, bowing to pressure from the mayor and local Italian-American groups—one last representation controversy for the road. The decision was overturned, and the shoot was rescheduled.)

"Normally when we shot, we shot onstage, or even when we shot outside, it was as if people didn't know what was going on," Iler says. "But the word got out that we were shooting 'the last scene,' the finale there. They

Jim, Edie Falco, and Robert Iler in the final scene of *The Sopranos*.
(Courtesy HBO/Photofest.)

blacked out the windows and all this stuff, and when you would go outside, it was Jersey—it couldn't be more of a place where people love the show. So that was something that was odd and not something you were used to. Normally you have the vibe of the scene, you walk in the door, you're ready to go; this threw you off. When you were outside, it was like, *Oh my God*, people yelling stuff at you and asking you questions. And then you kind of shut that door, like OK, now we're at your fucking *work*."

"It just felt like another average day," Chase said of that shoot. "It was all about the work, you know?" As far as Jim's performance: "I don't think I gave him any direction. I don't think he needed it."

At the end of every season, Jim had given generous gifts to the cast and crew. His final parting gift to his colleagues was the most extravagant yet: He gave every member of the company, every actor, writer, producer, and crew member—over two hundred in all—a special-edition Kobold watch, with the words "RIP Sopranos 1997–2007" engraved on the back. "He must have spent who knows how much money, I can't even imagine, over half a million dollars," Schirripa marvels. "I've never worn mine. It's in a safe deposit box."

He had another parting, and non-monetary, gesture of kindness in store. In a departure from production norms, the last scenes shot were not for the last episode of the show; after production wrapped on "Made in America," director Alan Taylor returned to shoot the closing scenes for the fourth-to-last show, "Kennedy and Heidi." "Because it was in Vegas, that was put at the end of the whole schedule for the last season," Taylor explained. "The entire series was done, and we flew out to Vegas and stayed at Caesars Palace."

In the closing scene, Tony watches the sun rise over Red Rock Canyon and cries, "I get it." The location was about an hour outside of Vegas, with pre-dawn call time. "It's the middle of the night, like 3:30 or 4:00 in the morning, and the gate is locked," recalls director of photography Alik Sakharov. "There's a caravan of trucks sitting outside, waiting. And we're going crazy. The sun is gonna rise in a couple of minutes, and we need to set up a shot." Finally the proper authority, who had overslept, showed up to unlock the gate. "And we now have literally about twenty-five minutes before sunrise, and we need to set the truck, we need to set the cameras, multiple cameras, we had to put Jim in clothes, we've got to line up everything, and we've got to shoot it. . . . Who's the first one to roll up his sleeves? Jimmy. He's in the fucking grip truck, throwing things out to the crew, helping out, basically—sandbags, track, dolly."

Sakharov tried to stop him: "Jimmy, man, go get dressed!"

"I just need a shirt, that's all," Gandolfini insisted. "Just a shirt and maybe some powder. That's it."

Finally, with three minutes to go before sunrise and the crew finishing their preparation, Jim went to his mark. Makeup patted him down—he'd worked up a coat of sweat during the setup—and powdered him up; the costumer threw his shirt on him. "Camera moves," Sakharov chuckles, "sun comes up, and Jimmy kills it in one take. Got it with two cameras. And that was it. That was Jimmy, man. That's what kind of person he was."

The last shot of the Vegas shoot was a solo image of Tony, sitting in a lawn chair by the hotel pool. Once Taylor called cut, Jim asked, "Do you have it?"

"Yes," Taylor assured him.

"Are you sure you have it?" he asked again—"because this was literally the last shot he was going to have to do as Tony Soprano," Taylor explained.

"Yes," the director repeated.

"And he picked me up and threw me into the swimming pool," Taylor said. "It was such a great way to end. Of course, David Chase being David Chase, we all went back and he had to do reshoots."

IN THE FIFTH EPISODE OF the seventh season of *The Sopranos*, Tony Soprano asks the big question, the biggest of them all: "Is this all there is?" It comes at the end of perhaps the most powerfully emotional of all his scenes of therapy with Dr. Melfi, in which he despairs over the attempted suicide of his son, summoning up a pain and empathy that never goes away; "When they're little and they're sick," he tells her, "you'd give anything in the world to trade places with them, so they don't have to suffer." And now, Tony Soprano must reckon with what all he—his personality, his neuroses, his way of life—has done to Anthony Jr. "My rotten putrid fuckin' genes have infected my kid's soul," he despairs, a moment of such torment and such sadness, his eyes wet but not leaking.

Gandolfini would find other new notes in this final year—emotional brutality with his character's wife, physical brutality with an associate who dares harass his daughter, new heights of feuding with Frank Vincent's Phil Leotardo, years of resentment and sadness in his last duets with Janice and Uncle Junior—but this scene finds the actor at the height of his powers, bringing his eighty-plus hours of screen time (and decade of work) to a head, powerfully conveying the complexities and contradictions of this impossible man.

The show around him was also firing on all cylinders, pulling its many through lines, subplots, conflicts, and characters onto a locomotive of character-driven crime drama, yet bleeding the genre of the vicarious thrills and winking enjoyment of the early years. Seasons 6 and 7, and especially the latter, are *bleak*, less like the electrical current of the early years than a funeral dirge; any hope of the completion of the moral and emotional turnaround Tony attempted after the shooting and coma has been hopelessly dashed. When he seizes on a fleeting opportunity to kill Christopher and make it look like an accident, he doesn't hesitate, and the most shocking quality of his often-expressive eyes as he takes the life of his nephew and protégé is that, at long last, there is nothing there but a void.

For the final premiere party on March 27, 2007, the company returned to Radio City Music Hall and Rockefeller Center, welcoming back departed cast members (including Drea de Matteo, Steve Buscemi, and Vincent Pastore) and paying tribute to the writers and crew. Gandolfini was greeted with a standing ovation, and in his simple but moving remarks, he reiterated that the show "brought a lot of blue-collar people together to make something great."

The traditional top-of-the-season hype was even more deafening for, as the *Guardian* put it, the "beginning of the end for the best TV ever." In an interview to promote his latest book, Norman Mailer likened the show to the Great American Novel. Jim, as usual, was resistant. "Maybe Archie Bunker was groundbreaking," he told *Variety*. "I don't know if we were necessarily groundbreaking. I think we talked about a lot of issues, and HBO was kind enough to let us go to a really dark place. It's good writing, you know?" He was similarly matter-of-fact in a series wrap-up with *TV Guide*: "I mean, c'mon, we did our best. You do the best you can, and we're all OK. We had a great time."

Perhaps Jim was merely attempting to tamp down expectations; after all, he knew how it would end. When the final episode, "Made in America," aired on June 10, writer-director Chase pulled one last fast one on his audience, concluding an episode (and season, and series) that seemed inextricably headed toward a final reckoning for our antihero with . . . nothing. Literally nothing. Tony, Carmela, and A. J. Soprano meet up for dinner at Holsten's, Meadow attempts (and fails, and tries again) to parallel park out front, Tony puts Journey's "Don't Stop Believin'" on the jukebox, onion rings arrive on the table, Tony eyes a handful of suspicious characters at the surrounding tables and counter, the front bell dings, he glances up, and . . . cut to black, a black screen, not even credits for several seconds. David Chase, the television groundbreaker who had never wanted to make television, ended the finest show in the medium's history with an anticlimax.

"It was summer, everybody's windows are open," Steve Kornacki, who was living in Manhattan, recalls. "Everybody was tuned to that show, you could hear the neighborhood. . . . And there was this, like, total silence for five seconds or so, ten seconds. And then I just heard people in the neighborhood, *You gotta be fucking kidding me! I don't believe this!* And I just sat down on my couch smiling."

Some viewers were merely confused; there were concerns that the cut to black was the result of a cable outage, and since the episode ran just a smidge over the typical sixty-minute time block, those watching it on DVRs thought their recordings had ended before the show was over. Some (especially critics) were delighted by the finale's subversion of expectations—nothing new for a show that had frequently thumbed its nose at the conventions of television drama. And some were intrigued, immediately flooding message boards and YouTube channels with detailed theories as to what the last scene *meant*, what had actually happened, who each of the (absolutely random) extras in the ice cream parlor could have been, how stylistic choices connected to throwaway comments Chase had made in long-forgotten interviews.

But many viewers were furious, blasting Chase for not giving them the kind of satisfactory bloodshed or, at the very least, the tidy conclusion they were longing for (even if that was something he'd never promised or provided). Was Tony dead or alive? And either way, why hadn't we *seen* it?

Ironically, considering all the ink and pixels spilled on a grand, *Lost*-style puzzle box explanation for those closing moments, Chase *had* planned on concluding the show that way from the beginning. During their first two weeks of work in a tiny office in Manhattan, cinematographer Alik Sakharov asked Chase, "So let's say this is a successful series. How are you going to end it?"

"I have no idea," Chase replied, "but I know that I'm gonna cut to black."

"Why?" Sakharov asked.

"I don't know," Chase said. "I have no idea. But it just *feels* right."

He was correct. It *did* feel right, for the kind of show they were doing, and the kind of impact he wanted to have. At the end of their journey that began in that little office all those years earlier, Chase asked Sakharov what he thought of the ending. "Of course it should be as enigmatic as possible," Sakharov agreed, "because you know if you're gonna give them a bloodbath, they're gonna forget about your show in twenty minutes. But if you give them a pure philosophy, that is not resolved, they will never forget the show. They will always be watching it."

Steve Kornacki concurs. "I think *Breaking Bad*'s an amazing show, but I think the worst episode is the last episode," he says. "It's just so *expected*. And the difference is, here we are, what, over fifteen years later, still talking about the ending of *The Sopranos*." Alas, that also meant poor David Chase would be stuck talking about that ending throughout those years, still trying to preserve its enigma, resisting the pleas to explain exactly what it meant, and articulate Tony Soprano's fate. "I never thought it would create that much of a stir," he later said. "I never thought, *Oh, they'll be talking about it for ten years because I want them to talk about it for ten years*. And the other thing about it is, as a corollary, no matter what I say about it, I always dig myself in deeper."

Jim, of course, kept it simple—and insightful. "When I first saw the ending, I said, 'What the fuck?,'" he said. "I mean, after all I went through, all this death, and then it's over like that? But after I had a day to sleep, I just sat there and said, 'That's perfect.'"

Viewers were still chewing over the big ending when Emmy nominations were announced a month later, with *The Sopranos* pulling fifteen nominations for its final season, including best drama, and best actor for Jim. The show won but, shockingly, Gandolfini didn't; he again lost to James Spader, prompting *Variety* to exclaim (in a headline, no less), OMG EVEN JAMES SPADER LOOKED EMBARRASSED.

The show had, over the course of its run, received a staggering 112 nominations, and took home 21 trophies. Falco was similarly (and bafflingly) passed over for one more best actress Emmy, but both actors received parting gift trophies at the following January's SAG Awards. Jim's acceptance speech was typically taciturn: "It's been ten years. It's an honor. That's all I can say." Five years later, he expressed no regrets that the show ended as, and when, it had. "You know, at no point, even at this point, have I ever said I wish I was still doing it," he said. "I've never missed it—which makes me think it was definitely time for it to end. . . . Obviously it was great, and the people we worked with were great, but we'd said everything we could, we'd done everything we could, it was time for everybody to move on. For us to go another year would have been a big mistake."

CHAPTER 19

HOST

WHEN JIM ATTENDED THE FINAL *Sopranos* premiere party, he had a new date on his arm. Deborah Lin was a beautiful model and actress, six years his junior, hailing from Honolulu, Hawaii. It was their first public appearance together, though they had been quietly dating for a few months; he'd drifted a bit after the engagement to Lora Somoza fell apart, his natural charisma and fame offset by his intense self-criticism and poor body image. "He didn't take anything for granted," Chiemi Karasawa says. "And I think he was desperately insecure." But Jim felt comfortable with Deborah, and after a year or so together, during a Christmas holiday vacation in Bermuda, he popped the question. The engagement hit the papers in January 2008, and they tied the knot that August 30 at the Central Union Church in Honolulu.

It was an intimate, twenty-minute ceremony, the church bedecked in white lilies and rhododendrons. Michael Gandolfini, then nine years old, served as the best man. At the reception, a source told *People*, "they both wore long, green leis around their necks. There were lots of white flowers on the tables and Gandolfini was beaming."

Even casual friends noticed a change in his demeanor. Marcy had invited the *Sopranos* cast and crew to Jim's surprise fortieth-birthday party back in 2001, and script supervisor Christine Gee notes, "they seemed OK—it was an off-and-on kind of thing, but I think sometimes that what was going on with them was a trigger for why he might go on a binge." They also attended his wedding to Deborah, Gee continues, "and it was just like, a whole different thing. You could see how really happy he was, and he became kind of calm, like he finally was ready to settle down." The following year, he and Deborah bought a $1.5 million, two-story colonial in the secluded, suburban community of Tewksbury, New Jersey. The 5,616-square-foot property sat on 8.76 acres and boasted two two-story fireplaces, a Jacuzzi, cathedral ceiling, open porch, attached garage, and a nice, long driveway, just like Tony Soprano's.

Deborah accompanied Jim to social and charity events around Manhattan. Mere days after "Made in America" aired, they joined Edie Falco,

Deborah Lin joins Jim on the red carpet for an HBO event, circa 2010.
(Courtesy Everett Collection Inc / Alamy Stock Photo.)

Steve Buscemi, and Aida Turturro at the opening of the solo dance show *Dining Alone*, starring Tricia Brouk, who had served as choreographer on *Romance & Cigarettes* (which would finally premiere in New York that September). They also attended the Bob Woodruff Family Fund benefit that November.

And that fall, Jim made an eight-hour round-trip journey to the Great Meadow Correctional Facility in Comstock, New York. He was there to pay a surprise visit to Martin Tankleff, who had been in the facility for seventeen years after confessing to the murder of his parents—a verbal confession he said he gave under duress and manipulation by the investigating detectives. Gandolfini heard about the case from Jay Salpeter, a former NYPD homicide detective who'd helped him research his role in *Lonely*

Hearts, and was now involved in efforts to get Tankleff's conviction overturned. "He was obviously compelled and moved by Marty's story and wanted to meet him," Lonnie Soury, also part of that effort, told the *New York Post*. "They really hit it off." (An appellate court overturned the conviction in December 2007; Tankleff was subsequently awarded a total of $13.4 million in settlements from Suffolk County and the State of New York.)

Jim also supported his Tribeca neighbors, and contributed his celebrity and resources, in protesting the construction of a 118-foot-high, three-district sanitation garage in the neighborhood. "I live down here and I'd rather not have all those trucks that are going to come down here," he told the *Villager*. "I don't think they're paying attention to what they're doing here, Mr. Bloomberg and the rest." His involvement had a palpable effect: "We couldn't get an entree into the mayor's office until Gandolfini got involved," said Richard Barrett, leader of the TriBeCa Community Association, "and suddenly the door was open." (At a rally for the cause, Jim compared the structure to the recently completed, supersized Trump SoHo condo-hotel, which he called a "piece of crap.")

There were still flashes of bad press, of course. Flying back from the 2008 SAG Awards on a red-eye to JFK, Gandolfini had an ugly confrontation at the airport with a self-proclaimed *Sopranos* superfan and autograph hound named Jason Ertischek. "I spoke to him in a kind of Tony Soprano accent, like, 'Yo, Tony.' All of a sudden, he turned around and choked me by the neck and punched me with a closed fist to the right side of my face," Ertischek told the *New York Post*. The tabloid granted that "some paparazzi" described Ertischek as "a pesky publicity seeker who taunts celebs to get reactions," but couldn't resist leading the report with the snarky taunt, "When push comes to shove, he'll always be Tony Soprano."

In fact, he was expending a considerable amount of energy figuring out how to remind people he was *not* Tony Soprano. "There's a lot of things that don't have anything to say," he said of the film scripts he was reading. "Just stories about nothing, that don't signify anything. A lot of things. Too violent."

"He very much wanted to leave the mobster character behind," says his friend and Attaboy Films collaborator Tom Richardson. "If it was very well written he would consider it, but for the most part, any kind of script where he's supposed to play Tony Soprano, or a Tony Soprano–like character, he would always just pass that by. He wanted to do other things."

But those "other things" were hard to pin down. Right after the conclusion of *The Sopranos*, HBO announced that Jim would play Sonny Vaccaro, the Nike scout who signed Michael Jordan to his lucrative endorsement deal, in a made-for-cable movie titled *ABCD Camp*. (That film wasn't made, but the story of Jordan's signing, with Matt Damon cast as Vaccaro, was told in the 2023 film *Air*.) Robin Williams handpicked Gandolfini to co-star in the buddy action cop comedy *A Couple of Dicks*, but that iteration of the project fell apart in 2008. (Kevin Smith directed it two years later under the new title *Cop Out*, with Bruce Willis in the Gandolfini role.) He took a small role in Spike Lee's World War II drama *Miracle at St. Anna*, but his role didn't make the film. Attaboy was set to produce the Marvin Gaye biopic *Sexual Healing*, with Jesse L. Martin as Gaye and Jim in the supporting role of promoter Freddy Cousaert, but that fell apart after the announcement of a bigger-budget competing project from director F. Gary Gray, titled *Marvin*. That competing film was ultimately scrapped as well.

"For a long time, you will continue to get material that echoes this other thing that you did," says Edie Falco, who battled post-*Sopranos* typecasting as well. "People say *Oh, who can do that tough-guy thing, get Gandolfini*, and all you have to do is say no. And little by little, other things start to present themselves, as started to happen with Jim. There were all other flavors of Jim that were just starting to be known to the public viewing audience, but yes, it would certainly take a while. The way I've always felt about it is, if you fully engage with a different character, the audience will come with you."

IN THE MEANTIME, JIM DECIDED to take his audience somewhere unexpected. "He saw things that he didn't like," according to Tom Richardson, "or that needed to change, and he would go change them and he didn't care who it pissed off or what he had to do, what kind of mountains he had to move. He would go tilt at that windmill." The USO tours he'd done during *The Sopranos* were of vital importance to him. "Whether you agree with the war or not," he explained, "what these kids do, their patriotism and sense of honor and duty—we forget about those things sometimes. So that's where that all started, talking about what they're facing and trying to make it a little easier for them, especially when they come home."

"He really saw them as America's Greatest Generation," Richardson says. When they'd go on those trips, manager Mark Armstrong recalls, "You would go into the little stores and the walls were lined with *Sopranos*

[DVDs] because when they weren't on duty, everyone said they'd come back and watch *Sopranos* together. . . . He would walk in unannounced in these very, very scary parts of town. He would just literally walk in and surprise them, and it was so magical to see their shock and reaction." Through his work with the USO, Jim became aware of the Wounded Warrior Project, a nonprofit organization that helped disabled soldiers return to civilian life.

Al Giordano, a former Marine and a veterans affairs activist, had co-founded the organization. "I grew up not so different than Jim," he said. "He was like a regular guy, you could talk with him about anything, he loved his Jets, Rutgers football, his son, his family, all of that, just like any-body. But I didn't know until I read about it, after he'd died, that his father had gotten a Purple Heart in World War II. He never mentioned it. And that kind of makes it all come together for me. He was quiet about certain things."

Gandolfini was struck by the fact that medical technology had grown by such leaps and bounds that soldiers who would've been killed in battle were now surviving, with the help of robotic limbs and other lifesaving procedures. "But because they saved so many people, that wasn't really shown as part of how much American people were losing," Richardson explains. "But really, so many of these people were losing so much. That was not the life they had before they had gone to war. So it was a story that he felt was interesting, and that needed to be told."

Jim decided to make his first post-*Sopranos* Attaboy Films project a documentary about these soldiers—using his cachet at HBO at the single moment when it was most valuable. He visited the Walter Reed Army Medical Center with HBO exec Sheila Nevins, and "Jim was great with everyone," she said. "He signed people's casts. Everybody knew the show; no one referred to him as Jim; they all referred to him as Tony." For once, he didn't mind. One mother asked him to sign her Bible as Tony Soprano. "He's willing to do anything for this kid and his mom," Nevins said. "We walk out of the room, and he rushes ahead of me through a door marked *laundry room*. When I get there, he's got his head buried in folded laundry, and he's sobbing like a baby."

They originally planned to shoot the documentary at Walter Reed, but the Department of Defense rescinded its permission at the eleventh hour. Instead, HBO and co-directors Jon Alpert and Ellen Goosenberg Kent arranged to bring their ten chosen soldiers to Jim, for intimate, one-on-one interviews. "We were in an East Village theater," Alpert recalls. "And the veterans were appearing onstage with Jim, one by one, and Jim had never done anything like this before. And you know, documentary filmmakers and documentary films are different from narrative films. We had no experience in his world, and he didn't have any experience in ours. And everybody was pretty nervous about whether this was going to work or not."

At first, it definitely did not. "Jim, as was proper, was very nervous about addressing the horrific injuries that the veterans had suffered, and sort of tiptoed all around with dealing with it," Alpert says. "And the first interview wasn't so great."

"Jim, how do you think that interview went?" Alpert asked.

"It wasn't very good!" Gandolfini replied.

"Well," Alpert said, delicately, "I know it's not easy, but you're gonna have to talk with the soldiers about the horrors that they suffered, and they're gonna have to show them to you."

"I can't do that."

"You're gonna have to," Alpert assured him, "because that's what the program is about." The filmmaker was beginning to worry, so he proposed a strategy: "Listen, I'm going to tap you on the shoulder because I know what injuries the next person has suffered. And when I tap you on the shoulder, you should ask this gentleman to roll up his pants leg." Jim looked at Alpert in horror; they both knew the soldier had no legs.

The second interview began much like the first, with Gandolfini respectful but not particularly penetrating. Alpert tapped his shoulder. Jim shook his head. Alpert tapped his shoulder again; Jim shook his head again. Finally, he leaned in to the soldier and gestured toward Alpert: "You know, this guy wants me to ask you if you'd roll up your pants legs."

The soldier nodded. "Sure."

"And with wonder," Alpert says, "Jim watches as he rolls up the legs and tells this really courageous story of the injury that he suffered, the sacrifices he made for our country, and the courage that he has, trying to move forward with his life. It was a revelatory moment for Jim. And every single other of the interviews was empathetic, inquisitive, caring. It was one of the most remarkable series of interviews that anybody's ever done."

The film was titled *Alive Day Memories: Home from Iraq*. According to the opening text, for survivors like these, "two days will forever immortalize their lives: their birthdays and their Alive Day, the day they narrowly escaped death." Gandolfini, dressed in casual clothes, sits in a big easy chair with a camera over his shoulder; he interviews these survivors one by one, mostly staying out of the way as they tell their stories. He's heard, offering up questions and moments of encouragement, occasionally a gentle and genuine chuckle at their jokes, but rarely seen full-on.

He is a marvelous interviewer, curious and conversational, which is ironic, considering his longtime aversion to interviews himself. But his skill was less about experience than humanity. Alpert explains:

> There was a real sincerity. Listen, I've been doing this type of work for a half century, I'm really lucky to have been able to do it. . . . But I've seen practitioners of this who throw on a switch and pretend that they care, and grab this, almost like an exsanguination—they suck the blood out of you for their interview, and then they're off to the next one. And Jim was *not* like that. He did not have to act; all he had to do was open up the door of his own soul, which he always shared with the people that he was interviewing. And it was always two ways, because you could feel the impact of what you were telling to him, in every part of his body. It was a big body, and it was a body that really exuded tremendous warmth, warmth and compassion. And the subject could feel it.

"He's an intense listener," said one of the film's subjects, Dawn Halfaker, first lieutenant, U.S. Army, retired. "And so it was very easy for me to feel comfortable and to open up. It wasn't about him. It was about telling our stories."

And as a documentarian, the perfectionism that could so often short-circuit him as an actor became a virtue. "He was always self-critical in a very constructive way," Alpert says. "He was always—whether it was an acting performance or whether it was working in a documentary—questioning whether he should be doing things better. And I think that was part of his accomplishment as an actor and as a person, is that he always kept pushing himself. . . . And so I think that was an important part of his progression as a documentarian—he wasn't taking any shortcuts, you know, he showed up when he was supposed to show up, and he worked hard."

Alive Day Memories screened for an invitation-only audience of military and political personnel in Washington, D.C., on September 6, 2007, two days before its HBO premiere. Eight of the ten subjects were in attendance, and they received a standing ovation. "No doubt wanting [to] keep the focus on the vets, Gandolfini did not speak and kept as low a profile as he could," *Variety* reported. But the response was heartfelt. According to Alpert, "Mike Mullen, who was the [about to become] chairman of the Joint Chiefs of Staff, said that this was the most important film that he thought has ever been made, and it needs to be seen by the military and by the public."

Critics were just as unequivocal in their praise. "Mr. Gandolfini functions here both as executive producer—through his company, Attaboy Films—and host, though 'host' seems too colloquial a term to describe a role that he approaches with a Calvinist dignity and reserve," wrote the *New York Times*' Ginia Bellafante. "If the film is without a maudlin moment, it is a credit not only to the subjects and to the process by which their accounts have been edited, but also to Mr. Gandolfini's refusal to attempt a sort of empathy that is inconceivable in this context."

It was Attaboy's first big project, and achieved exactly what Jim hoped. "The whole fame thing was always a double-edged sword," Tom Richardson says. "There's some good that comes with it, and some aggravation that comes with it. And he saw this as some of the good that came with it—to be able to shine a light on these folks and be able to tell their stories and let other people see that."

"These films and their stories are about service," Michael Gandolfini noted recently. "It's all-around service to something higher and something bigger, and it's incredibly inspiring to me, to not only hear these stories, but see how my dad just moved through his life in humility."

"He was very proud of that," Richardson says, of *Alive Day Memories.* "Very proud of that, and very proud of the people that were in it. And very proud that *he* was hardly in it!"

"And at that particular point, Jim fell in love with documentaries," Alpert says. "We collaborated with him on some very important work in which he was the major catalytic element. And he told me, and he told other people, that of all the work that he's done, the work that he's most proud of are his documentaries."

CHAPTER 20

CAROL

"ALL THE FUSS DURING *The Sopranos* really was pretty ridiculous," James Gandolfini told *Variety Fair*'s John Heilpern in 2009. "None of us expected it to last, and it lasted almost 10 years. Honestly? I don't think I'm that different. I've lived in the same apartment for years. I've kept a lot of the same friends. I'm still grumpy and miserable."

"You are?" Heilpern asked.

"But in a good way!" Jim replied.

With *The Sopranos* completed, Gandolfini was eager to embark on the next phase of his career. He knew it wasn't impossible to shake off the Tony Soprano character and persona, eventually. He liked to use Alan Alda as an example. "He was with *M*A*S*H* so long, and now you see him, that's not there that much anymore," he said around the same time, adding: "In my mind, you work hard, you'll be fine. Everybody's got their baggage."

In the years that followed, Jim rarely received a bad review. The same could not be said for the projects themselves; he was often at the mercy of his collaborators, his available choices, or just plain luck. "We were always chasing that role that was going to be as important, as well received, as Tony Soprano," explains manager Nancy Sanders. "But I will tell you that, as an actor, sometimes the work is literally the journey." He would always give his all, and was recognized for it. But a film or show where everything comes together is, in its own way, a kind of miracle—*The Sopranos* was one, *True Romance* another, and there would be a handful more in the post-Tony era.

The first, and one of the richest, of these new roles began while the show was still on the air, though its complicated production meant it wouldn't make its way to theaters until long after. Maurice Sendak's children's classic *Where the Wild Things Are* had been adapted to film before, as a short cartoon, faithful to the slender book. Spike Jonze's feature film adaptation greatly expanded the text (via a script he penned with novelist Dave Eggers) and was entirely live action; the "wild things" of the title would be voiced by actors, then brought to life via full-size practical wild-things costumes created by Jim Henson's Creature Shop. Those suits would be worn by different actors for the location photography on practical sets, with facial expressions subsequently enhanced via digital animation.

Jonze and Eggers's script gave names and personalities to each of the wild things; chief among them was a temperamental but sensitive tough guy, with the incongruent moniker of "Carol." Jonze initially cast Benicio Del Toro in the role, but quickly realized it wasn't working, and started looking for a replacement. Jim was a perfect fit. "It wasn't the texture of his voice as much as the feeling," Jonze wrote in the official companion book. "He made it electrical."

Jonze augmented this unconventional approach to family filmmaking with an unorthodox method of voice-over recording. Normally, actors providing voices for animated characters would spend a few days in a recording studio, laying down their dialogue tracks one at a time in a clean, sterile soundscape, to allow maximum manipulation by the film's editors. But Jonze didn't want these scenes to be clean or sterile. Instead, he arranged to have the actors record their dialogue together, on a soundstage equipped with platforms, foam blocks, and other tools for playing and roughhousing. The actors would use small, mobile microphones, taped to their faces, like the ones musical theater performers use onstage. "We needed the spontaneity of what the actors did in the moment," Jonze explained. "We'd feed off that spontaneity for the rest of the film for the suit actors' performances and the facial animation."

"The process was a little weird, a little odd, but a lot of fun," Jim said, "throwing big foam things at people's heads and whatnot. I would go home at the end of the night thinking, 'I'm a grown man. What the heck was I doing today?'"

Unlike with most voice-over work, Jonze found a way to use the actors' physicality to enhance their characters. "It was a bunch of people in a room in their day clothes, being photographed—being videotaped by a small camera while they physically interacted," says Chiemi Karasawa, who was the script supervisor on *Wild Things*. "So the puppeteers ultimately could use the physicality and spirit of the actual actor, and try to incorporate that in the character once they were engineered. It was pretty cool to watch."

Some actors have joked about the easy money of animated work, but Jim refused to phone it in; the fact that he was creating a voice-only performance didn't alter his approach to scene work and character building. "He was a genius, really, at understanding the chemistry of what made a scene work," Karasawa says. "And when it wasn't there, he would call it out right away." This once led to Jonze shutting down work for a half day, so he and Jim could walk through a key scene, line by line, beat by beat, and figure out why it wasn't playing in the moment. "He was right," Karasawa says. "It made much more sense when they reworked the scene." But that was just his way, she explains. "For an actor to care so much that they're going to stop everything, sit down with the director and say, *Let's work this out, let's figure out how we're going to get me from here to there. Because otherwise, I can't give you a true performance, I can't give you the real thing.*"

The fact that *Wild Things* was a family film also did nothing to temper Jim's usual intensity. "When Gandolfini didn't feel like he was imbuing the dialogue with something real, he would get so pissed off, so mad at himself, and yell obscenities and just rip the script out of my hands and read it and throw it back," Jonze said. "Working with him felt dangerous, not in a way that he was ever literally dangerous, but the level of emotion that he would bring felt dangerous, which is what the whole movie was about."

"Carol was a difficult part that changed all the time," Jim said. "He wants to feel safe, he wants a safe home. But a safe home is a difficult thing. Carol built the fort, but he still felt unsafe because he's still the same guy that lives in his temper, and that's a hard thing." It wasn't difficult to see how he found a way into the character.

His performance in *Where the Wild Things Are* is one of his finest: heart-wrenching and scary, tender and complicated. It's a role that requires so much sensitivity and so much vulnerability—so many of the qualities that weren't *immediately* associated with him—that he doesn't seem perfect for it, but he is. Using his everyday speaking voice (often an even softer, gentler variation), he draws on his teddy bear charm, and then shows his claws.

Moreover, his performance sets the tricky bar for the film around him, which must freely interweave childlike wonder and mature melancholy. His playfulness and childlike spirit are infectious; so are his pain, despair, and regret, never more than at the moment of young Max's departure, when Carol runs after the boy's boat in tears that turn to howls. The key to the performance, and to the movie, is that he's as much a child as Max—and as driven by the same needs and fears, just with an adult voice and a giant monster body.

"When I saw that movie, that was the person—that character that he was playing was so much like the man, in this kind of brightness and darkness," says filmmaker Robert Pulcini, who would direct Jim a few years later. "I was always curious, if it was written that way or if he made it that way. It really captured him."

COMING OUT OF *THE SOPRANOS*, Jim quickly realized that the kind of work he wanted to do was increasingly rare in big, studio pictures. "To be honest, I don't, you know—who's that guy that blows everything up? Michael Bay hasn't been calling too much," he explained. "I'm fine with doing what I'm doing, these little scripts, I'm lovin' them."

For his first post-*Sopranos* leading role, Jim went to work for some old friends. *Down the Shore*, originally titled *Kiddie Ride*, was written by Sandra Jennings, the wife of Jim's longtime acting coach Harold Guskin, who would direct the independently financed feature. Starring opposite Jim was another of Guskin's students, Famke Janssen, herself taking a break from the high-profile *X-Men* film franchise. "This was really a family project for us," she says, "something that we very much wanted to do for the sake of Harold realizing his dream."

Though they'd both studied with Guskin for years, Gandolfini and Janssen met for the first time to read scenes from the script on the couch of Jennings and Guskin's apartment in the West Village. That was also Jim's first interaction with a young actor named John Magaro. "It's *him*, Jim Gandolfini, who I only knew at that point as Tony from *The Sopranos*, which was a show that I watched religiously," Magaro says. "I was so afraid, I was like, *Oh, God, he's judging me, he thinks I'm terrible. I'm making a fool of myself in front of someone who I look up to.* But I didn't get fired. So I guess I did OK!"

"The script had been around for a long time," Janssen says, "but it wasn't until they found the financing, and Harold was trying to put the cast together, that he asked me to do it and asked Jim to do it." They shot in and around the Jersey Shore town of Keansburg in February 2008—"it's ice-cold, the beach has ice on it, freezing cold," Magaro recalls—and Janssen found tooling around the Garden State with Gandolfini to be a memorable experience. "You're basically with a rock star," she says, laughing. "When you're filming, all the cops, all the firemen, everyone comes up to him; he was their hero. So it's fun to see."

Janssen recalls the shoot as pleasurable, with lots of laughter, and low-pressure, even though the modest budget and abbreviated shooting schedule afforded little time for rehearsals. "We shared this common love for Harold and his approach to acting, and so that created a bond," she says. "It was a beautiful thing of not rehearsing it, really just letting the scene go where we wanted to take it, or wherever it went—and trusting that both of us had been trained properly, that we didn't need to go into any rehearsals for it, but just let it go and find it. And find each other during those moments."

"Watching him was just impressive, just his style," Magaro says. "He would beat himself up about his performance, but everything he did was *so good*. And I've heard that from other people, that he was tough on himself." Janssen agrees. "He was not only his own harshest critic, as I think most of us are, but I think where Jim got in trouble is when he stopped relying on these incredible instincts that he had as an actor, and started second-guessing," she says. "And the moment he started second-guessing himself, that's when things went awry. . . . It was tough to watch, because he was so gifted, and he didn't have to question anything. He just had to be present for him to be brilliant."

And it is, indeed, a brilliant performance. He's expected to come out of the gate at top volume—he's first seen reacting to his sister's death, and ends up wandering the beach, drinking and grieving, carrying an urn that he buries while sobbing—and does so admirably. But Gandolfini's best moments in *Down the Shore* are the quiet ones. Jennings's screenplay is a *Mystic River*–style tale of lifelong friends whose entire existence has been shaped by childhood trauma, and Jim is especially adept at playing a man who is clearly tortured, but unwilling to share why. So when he lets his guard down, in an emotional confession of love to Janssen, or in a devastating barstool monologue about their terrible fathers, it hits hard. And when he fully chokes up, when he allows himself to admit, simply and sadly, "I'm sorry, I fucked up so bad," it's seismic.

Down the Shore's low budget and limited resources decreased its visibility, which is unfortunate, as it would be one of Gandolfini's few honest-to-goodness leading roles in a feature film. It wasn't seen at all until nearly three years after its production, with an inauspicious debut at the 2011 Palm Springs International Film Festival; it didn't make its way to even a limited theatrical release until the spring of 2013, when reviews were mixed, but plaudits for Jim were unanimous. The *New York Daily News*' Elizabeth Weitzman praised his "extraordinary skill and sensitivity"; *Variety* said the film would remind audiences "why he's a genuine American acting treasure." As the film spent the intervening years crawling through festivals and sitting on shelves, Jim reached out to Guskin and Jennings to make sure they were "okay with money," Jennings said.

"Can you imagine anyone else saying that?" she added. "We'll be fine, but that's not the point. That was Jim. He could have made oodles of money instead of taking his time to do this film, and then he asks us if *we're* alright."

Shore does boast one other claim to fame: It marked the film debut of one Michael Gandolfini. "Michael had a little teeny part, he was like nine years old at the time," Magaro says. "We had a scene together, he's this little kid. And then it was great that it came back around, we got to work on *Many Saints of Newark* together, and to see him as a wonderful young man that Jim would be so proud of. Just a fully formed human being in so many ways."

"It was beautiful, just seeing him as a dad," Janssen says. "Just to witness the beauty of that relationship with the two of them and how much

Denzel Washington co-starred with Gandolfini for the third time in Tony Scott's remake of *The Taking of Pelham 123*. (Courtesy Columbia Pictures/Photofest.)

Michael looked up to him. Yeah, it was a beautiful thing. And I've seen him over the years and he's doing so well. Jim would be so proud."

WHEN SHOOTING WRAPPED ON *Down the Shore*, Jim went right into a picture that was its opposite in many ways: a supporting role in a big-budget, major studio production, fronted by giant stars. (It was the first deal that had been made for Jim since changing agents; he was now repped by the Endeavor Agency.) The commonality was that he was again working with a director he'd known and trusted for years: Tony Scott, who'd given him that first big break, all those years ago. Scott's latest was a remake of the 1974 Gotham classic *The Taking of Pelham 123*, starring Gandolfini's pal John Travolta as the leader of a criminal crew that takes a New York subway car hostage, and Jim and Scott's *Crimson Tide* collaborator Denzel Washington as the city employee who tries to foil his plot. (Frequent collaborators Michael Rispoli and John Turturro also appear in supporting roles.)

Gandolfini would star as the mayor. "I would think it would be quite different," said Lee Wallace, who originated the role in '74, and played him as an ineffectual bureaucrat in the mold of then mayor Abraham Beame. "I don't know that he would play that kind of buffoon." Indeed, screenwriter Brian Helgeland had revised the mayor into a millionaire businessman turned politico, a mirror image of then city CEO Michael Bloomberg, who inspired such details as the mayor's frequent subway patronage and his insistence on taking only a dollar-a-year salary for the job. But there were a few dashes of his predecessor, Rudy Giuliani, tossed in for flavor. In one scene, an aide suggests that the crisis could give the lame-duck mayor an opportunity to showcase his leadership skills, to which he semi-snarls, "I left my Rudy Giuliani suit at home." In a press availability, a pushy reporter asks, "How's about your divorce, do you have a statement on that, sir?"—a shout-out to Giuliani's very public divorce while in office, though the ferocity of Gandolfini's expression in that moment suggests that he might have used his own sense memory.

The role as written borders on caricature, a feckless, empty suit. But, as always, Gandolfini finds the character's moments of truth, and savors them. In this version, it's the mayor who figures out the Travolta character's hidden agenda, and the close-up as he puts that together is a mini-master class in how to let an audience see you think. And his reaction, horrified, when the first hostage goes down is genuine, troubling stuff.

Jim's breakneck work schedule continued apace once he wrapped *Pelham*, shooting in London, New York, and Washington, D.C., as part of the ensemble cast of Armando Iannucci's *In the Loop*. The film was an offshoot of Iannucci's acclaimed BBC series *The Thick of It*, expanding that satire of the inner workings of British government to include a host of American characters appealing to the Brits to join them in the mounting of war in the Middle East, a series of events reminiscent of the run-up to the 2003 invasion of Iraq. Gandolfini was cast as Lieutenant General George Miller, a military bigwig with the gravitas of "Stormin'" Norman Schwarzkopf, but the political spinelessness of Colin Powell.

Most of Miller's scenes were with U.S. Assistant Secretary of State Karen Clark, played by Mimi Kennedy. "My whole thing with James was like we were in Catholic school," she says, fondly. "I just felt like I was in fifth grade with him. He was the freest actor that I think I've ever worked opposite because of that eleven-year-old energy, just like, *Yeah, they think we're supposed to do this, but I'm gonna make you laugh.* And I always *would* laugh."

There were plenty of opportunities for that. Iannucci works in a loose, spontaneous manner, encouraging improvisation; he only asks actors to stick to the script on the first take. On the second go-round they can, in Kennedy's words, "loosen it up" a bit, and then, on the third, "take it wherever it's gonna go." ("I wanted the actors to be as exhausted and as stressed by the end as the characters they're playing," Iannucci said.) Jim found the Iannucci method, and its high stakes, invigorating. "He brought complete listening, complete attention, so you had to be right there in the moment," Kennedy says, adding that he could do the most wonderful thing you can do as an actor: "You surprise yourself *and* your scene partner."

He was also thrilled to take such chances on a relatively low-profile production. One day, Kennedy says, while waiting off camera for their entrance, Gandolfini confided to her, "I don't know what I'm doing, do you? I don't know what I'm doing in this movie. I interviewed these military guys. . . . I don't know what I'm doing."

"I don't know what I'm doing either," Kennedy assured him. "I'm right there with you."

"So nobody's ever gonna see this shit, right?" he chuckled. "Nobody's ever gonna see it. We don't have to worry about it, right? I mean, nobody's ever gonna come. Let's face it."

"I mean, who the hell ever heard of me?" she replied. "So what, they're not gonna see this movie." And with that, they made their entrance and did the scene. "But I did think, how interesting that Tony Soprano is standing there going, *I don't know what I'm doing and nobody's gonna see this, so I'm safe, right?*" she muses. "It was as if we were in an off-off-Broadway play, by some friends, that nobody would ever see." (Or, as he used to say to Susan Aston, "What's the worst that can happen? We suck?!")

Not that it ever felt like he had disappeared entirely. Kennedy and Gandolfini went to lunch while shooting near the U.N. building in New York, and he was greeted by passersby all along the way. "*Jim! Tony!* It didn't matter what they called him," Kennedy says. "They never stopped him. There was just this complete respect, and he responded every time—he didn't have any of that wall, *Don't talk to me, I don't want to be responsible for the acting I do.* He was right out there. Like *Yeah, I'm me. I've done that. I really appreciate that you're connected.*"

But the work he was doing continued his artistic journey away from the role they were identifying him with. As with *Pelham*, in *In the Loop* Jim uses his natural speaking voice, and plays a man who rarely so much as raises that voice. He carries the authority of a career military man, but his comic timing has never been sharper, he lands his punchlines and scene buttons

Mimi Kennedy with Jim in *In the Loop*. (Courtesy IFC Films/Photofest.)

with ease, and he understands and plays the character's affability and charisma. He can turn it to menace on a dime, of course, though always for comic effect.

In the Loop premiered in January 2009 at the Sundance Film Festival (where *Variety* called it "a feverish, sometimes hilarious fiction"), closing a U.S. distribution deal with IFC Films mere hours before its first screening. It hit theaters in July, just a few weeks after *Pelham 123*, and both films' notices rarely singled Jim out for special praise, which was probably his preference. The film had achieved its aim. "*In the Loop* changed everything for him," says manager Mark Armstrong. "I think that was the first time people thought he could be funny."

The picture had done something else for Jim, beyond that. "He had a moral righteousness inside him, and when you ticked him off in those terms, something that he didn't think was the right thing to do, you could feel it," Kennedy says. "At the time we were cast, we were very against the Iraq War, and very connected to the soldiers in that war. And we bonded on that completely. So what these two people were doing in the movie came from a deep well of passion where we didn't know what else to do about this. And yet we had these characters who were trying to stop the goddamn thing."

However, it was important to Jim that his portrayal not come off as mocking or condescending—to the military brass he'd talked to for research, to the soldiers he'd met through his work with the Wounded Warrior Project, and to the military contacts he'd made (and needed to maintain) for his documentary work. "He was really trying to honor the guys that he had talked to because he felt responsible for representing them," Kennedy explains. "And somehow our relationship made that all the better. Because he knew I cared. I knew he cared. We just were in this insane place."

Kennedy still treasures the time they spent together on the shoot. "He was generous, and he loved sharing. And if the experience was new, he had to take you there." She observed this firsthand while they were in London, when her daughter, who had just graduated from college, came over for a visit. "James wants to take us out to dinner, and we went to this fantastic restaurant, and he ordered everything on the menu that he'd never heard of. He's going like, *What's this? What's this? Quail eggs!* So we're eating quail eggs, and it was amazing. I think we went to a club later, and of course, nobody bought anything or even had a bill—there was just champagne brought to us all night long. That was James. And of course it was because everybody loved him."

Kennedy spent one other significant evening with him on that trip, taking in a new play in the West End. "You could play that part," she told him afterward. "You've *got* to play that part.

"And of course he did. He was brilliant." The play was called *God of Carnage*.

JIM'S NEXT LEADING ROLE, ANNOUNCED in February 2008, was originally targeted to begin production in April, but it was pushed back into the fall due to Jim's busy spring. *Welcome to the Rileys*, written by Ken Hixon and directed by Jake Scott, was a modest character study, mostly focusing on three people. Doug Riley (Gandolfini) is a sport-coat-and-khakis-clad Midwestern businessman in a strained marriage to an agoraphobe (Melissa Leo). Depressed on a business trip to New Orleans, originally intended as a getaway with his mistress before her unexpected death, he strikes up a conversation with Mallory (Kristen Stewart), an exotic dancer for whom he becomes something of a surrogate father, for reasons that she and (at least, initially) the audience don't quite understand.

Gandolfini was first drawn to the project because of Stewart's involvement. "I saw her in *Into the Wild*," he told the *New York Times*. "Some people kind of jump off the screen because they're actually—it had nothing to do with her beauty. She's beautiful, but her intelligence seemed to leap off the screen. I thought, this is a smart young girl. And Jake Scott, I know his uncle, Tony actually gave me my first big film. It was different from something I played before, and I thought the script had some humor in it."

The idea of playing new kinds of roles was key. "It was a kind of shedding of skins, to use Dylan Thomas as a reference," Jake Scott says. "He was kind of getting rid of [Tony], detoxifying. And I think part of the performance that he gave in *Welcome to the Rileys* was an exploration of other parts of himself. It was a very poignant thing to watch. Certainly, directing him, I had to be very aware of the deeper waters there."

Gandolfini and his young co-star had this in common: Her bad-girl character in *Rileys* was a pointed departure from her work in the wildly popular *Twilight* movies. Asked if he liked *Twilight*, Jim said, "I've never seen it"; asked if he told her that, he replied, "Well, she didn't ask. I don't think she watched *Sopranos* much."

But he felt a connection to her character—one rooted in his customary working-class ethos. "I've seen people like this," he explained, "girls like this, and you just shake your head and go, *How did it happen, so goddamn young*, and it's a bad path already at that age, 17, 18. That struck me. I hear people talk about, *Well, you know, I would never be in that position, and you've just got to do this or you've got to do that, and it's your own fault.* I go, no, not always. Some people get kicked in the teeth a lot, and sometimes we look down on that, and I don't think it's their fault a lot of the time. That's what was interesting to me, that struggle of *This is where I am now, how do I lift myself out of this and move on*." And with that, he grinned, and added, "We're getting pretentious."

Once he'd signed on, Jim took an active involvement in the preparation and revision of the screenplay. "We met in New York a few times," Scott says. "We spent a lot of time at the table going line by line: *I wouldn't say this. I wouldn't be like that.*" Emails of notes from those meetings, sent by Scott to screenwriter Hixon, reveal intense focus on details and motivations of the character. One reads, "Jim feels Doug would be more guarded about revealing he hadn't been to Gold Hill (cemetery) before. Instead he would remain silent and it would be that silence that reveals the truth." In another, Scott notes, "We talked about this scene but I also see now that Jim wants Doug to express how it is for him outside. . . . Jim was very motivated by this notion so I'd like to give it to him. He was doing good work in this regard."

"In my experience, he wasn't that keen on getting up on his feet with it, in terms of rehearsing," Scott says. "But he was really into discussing, and really into the detail, layering background—not even backstory, but sometimes just layering in an obstacle, all the workings of that character. And it was really interesting, I learned a lot, I have to say." This was the kind of laser-focused scene study and character work that he'd been doing for years with Susan Aston, and still did on most projects. But with his increased clout as a name above the title, he could do that work ahead of time, and steer scripts to better suit his conceptions of his characters.

Scott also saw these meetings as an opportunity to build their relationship, going into what would be a short and intense shoot. "You could never bullshit Jimmy," he says. "He needs to know that if you're going to answer a question, you better know the answer—and if you don't, you better be honest. And I think honestly, that was the big thing with him. Never tell

Jimmy that you know when you don't know. If you don't know, tell it to him. Have the courage to say, *I don't know, Jimmy, let's work it out.* But you better have matched him in terms of prep, because he expected that."

Scott, who had directed notable music videos in the 1990s, including for REM's "Everybody Hurts," was keenly aware that he was a young and relatively inexperienced filmmaker, and that while his familial connection might have opened a door with Gandolfini, he had to prove himself to the actor. "The first week of shooting I found that—this is my own experience—he tested me," Scott says. They'd had a disagreement, and neither had wanted to give in. Day stretched into night on that first Friday, and they were shooting in the French Quarter, with Jim behind the wheel of his car as they were setting up a shot. He called Scott over.

"You're right," Jim told him.

"Thank you," Scott replied, before quickly adding, "You were right too."

"No, no, no," Jim immediately responded. "You were right, you don't back down, I think you were right. You and me, we're gonna be all right." And that was it; they got along famously for the rest of the shoot.

The bulk of *Rileys* was shot on location in New Orleans, which offered up its own challenges. "The French Quarter being the place it is, especially when you're in the evening, shooting out in the streets, people would recognize him. And they'd even say, *Hey, Tony*! He was very good with that, but then I would see him get exasperated, and sometimes felt like he was trapped in it. So it must have been quite hard."

The more immediate struggle was with the accent. The director wanted Jim to do a Midwestern dialect; he settled on something a bit more Southern, which "worked better with his inflection and intonation, which was fine," Scott says. "James, rather like Brando, had this way of changing the shape of his mouth by using belt loops from jeans in his mouth. And it drove him crazy. And it was also very hot in New Orleans, in the Bywater, and the housing conditions, and he'd had enough of this accent, and really hated me for it." They were shooting a Gandolfini-Stewart duet scene and Jim, frustrated by the accent, blew a take. He stormed into the next room, and did what he'd done so often on *The Sopranos*: He yelled "FUCK" and punched a wall.

"The AD looks at me, Kristen looks at me, like, *What do you want to do?*" Scott says. "I go in the other room and there he is: He's got his arm in the wall, because he's punched this wall. But it's an old Bywater house that had been flooded in Katrina, and so the wood was all rotten. It was purely out of frustration, and he had his arm in the wall, it was like a cartoon. And he's just looking at me, and he starts giggling—and spitting out these belt loops. And I've got him, because his arm's in the wall. So I start tickling him." It defused the situation immediately.

Scott's fondest memories of their time together was Sundays, their days off. He was renting a house with several crew members, down below the Garden District, and on Sundays Jim would come over to make lunch. They'd eat, and play cards, and listen to jazz, and argue over who was the best jazz vocalist: Dinah Washington (Jim's choice) or Ella Fitzgerald (Jake's). Jim would have Italian food shipped in from the East Coast, big boxes of sausage and fresh ravioli and Parmesan; he'd show Scott these boxes when they arrived, excited about Sunday's sit-down. "That was Jimmy at his best," Scott says, fondly. "Sitting there enjoying a meal, talking, joking, telling stories, playing music, it was like—that was the best of him. He was a good soul."

Jim's performance in *Welcome to the Rileys* is lovely, low-key, and lived-in. The picture offers copious opportunities to simply regard him existing on-screen—watching, listening, thinking—but when he's required to go to raw, vulnerable places, even within the buttoned-up character, he doesn't falter. His scenes with Stewart are tender, and nicely defused of sexual tension (she doesn't understand why he doesn't want to bed her, and when she insists, "I'm pretty good," he replies, "I'm sure you are," with a delightful weariness). The healing of his relationship with Leo's Lois is nicely rendered as well. It's she who prompts his single best acting moment of the film, forcing him to understand and admit that this young woman cannot stand in for the daughter they've lost; the sadness in his eyes, his basset hound expression, when he is finally willing to admit it is staggering. Scott holds on that close-up, just for a moment, and Gandolfini fills it.

Rileys took Jim to Sundance for the second year in a row in January 2010; reviews there and in the film's eventual theatrical release the following October were mixed to negative, though Jim's notices were as strong as ever. (The *New York Daily News*' Joe Neumaier spoke for many when he wrote, "The only saving grace is the larger-than-life presence of James Gandolfini.") He did his best to promote the low-budget picture, even submitting to a few interviews with the equally media-adverse Stewart. "I like to support little movies like these, smaller movies that try to say something in a good, interesting way," he explained in one. "Sometimes I wonder how much this actually helps. But it really isn't that terrible. I've had much worse jobs."

If nothing else, the media tour strengthened the bond between the two actors; "I think he kind of wanted to take her under his big arm and protect her," says Mark Armstrong. Two years later, as one of several *Variety* pieces of actors praising actors in recent films, he wrote a brief but heartfelt rave for her work in that year's adaptation of *On the Road*—a performance he called "sexy and scary and reckless and smart. She can play all of these things. She has them at her fingertips. She is just beginning." (He was right.)

And, once again, his charitable instincts kicked in. Working on *Rileys* made him conscious of the plight of runaway kids; not long after, he found out about Ocean's Harbor House, a twelve-bed shelter for runaways and abused children in Toms River, near the Jersey Shore, where he was spending the summer with Michael. The younger Gandolfini's school had assigned its students community service work over the summer, so Jim reached out to Ocean's Harbor House to see what they could do. Discovering that they needed computers, the Gandolfinis purchased a baker's dozen laptops, loaded them with software, and brought them over. Walking the grounds, Jim noticed the property was badly in need of weeding and mulching. The next day, he and Michael returned with Tom Richardson and a healthy supply of mulch, and the trio spent the next three weeks landscaping, building fences, and painting picnic tables.

Jim was "completely down-to-earth, really likable," facilities director Ken Butterworth said. "Approachable, you know? You could tell he really loved his kid, and wanted him to know that not everybody is lucky with their families. And so we were working together, and I asked him, 'Where'd you go to college?'

"And he looked away, I think he said Rutgers, but I thought, 'Ah, so we're not going to talk about you, huh?'"

CHAPTER 21

MICHAEL

THE WEST END STAGING OF *God of Carnage* that Gandolfini had seen while shooting *In the Loop* was itself a transplant; French playwright Yasmina Reza had previously mounted productions in Germany and France. "I didn't know anything about it," Jim said. "Nothing. But we went and we laughed. When we came out of the theater after an hour and a half—which was a big selling point—all of us had grins on our faces, and the energy of the audience was good. I had wanted to try some theater, and this guy wasn't the king of England or anything so I figured I could play it. . . . I didn't want to come out and do a play about Ferdinand II with a wig and totally blow it."

He was so taken with the play—concerning a pair of parents meeting to discuss a playground fight between their sons, which devolves from a difficult-but-polite conversation to an emotional and intellectual brawl of its own—that he contacted his team after. "I don't know if they're going to move it to New York," he said. "But if they do, I'd love to audition for it."

"Audition? You must be joking."

"I've got no problem with auditioning or reading," he told *Vanity Fair*. "I want to make sure we're all on the same page."

He was not asked to audition, and initially, he wasn't worried about returning to the New York stage for the first time since the *On the Waterfront* fiasco. "He loved the theater," says Susan Aston. "But if you want a career even on Broadway, you can't get a great role unless you're a movie star now. And it's sad. But his roots were in the theater, and he was so proud to go back to the theater with *God of Carnage*. That was a really good experience for him."

"I hate to admit this, but I was looking for something to do," he explained. "I thought it would keep me home. I thought it was something that was probably easier than it actually ended up being."

Filling out the cast would be tricky; it was uniquely unsuited for actors with what director Matthew Warchus matter-of-factly dubbed "ego problems." "This is a play with four equal-sized roles, where each actor has

25 percent of the play and has to be silent for the other 75 percent whilst onstage," he said. "This is a really rare thing for a leading actor."

The cast was announced in January 2009. Gandolfini would share the stage with Jeff Daniels, Hope Davis, and Marcia Gay Harden, all of whom were also film and television actors with extensive stage experience. Harden and Jim had nearly worked together before; she had auditioned to play Janice on *The Sopranos*. Once they became friends during *God of Carnage*, that previous encounter came up.

"I remember you from that audition," he told her during rehearsals, once they'd become friendly and familiar. "You know why we couldn't cast you?"

"Why?" she replied.

"Because I can't want to fuck my sister."

"So, you know, *that* wasn't gonna work out," she says with a laugh. "And we just became super good friends, obviously, because you're working backstage and revealing yourself."

Warchus was thrilled to cast Gandolfini against type. "Certainly he has a strong signature physically and in the fact that he has been associated with that one role for so long," the director said. "But he's a real actor of great quality. And in the play itself, what I like is that, until he reaches a certain breaking point, his character is a mediator, a very mild, soothing, almost feminine presence." Though he would use his regular, non-Tony speaking voice, they decided to keep his basic physical type intact. ("I appreciate the fact that he has no funny beard or glasses," Davis noted.)

In an interview the day before rehearsals began, Jim was asked if he was nervous. "No, I'm not frightened by it at all," he insisted. "I got to figure out why. It's bothering me!" He would, soon enough. "I think I was probably kind of arrogant," he later said, "and it took me about a day or two to realize I didn't know what the hell I was doing." As usual, he called Warchus a few days in, to make sure he didn't want to cast someone else in the role; also as usual, the director declined.

"The rehearsal process is so vulnerable," Harden says. "And I think James especially felt vulnerable during that time. He had done stage before, but in his mind he was working with people who he maybe thought knew more than him—we didn't—and it was comedy. And he was a little nervous in the beginning, and very vulnerable."

The rehearsals were taxing—director Warchus gave the quartet "hundreds of pages of notes," according to Davis, to a point where, per

Daniels, "Every line, Matthew's had his hands on"—and the pacing was relentless, a breakneck ninety minutes in which not a line could be blown and not a cue could be dropped. "It keeps everybody on their toes," Jim said. "There's nobody snoozing." ("I thought I'd lose weight," he later joked. "I'm sweating like a farm animal up there, and I didn't lose a pound.")

"I came in thinking I was going to be fine," he said. "And it was not that fine for a little while. I was a little . . . I guess shellshocked is the word?" Eventually, he found that honesty was the best policy. "I did feel very out of sorts. And then I think we had a meeting, and essentially I was told this is the way you're supposed to feel, so don't drive yourself completely insane about it. And I said, *Oh, that's helpful!*"

He found plenty of support from his castmates. "There was an incredible humility about James," Harden said, "a kind of tilt your head down and look up, those little baby eyes of his. It was a sincere 'aw, shucks'-ness, you know?" He gravitated toward Daniels as a kind of mentor; "I don't want to make it out like it was big heart-to-heart discussions," he said. "It was more like, you got somebody who's been there before. If you have any

The original Broadway cast of *God of Carnage*: Marcia Gay Harden, James Gandolfini, Hope Davis, and Jeff Daniels. (Courtesy WENN Rights Ltd / Alamy Stock Photo.)

brains, you watch him and listen to him." ("Just like it would be for me guesting on *The Sopranos*," Daniels added.)

"He didn't know what the button was for a character," Harden explains. "And that's a terrifying moment for any actor. When you think, *I don't know what motivates them. I don't know what makes them tick. I don't know what they want*. And it's not clear on the page and you're not sure the director is telling you the right thing and it's just a very, very scary moment—and how each person handles it is different." He knew that his character, Michael, was "not the most positive human being on the planet," but the trick was figuring out how much of that to reveal and when, as the loaded silences, pregnant pauses, and doubled-back explanations of the script reveal more and more about this frustrated father and husband. "All of a sudden, one day, something clicks," Harden says. "You can't say what it was or how you got there. But something clicks and then it's just a tremendous relief. And I think that's what happens for James."

Once he locked in, and the show got in front of an audience, it became a deeply pleasurable experience. "Somehow I felt like an actor again," he said. "Being on stage fulfills you in a different way. I loved watching some 80-year-old woman in the front laughing so hard she can't catch her breath." This became one of the big takeaways of the production: Both Jim and his audiences were delighted to discover just how funny he could be. "I loved doing *Carnage*, listening to the audience really laugh all together, the belly laughs—that was really sweet," he said. "And I tell you, the older I get, the funnier-looking I get, the more comedies I'm offered. I'm starting to look like a toad, so I'll probably be getting even more soon." (Around this time, he was also in discussions to reunite with Sean Penn for the Farrelly Brothers' revamp of *The Three Stooges*, playing Curly to Penn's Larry. Penn eventually dropped out of the project, and Jim's interest followed.)

The audiences weren't the only ones laughing. "We buckled over in laughter, and laughed so hard that we peed our pants," Harden recalls. "How can you not love somebody that makes you do that? And each of us would make the other person do that. And then onstage it was just glorious to craft those; it's like music." This became the other thrill for Jim; after years of rehearsing in private and locking his performances in, on camera, for all posterity, here was acting that was fluid. The show, and the performance, could vary. "Everybody's a little different, every night," he said. "Even if it's the energy, and we tap into it. . . . You go into the chute, and you just go. And then all of a sudden you just realize that you're near the end."

"People have no idea what actors are thinking," Aston says, laughing. A fair amount of the pleasantries in the *Carnage* script revolve around the clafoutis that Veronica (Harden) has prepared for the quartet to nibble on while they chat. "People are thinking, *Oh, this great actor*, and I know he's just up there trying to remember: *clafoutis, clafoutis, clafoutis*," Aston says. "He was so afraid he was gonna fuck up that word, because he had never heard of it before."

God of Carnage began previews on February 28, 2009, at the Bernard B. Jacobs Theatre, opening on March 22. The critics went wild. "Never underestimate the pleasure of watching really good actors behaving terribly," wrote the *New York Times*' Ben Brantley; the *New Yorker* called it a "dark and hilarious farce" in which Gandolfini "brilliantly manages his character's arc from genteel to goniff. . . . his fine fury is sidesplitting." In their year-end wrap-up, the latter publication added, "It was an extra pleasure to watch James Gandolfini transition out of being America's great TV heavy into a deft stage comedian."

They weren't wrong. *Carnage* is spectacularly entertaining and delightfully pointed; its upstanding, responsible characters come to work out the problems of their children, but both couples bring in their own issues, baggage, and neuroses. Allegiances are shifted, old wounds are opened, and despite their high-minded ideals, they turn into their own children: beating up on each other, going into hysterics, screaming; throwing objects, imitations, accusations, insults.

The production is a beautifully orchestrated series of dips and valleys, tantrums and siestas, and no actor works those variations as skillfully as Gandolfini. His performance is an inspired bit of slow-burn character comedy work, in which Michael's affability—sometimes genuine, sometimes forced—slowly but steadily melts away into unapologetically roaring rage. His good, progressive wife spends the opening of the play (and, presumably, the past several years of their lives) trying to pass him off as a nice liberal, but (in his own words) "what I am and what I always have been is a total fuckin' Neanderthal!"

The combination of rave reviews and star power made the play into an immediate hit—not always guaranteed, even with those factors in play, for a new non-musical. Ticket sales were brisk for previews, and they stayed that way; grosses topped $700,000 per week before passing the $1 million mark per week in late July.

The intensity of the experience had a positive effect in his personal life as well. The demons that had so plagued him during the mid- to late *Sopranos* years had tapered off considerably, thanks to both the series' conclusion and the positive force of his relationship with Deborah. On *God of Carnage*, with its short but ferocious rehearsal period and then months of performing the tightly wound play eight times a week, going on benders and blowing off work weren't really an option. Being James Gandolfini, who took such pains to keep his private life private, there was no public announcement of his turnaround, no *People* magazine cover story of the beaming, now-sober family man. But the partying, the late arrivals, and no-shows were behind him. Aside from the cancellation of a Wednesday matinee during previews due to voice loss, Jim didn't miss a single show.

The run was mostly smooth sailing. Gandolfini and Daniels became regulars at Frankie & Johnnie's, the steakhouse and New York institution across West 45th Street ("though sometimes they have their steaks sent straight to their dressing rooms," the *Times* reported). He stayed close with his castmates; "I used to go to him for relationship advice," Harden says, "because he was so really, actually honest of the heart. It wasn't just in his jokey way or this sexual way. The two of us would sit and talk about trust and love and men and anthropology and women and just all of it, and he always just spoke from the heart and spoke so generously."

He got so comfortable onstage, he even bucked a few traditions. When Chiemi Karasawa came to see it, "he started the show over again," she says. "Some gag didn't work. And the actors were trying to make up for it onstage. . . . He was like, *Oh, wait a minute, can we just close the curtains and go back?* And like, they fucking did it. They closed the curtains!" It may not have been the norm ("You could hear the actors laughing, like, *What the hell is going on right now?*" Karasawa recalls), but this anecdote speaks to his relaxed mindset during the run. *Sopranos* cinematographer Phil Abraham also came to the show, and went out to dinner with Jim afterward. "Man, you are like . . . a different person," Abraham told him. "You just have this lightness to you."

"Yeah," Jim replied. "It's unreal."

He had further cause to celebrate when the awards nominations started coming in. Barely a month after opening, Gandolfini and Harden were nominated for Drama League Awards; the following month, all four were nominated for Tony Awards, the two men and two women each against each other in the lead actor and lead actress categories. Jim noted that this could make them competitive, "if you allow it," but that ultimately, it was all good for the show. "I'm very happy if somebody does (win), and it'd be nice to win best play for all of us together," he granted. "But if not, I think that we've accomplished putting something up that people like, they have a good time, they leave, generally, with a smile on their face—unless their marriage sucks. And that's more than enough for me."

He was also asked to present at the Tony Awards in June, alongside Daniels; their appearance followed a number from the Broadway adaptation of *Shrek*, prompting Jim to quip, "For the record, Shrek and I are no relation." The two men lost the Tony for best actor to *Exit the King*'s Geoffrey Rush, but Harden won the best actress award, and *God of Carnage* won the prize for best play.

The response was so good, and (perhaps even more important) receipts were so impressive that when the cast's original contractual run concluded on July 26, 2009, they weren't replaced with new actors, as was customary. Instead, the show shuttered for a six-week hiatus, allowing the original quartet to fulfill previous familial and professional commitments, before reopening with all four in place on September 8 and running through November 15. (Jim spent the hiatus at the house on the Jersey Shore.) It was a wise move financially; box office again topped $1 million during the last week of that run in November, then declined steeply (to about half) when new cast members Christine Lahti, Annie Potts, Jimmy Smits, and Ken Stott took over. The cast would shift again the following March, with Daniels returning but stepping into Gandolfini's role of Michael ("He couldn't have been nicer and more supportive, and actually came to see it," Daniels reported), before closing for good on June 6, 2010.

Perhaps in response to the less-than-stellar reception to the replacements, the show's producers did not opt for the touring production that would customarily follow such a commercial success on Broadway; not enough major cities were interested in hosting a show whose popularity was so tied to its original stars and their chemistry. But they were able to mount the next best thing: In April 2011, the original cast revived the production for a six-week run at the Ahmanson Theatre in Los Angeles. "I was sincerely, genuinely very happy to go back to the other role," Daniels said. "I felt like that's the role I owned. Doing Jim's role, I felt like I was renting it."

BY THE TIME OF *Carnage*'s Los Angeles run, Jim and Deborah were spending most of their time on the West Coast; his diehard devotion to the tristate area was proving an impediment to potential film and television opportunities. (It may have felt like an affirmation when, that June, he was one of the 135 performers and executives invited to join the Academy of Motion Picture Arts and Sciences.)

But he remained firmly bicoastal, still taking pains to invite his crew of friends out for summers down the Shore, for good times and big dinners, and going about his regular routines in Manhattan, even under extraordinary circumstances. Just after Christmas 2010, a brutal blizzard dumped several feet of snow on New York, surprising the city government and overwhelming the plows. Bedford Street in the West Village was buried under a three-foot snowdrift that evening, and a motorist attempting to pass through got stuck.

"And the next minute, James Gandolfini appeared from another car behind and offered to help out," reported Phil Casaceli, owner of the nearby bar and restaurant Daddy-O. "He helped dig their car out and then rocked it back and forth to get it out of the snow bank. He used a lot of old-school elbow grease." Jim worked at it for forty-five minutes, with the help of a few curious onlookers; "Some offered to help, and others just watched because you don't often see Tony Soprano digging people out of the snow," according to Casaceli. "It was a real New York moment. Somebody had the luck of the draw, and it was James Gandolfini who came to their rescue."

Once they'd dug the car out, Jim went into Daddy-O and asked if they could break a $100 bill. "He then took the $20 bills to thank the guys who helped them out," Casaceli told the *New York Post*'s Page Six. "He was a real gentleman." Even Page Six had to give him credit; its headline read, GANDOLFINI'S A BLIZZARD HERO.

"A COUPLE YEARS BEFORE HE passed," recalls manager Nancy Sanders, "we were in some negotiation. And he goes, *Hey, let's make our money now, because I don't know how long I'm gonna live*. It was a little prophetic." He was reasonably happy with the acting work he was getting, but Attaboy Films' deal with HBO wasn't proving as fertile as Jim would've liked; they had still only convinced the network to bite on *Alive Day Memories*. They developed a reality/cooking show called *MEN-U*, but HBO passed; Attaboy took it to Spike TV, which didn't pick it up for a series but did air the pilot as a one-time special in 2009.

His main focus for Attaboy was the long-gestating Ernest Hemingway project, in which he would both produce and star as "Papa." "I think I can play someone like that," he said. "I think he did all that stuff in his life for a reason—some of the reason I think was he was in pain a lot of the time, and he needed to keep moving." He was researching the role as early as 2004, but found himself at loggerheads with HBO over what, exactly, the film should be. "He'd always wanted to go to Cuba," Tom Richardson says, to play "that Hemingway, the older Hemingway that was in Cuba, questioning himself—past the heroic Hemingway of that movie. But I guess when it comes to what people want to see, what people are gonna pay money to see, that was the one that HBO really wanted to make. It had gone through a bunch of rewrites back and forth trying to find a way to bridge the two gaps."

Ultimately, Gandolfini dropped out as star, and Clive Owen stepped in to play "the heroic Hemingway" opposite Nicole Kidman in *Hemingway & Gellhorn*, which debuted in May 2012. "It won some awards, and it did very well for HBO," Richardson says. "So he was proud of it. But if he were holding all the purse strings, that wouldn't have been the movie that he would have made."

Jim and Attaboy turned their attention to another documentary—a kind of follow-up to *Alive Day Memories*, focusing on internal rather than external injuries. HBO's Sheila Nevins proposed that Jim reteam with Jon Alpert and Ellen Goosenberg Kent to explore the history of PTSD in the American military; he eagerly agreed. "One of the things that Jim really noticed is, no matter what the physical injuries were, the mental injuries were just as tough, if not tougher, to deal with," Richardson says. "The second one definitely has parts about physical injuries, but it was a lot more about the post-traumatic stress of it all. And the survivor's guilt of it all."

Thanks to the positive response to the first film, this time Jim, Tom, Jon Alpert, and the crew would be allowed to travel to active war zones in Afghanistan and Iraq to talk to military personnel, from foot soldiers to high-ranking generals. "We talked to a lot of guys, and they were pretty open with us," Gandolfini said. "Gen. Ray Odierno said he would talk to me, which I was reasonably astounded by. He has a lot to do, head of everything in Iraq."

"I really liked traveling with him," Alpert says. "First, because we got elevated to a much higher level of travel." When his crew had traveled to Baghdad or Kandahar for earlier documentaries, "it would take us a week—and it's a week without sleeping, it's a week lying on the floor on transport planes. Jim would get you there a lot faster. So I really enjoyed traveling with him because you would have energy to work on your stories that you would normally expend in logistics."

Which is not to say that the trip over wasn't difficult. Gandolfini, Alpert, Richardson, and their crew flew out of New Jersey on a large but comfortable transport plane, where the pilots let Jim come up and take the controls for a while, including during a midair fueling. Then they landed and changed planes, flying on Air Force Two with Admiral Mike Mullen, chairman of the Joint Chiefs of Staff. "Then we lost the USO guys and then we were starting to fly like soldiers," Richardson says, laughing. The next leg was on a giant transport plane with hundreds of infantrymen, "and they're sitting on top of the backpacks on top of chairs. They strapped me and Jim to the side of the plane, like stewardesses, in jump seats." From there they transferred to a smaller plane, and *then* to a Blackhawk helicopter, which would take them to the Forward Operating Base (FOB), and into potentially dangerous situations. "While it wasn't the heat of the war, there was still trouble going on there," according to Richardson. "And Jim ran to that trouble."

Once he was with the troops, Gandolfini was unhurried and attentive. "The generosity of the time that he would commit to these things, everybody appreciated it," Alpert says. "*We* appreciated it because it made the documentaries better—there was a depth to the encounters that's very, very important, because you really want to get past things that are superficial. But the people with whom we interacted, they're not dummies, they understand that everybody's pulling Jim to the left and they're pulling him to the right and all he's doing is sitting there talking to them. That was his whole world. And he was demonstrating to everybody that it was the most important thing to him."

That genuineness and generosity shows in the film, titled *Wartorn: 1861–2010*. Jim visits U.S. Army hospitals and barracks, dressed in unassuming black, again insisting on staying in the background; he's an interviewer, a journalist really, powered by both his curiosity and morality. He's at ease with the working-class soldiers, and his discussions with the brass are respectful but pointed. He sees the genuine injustice with which soldiers suffering from PTSD (previously called "battle fatigue," among other euphemisms) were treated; he shares the wrenching stories of families haunted by the suicides of their soldier sons, and lets teary-eyed World War II vets tell their stories for the first time. In interrogating the way this culture punished or ignored these men for their emotions, and the "weakness" they were told they represented, *Wartorn* is examining masculinity, as forcefully as *The Sopranos* had.

Shortly before its HBO debut on Veterans Day 2010, *Wartorn* screened at the Pentagon, with top military personnel (including General George Casey, chief of staff of the U.S. Army) in attendance, and participating in a panel discussion after. Admiral Mullen introduced the screening, calling the film "powerful and tough." Critics agreed. The *New York Times*' Mike Hale praised its "quietly devastating, haunting scenes, echoes of the nightmares that veterans are bringing home with them from Iraq and Afghanistan," noting that both of the team's documentaries "exhibit a respect for the individual soldier that borders on deference, though Mr. Gandolfini, who again conducts interviews, is not afraid to ask difficult questions." *Variety*'s Brian Lowry added, "Together, these documentaries create a compelling quilt of images about a war most Americans would seemingly prefer to ignore."

Jim was again proud—both of the film and of what it accomplished. "General [Peter] Chiarelli said that for however many years, it's always been, if somebody says, *I feel like I've got post-traumatic stress*, it's like, *Well, that's nice, prove it to me*," explains Richardson. "And half the time, these guys aren't able to prove it to him. He said, from now on, if somebody says they've got it, we're going to accept them at their word, and we're going to help them. Whether the timing was just fortuitous, or talking to Jim had something to do with it—however it worked out, I guess we'll never know. But it did happen that way."

Wartorn further cemented Jim's love for nonfiction filmmaking. He joined the board of directors at DCTV, a nonprofit community media center for documentary storytellers in downtown Manhattan. "He really was most enthusiastic about helping the high school kids that come here," says Jon Alpert, who is co-founder and co–executive director of DCTV. "He would sit with them, and they would show Jim Gandolfini their rough cuts, and he was giving them input. I mean, that's a side to him that nobody ever saw, except the people who were in the programs that he used to come and help."

But Jim was always up for acts of quiet advocacy and support. In 2010, he and Edie Falco briefly reprised their *Sopranos* characters to participate in a star-studded video, attempting to convince free agent LeBron James to join the New York Knicks. ("We got those requests all the time back then and Gandolfini, he did nothing," Falco revealed in 2021. "And somehow, he agreed to this thing, which I was shocked by. . . . He must have been a bigger basketball fan than I realized.") King James ultimately chose the Miami Heat, and the video was not seen publicly until 2024.

Other gestures were more personal. Robert Iler had been in some trouble with the law during the run of *The Sopranos*, and struggled with substance abuse, though Jim "never really spoke to me about that kind of stuff," Iler says. But after the show ended,

> Jim would call my manager and ask about me and tell him not to tell me. Which is so the fucking *opposite* of show business—normally, when people in show business do something, it's because they want to be seen. *Look what I'm doing*, social media, this kind of shit, where he was the opposite. He's like, *Don't ever tell Robert that I'm asking you these questions. But is he hanging out with the right people?* Even asking how much am I paying for rent, to make sure that I'm not being an asshole. That was exactly who he was.

Vincent Curatola remembers the phone ringing on Christmas morning, "I think it was 2010, '10 or '11," he says. Gandolfini was calling to wish his *Sopranos* castmate and his wife, Maureen, a merry Christmas.

"Jim, I'm on my way to the hospital," Curatola told him. "We put her in the hospital two days ago. She has something going on with vision, she's at Hackensack Hospital in New Jersey."

"I'm coming," Jim replied, immediately.

"No, Jim," Curatola insisted. "No, no, it's Christmas morning. Do what you gotta do."

"No, I'm coming," Jim said, firmly. "Fuck you. I'm gonna be there."

"Jimmy, stop!"

He didn't stop. "He shows up at the hospital with his wife, Deborah, sat in the room," Curatola says. "We were there about an hour and a half. We ordered coffee, doughnuts, whatever. And this was Christmas Day. My wife was great three days after that, but she had to spend Christmas in there. And Jimmy came."

CHAPTER 22

ALBERT

"PEOPLE SAY 'OH WE'RE LUCKY,'" James Gandolfini said in 2012. "Actually, I think I said it once to Brad Pitt, because I had nothing else to say. And he said, 'Oh, come on. You've worked for it.' And I have. I worked my ass off. I don't know anyone who's done really well and is lazy."

Jim had certainly never been lazy, but the pace at which he was going—and the sheer volume of projects he appeared in—between 2007 and 2013 was mind-boggling. Yet in many ways, the work he did in the years after *The Sopranos* was a matter of picking up where he left off before the show came along to change his life. Before he was Tony Soprano, he was a character actor, a valuable utility player, a specialist whom directors could bring in like a gunslinger to crush a handful of scenes and disappear. Now, he had the opportunity to do that again—but with his choice of high-profile projects for name directors. "I like the character parts I get now," he said. "I don't need to be the star. I've done it. Don't need to do it again."

Which was not to imply that he didn't mind being the star on occasion, for films that struck his interest. In July 2010, Jim began shooting his first acting role for HBO since the conclusion of *The Sopranos*, a fact-based drama titled *Cinema Verite*. It was based on the making of (and reception to) *An American Family*, the PBS documentary series that captured the slow-motion dissolution of the Louds, a seemingly typical California family. It was a nationwide sensation upon its airing in 1973, its reach extending from newspaper op-eds to *Tonight Show* monologues; it's now widely acknowledged as the grandfather of reality television.

The directors were Robert Pulcini and Shari Springer Berman, married documentarians who had crossed over to narrative filmmaking a few years earlier with the inventive hybrid film *American Splendor.* They were drawn to the material on an intensely personal level; much of the action centered on the relationships between the Louds and Alan and Susan Raymond, also married documentary filmmakers. "I was like, there's no one that knows this kind of material better than we did," Pulcini says, with some pride.

But the brain behind *An American Family* was Craig Gilbert, a New York–based television writer and producer, who conceived of the show and massaged (some said manipulated) its participants for maximum dramatic effect, only to disappear from public life after its stormy reception. As penned by screenwriter David Seltzer, Gilbert was perhaps the trickiest role in *Cinema Verite*, requiring an actor who could simultaneously project charm, intelligence, and ruthlessness. Gandolfini was Pulcini and Springer Berman's first choice, but they suggested him with some hesitation—after all, this was HBO, and this was Tony Soprano, even though the directors were drawn to what he'd done outside of that role.

Jim agreed to at least discuss it, but his people warned the directors that he was nervous to meet them. "I thought, why?" Pulcini says. "And they're like, *Well, he thinks you're cool.* And I said, Well, first of all, we're *not* cool."

"*He's* cool," Springer Berman adds.

Nevertheless, they headed to Jim's apartment in Tribeca for a meeting. "I remember like it was yesterday," Pulcini says. "We went down there, and he was standing outside."

"I've never met an actor where they give you an address and the actor's actually waiting for you outside the building," Springer Berman says with a laugh. They followed him up—"He seemed very not at ease," Pulcini says—sat down, and talked about the script. Gandolfini didn't have too many questions; he was mostly concerned that he wasn't right for the role. "It was purely like, *Why do you think I can do this?*" Pulcini recalls.

He had two key concerns, "which were both self-deprecating, which I think was a big thing for him," Springer Berman says. Much of the script hinged on an attraction, perhaps consummated, between Gilbert and Pat Loud, matriarch of the family; Diane Lane had just been cast in that role. "She's a goddess," Gandolfini told them, "and people are gonna laugh at me next to her. Nobody is gonna believe any kind of chemistry between us."

"Jim, you're a sex symbol!" Springer Berman assured him. "Do you understand how many women are in love with you? How could you say that?" But, she stresses, "It wasn't fake. It wasn't like he was looking for compliments. . . . In Jim's case, I think it was a sincere insecurity."

He was also worried about convincingly playing Gilbert, a Harvard-educated intellectual. Again, the directors assured him that he was credible. "We're not being forced to cast you," they insisted. "HBO isn't making us do this. It came from us. We really love you for the role." Jim signed on.

He first focused on the externals, knowing he would find the character's inner life once he settled on the right, specific look. Here, he had a real guy to model those elements on; early fittings to get comfortable in his authentic '70s wardrobe were key, and he would grow out his full beard. But the most important piece was finding the right wig to replicate Gilbert's full mane of hair. "Jim really wanted the wig," Springer Berman says. "He's like, *I don't feel like him unless I have that wig.*" In fact, he was fitted for two, one by the network's preferred wigmaker, one by a wig artist he'd used on a previous project. "One of the wigmakers was in New York and one was in LA," Springer Berman recalls. "It was a very time-consuming thing, and he didn't blink at doing it. He was like, *I'm going to do this because I need it right. I need this. This is gonna really help me.*" ("Hopefully people will get used to it," he said, while promoting the film. "My wife asked me to wear the wig a couple of times.")

But Jim knew that just looking like Craig Gilbert wouldn't be enough. While *Cinema Verite* was in preproduction, Gilbert, the surviving members of the Loud family, and the documentarian Raymonds were "all sort of at each other's throats," Springer Berman says. "They all had issues with each other, and they were suing each other." Only the Raymonds were cooperating with the production, so Springer Berman and Pulcini were not allowed to contact the Louds or Gilbert.

"Well, yeah, whatever," Jim said. "I'm gonna find Craig Gilbert. I'm hiring a detective."

"Okay, but HBO said you can't," his directors reminded him.

"Right, OK," Jim snorted. "I'm hiring somebody." And he did.

"He knocked on his door," Diane Lane said, laughing. "Can you imagine? I'm sorry, but can you imagine Jim Gandolfini knocking on your door? *Hey, I'm playing you in a movie. Can we spend some time together?* That would be very surreal." But Gilbert agreed to join Jim for lunch; one lunch turned into two, and then more. "He's a wonderful man, smart, honest, incredibly intelligent," Jim said. "Old-fashioned way about him, graduated from Harvard. He was an ambulance driver in World War II—he's old school. I enjoy him immensely.

"He's a bit of a freak, but a great guy," Gandolfini continued. "He tells me what an asshole I am every time he sees me. *You're an asshole, Jim, you're an idiot.* I say, *You're absolutely right*, and I laugh. He's a charming man!"

Their relationship was so affable, in fact, that when the production moved to New York for the last few days of shooting in August 2010, Jim brought Gilbert to the set. "I'm sure he had to drag him," Springer Berman says, "because he was not happy that they were making this movie. But I think he felt like he was in such good hands with Jim."

"We just loved working with him," Pulcini says of Jim, while noting that Gandolfini's habit of intense self-flagellation had not dissipated. He would berate himself openly, insisting, "I can't do this! I'm fucking up this whole movie!"

"It was never like, that actor that's always causing problems," Pulcini clarifies. "It was very real, this streak of disapproval he had for himself. And he was worth it all! He was giving an amazing performance. And I think he felt very comfortable with us. But it was impossible to convince him sometimes how good he was." Once, Jim had a particularly nasty, f-bomb-laden breakdown in front of the couple's visiting son, who was only a few years old. "He turned to me, he's like, *Daddy, why is that man saying 'fuck' over and over again?* It was the first time I ever heard that word come out of my son's mouth. And I was like, someday when you grow up, this will be a badge of honor—that the first time you said that word, it was because of Tony Soprano."

"But his instincts were brilliant," Springer Berman says. "His questions were always smart, useful." Tim Robbins, who played the father, Bill Loud, agreed. "You meet a lot of people that have pretenses and aspirations to be something they're not," Robbins said. "And Jim always was who he was, and always was genuinely in his own skin. Jim felt like a real breath of fresh air, someone that really understood what the process was."

Off the set, "he was very positive," Springer Berman recalls. "We talked about food and travel and his son. His son came to set a couple times, Michael—and his new wife came to set once or twice. . . . I think he felt free." And, as usual, he stunned his directors with his personal generosity. During the shoot, Pulcini's grandmother died; he left the production to Springer Berman and flew back to New Jersey for her funeral. "When I walked into the funeral home," he says, "there was this huge floral arrangement, just way bigger than anything else that was there. And I said, *Oh my God, who is that from?* And someone said to me, *Some guy named Jim Gandolfini, who has the same name as Tony Soprano.* I'm an Italian-American, so no one thought that it was the *real* Jim Gandolfini."

"There's probably another Jim Gandolfini in Philadelphia," Springer Berman says, laughing.

"No, it's really Jim Gandolfini," Pulcini assured them. "And that was the talk of the funeral, that Jim Gandolfini had sent this huge arrangement."

His work in *Cinema Verite* was no less impressive. Craig Gilbert is definitely a supporting role—he's off-screen for much of the action, back in New York supervising the editing as the Loud family falls apart—and most of his scenes are with Diane Lane. But they're electric together (his concerns about audiences buying their chemistry were entirely unfounded), slyly flirtatious, Gandolfini's strength as an on-screen listener dovetailing nicely with how the character would instinctively gain her trust as both a subject and a potential fling. Jim plays Gilbert as moody, mercurial, and manipulative; he knows when to lean back and let Bill talk himself into a confession, and when to give Pat the hard sell so he can get what he needs on camera.

The *New Yorker*'s Richard Brody was especially enamored of the performance ("Gandolfini lends Gilbert a quiet, ingratiating cunning"), which he championed as equal to any nominated for Best Supporting Actor at that year's Oscars. Pulcini and Springer Berman hoped to work with Jim again, as soon as possible, and asked if they could send him the script for their next project; they had a role in mind for him. He called to regretfully decline. "I just couldn't do it," he said. "I didn't like the character. I don't think I can do it." Pulcini knew "it wasn't the typical Jim thing," declining out of hesitation or modesty, but realized that "he wasn't connecting with it," so they cheerfully agreed to try again on something else, and hung up.

Fifteen minutes later, Pulcini's phone rang; it was Jim again. "Do you need me to say yes to get it financed?" he asked.

"No, of course not, I want to find something that you want to play," Pulcini assured him. "I would never ask you to do that." They again exchanged pleasant goodbyes. "I just couldn't believe he would do that, that he actually cared that much," Pulcini says. "But he just was that guy, you know?"

CINEMA VERITE WRAPPED IN AUGUST 2010 IN New York City, and Jim was at work on his next project, also in the city, the following month. *Violet & Daisy* was the feature directorial debut of Geoffrey Fletcher, who had just won the Oscar for his adapted screenplay *Precious*. That was a grim, realist drama about a young woman trapped in a life of poverty; *Violet & Daisy*, in stark contrast, was a fast, flashy, Tarantino-esque story of two blue-eyed teen girl contract killers, and the target (Gandolfini) who disarms them with his shrugging acceptance of his fate. Jim was drawn to it for similar reasons as *Welcome to the Rileys*. "Those were very sensitive men with a lot of heart," explains Mark Armstrong. In addition, "there was something about him being on the other side, being the mark of a hit man himself."

Bruce Willis was originally in talks for the role but dropped out at the last minute. "Fortunately, [Gandolfini] got ahold of the script and expressed interest in the part," Fletcher says. "I always knew he was a talent with untold range, so I thought he would excel in this role. He played far against type and did so remarkably while providing the film's moral foundation."

The character—never referred to by name, and only credited as "The Guy"—is a slacks-and-sweater-vest type, pleasant and balding, with an even softer variation on his regular speaking voice. The Guy, who has stolen a suitcase of mob money along with a shipment of cologne, has a death wish because he has pancreatic cancer: "I'm going to die and I don't want to take the scenic route," he explains, matter-of-factly. As such, he's all but sacrificing himself to the title characters, offering advice for completing the hit, and cookies to boot ("Who wants a snack? Careful, they're hot"). He plays it entirely as dry comedy, with just a touch of doomed inevitability, until the ending, which lands like a body shot: a heart-wrenching monologue in which he reads a goodbye letter to his estranged daughter. "I know I probably wasn't the best father in the world," he says, tenderly and genuinely. "But I tried the best I could."

It's the sequence that makes the entire character worth playing, but Jim was not precious about it. "After seeing the film for the first time, he shocked me when he suggested that his monologue might be a little long," Fletcher says. "This was regarding what is possibly his finest moment in the story, but he was more concerned about the movie's overall rhythm than the monologue that he had mastered. His idea inspired an unusual bit of intercutting that really worked."

Jim's co-stars, Saoirse Ronan and Alexis Bledel, got a peek at the Gandolfini Method right from the jump. "There's a scene when he meets Saoirse and Alexis, they were sleeping on the couch," explains manager Mark Armstrong. "He didn't want to meet them before, and told the director—there was no rehearsal. And so those two had to stay on the couch with their eyes closed for his first scene, when he came in and did all the stuff he was doing in the house. I remember them saying it was such a weird experience because they hadn't met him yet. . . . They actually didn't meet each other until they opened their eyes and they were filming."

Fletcher found Gandolfini to be a dream actor. "He was warm, genuine, and principled," the writer-director recalls. "He cared so deeply, not just about his role, but about all of the other roles and the film's quality as a whole. He was incredibly prepared every day and had terrific ideas. Any time he had a question, it was in service of the betterment of the film."

Violet & Daisy premiered at the Toronto International Film Festival in September 2011 to mostly negative reviews, though *Variety*'s Peter Debruge praised Jim for "bringing a soul to Fletcher's wink-wink style." The independently produced picture disappeared for more than a year after the festival before it was finally acquired in November 2012 by the small distributor Cinedigm, which gave it a limited release in June 2013. Critics were kind only to Jim. "Gandolfini scoops up another chance to show off the gentleness he left at home during six seasons of 'The Sopranos,'" wrote the *New York Daily News*' Joe Neumaier; A. O. Scott, in the *New York Times*, praised his "weary ease."

Sopranos chronicler Matt Zoller Seitz framed his two-star review with praise for Gandolfini, calling this "another indelible portrait" from "such a versatile and surprising performer that within a few minutes of watching him play a different character, you forget about his most famous role," and proclaiming that "the only thing predictable about Gandolfini is his excellence. He's an actor you're always happy to see." But, he concluded, "Gandolfini's quietly magnificent performance is the only reason to see 'Violet & Daisy.'"

It was becoming an unfortunate pattern of his post-*Sopranos* era: great work in films that were otherwise panned, if they were seen at all. "He was always hard on himself, for every performance, I would say," Armstrong says. "Was he disappointed the movies didn't do well? As an actor, I'm sure he was. But he never . . . he didn't blame himself. And there were a lot of wins in between as well. I don't think he regretted any of those decisions."

DAVID CHASE HADN'T BEEN NEARLY as busy as his leading man in the years since that notorious cut to black; he wanted to plan his post-*Sopranos* career methodically, and cash the blank check the show had given him with care. He would finally make the leap to feature filmmaking that he had longed for, over the course of all those years in television, by writing, directing, and producing a coming-of-age drama about a would-be rock musician growing up in New Jersey in the mid-1960s. It was originally titled *The Twylight Zones*, after the band at its center. Before its release, that distinctive moniker would give way to the more generic *Not Fade Away*.

Chase hadn't loved directing his bookending episodes of *The Sopranos*, but this story was so personal—based on his own rock dreams, as a Jersey kid in the '60s—that he felt he had to helm it himself. Considering the time, place, and milieu, reuniting with Steven Van Zandt (who would supervise the period music, as well as write and produce original songs) was a no-brainer. But casting his former leading man was trickier. John Magaro, Gandolfini's *Down the Shore* co-star, who was playing the leading role, says:

> I think David would admit this. I think when they left *The Sopranos*, the two of them had a contentious relationship. I think David felt like Jim hated him. And I think Jim probably did. I don't think he *hated* him—maybe he did, I don't know—but I think he gave so much to that role of Tony, and playing someone so dark left a lot of scars on him, I think. And part of having to give all that made him have some feelings toward David, when they wrapped that show. . . . I think it was like two guys who went to war. They didn't want to see each other again and talk about it, you know? We killed all those people, we don't want to get together and hash that out again.

But Chase had written a juicy role, of Douglas's tough-as-nails and overprotective father, that Jim would have been perfect for, and "there weren't that many candidates for it," according to Chase. Yet Gandolfini initially passed. "It wasn't his cup of tea," said Chase, "and I said, 'All right, that's that.'"

Some time passed. Jim called again. "How are you doing?" he asked.

"We still haven't cast it yet, I haven't gotten to that role yet," Chase replied.

"Who are you thinking of?" Jim asked, and Chase named another actor. "Oh, I can't let you do that!" Gandolfini immediately insisted. "I'll do it!"

Jim found his way in when he realized the character needn't only reflect Chase's old man. "I knew this guy," he said. "There's a lot of my dad in him." Douglas initially sees his father as an obstruction, discouraging his dreams and pushing him to make the kind of compromises he did. "As a kid, you never think, hey, I bet my father had other dreams," Gandolfini explained, "other things he thought of doing besides working at this job and raising a family and going on the vacations that I wanted to go on. That realization comes later, and when it does, I think your relationship changes, and deepens. So I drew a bit on that." These themes were never explicitly articulated, however, which was part of the role's appeal. "David can write things in a way that helps you understand a lot, with not a lot of words," he said.

Thankfully, that admiration was mutual. "Working with him on *Not Fade Away* was great," Chase said. "A lot of the stuff that washed up on the beach of *The Sopranos*, all that fame and all that attention, that was all gone. And it was just like, we were starting over again, as two guys starting another project. What I really liked about it, is that between takes, he and I were talking. He and I were friends between takes. That's what really made it so special."

Christine Gee, Chase's script supervisor on *The Sopranos*, returned to that role for *Not Fade Away*, and the relationship was "very easy between the two of them," she remembers. "At that point, Jim had settled down, and he was very happy and he was very relaxed—as if he was able to actually enjoy himself in a different way. He just was more at peace with himself, he didn't have that self-destructive, hard-on-himself kind of thing going on anymore."

"He was a pleasure to work with," Chase said. "He was rid of that cross he had to bear of playing Tony Soprano. I think he was more mellow."

"Jim came into that as kind of a different person," Magaro agrees. "Different actor. He was so happy. He would walk away from scenes just laughing, and you could tell he enjoyed what he was doing in the performance. It was just a different Jim." The young actor reveled in the opportunity to work so closely with Gandolfini (most of whose scenes were with Magaro), particularly when they shot an intimate, two-person dinner scene, in which the father tells his son that he's been diagnosed with cancer. "I really got to watch him, how he did it," Magaro says. "How he would just change little things, just to make it fresh, and how he kept me on my toes. There was one time where he asked me, *What would you do if I died? Would you take care of Mom?* And he just kept asking it and asking it, and wouldn't let me go, and it just opened up a whole different part of my performance. It was just so generous of him, to keep me going and give me it—because it was my coverage—give it to me over and over again, and let me just get to different places with it."

Not Fade Away premiered at the 2012 New York Film Festival and hit theaters late in the year, where it was buried among the avalanche of big, important, prestige pictures (a few of them also featuring Gandolfini in supporting roles). Critics weren't sure what to make of it, and reviews were mixed. *Time*'s Richard Corliss was one of many critics who advised Chase to "go back to doing what he did better than almost anyone: make great TV." Still, Corliss thought Jim's performance was "utterly convincing," and other critics agreed with that assessment, too: The *New York Times* said Jim was "wonderful as ever," while *Variety* praised his "knockout supporting performance" as a "brilliant turn." Because it's such a small role, his best moments are tiny ones: his little chuckle after Dean Martin zings the Stones; how he watches Douglas kiss his girl though their front window; the brief, pointed, unsentimental way he tells his wife his cancer diagnosis.

His best beat is his last, a quick interaction with his son before the kid drives away, pressing cash into the boy's hand and growling, "Now you keep your goddamn mouth shut." Despite his anger and impatience, there's goodness and love in his heart, and Gandolfini lets those qualities flash in his eyes as the camera volleys away from him, a father watching his son go, perhaps for the last time. It's a quick bit, fleeting even, but it lands like a thunderbolt. "He just stands there, and he just looks," Magaro marvels. "I don't know what's going on in his head. But whatever is going on expresses all that loss, all that hope for a child, and that regret that they're leaving your life. Whatever he's thinking in that moment—that's something Harold (Guskin) taught. As long as you're thinking *something*, as long as you're there and you're letting something catch you, it will feel right. And that's what he's doing in that moment. And it feels amazing."

ALL OF JIM'S SCENES FOR *Not Fade Away* were shot in the first eight days of that film's production in February 2011, so that he could hustle down to New Orleans to work on a new Brad Pitt movie. He only even considered *Killing Them Softly* as a favor to his friend, because it was the kind of role he had sworn off: a contract killer in a crime story. The character, a burned-out hit man named Mickey, "had some overtones, similarities to people I've played in the past," Gandolfini worried, but the writer-director, Andrew Dominik, wouldn't take no for an answer. "I think he said, *Shut up. You're the guy to do this. And you're going to do it.* And so after the 900th time he said that, I was like, *OK, I'll do it. Just leave me alone.* And I loved the dialogue, but [Mickey] is a disgusting human being. I did some pretty disgusting stuff during *The Sopranos* and I was hesitant to step back into those shoes."

Easing his hesitation was the fact that all his scenes would be with Pitt, and he "would do anything for Brad," Armstrong says. But he also came to realize that the performance could serve as an end point, his last word on the toll on the soul of a life of crime. "You put all the mob guys I've played together, that's who this guy is," he said. "At the end, the arc of his life is finished." It was a masterstroke: Mickey is Tony Soprano by way of Willy Loman, bitter, exhausted, paranoid, broken. Pitt's Jackie hires Mickey mostly as a favor to the busted-out old legend, and realizes almost immediately that he's not up to the job; "I need the Mickey from a couple of years ago," he fumes. "He's worthless now."

Gandolfini has only three scenes: an entrance (coming down the jetway, scowling face hidden behind his big, black tinted sunglasses, looking like a man out of time) and two dialogue scenes, one telling Jackie his sob

Gandolfini as the busted-out hitman Mickey in *Killing Them Softly*.
(Courtesy The Weinstein Company/Photofest.)

stories, one trying to justify his very existence. In that scant screen time, just like the old days, he steals the picture. The *New York Times'* A. O. Scott praised his "rancid swagger," while the *Boston Globe*'s Ty Burr wrote, "All of Gandolfini's scenes breathe a terrible sadness, and while 'Killing Them Softly' appears to slow to a crawl whenever Mickey's on-screen, it's actually coming close to its point. Which is that the weak suffer at the hands of the strong, and anyone who says otherwise is selling you something."

Reviews notwithstanding, *Killing Them Softly* tanked at the box office, much to the chagrin of its distributor, the Weinstein Company. Harvey Weinstein—who would topple from power a few years later when outed as a decades-long sexual predator—pressed Jim to do additional promotional work on its behalf. "Harvey Weinstein called. He wants me to do Letterman. I said I don't do talk shows," Jim told Steve Schirripa. When Harvey tried to turn up the heat, Jim turned it up back. "I will beat the *fuck* out of Harvey Weinstein, he fucking calls me again, I will beat the fuck out of him," Gandolfini fumed. "For the money he paid me, I'm not fucking doing it."

"Swear to God," Schirripa said. "And this is all before the Harvey Weinstein shit, when he was still king shit."

SEPTEMBER 18, 2011, MARKED JAMES GANDOLFINI's fiftieth birthday. He celebrated the night before with a bash at Hundred Acres in SoHo with nearly two hundred guests, including his old college buddy Mario Batali and *Sopranos* co-stars Michael Imperioli, Tony Sirico, and Steven Van Zandt. Michael and Deborah gave speeches; guests snacked on sliders, oysters, lobster rolls, mini-meatballs, and chicken empanadas; and Jim roared away at midnight on the back of Batali's Vespa.

He showed no signs of slowing down on the other side of that milestone. "I don't know, I just seek out good stories, basically." He shrugged. "That's it." Thanks to a shifting media landscape—a shift prompted, in no small part, by the ground broken on *The Sopranos*—those stories were increasingly being told on television instead of film. "He didn't want to do TV right away," explains manager Nancy Sanders, "because that felt a little bit like, *Get me off of this roller coaster, and let me prove myself.*" The films that followed all offered him *something*, a chance to show his versatility or work with an actor or director he respected. "But he wasn't Sean Penn, is the thing," Sanders continues. Jim realized he could have more control over the roles he played, and the collaborators he could command, in television—and with the deal he had in place with HBO, he could create those opportunities.

As usual, there were a few that didn't pan out. Attaboy was working with HBO on an American adaptation of the Canadian comedy series *Taxi 0-22* (retitled the simpler *Taxi 22*), with Jim attached not only to executive-produce, but also to star as "a politically incorrect cab driver in New York City," according to *Variety*. "He was always looking for an Archie Bunker–type role," Armstrong explains, "someone that might say things that make you cringe, but are sprinkled in truth." The show never made it to air; neither did the company's HBO movie project *Eating with the Enemy*, an adaptation of Hackensack restaurateur Bobby Egan's memoir, with Jim starring as Egan. He was also reportedly attached to star in a Boston-set ensemble cop drama for the network, penned by Peter Tolan (*Rescue Me*), and to lend his voice to the 3D animated adventure *Escape from Planet Earth*. He even shot scenes for Stephen Daldry's Oscar-nominated film adaptation of the novel *Extremely Loud and Incredibly Close*, playing a potential love interest for Sandra Bullock, but his character was cut after that subplot elicited a negative response from test audiences.

Most intriguingly, he met with brass at NBC to discuss joining the cast of its hit *The Office* when star Steve Carell departed in its seventh season. At the time, trades reported that Gandolfini "wasn't interested"; years later, on an episode of the podcast *Talking Sopranos*, Steve Schirripa revealed that they got as far as an offer from NBC of $4 million per season, but, according to Schirripa, "HBO paid him $3 million not to do it."

His desire to do more comedy was unsurprising to those who knew and worked with him. "I think he always wanted to be a comedic actor. Like, I think he would have been happy on a sitcom," John Magaro says. "I think he saw himself as more of a Jackie Gleason than he did a Tony Soprano." Asked about his own viewing habits, Jim told the *New York Times'* Melena Ryzik, "I watch stupid comedies. 'Role Models.' I love them. 'The Rocker.' I love that. I like idiotic comedies." When Ryzik asked why we hadn't seen him in one, he replied, "Nobody's asked."

Finally, in the fall of 2011, someone did. Don Scardino had been a producer and director for *30 Rock*, which shot at Silvercup Studios alongside *The Sopranos*. When he was casting his feature film *The Incredible Burt Wonderstone*, a broad comedy about rival Las Vegas magicians starring Jim Carrey, Steve Buscemi, and (coincidentally enough) Steve Carell, he kept hearing Gandolfini's voice in his head for the role of Doug Munny, a flamboyant casino owner. So he reached out to Jim's agent, and the actor came in for a meeting.

"Why do you guys want me in this?" Gandolfini asked, pointedly. "What do you want me for? I'm not funny."

"Have you seen your television show?" Scardino asked. "You're terrifying, but you're also hilarious."

"Don't get me wrong," Jim said. "I read it. I liked it. But I'm not this guy. I'm not funny and you've got all these funny guys. I think you've got the wrong guy."

So Scardino made his case. "I need a guy who I can believe owns a huge hotel in Vegas," he said. "He's a powerful guy. He's a charismatic guy. He's a wealthy guy. And right away the audience will go, *I believe this guy is a big sho*t. That's it. And as soon as they realize that the character is very different than Tony, that will also be a great surprise for people, you know?" Jim thought it over for a few days, and took the role.

"He's such an honest actor," Scardino says. "But I don't think he ever approached it in any other way than the truth of what he was playing. And I think he wanted to hear from me that I wasn't expecting him to *be funny*, that I wasn't expecting him to tell jokes."

All of that said, Gandolfini is very funny in *The Incredible Burt Wonderstone*. He uses a deep, gravelly voice, which renders his ridiculous dialogue even sillier, and again began his character work by "working on the outside details," Scardino recalls. "He wants to know the wig's gonna be right. He wants to know that the clothes are gonna be right, and the shoes are going to be right, and the glasses." As Munny, Gandolfini sports a series of ever-changing and increasingly wild looks, from silk bathrobes to Technicolor suits, in each scene. Those transformations were the actor's idea, Scardino says, executed in close collaboration with the film's hair, makeup, and wardrobe teams.

"His work ethic was amazing," Scardino says. "He's one of the most professional guys I've ever worked with. Always knew his lines, always right there, never a problem getting him out of the trailer, never a problem with he's late and hair and makeup or any of that crap. He's a total pro. And it's clear that he's having a good time." That good time is evident on-screen: It's a pleasurable performance and an inspired comic character, with Jim mining every laugh from Munny's gruff impatience ("I don't enjoy any of this shit"), lack of social graces ("I need you to dump Anton, he's homely," Gandolfini instructs Carell, before a clever cut revealing that Buscemi's

Anton is sitting right in front of him), and a juicy running gag concerning his inability to remember his own son's age ("Judah is turning . . . I don't know, he's turning something, and we're having a little birthday party at the house").

"Once we started rolling," Scardino says, "he never ever betrayed any nervousness, or thought that he wasn't doing a good job, or wasn't funny, or anything else. He was always right there. And in every scene, he was hilarious." On his last day, the director had only one simple thing for Jim to shoot: a background piece of promotional video for Munny's new casino, in which he's dancing and throwing money in the air.

"*What* do you want me to do?" Jim asked.

"Well," Scardino explained, meekly, "I thought it'd be very funny if you were dancing and throwing money."

"Come on, what do you mean, dancing? I don't dance. You seen me dance!"

"Sure."

Finally, Jim challenged his director: "All right, all right, big shot, show me. Show me what you want." Scardino, an actor in his early days, happily complied, dancing around and throwing the money in the air. Jim watched, amused, and then asked, "And this is gonna be *where?*"

"It's gonna be like forty feet high in the front of the hotel," the director replied, sheepishly.

"You gotta be kidding me, Scardino," Jim said with a laugh. "This is the limit."

But he got into place, and Scardino summoned the crew. "Come in and watch Gandolfini do this," he instructed them. "And then I want you to laugh and applaud." They did, and as they reacted, Jim got into it—throwing the money around, grinning from ear to ear, exclaiming, "Look at me! I'm dancing!" Everyone broke up, and Scardino called a wrap on James Gandolfini. The crew applauded, and Scardino noted that Gandolfini seemed visibly moved.

"I have this informal rep company," Scardino told him. "And you are now in it. It's not the last job we'll do together."

Jim smiled. "Any time you call me, pal, I'll be there."

"Gandolfini attacks his part with infectious delight," *Variety* raved, when *The Incredible Burt Wonderstone* debuted as the opening night selection at the SXSW Film and TV Festival in Austin the following March, a few days in advance of its theatrical bow; the *New York Times*' Stephen Holden wrote, "James Gandolfini has great fun as a jolly, avaricious casino owner." The gunslinger had done it again.

AFTER HE WRAPPED *BURT WONDERSTONE*, Jim moved into an even smaller role in a rather more prestigious production. *Zero Dark Thirty* reteamed Oscar-winning director Kathryn Bigelow with her *Hurt Locker* screenwriter, Mark Boal, to dramatize the CIA's years-long attempt to locate and execute Osama bin Laden after the terror attacks of September 11, 2001. It was a quick-turn job: SEAL Team Six had killed the al-Qaida leader in May 2011, Bigelow's film began production on March 5, 2012, and it was in theaters that December.

Jim would play agency head Leon Panetta, though he's only listed in the credits as "C.I.A. Director"; with his regular speaking voice, and wearing a hairpiece and glasses, the resemblance is uncanny. It's basically a cameo role, four short scenes, most of them reacting to the certainty and cojones of focal character Maya (Jessica Chastain), making fine use of one of Gandolfini's most effective tools, his bemused grin. In a long movie with a giant cast, the character has little time to establish his importance and gravity; luckily, as an actor, Jim comes with those qualities already in place.

"It wasn't a big part, but I wanted to be part of an important movie," Jim explained. "I liked the way it portrayed the military." Not everyone agreed; politicians and pundits criticized the film for its perhaps overly friendly portraiture of the government agencies involved, particularly the CIA, which cooperated heavily in its production. For his part, Panetta shrugged and said, "It's a movie. And it's a good movie. But I lived the real story. . . . people in the end have to understand that it isn't a documentary, it's a movie."

Jim was so worried about offending Panetta that he sent him an apology note on the film's release. "I sent a note to Leon saying, *I'm very sorry about everything. The wig, everything. You're kind of like my father. You'll find something to be angry about*," Gandolfini said at the National Board of Review Awards in January 2013. He got in a jab of his own, though, adding that screenwriter Boal had told him Panetta wanted his number but "doesn't know how to get in touch." Jim took a perfectly timed pause before deadpanning, "This is the head of the CIA."

Zero Dark Thirty opened in theaters on December 19, 2012, three weeks after *Killing Them Softly* and two days before *Not Fade Away*; *Burt Wonderstone* would be out in March, followed by the long-delayed limited releases of *Down the Shore* and *Violet & Daisy*. "I did all those things over the last two, three years," Jim explained, of his sudden theatrical ubiquity. "It's just that they're all coming out in the same two months. And they're not big parts, it's not like I'm in them for months. I work two, three weeks and I'm done." But the proximity of so many performances—characteristically excellent but also wildly wide-ranging in tone and tenor—underscored the effectiveness of his divergent choices.

His next would be even more of a departure: his first leading role in a romantic comedy. The writer and director was Nicole Holofcener, who made smart, thorny independent films, mostly about upper-class women in varying forms of personal and emotional crisis. Her latest, *Enough Said*, concerned Eva (Julia Louis-Dreyfus), a divorced massage therapist who begins dating a low-key nice guy named Albert, only to discover that her new client and friend (Catherine Keener) is Albert's ex-wife—and a source of endless criticisms of her new beau.

Gandolfini was an unconventional pick to play Albert, but one that made sense to Holofcener. "I think what made his performance in *The Sopranos* so brilliant is that it was so layered," she says. "He was so lovable at times. Eventually not lovable at all, but human, really human, and vulnerable. And then when I met with him, and he really wanted to do it, he didn't act like Tony Soprano at all. He acted like a lovely human being." She'd wanted to cast Jim in her previous film, *Please Give*, but worried that the adulterous turn of the character (eventually played by Oliver Platt) would remind viewers too easily of Tony Soprano. There was no danger of that here.

"That performance was really him," Louis-Dreyfus says. "Prior to making the movie with him, I didn't know him. So I didn't know if a big, blustery Tony Soprano was gonna come through the door. But it sure, sure wasn't. Sure wasn't. He was a teddy bear of a guy." Nancy Sanders concurs: "He was terrified because he was as vulnerable and real and James Gandolfini as he was ever gonna be. Those were his Birkenstocks. That's who he was—if anybody wants to know who Jim Gandolfini was, he was the closest to that character."

Jim was pleasantly surprised to have landed the role at all. "I don't get called for that kind of thing, you know, the parts when you get to kiss the girl," he said. "It's kind of like a buffalo kissing a rabbit when I'm kissing Julia, but it was nice that they gave the buffalo a chance."

"I was really surprised by his normal insecurity," Holofcener says. "I can't say he was an insecure person, but his normal insecurity as an actor playing something that he hasn't played before. And that surprised me. I figured he can do this with his eyes closed, and yet, I think he felt challenged."

"You're making me sound like a pussy!" Jim would complain, of his most vulnerable dialogue and scenes, to which Holofcener would fire back, "No, you're the right kind of pussy! All the women are going to love you, trust me." One day, after a bit of a back-and-forth on the set, Holofcener followed Gandolfini back to his trailer and put it to him bluntly: "I feel like you don't trust me." And then it all came out, all his insecurities about himself, as an actor and a person. "He was nervous about playing a romantic lead," Holofcener says. "He didn't think he was sexy. And we're all saying, *No, you're sexy! We all think so! Live with that!* No, he didn't believe that. So that was surprising, that someone that famous and that talented was still so vulnerable."

Nicole Holofcener directs Jim and Julia Louis-Dreyfus in *Enough Said.* (Courtesy Fox Searchlight Pictures/Photofest.)

After they talked it all over, Jim chilled out, though "sometimes Julia would have to whack him on the back and say, *Just do what she says. Trust her, we're not going to make a fool out of you*," Holofcener continues. Louis-Dreyfus observed his vulnerability more intimately. "We had a scene in bed together in *Enough Said*, and . . . I think this is okay for me to say," Louis-Dreyfus recalls, still sensitive to his needs, a decade later. "He had a scar on his arm. And he was embarrassed about it. So, and he told me, would I lay on top of him in such a way that it was covered up. And it was dear of him to tell me, and we worked it out."

Those small reassurances—par for the course for Jim—aside, both women were taken by the scope of his gifts. "What I loved about working with him, and on those scenes, was that he was very dedicated to the authenticity of it," Louis-Dreyfus said at the time. "It's like tuning an instrument. And that's how I think we both approached these scenes together. If it sounded just right, if he wanted to try something different, it was these slight adjustments that really were profound."

Holofcener was struck, as his colleagues so often were, by his thoughtfulness. "He was really attentive to people in smaller roles and the crew," she says. "There's always a PA or an AD that hangs around the trailers just to take care of the actors, and what they need, and walk them to the set. And there was this one woman who was sitting out there in the sun, day after day, and he showed up with a chair and an umbrella for her. Without asking, you know. He just was kind and generous that way."

"He brought total honesty," Louis-Dreyfus says. "I really feel like he had such depth as an actor, like a Marlon Brando." She's right, though Brando rarely crafted a performance as light and breezy as this. His comic timing is sharper than ever; he gets laughs even with the throwaway lines (watch the momentarily convincing way he asks, "Got any money?" when it's time to pay at the yogurt shop). But he's also got genuine rom-com chops. Holofcener wisely plays their first dates in something close to real time, hanging out with them as they build their rapport out of sparks of attraction and awkward pauses. His smile and laugh with her feels genuine, and they're so relaxed together that the most vital aim of a romantic comedy is achieved: You're pulling for them to end up together, no matter what complications may stand in the way.

That same offhand ease is present in their physical attraction. Gandolfini has such warmth and charm when he asks, "You wanna kiss?" that her "Yeah" seems like the only possible response. He puts his arm around her and kisses her; she smiles and he smiles, and then they kiss again. It's a lovely moment. But he can communicate more than sweetness; in the afterglow of their first sexual encounter, she says, of keeping the lights off, "I figured if I couldn't see you, you couldn't see me."

"Oh, I saw you," he responds, with the slightest but sexiest little purr to his voice.

Yet even these early, honeymoon-phase scenes hint at his capacity for pain. The first time he leans in for a kiss, she replies, "I'm not sure," and his facial response is devastating—which he quickly hides, taking the hit and moving on, as good-naturedly as he can. But when Eva turns on him, wielding the critiques his ex-wife has armed her with like a spiky sword, Jim plays the character's close-to-the-bone sensitivity. "I thought . . . you actually liked me," he says, with the hurt of a schoolboy.

Later, when Albert discovers Eva's betrayal, he goes at her with a combination of anger and pain. "She was poisoning our relationship," he fumes, "and poisoning your perception of me." It's an unbearably uncomfortable confrontation, and a tricky scene—in which Jim's open-wound acting allows a rather unorthodox moment of protagonist transference. "I know this sounds corny," he tells her, simply. "But you broke my heart." And in that moment, he breaks ours.

"My saddest moment about that," Mark Armstrong says, "is I remember leaving the studio from a screening and calling him and saying, 'I know, obviously, Tony Soprano is the role of a lifetime. But what you're doing in this movie, I cannot wait for people to see.'

"And he never saw it."

CHAPTER 23

MARV

"WE WERE WORKING ON *Enough Said*," Susan Aston recalls of that day in August 2012. "He had rented a little cottage in the hills, and he set up his office and I stayed there when we were working; he lived up the hill with his family. We were sitting there together when somebody called—maybe Travolta, I don't remember—to tell him that Tony Scott had killed himself. And you know, he fell apart."

The director—who had provided Jim his first major movie, then his breakthrough role, and then the chance to show his versatility after *The Sopranos*—had leaped from the Vincent Thomas Bridge in San Pedro, California, after leaving a note for his family in his Los Angeles office. He left another note in his car near the site of his plunge, with names and phone numbers for his family, presumably to assist officials on the scene.

"He was really deeply affected by it," Aston says. "He loved Tony Scott. He thought he was pretty amazing all the way around and couldn't believe . . ." She trails off. "I think all artists understand that level of depression, if that's what it was. So I think there's a lot of empathy among artists for getting so sad that you would take your own life, especially in such a brilliant career. He was really torn up about it."

Perhaps coincidentally, Jim found himself even more drawn to reconnecting with old friends and collaborators. He and Edie Falco met for dinner, catching up for the first time since the show had ended. "The two of us going to sit in the back of Tribeca Grill was deeply confusing to everybody there, I'm sure," she says, laughing. "But for the first time, I actually thought *Oh, who's this guy?* You know what I mean? I so did *not* feel close to him—my own doing, throughout the years. And all of a sudden I realized, *Oh, that's right. He was on that ride with me too*, you know?"

Falco not only felt more connected to Jim; she noticed a change in his overall demeanor. "He was just easier," she says. "He smiled a lot. The stress appeared to have lifted. I daresay he definitely seemed happier, for sure. But I *will* say that was a lot of years, and a lot of damage is done. And unless you are taking valiant steps in a wellness direction, it doesn't just go away."

Steve Schirripa, meanwhile, had written a pair of Young Adult novels about "Nicky Deuce," a goody-goody suburban kid thrust into his father's family (and, he believes, the gangsters within it) in the Bensonhurst section of Brooklyn. In 2012, the children's network Nickelodeon financed a film adaptation of the first book, *Nicky Deuce: Welcome to the Neighborhood*; Schirripa called in some favors and turned it into a *Sopranos* reunion, with supporting roles for himself, Tony Sirico, and Vincent Curatola, and a cameo for Michael Imperioli. "I hadn't seen Jim in a couple of years," Schirripa says. "We talked but I didn't see him much—you know, he had moved to LA." So Schirripa gave him a call and asked if he might be able to do a cameo, just a one-day shoot, for old times' sake.

"Let me see," Jim said. He was in the midst of *Enough Said*'s production in California, and *Nicky Deuce* was shooting in Montreal—but Labor Day was approaching, so he'd have a three-day weekend. He shot with Holofcener through Friday night, got on a plane Saturday, met Schirripa for dinner that night (it was Steve's birthday), shot all day Sunday, and flew back to California on Labor Day. "It's a long way to come from LA to Montreal, and he comes," Schirripa says. "He came all the way in to do that. That was a big favor, man. He didn't do it for the money. He did it to help a friend."

His cameo as "Bobby Eggs," a degenerate gambler deep in debt to the mob, was the most pure physical comedy Jim had ever done, an extended slapstick sequence in which he thinks the kid has come to harm him, and ends up badly injuring himself, over and over, as Nicky tries to help. Terrified, he finally gives up and hands over the money, begging, "Just stay away! Take it, tell him, it's all there!" It's only one short scene, but he's wonderful. Just like he always was.

He also made a brief appearance in *Elaine Stritch: Shoot Me*, directed by Chiemi Karasawa, who had been script supervisor on a handful of *Sopranos* episodes and several of his films—including *Romance & Cigarettes*, where he'd shared a memorable scene with the divine Ms. Stritch. (He was hungover at the time, according to the legendary actress, "and I love, love, love James Gandolfini, but not on a bad day. He's got more good days than bad days now. I'm very proud of him, he's doing fine.") He gets off one of the documentary's most quotable lines: "If we'd both met when we were thirty-five, I have no doubt that we'd have had a torrid love affair, which would have ended very badly."

While Karasawa was making the film, Stritch played the Walt Disney Concert Hall in Los Angeles, and Jim came to see her. Afterward, the director spotted Jim standing in a line, "probably one hundred people long," waiting to see Stritch in her dressing room.

"Oh, my God, I didn't even know you were in the audience," she said. "Come on, let's come up!"

"No, no," Jim insisted. "I want to wait. I mean, there's all these people."

"He wasn't going to take the privilege of being Jim Gandolfini," Karasawa says. "He didn't see himself as that kind of person."

FROM THE BEGINNING, JIM AND Deborah had wanted to start a family. Finally, through the IVF process, they were able to welcome a child into the world on October 10, 2012—a daughter, whom they named Liliana Ruth Gandolfini. Karen Duffy saw Jim a few months later. "I was asking about Michael, asking about Liliana," she recalls. "And he just was incandescent with happiness of where he was, and that was so beautiful."

They were at a birthday party at the home of *Sopranos* executive producer Brad Grey, who'd bought Frank Sinatra's former home. "I remember standing outside in LA, at the pool where Frank Sinatra was probably doing cannonballs with Sammy and Dean, and we were just—we couldn't believe it," she says. They'd both come a long, long way since Park Ridge High School.

"He liked living in LA," says Nancy Sanders. "He liked his Birkenstock shoes. He liked the uniform that he wore in LA. . . . He was happier." She and Armstrong visited him and Deborah at their home, shortly after Lily's birth. "It was like a Saturday or a Sunday," she recalls, "and he had wine and cheese, and he was running around like a little girl trying to make us happy, you know, *Do you want anything to drink?*"

Many of his East Coast friends and colleagues met Liliana for the first time on the day before Easter in 2013, at a get-together at the Tribeca apartment. Much of his family was there, along with some *Sopranos* cast and crew. After Steve Schirripa walked in, Tony Sirico immediately accosted him: "Hey, have you said hello to the boss yet?"

"He's not the boss anymore," Schirripa replied. When he glanced at Jim, he was struck by how relieved his friend was to be free of all that. "He was happy," Schirripa says. "He was really happy, in a good mood, and he loved that baby, and he loved his son Michael. Just loved, loved his kids."

Karasawa was struck by something else that day, beyond his sense of inner peace and happiness. "He was heavier than I've ever seen him," she says. He was likely substituting (as so many addicts do) food for substances; he was now modifying his old joke to call himself a "300-pound Woody Allen."

"And he was really pale," Karasawa says. "I remember thinking, *God, I hope somebody is on this, because he just does not look well.*"

GANDOLFINI HAD SPENT THE PAST year trying to get a project near and dear to his heart off the ground at HBO: a series adaptation of *Big Dead Place*, Nick Johnson's 2005 nonfiction account of life at McMurdo Station in Antarctica, where scientists, bureaucrats, and blue-collar grunts work side by side. It offered up endless possibilities for *M*A*S*H*-style satire, and pathos, but "what really interested Jim about it was that it was kind of like a high school," says Attaboy Films' Tom Richardson. "You're stuck in this location, you don't have a lot of ability to get out, your communication's limited . . . and you're all sitting around the same tables, eating dinner at the same time, and we go into the same room to watch the same movies, and you've got to talk to each other. You're all you have with each other."

Jim not only wanted to produce the show, but star in it. "*Big Dead Place* was honestly his passion project," Armstrong says. "He was hoping that was going to get to a place where it was going to be green-lit when *The Night Of* happened." In the latter, an adaptation of the BBC series *Criminal Justice*, he would play a down-on-his-luck defense attorney, desperate for a client, who gets wrapped up in a seemingly unwinnable murder case; the series would follow him on that one case throughout the season. The esteemed crime novelist and screenwriter Richard Price would write the script; Jim's *A Civil Action* and *All the King's Men* director Steven Zaillian would helm the pilot, after which point HBO would decide if it wanted to pick it up for more episodes.

"Since we originally thought of it as a series, he asked me, 'What's going to happen to my character in subsequent seasons?'" recalled Zaillian. "I said, 'I don't know, I'll be lucky to survive this first one, but if I have to guess, I'd say you'll probably end up in jail.' He lit up and said, 'That's good enough for me.'" They shot the pilot in the fall of 2012, and Zaillian edited it in early 2013, waiting for word from HBO to make more.

In the meantime, Attaboy began work on a third feature-length documentary with Jon Alpert and the DCTV crew. *From Schoolhouse to Jailhouse* would focus on literacy in prisons, and specifically the likelihood of students failed by public schools ending up incarcerated. It was an especially personal and important story to Jim. Michael Gandolfini explained:

> I have dyslexia and ADHD. My dad definitely had ADHD, and maybe a little bit of dyslexia, too, with some of those numbers and math. But it's a testament to my dad—he had sympathy for all different groups, right? The veterans, people in the jail system; it's anyone who feels that they're being held back for any reason, that there is a community of people that want to hear them speak, people that will be patient with them. Because sometimes if you just give them a moment, that's all they need to be remarkable and do remarkable things.

Alpert started setting up shoots and interviews for the summer, and Jim began recording voice tracks. "He would have been the narrator of the film, and done some interviews," Tom Richardson says, adding with a chuckle, "and him and Jon would have fought about how much he would be on camera. And we would see who would have won at the end of the day." In the meantime, in March 2013, he reported to Flatlands, Sheepshead Bay, and Marine Park, all in Brooklyn, to shoot what was then called *Animal Rescue*, a Dennis Lehane adaptation from director Michaël R. Roskam, a Belgian filmmaker whose feature *Bullhead* had crossed over to American art houses. Tom Hardy and Noomi Rapace would star; Jim would play the supporting role of "Cousin Marv," a bar owner and small-time criminal.

"I guarantee you," Susan Aston says, emotion taking over her voice, "I mean, this is me talking, not him. He would not have taken that role if he would have known it was his last one. Because he wouldn't want to be remembered as that. When he sent me the script, I said, 'OK, you told me you didn't want to play any more thugs. This is a thug. Do you want to play it? Why are you taking it?' And he said, 'Well, you know, it would fit into this, that, I don't know, life.'"

Wary of the inevitable comparisons, Jim focused on giving *this* thug his own distinctive look and sound. He alters the Tony Soprano dialect, making it more guttural, to give it a proper Brooklyn flavor. He retained his *Enough Said* beard, sprinkled with gray. Marv wears tracksuits, but older and uglier ones than Tony would, often under his leather jacket and page-boy cap. And then there are the glasses—it's like the entire character is in those glasses, which are big and uncool, a middle-aged man's glasses, the eyewear of a man who has all but given up. "Those were not slept on. Those were well thought out," Aston says. "We looked at *lots* of glasses. I don't remember who was bringing them over to the apartment, but somebody was bringing over different things for us to look at. It wasn't the production that supplied them."

Cousin Marv was a supporting role, but a large one—even larger once he was cast, and screenwriter Lahane started adding new lines and scenes for him. So Jim was present for much of the eight-week shoot in Brooklyn, where residents responded to him with the expected reverence, much to his embarrassment. "It was almost like he would try to hide among all the people, that was how he tried to disappear," said director Roskam. "And it was an irony, you know, that he was always the tallest guy in the room. He could not hide."

Mark Holstrom was the owner of the shuttered bar on Flatlands Avenue that doubled as Cousin Marv's home base in the film. "I was a big fan of 'The Sopranos' and thought Gandolfini was a tremendous actor," he told the *Daily News*. "When I came to the set it was hectic. I saw him but I didn't

Gandolfini with *The Drop* director Michaël R. Roskam. (Courtesy Fox Searchlight Pictures/Photofest.)

impose myself on him. Then he walks through the crowd, puts out his hand and says, 'Hi, I'm Jimmy.' He had such a regular-guy way about him."

During one of the shooting days at Holstrom's bar, Gandolfini was treated to a surprise visitor. "I pranced in the saloon door in the middle of a rolling scene," Tony Sirico said. "Jimmy had no idea I was coming. I slammed my palm on the bar and said, 'Wo, whadda I gotta do to get a drink around here?' Everybody was stunned. When Jimmy saw me, he broke up laughing and hugged me like a big teddy bear."

Jim was excited to work with Hardy, an energetic and chameleonic young British actor. The feeling was mutual—the intensely serious actor had a hard time keeping character during Jim's laugh lines. "There's a scene where he said to [my character], 'It's just a dog, it's not like your long-lost relative that turned up with a colostomy bag hanging out of his ass saying, "I'm yours now,"' Hardy said, laughing. "And the way he said it, even in the cut of the movie, you can see that I can't hold myself together. Normally I'm good at keeping a deadpan face, but Jimmy was funny in a way that was electric."

He's funny in the picture, and more often tragic—the performance isn't quite as much of a de-glammed inversion of Tony Soprano as *Killing Them Softly*, but it lands along the same lines. He portrays Marv as a grinder whose ship has never come in, and who cannot rise above his constant sense of disappointment. It's a good performance in a decent little crime thriller that, through no fault of its own, would play forevermore like an elegy.

"I FELT AFTER *SOPRANOS*," LORRAINE Bracco says, "Jimmy was a very happy man. He found Deborah, he just had a baby girl. He was living in LA. He had Michael. He was happy; he was accepting his success." New projects were continuing to line up at a rapid pace. In mid-May, after initially passing on the pilot, HBO announced that it had picked up *Criminal Justice* as a seven-episode limited series; Jim would stay on as star and executive producer, via Attaboy Films. The company had also set up an HBO original movie called *Bone Wars*, reuniting Jim and *Burt Wonderstone* co-star Steve Carell as rival paleontologists; *Big Dead Place* was also still in play there. A few weeks later, CBS picked up the *Taxi-22* series that Attaboy had developed at HBO, with Jim executive-producing but no longer starring.

On May 20, 2013, he joined his old *Sopranos* crew for the premiere of *Nicky Deuce* at the ArcLight Hollywood. "It was a little premiere, but there's a lot of great pictures," Steve Schirripa says. "That's the last time I saw him." In their book *Woke Up This Morning*, Schirripa and Michael Imperioli write that Jim "was in a wonderful mood at the premiere party. There's a photo somewhere of the two of us and Jim, smiling for the camera, looking like three guys without a care in the world. Which, for one brief moment in time, we were."

THAT SUMMER, JIM WAS INVITED to attend the 59th annual Taormina Film Fest in Sicily, where he would participate in an onstage conversation on June 22 with Italian director Gabriele Muccino (who'd crossed over to Hollywood success a few years earlier with *The Pursuit of Happyness*), receive the "Taormina City Prize," and appear at the closing ceremony alongside Marisa Tomei. He decided to make it into a family vacation, taking along

Michael Imperioli, Steve Schirripa, and Jim at the *Nicky Deuce* premiere. (Courtesy WENN Rights Ltd / Alamy Stock Photo.)

thirteen-year-old Michael for some father-son bonding. They'd fly into Rome, spend a couple of days sightseeing, and meet up with Jim's sister Leta (who would fly in from Paris) before heading to Taormina.

The Gandolfini boys landed on Tuesday, June 18. They had dinner that night at the Sabatini restaurant off Rome's Piazza di Santa Maria; an American tourist at a nearby table snapped a picture of a relaxed-looking Jim enjoying some gnocchi. On Wednesday, they went to the Vatican, exploring the Egyptian collection at the Musei Vaticani, where another American tourist, honeymooning Priscilla McGlaughlin of Philadelphia, snuck a few photos as well. "It's eerie because she took the picture through a glass case, and on either side of him, he's flanked by coffin lids with hieroglyphics from the Book of the Dead," said her husband, John McGlaughlin. "We didn't think anything of it at the time."

Jim and Michael went out for dinner, and then headed back to their hotel, the Boscolo Exedra Roma. And it was there, on the evening of June 19, 2013, that James Gandolfini's big heart finally gave out.

CHAPTER 24

JIM

MICHAEL GANDOLFINI FOUND HIS FATHER on the floor, in the bathroom of their suite, at approximately 10 P.M. He immediately called the front desk of the Boscolo Exedra for assistance; paramedics arrived quickly thereafter, wheeling Jim, still alive but in cardiac arrest, from room 449 into a waiting ambulance. They began resuscitation procedures while en route to Policlinico Umberto I hospital in central Rome, arriving at around 10:40 P.M.

"The resuscitation maneuvers, including heart massage etc., continued for 40 minutes," Claudio Modini, the emergency room chief, told Reuters. "Then, seeing no electric activity from the heart, this was interrupted and we declared James dead." He was fifty-one years old.

Leta Gandolfini's flight to Rome had landed just before Michael discovered Jim in distress, and she was in a taxi to the hotel while they were on their way to the hospital. She formally identified the body at the Rome morgue the following day, when the autopsy found that Jim had died of a massive heart attack. The body showed no signs that drugs or alcohol were a factor.

His managers, Mark Armstrong and Nancy Sanders, got the call shortly after he was pronounced dead. "I remember I kind of dropped to the floor, with my head in my hands," Sanders says, still emotional at the memory. They issued the official public statement: "It is with immense sorrow that we report our client James Gandolfini passed away today while on holiday in Rome, Italy. Our hearts are shattered and we will miss him deeply. He and his family were part of our family for many years and we are all grieving."

Marcy caught the first flight out of Los Angeles to be with Michael. Tom Richardson got on a plane from New York to ward off the media and coordinate the complicated process of getting Gandolfini's body back to the States, where word of his death was spreading to stunned friends, colleagues, and fans. David Chase issued one of the first and most eloquent statements:

> He was a genius. Anyone who saw him even in the smallest of his performances knows that. He is one of the greatest actors of this or any time. A great deal of that genius resided in those sad eyes. I remember telling him many times, "You don't get it. You're like Mozart." There would be silence at the other end of the phone. For Deborah and Michael and Liliana this is crushing. And it's bad for the rest of the world. He wasn't easy sometimes. But he was my partner, he was my brother in ways I can't explain and never will be able to explain.

"I was in my house with my kids, and I was just waking up from a nap when someone came upstairs," Edie Falco recalls. "I was still sort of half asleep, in a kind of a fog, and I couldn't make sense of what he was telling me. It took a while for me to actually understand what he was saying to me. It was one of those moments, and we all have them, when you feel your DNA shift a little bit."

Steve Schirripa was at a Yankees game when his business manager called with the news. "I felt my legs come out from under me a little bit," he says. "I was a mess. I was a mess for days. I don't know why, you know. I don't think you think about how would you feel when someone passes away, but I was a fucking mess. Boy, it really was close to home."

"I was at a poker table," Robert Iler says. "I got a phone call from Vince [Curatola], who besides Jamie[-Lynn] is probably the person I'm closest to now. And he told me what had happened, and I just kind of was like, *OK*, and I hung up the phone and I stayed at the poker table. I just stayed there playing poker, because it was just shock. . . . And I remember looking down, and my phone went off. And it was Jamie and it just said, *I love you*. And that was it. I can't even think about it now."

Chiemi Karasawa found out via a call from Elaine Stritch; her documentary on Stritch, with Jim's brief but memorable appearance, was awaiting distribution. "She goes *Chiem, listen*, and she was putting her phone up to the television," Karasawa says. "And she's like, *I can't believe it*. I can hear her crying. She's like, *How could he do this to us?*"

Testimonials and tributes poured forth from his fellow actors and friends. "When I heard of James' passing," Kristen Stewart wrote in a statement to *Entertainment Weekly*, "I was in New Orleans, where we met shooting, and every memory flooded back and gutted me. I'll hold that time near to me forever. He was immeasurably great." Brad Pitt wrote that he was "gutted by this loss," calling Gandolfini "a ferocious actor, a gentle soul and a genuinely funny man." His three-time director Steven Zaillian said, "I worked with Jim before 'The Sopranos' and after it, and throughout these many years he has always been the same man. A real man, like they don't make anymore."

On *Good Morning America*, John Travolta vowed to look out for Jim's family. "His little boy, I watched him grow up, and his new little girl. We'll just make sure they're taken care of. That's the whole idea." He saw this as repaying a debt of gratitude; when Travolta's son Jett died suddenly and tragically in 2009, he said, Jim turned up unannounced at Travolta's Florida home and "he would not leave Florida until I was okay, or he felt that I would be fine."

"It just didn't make sense to me," *Sopranos* director Terence Winter said. "I somehow was under the mistaken impression that this guy was indestructible." True enough, though some who knew him were careful to clarify the distinctions between "surprised" and "shocked." Karasawa explains, "I'll always remember Edie saying it's shocking, but it's not surprising. And everybody sort of agreed with that. Just because of the way he lived his life." David Chase concurred. "I wasn't as shocked as you might think. It was unbelievable, but I wasn't like, 'That's impossible,'" he explained. "He was hard on his body."

"He was a larger-than-life guy," says *Last Castle* director Rod Lurie. "He lived life very large. On the one hand, he seemed very athletically inclined. On the other hand, I never saw him pay particular attention to his health." *Sopranos* cinematographer Phil Abraham mostly felt that it was just unfair: "How could that be? He had just had a baby, he had just gotten married. . . . All these things were finally coming together for him."

"He was the healthiest, happiest, and most content toward the end, that's for sure," Sanders confirms. "Whether he knew it was ending, or whether he didn't and was reclaiming his life. . . . He just had grown up, you know? He had a new wife, a baby, all that kind of stuff. I think he died a happier man."

Those who knew him weren't mourning alone. "When he passed away, I remember we went to a place we used to hang out a lot—Walker's, it's called, in Tribeca," Steve Schirripa says. "We used to always be in there. I was eating dinner, and a guy came over to me and he said, *I'm sorry about your friend. The whole city is sad.* And it's true."

Front-page news: James Gandolfini's death in June 2013.
(Courtesy Richard Levine / Alamy Stock Photo.)

The whole state of New Jersey was equally crushed. Governor Chris Christie ordered government buildings in the Garden State to fly flags at half-staff on the Monday following Jim's passing. "James Gandolfini was a fine actor, a Rutgers alum and a true Jersey guy," Christie said. "I was a huge fan of his and the character he played so authentically, Tony Soprano." Holsten's, the ice cream parlor in Bloomfield where the final scene of *The Sopranos* had been shot, closed off the booth where the family had sat with a "reserved" sign, "out of respect for him," owner Chris Carley told the *Daily News*. Satin Dolls, the real-life strip club that doubled as the Bada Bing, put the message "THANK YOU JIMMY—FAREWELL BOSS" on its front signage, and placed a framed poster of Gandolfini in the spot at the bar where Tony typically perched.

But the biggest Jersey tribute came the night after Jim's death, when Bruce Springsteen stepped up to the mic twelve songs into a concert in Coventry, England (with Steven Van Zandt, of course, on guitar) and announced that he and the E Street Band would play their iconic album *Born to Run*, in its entirety, dedicating the performance to Jim. The Great White Way followed suit the following week, dimming the lights on Broadway at 8 P.M. on Wednesday, June 26, in Gandolfini's honor. "Dimming the lights is a special tribute to a great artist," said Paul Libin, executive vice president of Jujamcyn Theaters. "He was a special treasure."

THE TABLOIDS, AS WAS THEIR custom, infected their often thorough and reverential coverage of Gandolfini's death with shots of ghoulishness and bad taste. The *National Enquirer* re-ran its October 2002 interview, a PR move during the divorce from Marcy, with a new intro: "In an Exclusive ENQUIRER INTERVIEW with the late JAMES GANDFOLINI [*sic*] he revealed his debauched drug filled, boozy and sex-crazed lifestyle that may have caused his sudden death at age 51." The *New York Daily News* followed up its front-page TONY'S DEAD with interior headlines like "MOB" STAR'S SHOCK ENDING and HIS CAREER HIT LIST; the *New York Post* went with LAST ACT FOR TONY SOPRANO and GRIEVING FOR HEAD OF FAMILY. Both papers devoted multiple articles to the peculiar story of an Italian paramedic accused of stealing Gandolfini's $3,000 Submariner watch while he was in the ambulance in his last hour on earth; they also spilled copious ink on the inconsequential story of New York governor Andrew Cuomo's girlfriend Sandra Lee being the next inhabitant of Jim's suite at the Exedra.

But most vile, and typical, was the *Post*'s day two coverage. A front page headline blared THE LAST SUPPER below the subhead BIG TONY'S BIG BINGE IN ROME; the story by Rebecca Rosenberg, Jamie Schram, and Dan McCleod continued inside, with the secondary headline DEADLY BADA BINGE FOR TONY and the subhead ALCOHOLIC STAR BOOZED IT UP AND STUFFED SELF WITH FRIED FOOD AT FINAL MEAL, breathlessly reporting that "Gandolfini guzzled four shots of rum, two piña coladas, and two beers at dinner with his son—while he chowed down on two orders of fried king prawns and a 'large portion' of foie gras, a hotel source in Rome said."

Aside from the inaccuracy of the report—family spokesman Michael Kobold, in announcing the (natural causes) results of the autopsy, pointed out that "the piña coladas were virgin piña coladas; they were drunk by his son"—the *Post*'s big scoop was an astonishing example of the New York tabs' career-long insistence on having it both ways with Gandolfini. They had always ridden the train of the *Sopranos* popularity, while simultaneously taking every opportunity to cut Jim down for his weight, his looks, his addictions, or the storms of his personal life. Here, the *Post* was capitalizing on its readers' grief, paying homage out of one side of their collective mouths and whispering tacky slander from another; a Steve Schirripa–penned tribute, detailing Jim's generosity and kindness (including the story of the $36,000 checks), ran a few pages after the LAST SUPPER reporting. And that story, which all but accused Gandolfini of drinking himself to death in front of his kid, was accompanied by a tender photo of Jim kissing Michael on the top of his head. The wheels of New York media would continue to spin apace.

MARIO SESTI AND TIZIANA ROCCA, organizers of the Taormina Film Fest that had brought the Gandolfinis to Italy in the first place, told the Associated Press they had spoken to Jim hours before his death, "and he was very happy to receive this prize and be able to travel to Italy.

"He was the American actor that better than anyone else has been able to interpret the Italian-American with his personality full of contrasts, ambition, pain, humor. He was the face of the golden age of television, but also a memorable film actor," they commented in a statement. The festival hastily canceled his scheduled events and organized a closing-night tribute, emceed by *Variety* executive editor Steven Gaydos, who called Gandolfini "an actor who had in two decades established himself as an irreplaceable presence in television and film."

A much more elaborate tribute was being planned back in the States—once Gandolfini's body could be transported there. "In Italy it can take up to ten days to get all the necessary documents and paperwork to repatriate the body," Kobold told the press. "We are looking forward to working with the Italian government and officials to shorten that process. It looks like they're doing everything on their end, which is wonderful, so that we can get Jim's body back sooner." Ultimately, Bill and Hillary Clinton, as well as the latter's successor as secretary of state, John Kerry, intervened to expedite the matter; Gandolfini's remains would leave Rome via private plane on June 23, less than a week after his death, arriving at Newark Airport en route to a private, family wake at the Robert Spearing Funeral Home in Park Ridge on the 25th.

The following day, Thursday, June 26, the public service was held—not in New Jersey but in New York, and not at a Catholic church but an Episcopal one, the Cathedral of Saint John the Divine. "St. John's is the fourth-largest Christian church in the world," explained the *New Yorker*'s

Joan Acocella. "Whoever chose that venue knew that there was going to be a crowd."

And indeed there was. More than fifteen hundred friends, colleagues, family members, and fans turned up to say goodbye to a one-of-a-kind talent and man. "We thought we walked into the Vatican," Vincent Pastore recalls. "It was very, very sad, but a lot of people loved him. Lotta people loved him." Most of the *Sopranos* cast and crew reunited, somewhat surrealistically, considering how many fictional funerals they'd attended together over that decade; "It was like a scene we shot," Jamie-Lynn Sigler said. "We'd done this so many times before." (Robert Iler didn't attend. "I was like, *Jim's gone.* I just remember being angry and being like, *Jim's not there. Why the fuck would I go?*" he explains. "Just having zero understanding of what I have now, which is like, No, you go there for the other people, you go there for the family, you go there for yourself.")

Chris Christie showed up, and Jim's old friend Mario Batali. Alec Baldwin was there, and John Turturro, and Marcia Gay Harden; so were Steve Carell, Dick Cavett, Chris Noth, and Juliana Margulies. The coffin was wheeled in as the service began, covered in a purple and red shroud. Two hymns were sung: "O God, Our Help in Ages Past" and "Christ the Lord Is Risen Today." The baritone Jesse Blumberg sang "Bring Him Home" from *Les Misérables.* The Reverend Dean James A. Kowalski delivered the homily.

There were four eulogists. Deborah Lin Gandolfini spoke first. "My husband was an honest, kind, and loving man. Ironically," she said, indicating the crowd, "he was extremely private." She ended her remembrance with a simple, "I love you Jim, and I always will. Rest in peace." Then came Tom Richardson, who said Jim was "the most giving and generous person that everyone here has ever known." He described the intensity (in strength and duration) of his longtime friend and business partner's hugs, and asked everyone in attendance to hug those next to them in Jim's honor. "Close your eyes and think of Jim and hug too tight," he suggested.

Susan Aston spoke next, telling the "What's the worst that could happen? We suck?!" story from their days as struggling young actors. "These were liberating words of wisdom," she said, "his knowing that in order to create well, one has to be willing to make a mess of things. One has to be willing to miss the mark. One has to remain vulnerable and be willing to be seen as human every day, over and over again." And she recalled the last time they spoke, when he told her he'd turned down a good film role that would shoot over the summer, because he wanted to spend his traditional time at the Shore with his family. "I don't want to lose any time with Michael and Lily," he'd told her. "Quality of life, time with family and friends, that's more important than all of this stuff."

David Chase spoke last. "I don't like speaking in front of people, so I wasn't happy about that, but I knew I had to do it," he said, of that day. "I felt it was part of the job description. I couldn't face it. That's why I decided to make it a letter to him. I couldn't figure out how else to do it. Like I had to be in character or something."

"I am so honored and touched," he read, in his "letter" to Jim. "I'm also really scared, and I say that because you, of all people, understand this. I would like to run away and then call you four days from now from the beauty parlor. . . .

"I want to do a good job because I love you, and because *you* always did a good job," Chase continued. "I think your talent is that you can take in the immensity of humankind and the universe and shine it back out to the rest of us like a huge, bright light. And I believe that only a pure soul, like a child, could do that really well. And that was you."

The service ended, and the pallbearers carried Jim's coffin from the church. Among them was Michael Gandolfini, who took a moment to rest both hands atop his father's casket. Baby Liliana was in attendance as well. "I watched Deb bouncing Lily on her lap, this six-month-old baby," Chiemi Karasawa says. "And I just thought to myself, this has got to be the saddest day in the world."

"We all went to a restaurant afterward," Juliana Margulies recalls. "And (Michael) got up on a table and he started talking about his father in the most, I mean, I couldn't—everyone was sobbing. And he was talking to his little sister, saying *I will make sure you know who this man was.* Because she was only a baby. And I thought, it takes a special kind of parent to make that kind of kid."

"They were putting the coffin into the hearse," documentarian and friend Jon Alpert said. "And all the cars were lined up outside the church and they were gonna go to the cemetery and bury him." And then Alpert heard a whistle. "I look up, and this giant eagle comes swooping down over the hearse, and sits up on top of the church and looks down on everybody. And it was Jim. And it stayed there, and looked at everybody for about a minute. And as the cars drove away, it flapped away and went up to the sky."

THERE WOULD BE MORE TRIBUTES. The following September, Gandolfini received a special salute at the primetime Emmys, with a personal testimonial delivered by Edie Falco. Much of the cast reunited the following month for the Wounded Warrior Project's second annual Carry Forward Awards, where Chase introduced the inaugural James Gandolfini Award, christened for charitable considerations that extended even into his death—when funeral services were announced, the family asked that mourners make a donation to the organization in lieu of sending flowers. Deborah, Michael, and Jim's sister Johanna Antonacci were all in attendance; the award was given to Tony Sirico, Jim's traveling companion on all those USO trips. And that December, Michael and several members of the cast traveled to Park Ridge, New Jersey, for a tribute to its favorite son, including the dedication of a section of the town's Park Avenue; "James Gandolfini Way" sits at the intersection of Park and Kinderkamack Road, about ten minutes up the hill from where Jim grew up.

"James Gandolfini Way" in Park Ridge, as it looks today. (Author's collection.)

And there were projects in the pipeline to puzzle out. The most disappointing outcome was for his third documentary, *From Schoolhouse to Jailhouse*; according to Jon Alpert, "the day Jim died, HBO killed the film to collect the insurance. For them, he was worth more dead than alive. And they killed it." (He still hopes to complete the project. "The family has been asking us to resurrect this," he says, "to bring this out as one last tribute to the documentary work and the things that Jim was committed to.") *Taxi-22* finally moved forward at CBS the following year, with John Leguizamo in the leading role, but the pilot did not go to series.

Criminal Justice was another question mark. With only the pilot completed, Jim's death put the miniseries in limbo. A month later, HBO programming head Michael Lombardo told the Television Critics Association, "I can't imagine us airing the pilot with James in it," and they never have. As far as the show itself, Lombardo said, "It's taken some time to be able to have conversations with Steve about the future of that."

"I loved James and wasn't sure I wanted to continue without him," Steve Zaillian said. "HBO wasn't sure, either. We were all just so saddened by his death. Eventually, Richard and I continued working on the story and scripts. That would take about a year, and at some point during it, I started thinking about who might be able to play James's part."

That fall, HBO announced that Robert De Niro would take over the role, with Lombardo and HBO CEO Richard Plepler pinpointing Mr. De Niro as their only choice to fill Jim's shoes. They would rethink that when De Niro backed out due to concerns over the lengthy shooting schedule, instead offering the opportunity to Jim's friend and collaborator, *Romance & Cigarettes* director, and acclaimed character actor John Turturro.

"John was like, *I don't want to take a role that James Gandolfini had, I don't want to try and fill those shoes*," says Mark Armstrong, who was one of the show's executive producers. "And we explained to him that Jim would be so proud for him to take this part." Turturro watched the original pilot, and was relieved to find that Gandolfini only came in briefly, near the episode's end. "I didn't know how big a part he had done," Turturro said. "Say if he had done, like, the whole thing, I would have been 'Ahhh, oh my God, I have to erase that from my memory.' I had nothing really to erase." He wrote to Deborah, got her blessing, and signed on in 2014, visiting the same

Manhattan Criminal Court rooms that Jim had to research the role. The show premiered in the summer of 2016 under the new title *The Night Of*, and was such a hit for HBO that it also briefly resurrected *Big Dead Place*, with regular *Sopranos* director Tim Van Patten attached to helm and executive-produce, though it would again wither on the vine.

In the meantime, there were two more films to release. Fox Searchlight premiered *Enough Said* at the Toronto International Film Festival before releasing it to theaters on September 18, 2013, which would have been Jim's fifty-second birthday. At the New York premiere on September 16, when Nicole Holofcener brought the cast up for introductions, her emotions overwhelmed her. "Obviously, Jim is not here," Holofcener said, her voice breaking. "And I'm very sad that he's not standing here with us. He hadn't seen the movie. Maybe he's watching."

"This movie will make you laugh and leave you in tears," wrote the *New York Times*' A. O. Scott. "Some of the pathos is the accidental byproduct of seeing Mr. Gandolfini, so playful and alive, in one of his final major movie roles and feeling once again the loss of his remarkable gift." In the *New Yorker*, David Denby praised how "Gandolfini, without bullying his way through scenes or hiding Albert's need for love, makes his character a man who knows that dignity is something you must hold on to in life if any relationship is going to work at all." The *New York Daily News*' Joe Neumaier may have summed it up best: "What a treat it is to discover a totally new actor inside one we already loved. And how sad to know we won't see that from him again."

Animal Rescue arrived in theaters nearly a full year later, also debuting at Toronto, under the new title *The Drop*; critics were less kind to the movie, but just as taken with Gandolfini's performance in it, and thankful for one more opportunity to watch him work. Scott wrote, "The counterpoint between Mr. Hardy, compact and intense, and Mr. Gandolfini, expansive and subtle, is engaging (though also sad, of course)." Neumaier opined, "Gandolfini is on familiar territory here, but as always, he layers it with something extra."

"Unsurprisingly," wrote *Variety*'s Justin Chang, "it's Gandolfini who offers the most invaluable support here, putting across Cousin Marv's cynicism and capacity for reckless violence in a few deft, understated strokes, certainly all that's needed from an actor whose iconic tough-guy stature can hardly be overestimated. 'The Drop' may not be as moving or revelatory a final showcase for Gandolfini's talents as last year's 'Enough Said,' but it's a fitting, well-played note to end on nonetheless."

AND THERE WAS ALWAYS *THE SOPRANOS*, living on in perpetuity, thanks to reruns, DVDs and Blu-rays, and eventually, its omnipresence on HBO's various streaming services. "This is a show that's really obsessed, among other things, with mortality and legacy," noted longtime chronicler Alan Sepinwall, who asked Chase, "With Jim dying so young, do you feel differently about the show in any way?"

"Yes, there is an extra dimension," Chase said. "There is. And I should be the last person to say this, but that's also multiplied somehow because of how the show ended. Jim didn't have the death scene on the show, and yet he did have a real one, a surprising one where you thought, 'What? Who the fuck died? You're kidding me!'"

The Sopranos maintained an extraordinarily healthy fandom for a show that had been off the air for so long, with fans still flocking to *Sopranos* conventions and location tours. And then, in 2020, the show got an odd, unexpected boost from a global pandemic. Mere days into the COVID-19 lockdown, HBO made several of its signature shows available for free to quarantined Americans; chief among them was *The Sopranos*. Viewership went up 200 percent. Coincidentally, Michael Imperioli and Steve Schirripa had been planning to launch a "rewatch" podcast, revisiting the show episode by episode with guests from the cast and crew, and after briefly contemplating postponing, they dropped the first episode of *Talking Sopranos* on April 6. It grew to five million downloads by September, scoring the duo a deal to turn its segments into *Woke Up This Morning*, a best-selling oral history of the show.

The Sopranos found particular purchase among viewers who were too young to watch it when it originally aired—some who weren't even born yet. But they embraced it, often from an explicitly leftist perspective. Writing about this phenomenon in the *New York Times*, Willy Staley theorized, "The show's depiction of contemporary America as relentlessly banal and hollow is plainly at the core of the current interest in the show, which coincides with an era of crisis across just about every major institution in American life." Tony Soprano, bleary-eyed and bathrobed, had become a Millennial and Zoomer icon.

So there was a new hunger for *Sopranos*-related product. As early as 2014, Chase had indicated his interest in putting together a prequel film. "Even if I did it, it wouldn't be *The Sopranos* that was on the air—obviously at least one person is gone that we would need," he told the Associated Press. "There are a couple of eras that would be interesting for me to talk about, about Newark, N.J. One would be (the) late '60s, early '70s, about all the racial animosity, or the beginning, the really true beginning of the flood of drugs."

That idea grew into his screenplay *The Many Saints of Newark*. The primary focus was on Dickie Moltisanti (Alessandro Nivola), father to Imperioli's Christopher and cousin of Falco's Carmela. But there was a supporting role for young Tony Soprano, an impressionable and sensitive teenager, and in January 2019, Deadline reported that the no-brainer casting choice for the role was Michael Gandolfini, then nineteen and already an HBO vet thanks to his stellar supporting work on the network's '70s-set series *The Deuce*.

"I think David and I both knew it was right before we even auditioned him, in a way," explained Alan Taylor, the frequent *Sopranos* director who took on that job for *Many Saints*. "I think we did a pretty thorough session, we actually made him work. But karmically it was so strong, and then getting to know him, I just felt so confirmed in it. And then the day before we shot, we went out to dinner. And he stood up at one point and said, 'I just want to thank everybody here for giving me a chance to say hello to my dad again and say goodbye again.' And just the whole house was like, you know, not a dry eye."

The job presented a unique challenge for the young Gandolfini. "My dad really didn't want me to see Tony Soprano," he told *Esquire*. "I saw a very filtered version of the show. I'd watch scenes where someone was taking out the trash, or Tony was buttoning his shirt." So he watched *The Sopranos* from start to finish before auditioning to take on the role that had made his dad a star. He found the performance astonishing, overcome while describing Jim's sing-along to the Chi-Lites' "Oh Girl" in the season 4 episode "Watching Too Much Television." "He starts singing, and then he starts crying, and then he gets mad at himself because he's crying, and then he laughs at himself," the young Gandolfini marveled. "He literally spans like, four emotions in the matter of forty seconds! And they're all so grounded and I remember being blown away by him."

By the time *The Many Saints of Newark* was released in the fall of 2021, Michael could admit that the character wasn't all that he had in common with his father: He was a recovering alcoholic, with three years of sobriety.

"I had this disease in me, it runs in my family, and I'm so proud that I'm sober," he said. "I had to get sober young because I knew that from history and from just my acting out, I sort of have this disease. And I was depressed and low and it wasn't going to help me out. I'm very vocal about my sobriety, because it's saved my life and it's allowed me to have gratitude."

"HE WAS A BIG, LOVABLE motherfucker," Drea de Matteo says, with great emotion. "At the end of the day, that's what he was. He was a big, lovable, insanely talented man, you know?"

"I miss him every day," says Steven Van Zandt. "Personally, I just . . . We had big plans to do things together. And, you know, and I just—I just miss him. But the industry misses him, because he would have been just one of the greatest actors of all time. I mean, he *was* one of the greatest actors of all time, but he would have done a whole lot more work. And it's a real tragedy."

THE DEATH OF JAMES GANDOLFINI at such an early age is indeed a tragedy—a professional loss, to the art of acting, to documentary filmmaking, to whatever other endeavors he might have pursued in his fifties and beyond. And it was an unimaginable personal loss to the friends who loved him, to the son who adored him, and the new family he'd just begun. But perhaps there was some small comfort in framing his passing as the conclusion of his journey. The search that had begun back in Jersey, all those years ago, was finally over. He was no longer driven by drugs and alcohol and self-doubt; he was no longer defined by Tony Soprano. He could be Jim. Just Jim. And he could be at peace with that.

"This is the time of year that he would not be working that hard, where we'd be spending time with him, and we all miss it," says Jon Alpert. "And we've all kept together. It's very unusual—that friends who really weren't friends before they met Jim, and were only with each other because we were all included within this circle, we're all still in touch. My doorbell is ringing. It's somebody, they're all from New Jersey, that I never would have been friends with. And we're all still friends."

"I loved James with all my heart," Susan Aston says, simply. "We were friends for twenty-six years. So, it's just like, I miss him." In early 2023, she was diagnosed with breast cancer. "Yeah, so funny, when I got this cancer, I started dreaming about him, like, all the time. And I was like, *Fuck, you better not be coming to get me, you asshole.*"

In January 2019, Chase, his cast, and several members of the production staff reunited for a twentieth-anniversary event celebrating the *Sopranos'* debut on HBO. Stories were told, running jokes were revisited, the ending was re-litigated, and, of course, James Gandolfini was spoken of in glowing terms—his talent, his generosity, his consideration.

"As soon as we walked in, there's just like, a red carpet and there's all these people congratulating you on how great it was, oh my God, this must feel amazing, twenty years!" Robert Iler says, laughing. "And everybody was just like, *Man, he would fucking hate this.* Like, he would hate these people telling us what a great job we did, you know? And that was the way to smile and remember him and made it feel like he was there, you know?

"By the way, you know what?" Iler adds. "I hate to tell you: He'd probably hate your book. Just because of how nice everyone is gonna be in it, and how much we're gonna talk about how much we love him and how incredible he is. He's *so pissed* right now."

ACKNOWLEDGMENTS

RESEARCHING AND WRITING *GANDOLFINI* WAS the most challenging experience of my career, and I could not have done it without the endless support and encouragement of several wonderful people. First and foremost, I must always thank my best friend and collaborator, Mike Hull, who (as with all my previous books) is not credited as a co-writer but may as well be, so constant and sturdy are his commitment, advice, and motivation. Jori Frascino was an invaluable source of copy edits and general enthusiasm. Amy Dannenmueller had the unenviable task of listening to interviews, cleaning up transcripts, and pulling out good quotes. Hillary Busis was kind enough to work with me on a tribute to Jim for *Vanity Fair*, which provided my initial opportunity to talk to many of his friends and collaborators. And Mark Harris and Matt Zoller Seitz, two of my writing heroes, provided early and important advice on writing, respectively, a good biography, and a good *Sopranos* book.

My editor, Jamison Stoltz, saw this book through all sorts of difficulties—including an aborted first attempt on an entirely different subject—and was a beacon of patience and sage wisdom through all of them. My various hats are off to managing editor Annalea Manalili for her meticulous attention to detail; ditto to our copyeditor, Richard Slovak, and proofreader, Erin Slonaker. And I must also thank Sarah Masterson Hally in production and designer Eli Mock for making it look, well, like a real book, a thing that still excites me to no end.

And, of course, none of this could happen without my wonderful agent, Daniel Greenberg of Levine Greenberg Rostan Literary Agency, a trusted advisor and collaborator who really went through it on this one.

I'm greatly indebted to all of those who gave of their time (some of them on multiple occasions) to talk to me about working with and knowing Jim: Phil Abraham, Jon Alpert, Amy Appleyard, Mark Armstrong, Rosanna Arquette, Susan Aston, Shari Springer Berman, Lorraine Bracco, Rocky Carroll, Mary Collins, Ann Comarato, Vincent Curatola, Tony Danza, Drea De Matteo, Diana Doussant, Karen Duffy, Edie Falco, T.J. Forderaro, Elizabeth Forsyth, Robert Funaro, Christine Gee, Michael Greene, Marcia Gay Harden, Michael Harney, Nicole Holofcener, Robert

Iler, Famke Janssen, Mark Kamine, Chiemi Karasawa, Mimi Kennedy, Steve Kornacki, Julia Louis-Dreyfus, Rod Lurie, John Magaro, Julianna Margulies, Roberto Monticello, Joanna Mulkern, Joe Pantoliano, Vincent Pastore, Robert Pulcini, Kathleen Quinlan, Tom Richardson, Alik Sakharov, Nancy Sanders, Don Scardino, Steve Schirripa, Jake Scott, Steven Van Zandt, Mykelti Williamson, Patty Woo, and Josh Zuckerman. I thank them all for their candor and insight; I also thank the various publicists, agents, managers, and friends who helped make those interviews happen.

I also thank the many fine journalists and hosts who conducted the archival interviews quoted in these pages, particularly Chris Heath, James Lipton, Alan Sepinwall, and Matt Zoller Seitz.

And last, but not least, I appreciate to no end the love and support of my wife, Rebekah, who watched *The Sopranos* for the first time as I wrote this book, and my daughters Lucille and Alice, who I hope will do the same, but many years from now.

NOTES

Introduction

1 **The New York tabloids:** *Post* coverage: *New York Post*, June 20, 2013, New York Public Library (hereafter NYPL). *Daily News* coverage: *New York Daily News*, June 20, 2013, NYPL.

1 **"You can't go on saying . . .":** *James Gandolfini: Tribute to a Friend*, no director credited, HBO, 2013.

2 **I'm not trying to be difficult . . .":** Matt Zoller Seitz, "Gandolfini: Star Quality, Not Attitude," *Newark Star-Ledger*, June 14, 1999, www.nj.com/entertainment/2013/06/james_gandolfini_in_1999_interview_star_quality_not_attitude.html.

2 **"Now, this ain't a hatchet piece . . .":** Author interview with Steve Schirripa, May 12, 2023.

2 **"because it focused . . .":** Personal/private boundaries: Conversations with Michael Gandolfini and Tom Richardson, "James Gandolfini's Documentary Legacy," September 26, 2023, Firehouse: DCTV's Cinema for Documentary Film, New York, firehouse.dctvny.org/websales/pages/info.aspx?evtinfo=399296~2998286f-8e4b-4c31-9017-dcced8ffebb3.

2 **"She would prefer I respect . . .":** Email from Tom Richardson, November 4, 2023.

2 **"He was everything . . .":** Author interview with Joe Pantoliano, May 9, 2023.

2 **"He would say to me . . .":** Schirripa interview.

3 **"It's funny because you can tell . . .":** Author interview with Susan Aston, May 3, 2023.

3 **"One of my best friends . . .":** Author interview with Karen Duffy, May 9, 2023.

4 **a heartfelt testimonial in the *New York Post*:** Steve Schirripa, "Steve Schirripa Remembers James Gandolfini as a Truly Good Fella," *New York Post*, June 21, 2013, nypost.com/2013/06/21/steve-schirripa-remembers-james-gandolfini-as-a-truly-good-fella/.

4 **"He was a searcher . . .":** *James Gandolfini: Tribute to a Friend.*

Chapter 1

5 **1960 census:** Westwood and Park Ridge stats: www.nj.gov/labor/labormarketinformation/assets/PDFs/census/2kpub/njsdcp3.pdf#page=27.

5 **"My father was born . . .":** *Inside the Actors Studio*, "James Gandolfini," season 11, episode 2, aired October 17, 2004.

5 **"other obvious . . .":** Draft registration: Dated February 15, 1942.

5 **"In his youth he was . . .":** John Heilpern, "Curtains for Gandolfini," *Vanity Fair*, March 20, 2009, www.vanityfair.com/culture/2009/04/out-to-lunch-gandolfini200904.

5 **"He talked about 'the War' . . .":** Roger Moore, "Gandolfini Remembers His Father in 'Fade,'" McClatchy-Tribune News Service, January 3, 2013, www.post-gazette.com/ae/movies/2013/01/03/Gandolfini-remembers-his-father-in-Fade/stories/201301030377.

6 **"When they didn't want us . . .":** *Inside the Actors Studio.*

6 **"Loyalty to friends and family . . .":** Chris Heath, "Garden State Warrior: 11 Moments with James Gandolfini," *GQ*, December 2004, www.gq.com/story/james-gandolfini-profile-december-2004.

7 **"There were things . . .":** Stephen Whitty, "James Gandolfini Looms Large in Three Movies," *Newark Star-Ledger*, December 13, 2012, www.nj.com/entertainment/2012/12/james_gandolfini_opens_up_on_m.html.

7 **"My mother had an opinion . . .":** Paul Brownfield, "Married to This Mob," *Los Angeles Times*, April 3, 1999, www.latimes.com/archives/la-xpm-1999-apr-03-ca-23685-story.html.

7 **"Park Ridge, New Jersey, is a great . . .":** Author interview with Elizabeth Forsyth, August 29, 2023.

7 **"It's somewhat of a commuter town . . .":** Duffy interview.

7 **"Richard Nixon . . .":** Nixon in Park Ridge: David M. Zimmer, "President Nixon's North Jersey Home Hits the Market for $1.2 Million. Take a Look Inside,"

NorthJersey.com, April 26, 2023, www.northjersey.com/story/news/bergen/2023/04/26/richard-nixon-nj-real-estate-home-for-sale-park-ridge/70139114007/.

7 **"I think the thing about New Jersey . . .":** Whitty, "James Gandolfini Looms Large."

8 **"Jimmy and my brothers . . .":** Forsyth interview.

8 **"Not that much has changed . . .":** Patricia Winters Lauro, "Communities: A Mob Town, and Proud of It," *New York Times*, November 24, 2002, www.nytimes.com/2002/11/24/nyregion/communities-a-mob-town-and-proud-of-it.html.

8 **"Were you a well-behaved kid?":** *Inside the Actors Studio.*

8 **"When you're all in a room . . .":** Forsyth interview.

9 **"He had a great group . . .":** Author interview with Ann Comarato, August 29, 2023.

9 **"Jim definitely had an issue . . .":** Author interview with Tom Richardson, October 19, 2023.

9 **"At Park Ridge he could . . .": Dan** Bischoff, *James Gandolfini: The Real Life of the Man Who Made Tony Soprano* (New York: St. Martin's Press, 2014), 33.

11 **senior yearbook:** Provided by Ann Comarato, from the Park Ridge High School Yearbook, Park Ridge, New Jersey, 1979.

11 **"He wasn't a showboat . . .":** Duffy interview.

11 **"John Wayne . . .":** Seitz, "Gandolfini: Star Quality."

11 **"The first thing I remember . . .":** *Inside the Actors Studio.*

11 **"*Mean Streets* is . . .":** Ibid.

11 **"We had a small theater . . .":** Duffy interview.

11 **"A couple of his friends . . .":** Comarato interview.

12 **"Most of the kids . . .":** Ibid.

12 **"He had a natural knack . . .":** Author interview with Susan Coughlin, August 29, 2023.

12 **"Once again, he nailed . . .":** Comarato interview.

13 **"It was almost as if . . .":** Ibid.

13 **"I think he got detention . . .":** Ibid.

13 **"So my friend and I . . .":** Duffy interview.

13 **inscription to Comarato:** Provided by Ann Comarato, from the Park Ridge High School Yearbook, Park Ridge, New Jersey, 1979.

Chapter 2

14 **"Wasn't something my family . . .":** Beverly M. Reid, "Still Just a Regular Guy from Jersey, James Gandolfini Muscles His Way onto the Big Screen," *Newark Star-Ledger*, October 21, 2001, www.nj.com/sopranosarchive/2001/10/good_fella_still_just_a_regula.html.

14 **While he received:** Graduation: As reported in the *Hackensack Record*, June 21, 1979, www.newspapers.com/article/34802564/park-ridge-hs-grad-class/, and the *Ridgewood News*, July 12, 1979, ProQuest.

14 **"I basically went to college":** *Inside the Actors Studio.*

14 **"Whatever that is, I had no idea . . .":** Reid, "Still Just a Regular Guy."

14 **"I don't remember":** Seitz, "Gandolfini: Star Quality."

15 **"Rutgers College freshman . . .":** Paul Savage, "Window Shattered in Mettler Hall," *Rutgers Daily Targum*, April 11, 1980, ProQuest.

15 **"They were crazy . . .":** Author interview with T. J. Foderaro, August 24, 2023.

15 **"She was a smart, lovely girl . . .":** Heath, "Garden State Warrior."

15 **"I went to college . . .":** Ibid.

15 **"That hugely affected the color . . .":** Foderaro interview.

16 **"He was always interested in people . . .":** Richardson interview.

16 **"A kind of a literature/philosophy major . . .":** Foderaro interview.

17 **"That changed me a lot . . .":** Heath, "Garden State Warrior."

17 **"I'd like to dedicate this":** ""James Gandolfini Wins 2003 Emmy Award for Lead Actor in a Drama Series," YouTube, youtu.be/ZprT43m1jmY?si=A-1_4ZsSY3z9epKO.

17 **"I dabbled a little bit . . ."** Sam Kashner and Jim Kelly, *The Sopranos: The Vanity Fair Oral History* (New York: Vanity Fair, 2012), 10.

17 **"Even then, Jim Gandolfini wanted . . .":** Mark Di Ionno, "When James Gandolfini Was Just a Rutgers Student from Park Ridge," *Newark Star-Ledger*, June 20, 2013, blog.nj.com/njv_mark_diionno/2013/06/james_gandolfini_dead_rutgers.html.

17 **"And he failed . . .":** Bischoff, *James Gandolfini*, 45.

17 **"I didn't know what I was doing . . .":** Di Ionno, "When James Gandolfini Was Just a Rutgers Student."

17 **"I do think that the death . . .":** Foderaro interview.

17 **"It didn't make much sense . . .":** Heath, "Garden State Warrior."

Chapter 3

19 **THE APARTMENT GYPSIES OF MANHATTAN:** First *New York Times* appearance: Lisa W. Foderaro, "The Apartment Gypsies of Manhattan," *New York Times*, May 29, 1988, www.nytimes.com/1988/05/29/realestate/the-apartment-gypsies-of-manhattan.html.

19 **"He didn't know a lot about wine . . .":** Foderaro interview.

20 **"Like a department store . . .":** Amy Virshup, "The Club Beat," *New York*, July 2, 1984, books.google.com/books?id=X-UCAAAAMBAJ&dq=%22private+eyes%22+video+%2221st+street%22&pg=PA70#v=onepage

20 **"It was the first nightclub . . .":** Heath, "Garden State Warrior."

20 **"He might have literally been . . .":** Foderaro interview.

20 **"That speaks volumes . . .":** Ibid.

20 **"I was way too young . . .":** Heath, "Garden State Warrior."

20 **"I got a lot of great research . . .":** *Inside the Actors Studio.*

20 **"I got drunk . . .":** Heath, "Garden State Warrior."

20 **"When I visited him . . .":** Foderaro interview.

21 **"I looked at him . . .":** Matthew Kassel, "The Man Who Brought Gandolfini to Acting," *New York Observer*, June 25, 2013, observer.com/2013/06/the-actor-who-brought-gandolfini-to-acting/.

21 **"I'd talked about taking acting classes . . .":** *Inside the Actors Studio.*

21 **"He asked what no other . . .":** Bischoff, *James Gandolfini*, 56.

21 **"I went in . . .":** *Inside the Actors Studio.*

21 **"It really made me very nervous . . .":** Reid, "Still Just a Regular Guy."

22 **"I had such anger . . .":** *Inside the Actors Studio.*

22 **"Listening and paying attention . . .":** Ibid.

22 **"Waiter, bartender, bouncer . . .":** Heilpern, "Curtains for Gandolfini."

23 **"All kinds of crap . . .":** Chris Heath, "Mooners, Misbehavior and Mobbed-Up Actors: The Sopranos Tell All," *Rolling Stone*, March 29, 2001, www.rollingstone.com/tv-movies/tv-movie-features/the-sopranos-tell-all-113159/.

23 **American Drama Group Europe:** Background: www.adg-europe.com/about-us/.

23 **"We met on Theatre Row . . .":** Author interview with Robert Funaro, August 15, 2023.

23 **"He originally auditioned for Stanley . . .":** Author interview with Joanna Mulkern, September 4, 2023.

23 **"It really was my first . . .":** Funaro interview.

23 **"A caravan of New York actors . . .":** Mulkern interview.

24 **"I remember us having a break . . .":** Funaro interview.

25 **"He never lapsed . . .":** Mulkern interview.

25 **"There was a ten-foot drop . . .":** Moody, "James Gandolfini Comes Home."

26 **"He was laughing . . .":** Mulkern interview.

26 **"I had a girlfriend . . .":** Aston interview.

26 **"There's a woman . . .":** *Inside the Actors Studio.*

27 **"The other woman . . .":** Aston interview.

27 **"About two people . . .":** *Inside the Actors Studio.*

27 **"A writer who saw us . . .":** Aston interview.

27 **"I think he got used . . .":** Ibid.

27 **"We both were very much invested . . .":** Ibid.

27 **"Neither of us . . .":** Ibid.

28 **"Particularly good":** "*Doogan's:* Reviewed by David Sheward," *Back Stage*, August 11, 1989, ProQuest.

29 **"In the eighties . . .":** Seitz, "Gandolfini: Star Quality."

29 **"I don't think anybody in my family . . .":** Kashner and Kelly, *The Sopranos*, 10.

29 **"I said, 'If I get famous . . .'":** Heath, "Garden State Warrior."

29 **"I got up to go . . .":** Rebecca Brill Moody, "James Gandolfini Comes Home," *New Jersey Monthly*, March 2004, njmonthly.com/articles/jersey-living/jersey-celebrities/james-gandolfini/.

29 **"He didn't want to play a mob guy . . .":** Aston interview.

29 **"There was something about James . . .":** Funaro interview.

29 **Gandolfini made his very:** *Shock! Shock! Shock!*, directed by Arn McConnell and Todd Rutt, Rhino Home Video, 1987.

30 **"None of them were very convincing . . .":** Gabriel Falcon, "See James Gandolfini's 1989 Screen Debut," CNN.com, June 26, 2013, www.cnn.com/2013/06/26/showbiz/gandolfini-debut/index.html.

30 **"She called me up . . .":** Author interview with Michael Greene, March 29, 2024.

30 **"the most lucrative script deal . . .":** Claudia Eller, "Geffen Co. Comes Prepared, Pays Record $1.75-Mil for 'Last Boy Scout' Script," *Variety*, April 25, 1990, NYPL.

30 **Black and Silver:** *Last Boy Scout* background: Official press notes, NYPL; Lawrence Van Gelder, "Tony Scott's Project," *New York Times*, July 12, 1991, www.nytimes.com/1991/07/12/movies/at-the-movies.html.

30 ***The Last Boy Scout* went:** *The Last Boy Scout*, directed by Tony Scott, Warner Bros., 1991.

31 **"So he went in . . .":** Greene interview.

31 **"*Stranger Among Us* was different . . .":** Aston interview.

31 **"I really didn't have a clue . . .":** *Inside the Actors Studio*.

31 **"Stage acting is . . .":** Moody, "James Gandolfini Comes Home."

31 ***Stranger* is a loose:** *A Stranger Among Us*, directed by Sidney Lumet, Hollywood Pictures, 1992.

Chapter Four

33 **"He never asked about money . . ."** and background on *Streetcar*: Patrick Pacheco, "Alec Baldwin's Career Rides a 'Streetcar,'" *New York Times*, April 5, 1992, www.nytimes.com/1992/04/05/archives/theater-alec-baldwins-career-rides-a-streetcar.html.

33 **"the part he *should* have played . . .":** Aston interview.

33 **Even better:** Filled in four times: According to Gandolfini's casting card from Marion Dougherty's files, Marion Dougherty Collection, Margaret Herrick Library, AMPAS.

34 **"He played my husband . . .":** Aida Turturro, "James Gandolfini's TV Sister Aida Turturro Remembers 'Sopranos' Star as Someone Who Always Had Your Back," *New York Daily News*, June 23, 2013, www.nydailynews.com/entertainment/james-gandolfini-tv-sister-back-article-1.1380339.

34 **"Very open and great . . .":** *Talking Sopranos* (blog), episode 88, November 29, 2021, youtu.be/erUHOKep4sE?si=frRLu4BR3FHTXEh2.

34 **"His Stanley is . . .":** Frank Rich, "Review/Theater: *A Streetcar Named Desire*; Alec Baldwin Does Battle with the Ghosts," *New York Times*, April 13, 1992, www.nytimes.com/1992/04/13/theater/review-theater-a-streetcar-named-desire-alec-baldwin-does-battle-with-the-ghosts.html.

35 **"lethargic and bland . . .":** "A Streetcar Named Desire," *Newsday*, April 13, 1992, ProQuest.

35 **"In the first act . . .":** Author interview with Mary Collins, March 25, 2024.

35 **"He knew nothing about the business . . .":** Author interview with Patty Woo, March 1, 2024.

35 **Money for Nothing, co-written:** *Money for Nothing*, directed by Ramón Menéndez, Hollywood Pictures, 1993. Background: Tommy Rowan, "1981: Joey Coyle Wasn't Looking for $1 million. Until It Fell Off a Truck," *Philadelphia Inquirer*, January 12, 2017, web.archive.org/web/20230826002840/https://www.inquirer.com/philly/blogs/real-time/1981-Joey-Coyle-wasnt-looking-for-1-million-Until-it-fell-off-a-truck.html.

36 **On August 15, 1993:** Joey Coyle's suicide: Diana Marder, "Coyle Showed No Despair in Final Hours, Friend Says," *Philadelphia Inquirer*, August 17, 1993, NYPL.

36 **"This tragic event . . .":** Carrie Rickey, "'Money' Is a Misshapen Moral Tale That's Duller Than It Had to Be," *Philadelphia Inquirer*, September 10, 1993, ProQuest.

36 **"with various unattractive characters . . .":** Brian Lowry, "Money for Nothing," *Variety*, September 10, 1993, variety.com/1993/film/reviews/money-for-nothing-1200433419/.

36 **"there are some special . . .":** Phillip Wuntch, "'Money for Nothing' Not Worth It," *Dallas Morning News*, syndicated to *the Arizona Republic*, September 11, 1993, ProQuest.

37 **barely $1 million:** *Money for Nothing* box office: Box Office Mojo, www.boxofficemojo.com/title/tt0107594/?ref_=bo_se_r_1.

37 **"I never had a date . . .":** *Mr. Wonderful*, directed by Anthony Minghella, the Samuel Goldwyn Company, 1993.

37 **It's a short, slight:** *Mr. Wonderful* as showcase: Author interview with Mark Armstrong, January 9, 2024.

37 **"Well cast and convincingly played . . .":** Janet Maslin, "A Story of Electricity: Men, Women and Con Ed," *New York Times*, October 15, 1993, www.nytimes.com/1993/10/15/movies/a-story-of-electricity-men-women-and-con-ed.html.

37 **$3 million domestic:** *Mr. Wonderful* box office: Box Office Mojo, www.boxofficemojo.com/title/tt0107613/?ref_=bo_se_r_1.

Chapter 5

38 **Quentin Tarantino had:** *True Romance* background: Jason Bailey, *Pulp Fiction: The Complete History of Quentin Tarantino's Masterpiece* (Minneapolis: Voyageur Press, 2013), 24–25.

38 **"I had read the script . . .":** Greene interview.

38 **"When James came in . . .":** Tony Scott, *True Romance* DVD audio commentary, Warner Home Video, released December 13, 2005.

39 **"Someone I knew . . .":** *Inside the Actors Studio.*

39 **"He lived in a shitty motel . . .":** Scott, *True Romance* commentary.

39 **Jim is first seen:** *True Romance*, directed by Tony Scott, Warner Bros., 1993.

39 **"the most romantic scene . . .":** Quentin Tarantino, *True Romance* DVD audio commentary, Warner Home Video, released December 13, 2005.

40 **"Now I do it . . .":** Added dialogue and business: Richardson interview; Scott, *True Romance* commentary.

40 **"He is so perfect . . .":** Scott, *True Romance* commentary.

40 **"It was like a dance . . .":** Seitz, "Gandolfini: Star Quality."

40 **"Get James to really bash me . . .":** Scott, *True Romance* commentary.

40 **"Even though sometimes . . .":** Patricia Arquette, *True Romance* DVD audio commentary, Warner Home Video, released December 13, 2005.

41 **"That's how much he was getting . . .":** Scott, *True Romance* commentary.

41 **"a vile, soulless fairy tale . . .":** Julie Salamon, "True Romance," *Wall Street Journal*, September 23, 1993, NYPL.

41 **"provides some amazing encounters . . .":** Leonard Klady, "True Romance," *Variety*, August 27, 1993, variety.com/1993/film/reviews/true-romance-2-1200432880/.

41 **"a vibrant, grisly, gleefully . . .":** Janet Maslin, "Desperadoes, Young at Heart with Gun in Hand," *New York Times*, September 10, 1993, www.nytimes.com/1993/09/10/movies/reviews-film-desperadoes-young-at-heart-with-gun-in-hand.html.

41 **"He said he wasn't proud . . .":** Aston interview.

41 **"Everybody was calling me . . .":** Greene interview.

41 **"He was just getting great little . . .":** Armstrong interview, January 9, 2024.

41 **low-budget New York indie:** *Italian Movie*, directed by Roberto Monticello, Janson Media, 1995.

42 **"was really like . . .":** Author interview with Michael Harney, January 23, 2024.

42 **"How bad am I? . . .":** Author interview with Roberto Monticello, August 3, 2023.

42 **"He was truthful . . .":** Harney interview.

42 **"You can see the guy . . .":** Monticello interview.

42 **"He wanted to play quality roles . . .":** Greene interview.

43 ***Angie, I Says*; outstanding offers:** Armstrong interview, January 9, 2024; Greene interview.

43 **solid, juicy role:** *Angie*, directed by Martha Coolidge, Hollywood Pictures, 1994.

43 **"In *Angie* . . .":** Seitz, "Gandolfini: Star Quality."

43 **"We worked like the devil . . .":** Woo interview.

44 **"He had all this heat . . .":** Armstrong interview, January 9, 2024.

44 **"a skin-deep . . .":** Todd McCarthy, "Angie," *Variety*, March 6, 1994, variety.com/1994/film/reviews/angie-2-1200436472/.

44 **"is saved from condescension . . .":** Janet Maslin, "Emotional Adventures of a Spunky Heroine," *New York Times*, March 4, 1994, www.nytimes.com/1994/03/04/movies/reviews-film-emotional-adventures-of-a-spunky-heroine.html.

44 **"It's just a matter of showing up . . .":** *Inside the Actors Studio.*

44 **"It was a rough shoot . . .":** Woo interview.

44 **As Deputy District Attorney:** *Terminal Velocity*, directed by Deran Sarafian, Hollywood Pictures, 1994.

44 **"a rousing, good-looking . . .":** Kevin Thomas, "'Terminal Velocity' Races into Romance and Comedy," *Los Angeles Times*, September 23, 1994, www.latimes.com/archi

ves/la-xpm-1994-09-23-ca-41881-story .html.

44 **"a snappy, thrill-packed . . .":** Steven Gaydos, "Terminal Velocity," *Variety*, September 23, 1994, variety.com/1994/film /reviews/terminal-velocity-1200438449/.

44 **$37 million return:** *Terminal Velocity* box office: "World's Champs and Chumps," *Variety*, February 13, 1995, NYPL.

45 **"a really low-budget thing . . .":** Aston interview.

45 **"Maybe tonight . . .":** *Mint Julep*, directed by Kathy Fehl and Ian Teal, Zoolooki, 2010.

45 **The filmmakers spent:** *Mint Julep* background: Dan Sallitt, "Diary of a Lost Film: 'Mint Julep,'" MUBI Notebook, June 7, 2011, mubi.com/en/notebook/posts/diary -of-a-lost-film-mint-julep.

45 **"So now I got . . .":** *Le Nouveau Monde* (aka *New World*), directed by Alain Corneau, Film Par Film, 1995.

46 **He was working with Tony Scott:** *Crimson Tide* background: Armstrong interview, January 9, 2024; "Hackman Fever Turns Denzel 'Crimson,'" *Premiere* magazine, December 1994; *Crimson Tide* production notes, NYPL.

46 **Lieutenant Bobby Dougherty:** *Crimson Tide*, directed by Tony Scott, Hollywood Pictures, 1995.

46 **"We were all . . .":** Author interview with Rocky Carroll, August 14, 2023.

46 **refused to assist:** *Crimson Tide* and the Navy: "'Crimson Tide' Goes Continental," *Variety*, February 13, 1995, NYPL.

46 **exchanged tense words:** Washington vs. Tarantino: "Denzel Sees Red on 'Crimson' Set," *New York Post*, June 12, 1995, NYPL.

47 **"James Gandolfini, the actor . . .":** Ari Posner, "The Princes of Tide," *Premiere* magazine, June 1995, NYPL.

47 **"It got really heated . . .":** Carroll interview.

47 **"Because he arrived late . . .":** Armstrong interview, January 9, 2024.

47 **"Hey, I'm calling . . .":** Woo interview.

48 **"'What the fuck . . .'":** Posner, "The Princes of Tide."

48 **"I almost feel . . .":** Armstrong interview, January 9, 2024.

48 **"an NFL locker room . . .":** Carroll interview.

48 **"John is actually responsible . . .":** "How Tony Caught the Fever," *New York Daily News*, December 7, 2004, NYPL.

48 **book by Elmore Leonard:** *Get Shorty*, directed by Barry Sonnenfeld, MGM, 1995.

49 **Hackman co-stars:** *Get Shorty* background: Patrick Goldstein, "Hey, Crime Does Pay," *Los Angeles Times*, October 15, 1995, www.latimes.com/archives/la-xpm -1995-10-15-ca-57239-story.html; Bernard Weinraub, "Getting 'Get Shorty' off the Page to the Screen," *New York Times*, October 26, 1995, www.nytimes.com/1995/10 /26/movies/getting-get-shorty-off-the -page-to-the-screen.html.

49 **"because I didn't know what to do . . .":** Moody, "James Gandolfini Comes Home."

49 **"Jim had built an entire character . . .":** Woo interview.

50 **"the first time he acted opposite . . .":** Harold Guskin, *How to Stop Acting* (New York: Farrar, Straus and Giroux, 2003), 146.

50 **"The response from film people . . .":** Collins interview.

50 **"I like when you go to a movie . . .":** Seitz, "Gandolfini: Star Quality."

50 **"He liked being the character actor . . .":** Author interview with Steven Van Zandt, May 26, 2023.

50 **"Sometimes your character's . . .":** Guskin, *How to Stop Acting*, 151–52.

51 **"There was rarely . . .":** Author interview with Diana Doussant, March 25, 2024.

51 **"They wanted James to audition . . .":** Collins interview.

51 **"This will sound crazy . . .":** Greene interview.

51 **"It wasn't like he was going out . . .":** Doussant interview.

51 **"He definitely didn't want . . .":** Collins interview.

51 **"TV didn't exist . . .":** Doussant interview.

51 **"He kept making his mark . . .":** Collins interview.

52 **"I think he didn't feel he belonged . . .":** Doussant interview.

Chapter 6

53 **"it was just a disaster . . .":** Doussant interview.

53 **"really trying to make this thing work . . .":** Author interview with Amy Appleyard, April 3, 2024.

53 **"Jim Gandolfini was a very strong personality . . .":** Woo interview.

54 **"The thing that I remember . . .":** Doussant interview.
54 **"I think he had just . . .":** Aston interview.
54 **"a lovely discussion . . .":** Heilpern, "Curtains for Gandolfini."
54 **"I brought Jimmy a bottle . . .":** Harney interview.
54 **"the rockiest tryout . . .":** Jeremy Gerard, "On the Waterfront," *Variety*, May 2, 1995, variety.com/1995/legit/reviews/on-the-waterfront-3-1200441748/.
54 **"the costliest nonmusical . . .":** Greg Evans, "'Waterfront' Sinks as Tony Season Ends," *Variety*, May 8, 1995, variety.com/1995/legit/news/waterfront-sinks-as-tony-season-ends-99127509/.
54 **"He was really surprised . . .":** Aston interview.
54 **John Grisham-esque thriller:** *The Juror*, directed by Brian Gibson, Columbia Pictures, 1996.
55 **"number of fine actors . . .":** Dave Kehr, "'Juror' Demi in Distress," *New York Daily News*, February 2, 1996, NYPL.
55 **"strong supporting cast":** Janet Maslin, "Case of the Suave Creep vs. the Feisty Mom," *New York Times*, February 2, 1996, www.nytimes.com/1996/02/02/movies/film-review-case-of-the-suave-creep-vs-the-feisty-mom.html.
55 **"A performance that . . .":** Roger Ebert, "The Juror," *Chicago Sun-Times*, February 2, 1996, www.rogerebert.com/reviews/the-juror-1996.
56 **"He hated that . . .":** Doussant interview.
56 **"We got the offer . . .":** Woo interview.
56 **"He pulled out . . .":** Doussant interview.
56 **"There was a pool table . . .":** Appleyard interview.
57 **"The thing about dating Jim . . .":** Email from Amy Appleyard, April 4, 2024.
57 **"I do remember being really surprised . . .":** Appleyard interview.
58 **"the biggest crackhead . . .":** Greene interview.
58 **"Susan got me in . . .":** *Inside the Actors Studio*.
58 **"He was nobody . . .":** Cindy Adams, "BADFELLA: Spurned 'Soprano' Wife Bears Anguish," *New York Post*, March 18, 2002, NYPL.
58 **"She was very helpful . . .":** Appleyard interview.
59 **"But Jim would always ask . . .":** Armstrong interview, January 9, 2024.
59 **"The writing, the writing . . .":** *Inside the Actors Studio*.
59 **"You should have your own idea . . .":** Guskin, *How to Stop Acting*, 135.
59 **"Sidney Lumet called . . .":** *Inside the Actors Studio*.
59 **films about corruption:** *Night Falls on Manhattan*, directed by Sidney Lumet, Paramount Pictures, 1997.
60 **the film's premiere:** Carol Diuguid, "'Night' Takes Flight at Gotham Preem,' *Variety*, May 19, 1997, variety.com/1997/scene/vpage/night-takes-flight-at-gotham-preem-1116679745/.
60 **"complexity and artistry":** Leonard Klady, "Night Falls on Manhattan," *Variety*, May 18, 1997, variety.com/1997/film/reviews/night-falls-on-manhattan-1117329798/.
60 **"stellar supporting actors":** Jami Bernard, "A Prosecution Complex," *New York Daily News*, May 16, 1997, NYPL.
60 **"I remember we had a reading . . .":** *James Gandolfini: Tribute to a Friend*.
60 **"Whenever he would agree . . .":** Richardson interview.
61 **"I realized that perhaps . . .":** *She's So Lovely* production notes, NYPL.
61 **"I knew Nick Cassavetes . . .":** *Inside the Actors Studio*.
61 **"I find them difficult . . .":** Ibid.
61 **"I'm sorry but . . .":** *She's So Lovely*, directed by Nick Cassavetes, Miramax, 1997.
61 ***Perdita Durango*:** *Perdita Durango* (aka *Dance with the Devil*), directed by Álex de la Iglesia, Lolafilms / Mirador Films, 1997.
62 **a much more conventional effort:** *Fallen*, directed by Gregory Hoblit, Turner Pictures, 1998.

Chapter 7

63 **ran the obituary:** Santa Gandolfini obit: *Record (North Jersey)*, January 11, 1997, ProQuest.
63 **"A lot of actors . . .":** Jefferson Graham, "Altman Gives TV Another Shot with 'Gun,'" *USA Today*, April 9, 1997, NYPL.
63 **"Columbus Day":** *Gun*: "Columbus Day," directed by James Steven Sadwith, ABC, 1997.
63 **"He has those very compassionate . . .":** Author interview with Rosanna Arquette, May 19, 2023.
64 **"I loved him . . .":** Ibid.

64 **"I think it was because he did the *Gun* . . .":** Armstrong interview, January 9, 2024.

64 ***12 Angry Men* was first presented:** *12 Angry Men* background: Cathy Lubenski, "'12 Angry Men's' Mad Rush," *New York Daily News*, August 17, 1997, NYPL; Susan King, "In the Jury Room," *Los Angeles Times*, August 17, 1997, www.latimes.com/archives/la-xpm-1997-aug-17-tv-23111-story.html; Army Archerd, "O.J. Trial Gives 'Angry Men' New Appeal," *Variety*, February 26, 1997, variety.com/1997/voices/columns/o-j-trial-gives-angry-men-new-appeal-1117863032/.

65 **"I think he felt like he was invited . . .":** Armstrong interview, January 9, 2024.

65 **"I'd seen his work . . .":** Author interview with Mykelti Williamson, May 12, 2023.

65 **"We had a good time . . .":** Ibid.

65 **"First of all, Jack Lemmon . . .":** Author interview with Tony Danza, May 16, 2023.

65 ***12 Angry Men* is a work of high drama:** *12 Angry Men*, directed by William Friedkin, Showtime, 1997.

66 **"The guy was really . . .":** Danza interview.

66 **"I gave him a really great meeting . . .":** Author interview with Nancy Sanders, January 10, 2024.

66 **"He had reverence . . .":** Ibid.

66 **Peter Chelsom's adaptation:** *The Mighty*, directed by Peter Chelsom, Miramax, 1998.

67 **"He wanted to go up . . .":** Armstrong interview, January 9, 2024.

67 **Los Angeles stage debut:** *Remembrance* background: Diane Haithman, "Their Son, the Producer," *Los Angeles Times*, September 21, 1997, www.latimes.com/archives/la-xpm-1997-sep-21-ca-34459-story.html.

67 **"He called me . . .":** Aston interview.

68 **"I was racing someone . . .":** Barry Levine, "Exclusive Interview! James Gandolfini's Secret Life of Drugs & Booze," *National Enquirer*, republished June 20, 2013, www.nationalenquirer.com/celebrity/exclusive-interview-james-gandolfinis-secret-life-drugs-booze/.

68 **"I'm sorry to say . . .":** Woo interview.

68 **"Gandolfini's loutishness gives . . .":** Charles Isherwood, "Remembrance," *Variety*, October 8, 1997, variety.com/1997/legit/reviews/remembrance-1200451631/.

68 **"the roles you'd expect . . .":** Seitz, "Gandolfini: Star Quality."

68 **"My parents worked hard . . .":** *Inside the Actors Studio.*

69 **"James Gandolfini is in final . . .":** "Gandolfini Set to Get 'Civil' with Travolta," *Variety*, August 11, 1997, variety.com/1997/film/news/gandolfini-set-to-get-civil-with-travolta-1116676163/.

69 **"He was thrilled . . .":** Sanders interview, January 10, 2024.

69 **"I'm very sorry about your son":** *A Civil Action*, directed by Steven Zaillian, Touchstone Pictures, 1998.

69 **"I do remember . . .":** Author interview with Kathleen Quinlan, May 12, 2023.

69 **"I remember him getting really mad . . .":** Ibid.

69 **among the "effective":** Kenneth Turan, "Legal Entanglements," *Los Angeles Times*, December 25, 1998, www.latimes.com/archives/la-xpm-1998-dec-25-ca-57386-story.html.

70 **"shrewd, first-rate performances":** Janet Maslin, "Lawyer Errs on the Side of Angels," *New York Times*, December 25, 1998, www.nytimes.com/1998/12/25/movies/film-review-lawyer-errs-on-the-side-of-angels.html.

70 **"I was very proud . . .":** *Inside the Actors Studio.*

70 **"A dark, dark film":** Seitz, "Gandolfini: Star Quality."

70 **"He loved Schumacher":** Sanders interview, January 10, 2024.

70 **an attempt at an edgy, gritty comeback:** *8MM*, directed by Joel Schumacher, Columbia Pictures, 1999.

71 **"Once *A Civil Action* . . .":** James Andrew Miller, *Tinderbox: HBO's Ruthless Pursuit of New Frontiers* (New York: Henry Holt, 2021), 757–58.

Chapter 8

72 **didn't want to work in television:** David Chase background: David Bianculli, *The Platinum Age of Television: From* I Love Lucy *to* The Walking Dead, *How TV Became Terrific* (New York: Doubleday, 2016); Felix Gillette and John Koblin, *It's Not TV: The Spectacular Rise, Revolution, and Future of HBO* (New York: Viking, 2022); Brett Martin, *Difficult Men: Behind the Scenes of a Creative Revolution* (New York: Penguin Press, 2013); Alan Sepinwall, *The Revolution Was Televised: How* The Sopranos, Mad Men, Breaking Bad, Lost, *and Other*

Groundbreaking Dramas Changed TV Forever (New York: Gallery Books, 2013).

72 **"It was funny . . .":** Bianculli, *The Platinum Age*, 224.

72 **"I'm Italian-American . . .":** Ibid.

73 **"That was the last thing . . .":** Gillette and Koblin, *It's Not TV*, 100.

73 **"Then I was driving home . . .":** Matt Zoller Seitz & Alan Sepinwall, *The Sopranos Sessions*, (New York: Abrams Press, 2019), 503.

73 **"Mafia Mother and Son . . .":** Martin, *Difficult Men*, 70.

73 **"'I'm not getting the feeling . . .":** Seitz & Sepinwall, *The Sopranos Sessions*, 503.

73 **"I don't really have a problem . . .":** Gillette and Koblin, *It's Not TV*, 102.

74 **"We sent the script over . . .":** Martin, *Difficult Men*, 72.

74 **room for more:** HBO deal background: Gillette and Koblin, *It's Not TV*, 103–5; Sepinwall, *The Revolution Was Televised*, 34.

74 **up for a job:** Connecting with Chase: Gillette and Koblin, *It's Not TV*, 102; Sanders interview, January 10, 2024; Armstrong interview, January 9, 2024.

74 **"I read it . . .":** Sanders interview, January 10, 2024.

75 **"In the movie version . . .":** Kashner and Kelly, *The Sopranos*, 10.

75 **"We didn't know . . .":** *Talking Sopranos*, episode 10, June 1, 2020, youtu.be/sDrkc6-_sjo?si=3neSITKldzzCa7Y_.

75 **"We had only seen Jim Gandolfini . . .":** Michael Imperioli and Steve Schirripa with Philip Lerman, *Woke Up This Morning: The Definitive Oral History of 'The Sopranos'* (New York: William Morrow, 2021), 29.

75 **"I think my exact words were . . .":** Lorraine Bracco and Emily McDermott, "The Mobster and the Shrink," *Interview*, March 1999, www.interviewmagazine.com/film/1999-the-mobster-and-the-shrink-james-gandolfini-and-lorraine-bracco.

75 **"Everybody had to be Italian . . .":** *Talking Sopranos*, episode 10, June 1, 2020.

75 **"We said, 'No, you should know' . . .":** Armstrong interview, January 9, 2024.

75 **"At the time I was younger . . .":** Kashner and Kelly, *The Sopranos*, 10.

75 **"and then he . . .":** Armstrong interview, January 9, 2024.

75 **"I was born to play Tony . . .":** Jack Newfield, "Even Wiseguys Get the Blues," *New York Post*, April 4, 1999, nypost.com/1999/04/04/even-wiseguys-get-the-blues-runaway-hit-series-the-sopranos-and-its-mobster-on-prozac-were-created-by-a-jersey-boy-inspired-by-guys-back-in-the-old-neighborhood-and-his-mom/.

75 **"agreed to audition for it":** Jim's audition: Imperioli, Schirripa, and Lerman, *Woke Up This Morning*, 30.

76 **"He was very good.":** Seitz & Sepinwall, *The Sopranos Sessions*, 505.

76 **"I'm not doing this right . . .":** *Inside the Actors Studio.*

76 **"and then Friday . . .":** Seitz & Sepinwall, *The Sopranos Sessions*,,505.

76 **"He was really our favorite . . .":** *Talking Sopranos*, episode 10, June 1, 2020.

76 **"When he finally settled down . . .":** Gillette and Koblin, *It's Not TV*, 107.

76 **"It was audition after audition . . .":** Kashner and Kelly, *The Sopranos*, 10.

76 **"There were three people testing . . .":** Miller, *Tinderbox*, 332.

76 **"the minute he walked in . . .":** Ibid.

76 **"took some convincing . . .":** Martin, *Difficult Men*, 75.

76 **"Rispoli was great . . .":** Sepinwall, *The Revolution Was Televised*, 36.

77 **"This was an incredible leap . . .":** Martin, *Difficult Men*, 75.

77 **"Why am I doing this? . . .":** Sanders interview, January 10, 2024.

77 **"Oh my God, Roberto . . .":** Monticello interview.

77 **"The first time . . .":** Author interview with Lorraine Bracco, May 26, 2023.

77 **"I had been told that . . .":** Author interview with Edie Falco, May 17, 2023.

78 **"I loved Tony Sirico . . .":** Author interview with Vincent Pastore, May 19, 2023.

78 **"I knew who all the different people . . .":** Author interview with Drea de Matteo, March 22, 2024.

78 **"David committed his life . . .":** Sepinwall, *The Revolution Was Televised*, 35.

78 **"David Chase, even though his background . . .":** Author interview with Phil Abraham, August 7, 2023.

79 **"I had no interest in doing . . .":** Bracco and McDermott, "The Mobster and the Shrink."

79 **"We didn't know what it was gonna be . . .":** Aston interview.

79 **"I met a few mob guys . . .":** Reid, "Still Just a Regular Guy."

79 **"It wasn't that hard . . .":** Brett Martin, *The Sopranos: The Complete Book* (New York: Liberty Street, 2007), 12.

79 **"Once you identify . . .":** Aston interview.

79 **"I was concerned . . .":** Van Zandt interview.

80 **"The whole thing about Jimmy . . .":** Pastore interview.

80 **"I think we bonded . . .":** Van Zandt interview.

80 **"I can't do this . . .":** Armstrong interview, January 9, 2024.

80 **"The first day we were shooting . . .":** Jeremy Egner, "David Chase on 'The Sopranos,' Trump and Yes, That Ending," *New York Times*, January 7, 2019, www.nytimes.com/2019/01/07/arts/television/david-chase-sopranos-interview.html.

80 **"I had questions myself . . .":** Seitz & Sepinwall, *The Sopranos Sessions*, 507.

81 **"My first day . . .":** Miller, *Tinderbox*, 333.

81 **"The first thing I remember . . .":** Author interview with Robert Iler, August 1, 2023.

81 **"Jimmy and Edie made everybody better . . .":** *James Gandolfini: Tribute to a Friend.*

81 **The hour of television they created:** *The Sopranos*, various directors, HBO, 1999–2007.

82 **"This is it . . .":** Iler interview.

83 **"Nobody knew it was going to become . . .":** Author interview with Alik Sakharov, August 15, 2023.

83 **"not a good waiter":** Martin, *Difficult Men*, 78.

83 **"I remember us sitting down . . .":** Armstrong interview, January 9, 2024.

83 **"He had concerns . . .":** Sanders interview, January 10, 2024.

84 **"It was like a big Christmas present":** Imperioli, Schirripa, and Lerman, *Woke Up This Morning*, 54.

84 **"HBO has committed . . .":** Ray Richmond, "HBO Goes for Drama with 'The Sopranos,'" *Variety*, January 12, 1998, NYPL.

Chapter 9

85 **"We had to figure out . . .":** Seitz & Sepinwall, *The Sopranos Sessions*, 513.

85 **Chase staffed up:** Season 1 writing particulars: Martin, *Difficult Men*, 84.

85 **"In the beginning . . .":** Martin, *The Sopranos*, 12.

85 **"David was very specific . . .":** Kashner and Kelly, *The Sopranos*, 22.

85 **"Those were his choices . . .":** Aston interview.

88 **"The network didn't . . .":** Seitz & Sepinwall, *The Sopranos Sessions* , 516.

88 **"David, you can't . . .":** Sepinwall, *The Revolution Was Televised*, 39.

88 **"Jim, Edie, all of us . . .":** Martin, *Difficult Men*, 87.

88 **"The character is a good fit . . .":** Seitz, "Gandolfini: Star Quality."

88 **"It's a man in struggle . . .":** *Inside the Actors Studio.*

89 **"They went to an ad agency . . .":** Miller, *Tinderbox*, 333–34.

89 **"'Arliss,' 'Oz' and . . .":** John Dempsey, "'Arliss' Stays Alive,' *Variety*, October 25, 1998, variety.com/1998/tv/news/arliss-stays-alive-1117481799/.

89 **"By that time . . .":** Miller, *Tinderbox*, 333–34.

89 **"We had no idea . . .":** Abraham interview.

89 **season 1 premiere party:** Gillette and Koblin, *It's Not TV*, 121; Jay Lustig, "Remembering the Premiere of 'The Sopranos,' 20 Years Later," NJ Arts, January 6, 2019, www.njarts.net/remembering-the-premiere-of-the-sopranos-20-years-later/.

89 **"Just very proud of him . . .":** Aston interview.

89 **"Out of the hard work . . .":** *James Gandolfini: Tribute to a Friend.*

89 **called it "audacious . . .":** Tom Carson, "Mean Driveways," *Village Voice*, January 12, 1999, NYPL.

89 **"Subtle, droll, and . . .":** Matt Roush, "All in the Family: Suburban Mobsters," *TV Guide*, January 16, 1999, NYPL.

89 **"Hands down, it's . . .":** Howard Rosenberg, "'Providence' Is Flat but 'Sopranos' Really Sings," *Los Angeles Times*, January 8, 1999, www.latimes.com/archives/la-xpm-1999-jan-08-ca-61442-story.html.

89 **"magnificent megamovie":** Vincent Canby, "From the Humble Miniseries Comes the Magnificent Megamovie," *New York Times*, October 31, 1999, www.nytimes.com/1999/10/31/arts/from-the-humble-mini-series-comes-the-magnificent-megamovie.html.

90 **"brilliantly subtle, always . . .":** David Bianculli, "'Sopranos' Has Makings of a Hit," *New York Daily News*, January 8, 1999, www.nydailynews.com/entertainment/tv/sopranos-makings-hit-1999-review-article-1.822131.

90 **"Gandolfini does a lot . . .":** Phil Gallo, "The Sopranos," *Variety*, January 5, 1999, variety.com/1999/tv/reviews/the-sopranos-4-1200456522/.

90 **"Gandolfini joins the club . . .":** Michele Greppi, "Goodfella Goes Bad: HBO's Depressed Mobster Is Reason to Be Cheerful," *New York Post*, January 8, 1999, nypost.com/1999/01/08/goodfella-goes-bad-hbos-depressed-mobster-is-reason-to-be-cheerful/.

90 **"In an era . . .":** Matt Zoller Seitz, "The Godfather Meets Ralph Kramden in 'Sopranos,'" *Newark Star-Ledger*, February 2, 1999, www.nj.com/sopranosarchive/1999/02/the_godfather_meets_ralph_kram.html.

90 **"negative, cartoonish images . . .":** Bill Dal Cerro, "Why No Outrage over the Offensive Stereotypes on 'Sopranos'?," *Los Angeles Times*, July 26, 1999, www.latimes.com/archives/la-xpm-1999-jul-26-ca-59628-story.html.

90 **"Come on, you . . .":** *Inside the Actors Studio*.

90 **ten million viewers per episode:** Season 1 ratings: Gillette and Koblin, *It's Not TV*, 133; John Dempsey, "'Sopranos' Has HBO on Ratings High," *Variety*, April 5, 1999, NYPL.

90 **"We didn't know . . .":** Iler interview.

90 **"I think having to go . . .":** De Matteo interview, March 22, 2024.

91 **"The fuss started . . .":** Kashner and Kelly, *The Sopranos*, 31.

91 **"We went down . . .":** Armstrong interview, January 9, 2024.

91 **"It was this crazy . . .":** Sanders interview, January 10, 2024.

91 **"So that was like, O.K. . . .":** Kashner and Kelly, *The Sopranos*, 31.

91 **"I feel like I'm being . . .":** Seitz, "Gandolfini: Star Quality."

91 **"We looked at each other . . .":** Miller, *Tinderbox*, 338–39.

92 **"network executives are . . .":** Bill Carter, "A Cable Show Networks Truly Watch," *New York Times*, March 25, 1999, www.nytimes.com/1999/03/25/arts/a-cable-show-networks-truly-watch.html.

92 **"no longer the . . .":** Frank Decaro, "No Longer the Punch-Line State," *New York Times*, April 4, 1999, www.nytimes.com/1999/04/04/style/no-longer-punch-line-state-lauryn-hill-sopranos-others-are-unapologetic-new.html.

92 **"It's a great show and I enjoy it very much":** Frank Lombardi, "Rudy 'Loves' TV Mafia," *New York Daily News*, August 26, 1999, NYPL.

92 **"What characters . . . great acting":** Al Guart, "'Sopranos' Strikes Chord with Jersey Mob: Tapes," *New York Post*, December 16, 1999, nypost.com/1999/12/16/sopranos-strikes-chord-with-jersey-mob-tapes/.

92 **When the Emmy nominations:** Lawrie Mifflin, "In a Coup for Cable, HBO's 'Sopranos' Receives 16 Nominations," *New York Times*, July 23, 1999, www.nytimes.com/1999/07/23/movies/in-a-coup-for-cable-hbo-s-sopranos-receives-16-emmy-nominations.html.

92 **"obviously unhappy":** Bernard Weinraub, "The Emmys, Still Favoring More of the Same," *New York Times*, September 14, 1999, www.nytimes.com/1999/09/14/arts/the-emmys-still-favoring-more-of-the-same.html.

92 **"wuz robbed":** Austin Smith, "They Wuz Robbed! H'wood Bias Whacked Emmy Chances of 'Sopranos' Mob," *New York Post*, September 14, 1999, nypost.com/1999/09/14/they-wuz-robbed-hwood-bias-whacked-emmy-chances-of-sopranos-mob/.

92 **"She couldn't be . . .":** Maggie Haberman, "Sopranos Makes It a Real Mob Scene," *New York Post*, January 24, 2000, nypost.com/2000/01/24/sopranos-makes-it-a-real-mob-scene/.

92 **"I don't think any of us . . .":** Dave McNary, "Spacey, Bening Take SAG Honors," *Variety*, March 12, 2000, variety.com/2000/film/news/spacey-bening-take-sag-honors-1117779359/.

93 **"I think the interesting thing . . .":** Kashner and Kelly, *The Sopranos*, 26.

93 **"I think you cared about Tony . . .":** *Ibid.*, 55.

94 **"The casting of Gandolfini . . .":** *Ibid.*, 56.

94 **"I think a lot of people feel powerless . . .":** *Inside the Actors Studio*.

94 **"Tony just sits . . .":** Bracco and McDermott, "The Mobster and the Shrink."

94 **"I see the show . . .":** Matt Zoller Seitz, "Married to the Mob," *Newark Star-Ledger*, January 9, 1999, www.nj.com/sopranosarchive/1999/01/married_to_the_mob_a_harried_g.html.

95 **"What you see in Tony . . .":** Martin, *The Sopranos*, 63.

95 **"For whatever reason . . .":** Kashner and Kelly, *The Sopranos*, 53.

95 **"He was extremely emotional . . .":** Seitz & Sepinwall, *The Sopranos Sessions*, 614.

95 **"It's like showing . . .":** Seitz, "Gandolfini: Star Quality."

95 **"There is something sad . . .":** Seitz & Sepinwall, *The Sopranos Sessions*, 584.

96 **"You can tell when something's . . .":** Author interview with Christine Gee, August 9, 2023.

Chapter 10

97 **"When I sat . . .":** Bill Carter, "He Engineered a Mob Hit, and Now It's Time to Pay Up; Entering a 2nd Season, 'The Sopranos' Has a Hard Act to Follow," *New York Times*, January 11, 2000, www.nytimes.com/2000/01/11/arts/he-engineered-mob-hit-now-it-s-time-pay-up-entering-2nd-season-sopranos-has-hard.html.

97 **$55,000 per episode:** salary background: Bischoff, *James Gandolfini*, 93.

97 **"Reps for HBO . . .":** Cynthia Littleton, "Gandolfini Gets Raise," *Variety*, June 21, 1999, variety.com/1999/tv/news/gandolfini-gets-raise-1117503312/.

97 **overall boost:** Budget and Naples shoot background: Eric Mink, "'Sopranos' to Get More Mugs & Money," *New York Daily News*, April 29, 1999, NYPL; Army Archerd, "'Sopranos' to visit Italy," *Variety*, October 26, 1999, variety.com/1999/voices/columns/sopranos-to-visit-italy-1117756993/.

98 **"A hand-delivered . . .":** *New York Post*, May 11, 1999, NYPL.

98 **"She was coughing . . .":** Seitz & Sepinwall, *The Sopranos Sessions*, 509.

98 **"I've known I've had cancer . . .":** Don Kaplan, "'Sopranos' Mom Loses Her Fight for Life," *New York Post*, June 20, 2000, nypost.com/2000/06/20/sopranos-mom-loses-her-fight-for-life/.

98 **"had no belief . . .":** Seitz & Sepinwall, *The Sopranos Sessions*, 509.

98 **"Her attitude is . . .":** "'Sopranos' Star Diagnosed with Cancer," Mr. Showbiz, September 29, 1999, NYPL.

98 **"I worked with her a lot . . .":** Kashner and Kelly, *The Sopranos*, 15.

98 **"Listen, Jimmy . . .":** Imperioli, Schirripa, and Lerman, *Woke Up This Morning*, 130.

98 **second season began:** Season 2 background: Army Archerd, "'Sopranos' Hits High Note," *Variety*, April 21, 1999, variety.com/1999/voices/columns/sopranos-hits-high-note-1117493450/.

98 **"The non-stop click-click . . .":** Matt Zoller Seitz, "The Royal Treatment," *Newark Star-Ledger*, August 28, 1999, NYPL.

99 **"A lot of this stuff . . .":** Author interview with Steve Kornacki (not to be confused with the NBC political analyst of the same name), August 7, 2023.

99 **developed a method:** Production background: Martin, *The Sopranos*, 145.

100 **"But these guys . . .":** Kornacki interview.

100 **"Then it was just off . . .":** Ibid.

100 **"You'll start Monday . . .":** *Inside the Actors Studio.*

101 **"We would call . . .":** Gee interview.

102 **"The first day of shooting . . .":** Imperioli, Schirripa, and Lerman, *Woke Up This Morning*, 139.

102 **"and he's trying . . .":** Schirripa interview.

102 **"He knew that I was . . .":** Ibid.

103 **"We do this long . . .":** Imperioli, Schirripa, and Lerman, *Woke Up This Morning*, 139.

103 **"We get to the island . . .":** Bischoff, *James Gandolfini*, 100.

103 **From his office:** Chase's control: Martin, *Difficult Men*, 17.

103 **"He was always upstairs . . .":** Gee interview.

103 **"Some new actors would come in . . .":** Kashner and Kelly, *The Sopranos*, 49.

104 **"Look, they had a great relationship . . .":** Abraham interview.

104 **"What's good about David . . .":** Sakharov interview.

104 **"People would probably . . .":** Allen Rucker, *The Sopranos: A Family History*, (New York: NAL Books, 2001).

104 **pushed back "all the time . . .":** Seitz & Sepinwall, *The Sopranos Sessions*, 537.

104 **"He said in front of . . .":** Author interview with Mark Kamine, January 22, 2024.

104 **"It was rare that I didn't understand . . .":** Kashner and Kelly, *The Sopranos*, 49.

105 **"He never, ever . . .":** Sanders interview, January 10, 2024.

105 **"We'd go around . . .":** Seitz & Sepinwall, *The Sopranos Sessions*, 537.

105 **"take the acting seriously . . .":** Iler interview.

105 **"Jim had a mantra . . .":** Author interview with Vincent Curatola, May 19, 2023.

105 **"I've heard him talk sometimes . . .":** Aston interview.

105 **"It's rote. . . .":** Ibid.

106 **"It was really hard for him . . .":** Panel discussion, "James Gandolfini's Documentary Legacy," September 26, 2023, Firehouse:

DCTV's Cinema for Documentary Film, New York, firehouse.dctvny.org/websales/pages/info.aspx?evtinfo=399296~2998286f-8e4b-4c31-9017-dcced8ffebb3.

106 **memorization method:** Aston interview; Pastore interview.

106 **"it was just that kind of sensory . . .":** Gee interview.

106 **He taught this technique:** Pastore interview.

106 **"It's kind of like when you do a play . . .":** Guskin, *How to Stop Acting*, 136–37.

106 **"You would be in the middle . . .":** Aston interview.

106 **"Susan is as much a part . . .":** *Inside the Actors Studio.*

107 **"We both were highly intelligent . . .":** Aston interview.

107 **"There's where your . . .":** Martin, *Difficult Men*, 12.

107 **"Jim was very serious . . .":** Schirripa interview.

107 **"I don't want to give the impression . . .":** Aston interview.

107 **"picking up whatever . . .":** Guskin, *How to Stop Acting*, 157.

107 **"It throws everything . . .":** Ibid.

107 **"Lack of sleep . . .":** *Inside the Actors Studio.*

107 **"I've always wondered . . .":** Nick Pope, "The Making of Michael Gandolfini," *Esquire*, September 20, 2021, www.esquire.com/uk/culture/a37617783/michael-gandolfini-the-many-saints-of-newark/.

108 **"I'll do a lot of weird things . . .":** *Inside the Actors Studio.*

108 **"He tucked it . . .":** Gee interview.

108 **"he wasn't a smoker . . .":** *Talking Sopranos*, episode 1, April 6, 2020, youtu.be/z1ZFm_7WaeU?si=xnwKfh2AVAdm4g5-.

108 **"Especially in the morning . . .":** Heath, "Mooners, Misbehavior and Mobbed-Up Actors."

108 **"I saw nothing but the good . . .":** Van Zandt interview.

108 **"He'd be walking . . .":** Iler interview.

108 **"It's almost like, you are about . . .":** Heath, "Mooners, Misbehavior and Mobbed-Up Actors."

108 **"When you get to a certain level . . .":** Aston interview.

109 **"I remember going to him . . .":** *Talking Sopranos*, episode 78, September 20, 2021, youtu.be/9GNE-5hxTIc?si=tCtL3dgFOGV-Dp3a.

109 **"To me," he says, "that's very telling . . .":** Abraham interview.

109 **"clocking it all . . .":** Sakharov interview.

109 **"I worked with him first . . .":** Panel discussion, "James Gandolfini's Documentary Legacy."

109 **"He was willing to do . . .":** Aston interview.

109 **"There's a corny saying . . .":** Iler interview.

109 **"I winged the . . .":** Guskin, *How to Stop Acting*, 150.

110 **"Jamie-Lynn Sigler told me . . .":** Schirripa interview.

110 **"he's free to be . . .":** Aston interview.

110 **"He didn't let himself . . .":** Falco interview, May 17, 2023.

110 **"He did that all the time . . .":** *James Gandolfini: Tribute to a Friend.*

110 **"You've got to be present . . .":** Falco interview, May 17, 2023.

110 **"He was a great Ping-Pong player . . .":** Bracco interview.

110 **"It doesn't matter what you throw . . .":** *Talking Sopranos*, episode 38, December 14, 2020, youtu.be/iDGg7jtKskE?si=hFiz8M191c1RVthv.

110 **"It's almost as if . . .":** Curatola interview.

110 **"We kind of stayed out of . . .":** Falco interview, May 17, 2023.

111 **"Once you would hear *cut* . . .":** Curatola interview.

111 **"Listen, I didn't start acting . . .":** Pastore interview.

111 **"He was always there . . .":** Aston interview.

111 **"Typically, number one . . .":** Abraham interview.

111 **"He would say to you . . .":** Schirripa interview.

111 **"I said I dunno . . .":** Pastore interview.

112 **"We had very long scenes . . .":** Bracco interview.

112 **"We would end up doing . . .":** *Inside the Actors Studio.*

112 **"she would always . . .":** Kashner and Kelly, *The Sopranos*, 29.

112 **"reached into the back . . .":** Gee interview.

112 **"It was late . . .":** *Inside the Actors Studio.*

112 **"He was a pain in my ass . . .":** Bracco interview.

113 **"One you're not . . .":** *Inside the Actors Studio.*

113 **"Mooning occurred . . .":** Bracco interview.

113 **"I used to call David . . .":** Martin, *The Sopranos*, 12.
113 **"Doing a show . . .":** *James Gandolfini: Tribute to a Friend.*
113 **"He worked so hard . . .":** Bischoff, *James Gandolfini*, 96.
113 **"For nine months . . .":** Schirripa interview.
113 **"What I witnessed . . .":** Van Zandt interview.
114 **"Naturally you hear . . .":** Author interview with Don Scardino, August 3, 2023.
114 **"Well, that whole group of actors . . .":** Reid, "Still Just a Regular Guy."
114 **"There were no . . .":** Kashner and Kelly, *The Sopranos*, 48.
114 **"I think of him . . .":** Heath, "Mooners, Misbehavior and Mobbed-Up Actors."
114 **"I think he was the patriarch . . .":** Iler interview.
114 **"I really didn't have much . . .":** Falco interview, May 17, 2023.
115 **"Jim, as we know . . .":** *Talking Sopranos*, episode 21, August 17, 2020, youtu.be/f4xb4XzmkQY?si=hJoFN1WzeoZk7n4A.
115 **"I'm the messenger . . .":** Author interview with Chiemi Karasawa, August 3, 2023.
115 **"We were working . . .":** Abraham interview.
115 **"not in his trailer . . .":** Sakharov interview.
115 **"The crew would try . . .":** Gee interview.
116 **"Listen, anytime that you're getting . . .":** Abraham interview.
116 **"the working-class thing":** Iler interview.
116 **"just the way he related . . .":** Foderaro interview.
116 **"Always getting presents . . .":** Falco interview, May 17, 2023.
116 **"There would be a spread . . .":** Sakharov interview.
116 **"A huge box . . .":** Author interview with Mark Armstrong, January 23, 2024.
116 **"I never saw him . . .":** Iler interview.
116 **"I mean, he punched holes . . .":** Gee interview.
116 **"Yeah, he definitely would lose . . .":** Author interview with Drea de Matteo, May 22, 2023.
116 **"I remember once, he was messing . . .":** Abraham interview.
117 **"He would punch . . .":** Schirripa interview.
117 **"I did witness . . .":** Falco interview, May 17, 2023.
117 **"He's a perfectionist . . .":** Curatola interview.
117 **"On the second day . . .":** Iler interview.
117 **"He was gentle . . .":** Falco interview, May 17, 2023.
117 **"For some strange reason . . .":** Curatola interview.
118 **"One time they had to make quail . . .":** Gee interview.
118 **"They were having steak . . .":** Ibid.
118 **"We did it . . .":** Falco interview, May 17, 2023.

Chapter 11

119 **"I remember at the end . . .":** Abraham interview.
119 **no such modesty:** Season 2 ad campaign: Bill Carter, "HBO Wants to Make Sure You Notice," *New York Times*, January 11, 2000, www.nytimes.com/2000/01/11/arts/hbo-wants-to-make-sure-you-notice.html.
120 **legendary Ziegfeld Theatre:** Season 2 premiere: Glenn Collins with Joe Brescia, "These Sopranos Usually Don't Sing," *New York Times*, January 7, 2000, www.nytimes.com/2000/01/07/nyregion/public-lives.html; Carol Diuguid, "'Sopranos' Tuning Up," *Variety*, January 9, 2000, variety.com/2000/scene/vpage/sopranos-tuning-up-1117760662/; Paul Lieberman, "Godfather to This Bunch of Gangsters," *Los Angeles Times*, January 14, 2000, www.latimes.com/archives/la-xpm-2000-jan-14-ca-53798-story.html; Linda Stasi, "Stars Sing Praises of 'Sopranos' at Premiere," *New York Post*, January 6, 2000, nypost.com/2000/01/06/stars-sing-praises-of-sopranos-at-premiere/.
120 **"At that point, I was working . . .":** Duffy interview.
120 **"The evolution of Jimmy . . .":** Forsyth interview.
120 **"the most talked-about show . . .":** Caryn James, "Be Patient: The Best May Be Last, After the Fall," *New York Times*, September 12, 1999, www.nytimes.com/1999/09/12/arts/new-season-television-radio-be-patient-best-may-be-last-after-fall.html.
120 **"As startling and . . .":** Matt Roush, "Mesmerized by the Mob," *TV Guide*, January 15, 2000, NYPL.
120 **"'The Sopranos' is perhaps . . .":** Verne Gay, "Family Dynamics," *Newsday*, January 13, 2000, NYPL.
121 **"'The Sopranos remains . . .":** Eric Mink, "'Sopranos' II: All Hail the Gang," *New York Daily News*, January 14, 2000, NYPL.
121 **"James Gandolfini continues . . .":** Phil Gallo, "The Sopranos," *Variety*, January 12,

2000, variety.com/2000/tv/reviews/the-sopranos-6-1117775557/.

121 **"How magically James . . .":** Caryn James, "The Ziti's in the Oven and the Matriarch's Still Not Dead," *New York Times*, January 14, 2000, www.nytimes.com/2000/01/14/movies/tv-weekend-the-ziti-s-in-the-oven-and-the-matriarch-s-still-not-dead.html.

121 **"James Gandolfini's brutal . . .":** Howard Rosenberg, "'Sopranos,' Still Supreme," *Los Angeles Times*, January 14, 2000, www.latimes.com/archives/la-xpm-2000-jan-14-ca-53800-story.html.

121 **"We'd get accused . . .":** Kashner and Kelly, *The Sopranos*, 56.

121 **"Why America Loves 'The Sopranos'":** Verlyn Klinkenborg, *New York Times*, January 16, 2000, www.nytimes.com/2000/01/16/opinion/editorial-notebook-why-america-loves-the-sopranos.html.

121 **"Without Jim Gandolfini . . .":** "Gandolfini Through the Eyes of Those He Worked With," *Fresh Air*, June 20, 2013, www.npr.org/2013/06/20/193865792/gandolfini-through-the-eyes-of-those-he-worked-with.

121 **ratings continued to soar:** Season 2 ratings /HBO response: Bill Carter, "'Sopranos' Remains Boss at Season's End," *New York Times*, April 10, 2000, www.nytimes.com/2000/04/10/business/media-sopranos-remains-boss-at-season-s-end.html.

121 **THE BRAINS BEHIND THE TALKING FISH:** Eric Mink, *New York Daily News*, April 13, 2000, NYPL.

122 **"'He was a very down-to-earth . . .'":** Claudia Rowe, "Permanent Summer or Just a Rental?" *New York Times*, May 21, 2000, www.nytimes.com/2000/05/21/nyregion/permanent-summer-or-just-a-rental.html.

122 **"He was married . . .":** Sanders interview, January 10, 2024.

122 **"apparently up for . . .":** George Rush & Joanna Molloy, "'Sopranos' Star Is Off in a Flash," *New York Daily News*, February 6, 2000, NYPL.

122 **his co-op board:** *New York Post*, April 19, 1999, NYPL.

122 **"MOB" CONTRACT WAR:** Laura Italiano, "'Mob' Contract War: Film-Star Couple Sues 'Soprano' Over House": *New York Post*, October 27, 2001, nypost.com/2001/10/27/mob-contract-war-film-star-couple-sues-soprano-over-house/.

122 **ACID REFLUX, CHIC GASTRIC AILMENT, REPLACES THE ULCER—ASK GANDOLFINI:** Ian Blecher, *New York Observer*, March 12, 2001, observer.com/2001/03/acid-reflux-chic-gastric-ailment-replaces-the-ulcerask-gandolfini/.

122 **EAT! IT'S TUBBY TOWN:** Alexandra Wolfe, *New York Observer*, September 30, 2002, observer.com/2002/09/eat-its-tubby-town-2/.

123 **"He hated it . . .":** Aston interview.

123 **"He definitely tried . . .":** Sanders interview, January 10, 2024.

123 **"Gandolfini's goodfella stirs . . .":** Michelle McPhee, "Soprano's Hot Number," *New York Daily News*, April 8, 1999, NYPL.

123 **"We all had crushes . . .":** De Matteo interview, May 22, 2023.

123 **"It's true that Tony's . . .":** Reid, "Still Just a Regular Guy."

123 **"that happened when . . .":** *Inside the Actors Studio*.

124 **"And that couch-potato . . .":** McPhee, "Soprano's Hot Number."

124 **"women that were hitting on him . . .":** Author interview with Rod Lurie, June 29, 2023.

124 **"I don't think he ever really wanted . . .":** Armstrong interview, January 9, 2024.

124 **"I said, you . . .":** Van Zandt interview.

125 **Jim and Meryl Streep:** Sanders interview, January 10, 2024; Armstrong interview, January 9, 2024.

125 **"I think there was a certain amount . . .":** Schirripa interview.

125 **"I'm under no delusions . . .":** Reid, "Still Just a Regular Guy."

125 **"I think, given how he grew up . . .":** Doussant interview.

126 **"He was just a regular guy . . .":** Williamson interview.

126 **"I know that he missed . . .":** Aston interview.

126 **"I remember being out with him . . .":** Author interview with Robert Pulcini and Shari Springer Berman, August 10, 2023.

126 **"Jim Gandolfini was just part . . .":** Woo interview.

126 **"For the first two days . . .":** Heath, "Mooners, Misbehavior and Mobbed-Up Actors."

126 **"He was adamant . . .":** Armstrong interview, January 9, 2024.

127 **"I'm saying that . . .":** Heath, "Garden State Warrior."

127 **"It's just not comfortable . . .":** Aston interview.

127 **"I actually learned . . .":** De Matteo interview, May 22, 2023.

127 **"When we went . . .":** Pastore interview.
127 **"We were in West Virginia . . .":** *James Gandolfini: Tribute to a Friend.*
127 **"We'd be in the bathroom . . .":** Ibid.
128 **"God love him . . .":** Richardson interview.
128 **"When it came down to it . . .":** Falco interview, May 17, 2023.
128 **"I would call . . .":** *Talking Sopranos*, episode 62, May 31, 2021, youtu.be/9uAYrPwpR5k?si=akPv471qJBmnd7GL.
128 **"I've been in . . .":** *Inside the Actors Studio.*

Chapter 12

129 **IS TONY GETTING TOO BIG FOR TV?:** Don Kaplan, *New York Post*, August 13, 2001, nypost.com/2001/08/13/is-tony-getting-too-big-for-tv/.
129 **Caruso was the white-hot lead:** David Caruso background: Daniel Howard Cerone, "Det. Kelly's Public Hell," *Los Angeles Times*, March 12, 1995, www.latimes.com/archives/la-xpm-1995-03-12-ca-41938-story.html.
129 **after season 2 wrapped:** Season 2–3 hiatus: Bill Carter, "'Sopranos' Remains Boss at Season's End," *New York Times*, April 10, 2000, www.nytimes.com/2000/04/10/business/media-sopranos-remains-boss-at-season-s-end.html.
129 **"Jim's natural vernacular . . .":** Curatola interview.
129 **"He played tough . . .":** Author email interview with Geoffrey Fletcher, May 24, 2023.
130 **opposite Leonardo DiCaprio:** *Catch Me If You Can*: Claude Brodesser and Dana Harris, "Inside Move: DiCaprio Misses 'Catch,'" *Variety*, November 5, 2000, variety.com/2000/film/news/inside-move-dicaprio-misses-catch-1117788759/.
130 **He "looked likely":** *I Now Pronounce You Chuck and Larry / The Honeymooners*: Michael Fleming, "Gandolfini Pining for Kramden Duty," *Variety*, April 15, 2002, variety.com/2002/voices/columns/it-s-all-about-a-remake-as-par-preps-new-alfie-1117865504/.
130 **Most tantalizing:** *Scared Guys*: Michael Fleming, "Dream Casting," *Variety*, August 8, 2001, variety.com/2001/voices/columns/fox-hooks-fisher-lead-1117850965/; Michael Fleming, "De Niro Thinks Shrink," *Variety*, October 17, 2001, variety.com/2001/film/columns/de-niro-thinks-shrink-1117854478/.
130 **"He wanted to diversify . . .":** Pastore interview.
130 **"He was always worried . . .":** Aston interview.
131 **"I couldn't play another thug . . .":** Bracco and McDermott, "The Mobster and the Shrink."
131 **story of a nice girl:** *The Mexican* background: Michael Fleming, "Pitt Giving Books Looks for Par & U," *Variety*, March 9, 2000, variety.com/2000/film/news/pitt-giving-books-look-for-par-u-1117779297/.
131 **"It's so amazing . . .":** John Hiscock, "Pretty Woman Made Me Gay; How Julia Roberts Convinced Sopranos' Star James Gandolfini to Play a Gay Hitman in The Mexican," accessed October 30, 2023, www.thefreelibrary.com/Film%3a+PRETTY+WOMAN+MADE+ME+GAY%3b+How+Julia+Roberts+convinced+Sopranos%27-a073697430.
131 **"He loved Brad . . .":** Sanders interview, January 10, 2024.
132 **"Julia wanted me to do it . . .":** Hiscock, "Pretty Woman Made Me Gay."
132 **"Talk about not . . .":** Mitchell Fink, "New Side of Tony Soprano?," *New York Daily News*, May 8, 2000, NYPL.
132 **"Basically, I worked out . . .":** Mitchell Fink, "Soprano Slims Down on 'Mexican' Food," *New York Daily News*, June 1, 2000, NYPL.
132 **"I started to slim . . .":** Hiscock, "Pretty Woman Made Me Gay."
132 **"He usually called . . .":** Armstrong interview, January 9, 2024.
132 **"I didn't think it was going well . . .":** *Inside the Actors Studio.*
133 **"It was nowhere in the writing . . .":** Aston interview.
133 **"He's a liar . . .":** Rush & Molloy, "A Regular Wise Guy," *New York Daily News*, March 7, 2001, NYPL.
133 **"This is a smart lady . . .":** *Inside the Actors Studio.*
133 **"She's one of the good ones":** Kevin Giordano, "Moving Tribute to Julia," *Variety*, March 5, 2001, variety.com/2001/scene/vpage/moving-tribute-to-julia-1117794805/.
133 **Gandolfini shows up about:** *The Mexican*, directed by Gore Verbinski, DreamWorks Pictures, 2001.
133 **"No one in . . .":** Andrew Sullivan, "The Way We Live Now: 3-18-01; Life After Wartime," *New York Times Magazine*, March 18, 2001, www.nytimes.com/2001/03/18/magazine/the-way-we-live-now-3-18-01-life-after-wartime.html.

134 **"it wants ever so desperately . . .":** Kenneth Turan, "Roberts and Pitt Take Dead Aim," *Los Angeles Times*, March 2, 2001, www.latimes.com/archives/la-xpm-2001-mar-02-ca-32062-story.html.

134 **"surprising depth of . . .":** Mike D'Angelo, "The Mexican," *Time Out New York*, March 1, 2001, NYPL.

134 **"Thank god for . . .":** Bob Graham, "The Brad and Julia Show," *San Francisco Chronicle*, March 2, 2001, NYPL.

134 **$20 million weekend:** *The Mexican* box office: Carl DiOrio, "'Mex' Numero Uno," *Variety*, March 3, 2001, variety.com/2001/film/news/mex-numero-uno-1117794595/.

134 **"He sort of . . .":** Armstrong interview, January 9, 2024.

135 **"He was never gonna say no . . .":** Sanders interview, January 10, 2024.

135 **"The script was unlike . . .":** *The Man Who Wasn't There* production notes, NYPL.

135 **"a very smart guy . . .":** *Inside the Actors Studio.*

135 **"It was a worthwhile experience . . .":** Sanders interview, January 10, 2024.

135 **"terrific," per:** A. O. Scott, "First Passive and Invisible, Then Ruinous and Glowing," *New York Times*, October 31, 2001, www.nytimes.com/2001/10/31/movies/film-review-first-passive-and-invisible-then-ruinous-and-glowing.html.

136 **"a force of nature":** Peter Travers, "The Man Who Wasn't There," *Rolling Stone*, November 22, 2001, NYPL.

136 **"he was really reluctant . . .":** Author interview with Rod Lurie, May 12, 2023.

136 ***The Castle*:** *The (Last) Castle* background: Michael Fleming, "Gandolfini Reaches D'Works' 'Castle,'" *Variety*, January 7, 2001, variety.com/2001/film/news/gandolfini-reaches-d-works-castle-1117791409/; *The Last Castle* production notes, NYPL.

136 **"Tony's emotions just . . .":** Lou Lumenick, "Tony, Tony, Tony: TV Mob Boss Now Gets Film Roles No One Could Refuse," *New York Post*, October 14, 2001, nypost.com/2001/10/14/tony-tony-tony-tv-mob-boss-now-gets-film-roles-no-one-could-refuse/.

136 **"Usually I play characters . . .":** Reid, "Still Just a Regular Guy."

137 **"ferocious in his commitment . . .":** Lurie interview, May 12, 2023.

137 **"like for a full minute . . .":** Lurie interview, June 29, 2023.

317 **"The other thing that was dichotomous . . .":** Lurie interview, May 12, 2023.

137 **"I play chess . . .":** Lurie interview, June 29, 2023.

138 **"It's not Bob's style . . .":** Ibid.

138 **"Often actors will . . .":** Lurie interview, May 12, 2023.

139 **"I thought it was a very good script . . .":** *Inside the Actors Studio.*

139 **"There was no such thing . . .":** Lurie interview, May 12, 2023.

140 **Colonel Winter:** *The Last Castle*, directed by Rob Lurie, DreamWorks Pictures, 2001.

140 **"an about-face for . . .":** Matt Zoller Seitz, "The Last Castle," *New York Press*, October 24–30, 2001, NYPL.

140 **"Mr. Gandolfini shows . . .":** Elvis Mitchell, "Manning the Ramparts for Old Glory," *New York Times*, October 19, 2001, www.nytimes.com/2001/10/19/movies/film-review-manning-the-ramparts-for-old-glory.html.

140 **"Redford's chiseled nobility . . .":** Jan Stuart, "An Ex-Officer and a Not-So-Gentle Man," *Newsday*, October 19, 2001, NYPL.

140 **"creates not simply . . .":** Roger Ebert, "The Last Castle," *Chicago Sun-Times*, October 19, 2001, www.rogerebert.com/reviews/the-last-castle-2001.

140 **"there's been a lot of money . . .":** Reid, "Still Just a Regular Guy."

141 **"This is why it's very rare . . .":** Lurie interview, June 29, 2023.

141 **a bust:** *The Last Castle* budget and box office: Box Office Mojo/IMDb Pro, pro.imdb.com/title/tt0272020?ref_=mojo_rl_summary&rf=mojo_rl_summary.

141 **"The first poster . . .":** Lurie interview, May 12, 2023.

141 **"Please note that . . .":** "DreamWorks Rights 'Castle's' Flag," *Los Angeles Times*, October 15, 2001, www.latimes.com/archives/la-xpm-2001-oct-15-ca-57394-story.html.

141 **"They tried to seize . . .":** Liz Smith, "Redford Sounds Off," *Newsday*, January 4, 2002, NYPL.

141 **"I was a little . . .":** Lumenick, "Tony, Tony, Tony."

142 **"They loved him . . .":** Ibid.

142 **"The guys who were working . . .":** Bischoff, *James Gandolfini*, 141.

142 **Helping Hands II: Handmade in America:** Rebecca Traister, "Paint & Suffering," *New York Observer*, December 24, 2001,

observer.com/2001/12/aoltime-warners-new-chief-richard-parsons-makes-his-social-debut/.

142 **"The baby has . . .":** Hiscock, "Pretty Woman Made Me Gay."

142 **"I'm up in the warden's office . . .":** Lurie interview, May 12, 2023.

142 **"I just like the house . . .":** Deborah Netburn, "Soprano Suburb?," *New York Observer*, April 29, 2002, observer.com/2002/04/sopranos-suburb/.

142 **fortieth-birthday party:** Mitchell Fink, "Why Gandolfini & the Gang Couldn't Make It to Awards," *New York Daily News*, July 24, 2001, NYPL.

143 **"I think a lot of it . . .":** Aston interview.

143 **"I had it put this way . . .":** Author interview with Edie Falco, March 29, 2024.

Chapter 13

144 **"most of my time talking . . .":** Van Zandt interview.

144 **"He likes to have a good time . . .":** Gee interview.

144 **"So that could throw a day . . .":** Kornacki interview.

144 **As updates were relayed:** Late days routine: Mark Kamine, *On Locations: Lessons Learned from My Life on Set with "The Sopranos" and in the Film Industry* (Lebanon, N.H.: Steerforth, 2024), 117.

145 **"Find something else . . .":** Kamine interview.

145 **"After the first time . . .":** Kornacki interview.

145 **"Look, it was difficult . . .":** Abraham interview.

145 **"Time would pass . . .":** Gee interview.

145 **"It's a hard scheduling thing . . .":** Miller, *Tinderbox*, 415.

145 **"I can't say . . .":** Abraham interview.

146 **"I'm not sane . . .":** Reid, "Still Just a Regular Guy."

146 **"The guy was . . .":** Miller, *Tinderbox*, 415.

146 **"I was concerned . . .":** Ibid., 414.

146 **"It was infuriating . . .":** Gee interview.

146 **"Someone like Edie . . .":** Kamine interview.

146 **"As I remember . . .":** Falco interview, March 29, 2024.

146 **"sort of like an apology . . .":** Gee interview.

147 **"there were regrets . . .":** Armstrong interview, January 9, 2024.

147 **"It kind of peaked . . .":** Gee interview.

147 **"I just think . . .":** Karasawa interview.

148 **"Jim did not spend . . .":** Falco interview, March 29, 2024.

148 **"Sweet guy. Listen . . .":** Schirripa interview.

148 **"He was the sun . . .":** Pantoliano interview.

148 **"It was a product . . .":** Gee interview.

148 **TONY SOPRANO HITS JACKPOT:** *New York Post*, September 19, 2000, NYPL.

148 **"said to include . . .":** Michael Fleming, "HBO Pays Off Mob Boss," *Variety*, September 18, 2000, variety.com/2000/tv/news/hbo-pays-off-mob-boss-1117786550/.

148 **"It wasn't really to find stuff . . .":** Armstrong interview, January 9, 2024.

148 **"Being an actor . . .":** Richardson interview.

149 **Nancy Marchand died:** Myrna Oliver, "Nancy Marchand; Actress Starred in TV's 'Sopranos' and 'Lou Grant,'" *Los Angeles Times*, June 20, 2000, www.latimes.com/archives/la-xpm-2000-jun-20-me-42824-story.html; Bob Heisler, "'Sopranos' Handling Its Loss," *New York Daily News*, July 11, 2000, NYPL.

149 **"Jim loved the scenes . . .":** Gee interview.

149 **"If I die . . .":** Kaplan, "'Sopranos' Mom Loses Her Fight for Life."

149 **final scene for Livia:** Andy Geller, "Hi-Tech Livia Lives On in 'Sopranos' Debut," *New York Post*, February 28, 2001, nypost.com/2001/02/28/hi-tech-livia-lives-on-in-sopranos-debut/; Gee interview.

150 **"I can't get the job for you . . .":** Robert Funaro's audition: Funaro interview.

150 **"Doing an hour-long drama . . .":** Whitty, "James Gandolfini Looms Large."

150 **"It was dark . . .":** Sanders interview, January 10, 2024.

150 **"an all-day sucker . . .":** Seitz & Sepinwall, *The Sopranos Sessions*, 538.

151 **"We had been . . .":** *Talking Sopranos*, episode 38, December 14, 2020.

151 **"At the beginning . . .":** Kashner and Kelly, *The Sopranos*, 42.

151 **"We'd have a director . . .":** Karasawa interview.

151 **"My first day . . .":** Pantoliano interview.

152 **"You hold your head high . . .":** Todd A. Kessler story: Libby Torres, "A 'Sopranos' Screenwriter Who Was Fired from the Show Reveals That James Gandolfini Insisted on Taking Him Out to Dinner the Night He Was Let Go," Insider.com,

November 22, 2021, www.insider.com/james-gandolfini-took-fired-sopranos-writer-to-dinner-2021-11.

152 **"So I told the prop guy . . .":** *James Gandolfini: Tribute to a Friend.*

152 **"Once you got . . .":** Seitz & Sepinwall, *The Sopranos Sessions*, 620.

152 **"When Michael was . . .":** Falco interview, May 17, 2023.

153 **"He had his dad . . .":** Gee interview.

153 **In February 2001:** Leaving Marcy: Dareh Gregorian, "'Tony Soprano' Divorces for Real," *New York Post*, December 19, 2002, nypost.com/2002/12/19/tony-soprano-divorces-for-real/.

153 **feverish sense of anticipation:** Season 3 hype: Martin, *Difficult Men*, 164; Howard Rosenberg, "They Keep Pulling Us Back In," *Los Angeles Times*, March 2, 2001, www.latimes.com/archives/la-xpm-2001-mar-02-ca-32063-story.html.

153 **"A mob of . . .":** Chris Wilson, "The Son Also Falls—Gala Shocker," *New York Post*, February 22, 2001, nypost.com/2001/02/22/the-son-also-falls-gala-shocker-sopranos-kid-to-take-turn-for-worse/.

154 **"'The Sopranos' retains . . .":** Phil Gallo, "The Sopranos," *Variety*, March 1, 2001, variety.com/2001/tv/reviews/the-sopranos-7-1200467553/.

154 **LIKE IBSEN OR DICKENS, *SOPRANOS* IS OUR PEAK:** Michael M. Thomas, *New York Observer*, June 4, 2001, observer.com/2001/06/like-ibsen-or-dickens-sopranos-is-our-peak/.

154 **restaurants mentioned on the show:** Rebecca Traister, "Sopranos in Manhattan, Without Reservations," *New York Observer*, March 19, 2001, observer.com/2001/03/sopranos-in-manhattan-without-reservations/.

154 **guided tours:** Debra Galant, "Guides Finger 'Sopranos' Sites," *New York Times*, July 22, 2001, www.nytimes.com/2001/07/22/travel/guides-finger-sopranos-sites.html; Steve Parks, "Crook's Tour," *Newsday*, April 6, 2001, NYPL.

154 **"Joey Flowers" Tangorra:** Jerry Capeci, "Capo's Life Imitates Art," *New York Daily News*, April 23, 2001, NYPL.

154 **"If this kind of ethnic profiling . . .":** Raymond Hernandez, "Congresswoman Takes a Whack at 'The Sopranos' Stereotype," *New York Times*, May 24, 2001, www.nytimes.com/2001/05/24/nyregion/congresswoman-takes-a-whack-at-the-sopranos-stereotype.html.

154 **schools refused:** AP, "An Offer They Refused: School Kills HBO Shoot," *Newsday*, November 3, 2000, NYPL; Dexter Filkins, "'Sopranos' Makes Offer Several Schools Refuse," *New York Times*, November 8, 2000, www.nytimes.com/2000/11/08/nyregion/sopranos-makes-offer-several-schools-refuse.html.

154 **Officials in Essex County:** County property controversies: AP, "'Sopranos' Banned from County Property," *New York Times*, December 17, 2000, NYPL; Michael Starr, "Gang-Ho for 'Sopranos': Rival Jersey Counties Put Out Welcome Mat for Tony and His Mob After Film Ban," *New York Post*, December 21, 2000, nypost.com/2000/12/21/gang-ho-for-sopranos-rival-jersey-counties-put-out-welcome-mat-for-tony-and-his-mob-after-film-ban/; Ronald Smothers, "Former Essex County Official Sentenced in Corruption Case," *New York Times*, October 18, 2003, www.nytimes.com/2003/10/18/nyregion/former-essex-county-official-sentenced-in-corruption-case.html.

154 **"individual dignity":** Austin Smith, "Group Sues 'Sopranos' as Defamatory," *New York Post*, April 6, 2001, nypost.com/2001/04/06/group-sues-sopranos-as-defamatory/); AP, "'Sopranos' Suit Is Thrown Out," *Newsday*, September 20, 2001, NYPL.

155 **"Arrant exploitation of . . .":** William F. Buckley, "Exercises in Infamy," *New York Post*, April 4, 2001, NYPL.

155 **"unusually sleazy and gratuitous":** Austin Smith, "Did 'Sopranos' Go Too Far?," *New York Post*, April 5, 2001, nypost.com/2001/04/05/did-sopranos-go-too-far-young-girls-brutal-death-stirred-up-backlash-among-mob-opera-fans/.

155 **"the first three weeks . . .":** Marvin Kitman, "No More Mr. Nice Wiseguy," *New York Daily News*, April 15, 2001, NYPL.

155 **"Just a lot . . .":** Austin Smith, "'Sopranos' Finale Hits Sour Note," *New York Post*, May 21, 2001, nypost.com/2001/05/21/sopranos-finale-hits-sour-note/.

155 **The ratings, however:** Bill Carter, "Bada-Bing Go the Ratings," *New York Times*, March 7, 2001, www.nytimes.com/2001/03/07/arts/tv-notes-bada-bing-go-the-ratings.html; Bill Carter, "A Big 'Sopranos' Finale," *New York Times*, May 23, 2001, www.nytimes.com/2001/05/23/arts/tv-notes-a-big-sopranos-finale.html.

155 **Emmy nominations were announced that summer:** Bernard Weinraub, "Emmy Award Nominations Favor Established Hits," *New York Times*, July 13, 2001, www.nytimes.com

/2001/07/13/movies/emmy-award-nominations-favor-established-hits.html; Bernard Weinraub, "Subdued Patriotism Replaces Glitter as Television Finally Presents Its Emmys," *New York Times*, November 5, 2001, www.nytimes.com/2001/11/05/us/subdued-patriotism-replaces-glitter-as-television-finally-presents-its-emmys.html.

155 **"he hit Richard . . .":** *Talking Sopranos*, episode 34, November 16, 2020, youtu.be/ASlfHgqqdfs.

155 **"They serve liquor . . .":** Ibid.

Chapter 14

156 **"What're they going to do . . .":** Steven Van Zandt on the hiatus: Kashner and Kelly, *The Sopranos*, 46.

156 **targeted to debut:** Hiatus: Bill Carter, "Sopranos Go Mute," *New York Times*, September 5, 2001, www.nytimes.com/2001/09/05/arts/tv-notes-an-awards-host-deep-in-training.html.

156 **"I'm just speaking for myself . . .":** David Bianculli, "'Sopranos' Endgame," *New York Daily News*, July 15, 2002, NYPL).

156 **extend his contract:** Chase's deal: Michael Fleming, "HBO, Chase Eyeing More 'Sopranos,'" *Variety*, July 9, 2001, variety.com/2001/film/columns/miramax-opens-an-english-lingo-closet-1117802489/; Jim Rutenberg, "'Sopranos' Creator Expected to Remain for a Fifth Season," *New York Times*, July 17, 2001, www.nytimes.com/2001/07/17/business/sopranos-creator-expected-to-remain-for-a-fifth-season.html.

156 **"numb parody":** Heath, "Mooners, Misbehavior and Mobbed-Up Actors."

156 **Production commenced on season 4:** Lumenick, "Tony, Tony, Tony."

156 **"While Taylor calmly listens . . .":** Stephen Battaglio, "'Sopranos,' Behind the Music," *New York Daily News*, May 16, 2002, NYPL.

157 **According to Riegert:** Imperioli, Schirripa, and Lerman, *Woke Up This Morning*, 291–92.

157 **Jim's work stoppages had become a pattern:** Martin, *Difficult Men*, 26.

157 **"There was probably a peak . . .":** Kamine interview.

157 **"So first, you worry about . . .":** Miller, *Tinderbox*, 415.

157 **"It was an annoyance . . .":** Martin, *Difficult Men*, 11.

158 **"Nobody could find him . . .":** Gee interview.

158 **"It was some drummer . . .":** Martin, *Difficult Men*, 26.

158 **"And we just said . . .":** Miller, *Tinderbox*, 415.

158 **"He had real struggles . . .":** Aston interview.

158 **"I wouldn't want . . .":** Abraham interview.

158 **"What I think is interesting . . .":** De Matteo interview, March 22, 2024.

158 **"He was a man . . .":** Gee interview.

158 **"You cannot protect them . . .":** Woo interview.

159 **"It didn't strike . . .":** De Matteo interview, March 22, 2024.

159 **"He was fun . . .":** Kamine interview.

160 **"Props would give . . .":** Gee interview.

160 **"If there was drinking . . .":** Abraham interview.

160 **"We were all having a blast . . .":** De Matteo interview, March 22, 2024.

160 **"I didn't see him drunk . . .":** Kamine interview.

160 **"He and Michael . . .":** Abraham interview.

160 **"Jim was drinking . . .":** Gee interview.

160 **"I was nervous . . .":** Falco interview, March 29, 2024.

161 **"I used to call them the vampires . . .":** Kashner and Kelly, *The Sopranos*, 23.

161 **"I know Jim . . .":** Abraham interview.

161 **"Jim always said that . . .":** Kashner and Kelly, *The Sopranos*, 24.

161 **"In all of these serial . . .":** Ibid.

161 **"TONY SOPRANO" WHACKS HIS MARRIAGE:** Richard Johnson, *New York Post*, March 13, 2002, nypost.com/2002/03/13/tony-soprano-whacks-his-marriage/.

161 **"had trouble right . . .":** George Rush & Joanna Molloy, "A Soprano Split," *New York Daily News*, March 14, 2002, NYPL.

162 **full-cover spread:** Adams, "BADFELLA."

162 **rumored affair:** Chris Wilson, "Splitsville: 'Soprano' Wife Never Saw It Coming," *New York Post*, March 14, 2002, nypost.com/2002/03/14/splitsville-sopranos-stars-wife-never-saw-it-coming/.

162 **"wild sexual affair":** "Ba-da-bing! Tony Soprano Caught in Real-Life Cheating Scandal," *National Enquirer*, March 27, 2002, www.nationalenquirer.com/celebrity/ba-da-bing-tony-soprano-caught-real-life-cheating-scandal/.

162 **Page Six would subsequently report:** Lora Somoza on Page Six: Richard Johnson, "Gandolfini Met Lover on Set," *New York Post*, April 4, 2002, NYPL; Richard

Johnson, "Tony's Girl Is Right at Home," *New York Post*, May 20, 2002 (NYPL).

162 **"My husband basically . . .":** Adams, "BADFELLA."

162 **leaked to the *Enquirer*:** *Enquirer* reporting of divorce filings: The original *Enquirer* story is no longer available online, but it was quoted in George Rush, "Tony's Drug Woes," *New York Daily News*, October 17, 2002, NYPL; and Richard Johnson, "Gandolfinis' Split Gets Uglier," *New York Post*, October 11, 2002, NYPL.

163 **"God, I can't believe . . .":** Levine, "Exclusive Interview!".

163 **"We're getting along . . .":** Richard Johnson, "Friends Again," *New York Post*, October 12, 2002, NYPL.

163 **"almost record time":** Brian Hiatt, "James Gandolfini Finalizes Divorce," *Entertainment Weekly*, December 19, 2002, ew.com/article/2002/12/19/james-gandolfini-finalizes-divorce/.

164 **"they appeared to be abandonment":** Associated Press, "Judge Grants Gandolfini Divorce," *Newsday*, December 19, 2002, NYPL.

164 **"Perp walk . . .":** Helen Peterson, "Divorce, Soprano-Style," *New York Daily News*, December 19, **2002, NYPL.**

164 **$1.05 million deal:** Condo purchase: Netburn, "Soprano Suburb?"

164 **a restaurant and bar:** Vines investment: Denise Richardson, "Gandolfini's Sudden Death Hits Home," *Daily Star* (Oneota), June 21, 2013, www.thedailystar.com/news/local_news/gandolfinis-sudden-death-hits-home/article_7c16c975-852c-53d9-a776-4b58da86df1e.html.

164 **grand opening party:** The Vines opening: Paul Tetley and Bill Hoffman, "Goodfella 'Mixes' It Up Again," *New York Post*, April 19, 2002, NYPL.

164 **out and about:** *New York Post*, October 11, 2002, photo by Helayne Seidman, NYPL.

164 **"I catch a lot of grief . . .":** Heath, "Garden State Warrior."

164 **Video Music Awards:** Glenn Collins with James Barron, "Mob Connections," *New York Times*, September 3, 2002, www.nytimes.com/2002/09/03/nyregion/boldface-names-684414.html.

164 **"highly exaggerated . . .":** George Rush & Joanna Molloy, "Gandolfini's Not Acting All Broken Up," *New York Daily News*, October 23, 2002, NYPL.

164 **"They have some issues . . .":** George Rush & Joanna Molloy, "Looks Like Tony's a Hit with the Ladies," *New York Daily News*, June 1, 2003, NYPL.

164 **"He's hitting downtown . . .":** Richard Johnson, "Freedom Rings," *New York Post*, July 31, 2003, NYPL.

164 **"He was always a smart ass . . .":** Caroline Graham, "Tony Soprano Drove My Gentle Giant to Binge His Life Away," *Daily Mail Online*, June 22, 2013, www.dailymail.co.uk/news/article-2346673/James-Gandolfini-dead-Tony-Soprano-drove-gentle-giant-binge-life-away-says-sex-therapist-ex-girlfriend.html.

164 **split custody:** Rush & Molloy, "Gandolfini's Not Acting All Broken Up."

164 **Paparazzi caught them:** Out and about with Michael: "He's a Wisedaddy," *New York Daily News*, April 2, 2002, NYPL; *New York Post*, December 16, 2012, photo by Albert Ferreira, NYPL; *New York Daily News*, October 20, 2003, photo by Richard Corkery, NYPL.

165 **"He just was generous . . .":** Richardson interview.

165 **"One day I get a call . . .":** *James Gandolfini: Tribute to a Friend.*

165 **"FDNY Is Worth It" campaign:** Alice McQuillan, "Sopranos Star Aids Push to Raise Bravest Pay," *New York Daily News*, October 29, 2002, NYPL.

165 **"He came every year . . .":** Comarato interview.

165 **left his talent agency:** Dana Harris and Michael Fleming, "Gandolfini Whacks W&A," *Variety*, June 19, 2003, variety.com/2003/scene/markets-festivals/inside-move-gandolfini-whacks-w-a-1117888235/; Don Kaplan, "'Sopranos' Star Stands by Whacked Goombah," *New York Post*, June 25, 2003, nypost.com/2003/06/25/sopranos-star-stands-by-whacked-goombah/.

166 **boxing drama:** *The Set-Up*: Charles Lyons, "Lumet 'Set-Up' Again," *Variety*, September 19, 2002, variety.com/2002/film/news/lumet-set-up-again-1117873050/.

166 **2002 iteration:** *Before the Devil Knows You're Dead*: Claude Brodesser and Marc Graser, "Gandolfini Wants Pic Deal for 'Christmas,'" *Variety*, December 17, 2002, variety.com/2002/film/markets-festivals/gandolfini-wants-pic-deal-for-christmas-1117877614/.

166 **Glenn Ficarra and John Requa:** *Bad Santa*: Bruce Fretts, "How the First 'Bad Santa'

Boozed Down the Chimney," November 4, 2016, www.nytimes.com/2016/11/06/movies/how-the-first-bad-santa-boozed-down-the-chimney.html.

166 **DreamWorks comedy:** *Shark Tale:* Dade Hayes and Marc Graser, "'Toon Turf Tussle," *Variety*, June 26, 2002, variety.com/2002/film/markets-festivals/toon-turf-tussle-1117869082.

166 **"I will respectfully . . .":** Armstrong interview, January 9, 2024.

167 ***Sesame Street*:** "Oscar's Road Trip," season 33, episode 50, aired April 12, 2002, www.youtube.com/watch?v=Y-v6T4gUmkw.

167 **Global Crossing:** Simon Romero, "You Kidding Me? How Global Crossing Pursued Tony Soprano," *New York Times*, June 10, 2002, www.nytimes.com/2002/06/10/business/you-kidding-me-how-global-crossing-pursued-tony-soprano.html.

167 **"It's like we have to . . .":** Noel Holston, "Few Clues on New 'Sopranos,'" *Newsday*, July 14, 2002, NYPL.

167 **story about the conclusions:** Photo fan theories: Don Kaplan, "Mob Picture Puzzle—Fans Hunt for Clues in New 'Sopranos' Photo," *New York Post*, August 16, 2002, nypost.com/2002/08/16/mob-picture-puzzle-fans-hunt-for-clues-in-new-sopranos-photo/.

167 **tie-ins:** Coeli Carr, "Wise Guys, and Their Fans, Gotta Eat, Too," *New York Times*, August 5, 2002, www.nytimes.com/2002/08/05/business/mediatalk-wise-guys-and-their-fans-gotta-eat-too.html.

167 **big premiere and party:** Season 4 premiere: James Barron with Alison Leigh Cowan and Wendell Jamieson, "All in the Family," *New York Times*, September 10, 2002, www.nytimes.com/2002/09/10/nyregion/boldface-names-810703.html.

167 **"She's *everything* . . .":** George Rush & Joanna Molloy, "Amore the Merrier for Gandolfini," *New York Daily News*, September 8, 2002, NYPL.

168 **"That was like . . .":** Pantoliano interview.

169 **"as subtle, explosive . . .":** Steve Johnson, "In Season 4, 'Sopranos' Still Hits All the High Notes," *Chicago Tribune*, September 12, 2002, www.chicagotribune.com/news/ct-xpm-2002-09-12-0209120011-story.html.

169 **most-watched show:** Season 4 ratings: Bill Carter, "'Sopranos' Draws Record Viewers to HBO," *New York Times*, September 18, 2002, www.nytimes.com/2002/09/18/business/the-media-business-sopranos-draws-record-viewers-to-hbo.html.

169 **"monotonous, aimless, and . . .":** Austin Smith, "Whack Somebody!—'The Sopranos' Has Become Aimless and Deadly Dull. It Needs a Nasty Death—Fast," *New York Post*, October 15, 2002, nypost.com/2002/10/15/whack-somebody-the-sopranos-has-become-aimless-and-deadly-dull-it-needs-a-nasty-death-fast/.

169 **"basically has been . . .":** Marvin Kitman, "Give 'Sopranos' a Big Whack," *New York Daily News*, March 20, 2003, NYPL.

169 **"in a bit . . .":** Tunku Varadarajan, "Surfer's Guide," *Wall Street Journal*, October 25, 2002, NYPL.

169 **nabbed sixteen nominations:** Season 4 Emmys: Bernard Weinraub, "'Six Feet Under' Leads Emmy Nominations," *New York Times*, July 17, 2003, www.nytimes.com/2003/07/17/arts/television/six-feet-under-leads-emmy-nominations.html; Bill Carter, "Despite Losing Some Biggies, Cable Triumphs at the Emmys," *New York Times*, September 23, 2003, www.nytimes.com/2003/09/23/arts/despite-losing-some-biggies-cable-triumphs-at-the-emmys.html.

169 **button for Joe Renna:** Neil Graves, "Gandolfini's N.J. Pol Pal Stunned by Emmy Plug," *New York Post*, September 23, 2003, NYPL.

169 **"I did have some conversations . . .":** Falco interview, March 29, 2024.

170 **"We had an intervention . . .":** Miller, *Tinderbox*, 417.

170 **According to Miller:** Intervention story: Ibid.

Chapter 15

171 ***Surviving Christmas* sounded:** Background: Brodesser and Graser, "Gandolfini Wants Pic Deal for 'Christmas.'"

171 **"the most passionate . . .":** *Surviving Christmas* production notes, NYPL.

171 **pulled strings:** Affleck and HBO: Armstrong interview, January 9, 2024.

171 **"kind of a disaster . . .":** Sanders interview, January 10, 2024.

171 **"It was a little chaotic . . .":** Author interview with Josh Zuckerman, August 28, 2023.

172 **"This one [Jim] . . .":** Sanders interview, January 10, 2024.

172 **"I remember him smiling . . .":** Zuckerman interview.

172 **The production shot:** *Surviving Christmas* shooting: *Surviving Christmas* production notes, NYPL.

172 **"It never felt . . .":** Zuckerman interview.

173 **is a mess:** *Surviving Christmas*, directed by Mike Mitchell, Dreamworks Pictures, 2004.

173 **"just ten months . . .":** Bill Higgins, "'Tis the Season to Be Early," *Variety*, October 18, 2004, variety.com/2004/scene/vpage/tis-the-season-to-be-early-1117912149/.

173 **"Nobody survives 'Surviving Christmas' . . .":** Lou Lumenick, "Surviving Christmas," *New York Post*, October 20, 2004, NYPL.

173 **"Mr. Gandolfini's Tom . . .":** Stephen Holden, "You Can't Go Home, or Perhaps You Just Shouldn't," *New York Times*, October 22, 2004, www.nytimes.com/2004/10/22/movies/you-cant-go-home-or-perhaps-you-just-shouldnt.html.

173 **It opened in seventh:** *Surviving Christmas* box office: Gabriel Snyder, "'Grudge' Match," *Variety*, October 24, 2004, variety.com/2004/film/box-office/grudge-match-1117912389/.

173 **"an almost mirth-free . . .":** Brian Lowry, "Surviving Christmas," *Variety*, October 21, 2004, variety.com/2004/film/markets-festivals/surviving-christmas-1200530060/.

173 **In late 2002:** Season 5 salary squabble background: David Bianculli, "Spoiling for a Pay Hike," October 19, 2002, NYPL; Bill Carter, "HBO Files Countersuit Against Star of 'The Sopranos,'" *New York Times*, March 12, 2003, www.nytimes.com/2003/03/12/business/hbo-files-countersuit-against-star-of-the-sopranos.html; Michael Starr, "Who's Whacking Who—The Inside Story of James Gandolfini's War with HBO," *New York Post*, March 12, 2003, nypost.com/2003/03/12/whos-whacking-who-the-inside-story-of-james-gandolfinis-war-with-hbo/; Melissa Grego, "Bada-Bing vs. Cha-Ching," *Variety*, March 17, 2003, NYPL; Bill Carter, "In 'Sopranos' Staredown, Both Sides Blink," *New York Times*, March 17, 2003, www.nytimes.com/2003/03/17/business/in-sopranos-staredown-both-sides-blink.html; Bill Carter, "'Sopranos' Star Drops Suit and Will Return to Series," *New York Times*, March 19, 2003, www.nytimes.com/2003/03/19/business/the-media-business-sopranos-star-drops-suit-and-will-return-to-series.html.

173 **"James Gandolfini is said . . .":** Michael Starr, "'Soprano' Co-Stars Gang Up for a Rai$e," *New York Post*, October 18, 2002, nypost.com/2002/10/18/soprano-co-stars-gang-up-for-raie/.

174 **By late February:** Initial deals made: Austin Smith, "Meet the $opranos: Cast Whacks HBO for Big-Bucks Raises," *New York Post*, February 27, 2003, nypost.com/2003/02/27/meet-the-opranos-cast-whacks-hbo-for-big-bucks-raises/.

174 **What's more:** *Sopranos* vs. *Friends* math: Armstrong interview, January 9, 2024.

174 **"He wasn't making that much . . .":** Aston interview.

174 **"A lot of us came . . .":** Kashner and Kelly, *The Sopranos*, 48.

174 **"Our legal position . . .":** Michael Fleming, "'Sopranos' Boss Sues to Whack HBO Pact," *Variety*, March 6, 2003, variety.com/2003/biz/markets-festivals/sopranos-boss-sues-to-whack-hbo-pact-1117881853/.

175 **"We are exposing . . .":** Janet Shprintz, "HBO Set to Whack Back," *Variety*, March 10, 2003, variety.com/2003/biz/markets-festivals/hbo-set-to-whack-back-1117882037/.

175 **"It became a public fight . . .":** Miller, *Tinderbox*, 444.

175 **"greedy pig":** Joanna Molloy, "'Sopranos' Ceasefire: HBO and Tony to Talk Salary," *New York Daily News*, March 17, 2003, www.nydailynews.com/2003/03/17/sopranos-ceasefire-hbo-and-tony-to-talk-salary/.

175 **"That just rocked . . .":** Armstrong interview, January 9, 2024.

175 **"was really offended . . .":** Miller, *Tinderbox*, 444.

175 **"Jim was a brilliant . . .":** Ibid.

176 **"Production on season . . .":** Melissa Grego, "Mob Showdown at HBO," *Variety*, March 12, 2003, variety.com/2003/biz/markets-festivals/mob-showdown-at-hbo-1117882187/.

176 **"Gandolfini's agents believe . . .":** Ibid.

176 **"He had a lot of people . . .":** Sanders interview, January 10, 2024.

176 **But there was more:** Additional contract negotiations: Smith, "Meet the $opranos."

176 **"I remember at one point . . .":** *Talking Sopranos*, episode 10, June 1, 2020.

176 **"In contract negotiations . . .":** Iler interview.

176 **Finally, with the clock:** Brad Grey intercedes: Michael Fleming, "Diplomatic Push in 'Sopranos' Spat," *Variety*, March 16, 2003, variety.com/2003/biz/markets-festivals/diplomatic-push-in-sopranos-spat-1117882403/.

177 **"Lawyers for the . . .":** Michael Shain, "HBO to Cut Tony In on Piece of 'Sopranos'

Action," *New York Post*, March 17, 2003, nypost.com/2003/03/17/hbo-to-cut-tony-in-on-piece-of-soprano-action/.

177 **"I'm very happy . . .":** Melissa Grego and Michael Fleming, "'Sopranos' Sing Sweetly," *Variety*, March 19, 2003, variety.com/2003/scene/markets-festivals/inside-move-sopranos-sing-sweetly-1117882846/.

177 **"I have nothing . . .":** Alison Hope Weiner, "The Bold Soprano," *Entertainment Weekly*, March 28, 2003, ew.com/article/2003/03/28/bold-soprano/.

177 **"His fat salary . . .":** Austin Smith, "Tony's Sorry State: Gandolfini Issues HBO a Big Fat Apology for Contract Rift," *New York Post*, March 22, 2003, NYPL.

177 **The deal they hammered out:** Michael Fleming and Melissa Grego, "'Sopranos' Kingpin Set for Raise," *Variety*, March 17, 2003, variety.com/2003/scene/markets-festivals/sopranos-kingpin-set-for-raise-1117882566/; Stuart Levine, "Gandolfini Fracas: Business, Not Personal," *Variety*, August 24, 2003, variety.com/2003/scene/markets-festivals/gandolfini-fracas-business-not-personal-1117891209/.

177 **"He got paid . . .":** Sanders interview, January 10, 2024.

177 **"The deals that were made . . .":** De Matteo interview, May 22, 2023.

177 **"He pulled each . . .":** Ibid.

177 **"That's all he said . . .":** Schirripa interview.

178 **"Jim, I'm not . . .":** De Matteo interview, May 22, 2023.

178 **"He wrote checks . . .":** Pantoliano interview.

178 **"Nobody knew at that time . . .":** Armstrong interview, January 9, 2024.

178 **"Especially in show business . . .":** Iler interview.

178 **"that part we couldn't talk about . . .":** Armstrong interview, January 9, 2024.

178 **"He split it up . . .":** Van Zandt interview.

178 **"His generosity was unparalleled . . .":** De Matteo interview, May 22, 2023.

178 **Robert Funaro remembers shooting:** Funaro interview.

179 **"There was no ad-libbing . . .":** Schirripa interview. See also Dave McNary, "Oscar-Nominated Actor Robert Loggia Dies at 85," *Variety*, December 4, 2015, variety.com/2015/film/news/robert-loggia-scarface-dies-dead-1201654545/.

179 **"When I was acting . . .":** Imperioli, Schirripa, and Lerman, *Woke Up This Morning*, 332.

180 **"I was nervous . . .":** De Matteo interview, May 22, 2023.

180 **"This doesn't put an end to it . . .":** Kamine, *On Locations*, 129.

180 **"It's like a muscle . . .":** Moody, "James Gandolfini Comes Home."

181 **dance of a new season:** Waiting for season 5: Ted Johnson, "What's the Holdup," *TV Guide*, March 29, 2003, NYPL; David Bianculli, "'Sopranos' No-Show," *New York Daily News*, June 9, 2003, NYPL.

181 **"Can a hit series . . .":** *TV Guide*, March 6, 2004, NYPL.

181 **"SOPRANOS" ACTORS SLEEP WITH THE FISHES IN PROMO PIC:** Don Kaplan, *New York Post*, February 4, 2004, nypost.com/2004/02/04/mob-keeling-spree-sopranos-actors-sleep-with-fishes-in-promo-pic/.

181 **the star-studded premiere:** Season 5 premiere party: Campbell Robertson, "We Feel the Same Way About Gossip Columns," *New York Times*, March 4, 2004, www.nytimes.com/2004/03/04/nyregion/boldface-names-654043.html.

181 **"'The Sopranos' returns . . .":** Alessandra Stanley, "Bullies, Bears and Bullets: It's Round 5," *New York Times*, March 5, 2004, www.nytimes.com/2004/03/05/movies/tv-weekend-bullies-bears-and-bullets-it-s-round-5.html.

181 **dream sequence:** Julie Salamon, "Analyze This: Tony Soprano Had a Dream. A Long One," *New York Times*, May 18, 2004, www.nytimes.com/2004/05/18/arts/analyze-this-tony-soprano-had-a-dream-a-long-one.html.

181 **"Wake me when . . .":** Austin Smith, "Hard Target—Analyzing Tony's 23-Minute Dream," *New York Post*, May 18, 2004, nypost.com/2004/05/18/hard-target-analyzing-tonys-23-minute-dream/.

181 **ratings record-breaker:** Bill Carter, "'Sopranos' Premiere Sets a Record (Sort Of)," *New York Times*, March 10, 2004, www.nytimes.com/2004/03/10/arts/sopranos-premiere-sets-a-record-sort-of.html; Bill Carter, "Sopranos Score in Finale," *New York Times*, June 9, 2004, www.nytimes.com/2004/06/09/theater/arts-briefing-highlights-sopranos-score-in-finale.html.

181 **When the Primetime Emmys:** Season 5 Emmys: Bernard Weinraub, "HBO Is Big Winner at Emmy Awards," *New York Times*, September 20, 2004, www.nytimes.com/2004/09/20/arts/television/hbo-is-big-winner-at-emmy-awards.html.

182 **renewal for a sixth:** Bill Carter, "Producer Says 'Sopranos' Will Have a 6th Season," *New York Times*, June 18, 2003, www.nytimes.com/2003/06/18/business/producer-says-sopranos-will-have-a-6th-season.html.

Chapter 16

183 **"He did a reading . . .":** Addie Morfoot, "Turturro's 'Romance' Premieres," *Variety*, September 5, 2007, variety.com/2007/scene/vpage/turturro-s-romance-premieres-1117971410/.

183 **"It was like, dude . . .":** Sanders interview, January 10, 2024.

183 **"'Pennies from Heaven' . . .":** Michael Fleming, "Coens Croon Feature Tune for Turturro," *Variety*, July 22, 2002, variety.com/2002/film/columns/coens-croon-feature-tune-for-turturro-1117870112/.

183 **"Jim was, you know, Jim . . .":** Karasawa interview.

184 **"There's something about James . . .":** "Gallopin' Gandolfini," *New York Observer*, September 10, 2007, NYPL.

184 **"He would absorb . . .":** Karasawa interview.

184 **"We'd do these . . .":** Ibid.

185 **"He just never saw himself . . .":** Ibid.

185 **"One of my former students . . .":** Aston interview.

185 **occasionally wonderful picture:** *Romance & Cigarettes*, directed by John Turturro, United Artists, 2005/2007.

186 **The film's road:** *Romance & Cigarettes* release: David Rooney, "United Artists," *Variety*, September 7, 2004, variety.com/2004/scene/markets-festivals/united-artists-3-1117910090/; Ian Mohr, "Seconds Count at Fest," *Variety*, September 11, 2005, variety.com/2005/film/news/seconds-count-at-fest-1117928906/; Frank Lidz, "The Actors Sing, the Director Suffers, the Film Survives," *New York Times*, September 2, 2007, www.nytimes.com/2007/09/02/movies/02lidz.html; David M. Halbfinger, "Turturro Film Goes On," *New York Times*, October 5, 2007, www.nytimes.com/2007/10/05/arts/05arts.html.

186 **"There is more . . .":** Stephen Holden, "Blue Collar Guy Loses His Heart and Ruins His Lungs," *New York Times*, September 7, 2007, www.nytimes.com/2007/09/07/movies/07roma.html.

186 **"the most original . . .":** Andrew O'Hehir, "Beyond the Multiplex," *Salon*, September 6, 2007, www.salon.com/2007/09/06/btm_8/.

186 **"the real thing . . .":** Roger Ebert, "Romance & Cigarettes," *Chicago Sun-Times*, November 8, 2007, www.rogerebert.com/reviews/romance-and-cigarettes-2007.

186 **"It's one of the things . . .":** Armstrong interview, January 9, 2024.

186 **"He liked to gather his friends . . .":** Author interview with Jon Alpert, May 19, 2023.

187 **"My grandmother has . . .":** Joyce Wadler, "We're Thinking She's New to the Business," *New York Times*, June 4, 2004, www.nytimes.com/2004/06/04/nyregion/boldface-names-847453.html.

187 **Pediatric AIDS Foundation:** Joyce Wadler, "Leave the Balloon, Take the Cannoli," *New York Times*, May 4, 2004, www.nytimes.com/2004/05/04/nyregion/boldface-names-465283.html.

187 **OctoberWoman:** Michael Starr, "Starr Report," *New York Post*, September 30, 2004, nypost.com/2004/09/30/starr-report-815/.

187 **Bill Clinton:** "Bubba & 'Da Boss': Goofball Bigshots' Beastly Fashion," *New York Post*, August 21, 2004, nypost.com/2004/08/21/bubba-goofball-bigshots-beastlyfashion/.

187 **Republican National Convention:** Michael Slackman and Diane Cardwell, "Tactics By Police Mute the Protestors, and Their Messages," *New York Times*, September 2, 2004, www.nytimes.com/2004/09/02/politics/campaign/tactics-by-police-mute-the-protesters-and-their-messages.html.

187 **African Rainforest Conservancy's:** Campbell Robertson, "And the Other Was 'Mr. Alimony,'" *New York Times*, May 18, 2005, www.nytimes.com/2005/05/18/nyregion/and-the-other-was-mr-alimony.html.

187 **Mario Batali:** Florence Fabricant, "Calendar," *New York Times*, November 1, 2006, www.nytimes.com/2006/11/01/dining/arts/calendar.html.

187 **Rutgers Hall of Distinguished Alumni:** Serena Kappes, "The Week Ahead," *People*, April 30, 2004, people.com/celebrity/the-week-ahead-friends-says-farewell/.

187 **"So the two . . .":** Heath, "Garden State Warrior."

187 **"Lipton did ask . . .":** Aston interview.

188 **inaugural episode:** *The Wiseguy Show*: *Variety* staff, "Mob Scene," *Variety*, June 2, 2004, variety.com/2004/scene/markets-festivals/mob-scene-1117905918/.

188 **He popped up:** *Club Soda*, directed by Paul Carafotes, released as part of *Stories USA* (aka *American Breakdown*), Phase 4 Films, 2007/2010.

188 **And he did a favor:** *The Tony Danza Show*: Virginia Heffernan, "A Heaping Portion of Talk Show Parmigiana," *New York Times*, September 14, 2004, www.nytimes.com/2004/09/14/arts/television/a-heaping-portion-of-talk-show-parmigiana.html.

188 **"He tells the guy . . .":** Danza interview.

188 **"On one level . . .":** Moody, "James Gandolfini Comes Home."

188 **"it's 270 now.":** Heath, "Garden State Warrior."

188 **"I used to say . . .":** *Post* staff, "'Too Old to Lose Weight': Gandolfini," *New York Post*, December 28, 2006, NYPL.

188 **Ernest Hemingway:** *Hemingway and Gellhorn* announcement: Michael Fleming, "Thesp Comes to Papa," *Variety*, August 15, 2004, variety.com/2004/film/markets-festivals/thesp-comes-to-papa-1117909115/.

188 ***All the King's Men*:** Background: Nicole LaPorte, "'King's' Remake Rounds Out Court," *Variety*, November 21, 2004, variety.com/2004/film/markets-festivals/king-s-remake-rounds-out-court-1117913845/; David M. Halbfinger, "The Soul of Willie Stark, Found in the Cutting Room," *New York Times*, September 10, 2006, www.nytimes.com/2006/09/10/movies/moviesspecial/10halb.html.

189 **The high-profile production:** *All the King's Men*, directed by Steven Zaillian, Columbia Pictures, 2006.

189 ***Lonely Hearts*:** Background: Dana Harris, "'Lonely' Finds Company," *Variety*, January 5, 2005, variety.com/2005/film/markets-festivals/lonely-finds-company-1117915840/; *Jacksonville Film & Television Office E-Newsletter* 8, no. 1 (2006), archived at web.archive.org/web/20090224070601/http://www.coj.net/Departments/Jacksonville+Economic+Development+Commission/Film+and+Television/NewsLetters/2006+Newsletter.htm#article1.

189 **"That was a mistake . . .":** Sanders interview, January 10, 2024.

189 **This time they:** *Lonely Hearts*, directed by Todd Robinson, Millennium Films, 2007.

190 **"I saw him . . .":** George Rush & Joanna Molloy, "Joltin' Joe Still a Hit," *New York Daily News*, June 27, 2005, NYPL.

190 **James Gandolfini Sr. died:** "Gandolfini Talks," *Passaic Herald-News*, May 5, 2007, northjersey.newspapers.com/article/the-herald-news-gandolfini-2007/116243400/.

190 **"Of course we . . .":** Curatola interview.

190 **"They are still . . .":** George Rush & Joanna Molloy, "Gandolfini Going Solo as Fiancee Goes to L.A.," *New York Daily News*, February 4, 2005, NYPL.

190 **"Sometimes love does . . .":** Graham, "Tony Soprano Drove My Gentle Giant to Binge His Life Away." Somoza gave this interview shortly after Gandolfini's death; in an odd and tragic coincidence, she too would die at fifty-one, in a freak accident; Kana Ruhalter, "James Gandolfini's Ex-Fiancée Dead in Freak Swimming Pool Accident," *Daily Beast*, November 2, 2021, www.thedailybeast.com/the-sopranos-star-james-gandolfinis-ex-fiancee-lora-somoza-died-in-freak-swimming-pool-accident-at-51.

190 **"My son. And . . .":** Heath, "Garden State Warrior."

191 **"I ran my body . . .":** Ibid.

191 **"I told Patricia . . .":** Golden Globes story: Miller, *Tinderbox*.

191 **slated for Christmas:** *All the King's Men* release: Nicole LaPorte and Gabriel Snyder, "Docket Rocked," *Variety*, October 20, 2005, variety.com/2005/film/markets-festivals/docket-rocked-1117931361/; Nicole LaPorte, "'Men' Shot to Fall Slot," April 12, 2006, variety.com/2006/film/features/men-shot-to-fall-slot-1117941460/; Halbfinger, "The Soul of Willie Stark, Found in the Cutting Room."

191 **"Overstuffed and fatally . . .":** Todd McCarthy, "All the King's Men," *Variety*, September 10, 2006, variety.com/2006/film/awards/all-the-king-s-men-5-1200513573/.

191 **"it's portentous and vague . . .":** David Denby, "Power Players," *New Yorker*, October 2, 2006, www.newyorker.com/magazine/2006/10/02/power-players.

191 **$55 million movie:** *All the King's Men* box office: Scott Martelle, "A 'King'-Sized Collapse," *Los Angeles Times*, October 3, 2006, www.latimes.com/archives/la-xpm-2006-oct-03-et-zaillian3-story.html.

191 **"superb":** David Denby, "Dearly Departed," *New Yorker*, April 23, 2007, www.newyorker.com/magazine/2007/04/23/dearly-departed.

191 **"formidable":** Stephen Holden, "In 'Lonely Hearts,' Crimes' Visceral Side Trumps the Mela[n]cholic," *New York Times*, April 19, 2007, www.nytimes.com/2007/04/19/arts/19iht-fmreview20.1.5350161.html.

191 **"Gandolfini, in classic character actor . . .":** Ronnie Scheib, "Lonely Hearts," May 1, 2006, variety.com/2006/film/markets-festivals/lonely-hearts-2-1200516597/.

192 **a miserable $188,000:** *Lonely Hearts* box office: Box Office Mojo, www.boxofficemojo .com/release/rl1667335681/weekend/.

Chapter 17

193 **execution of its conclusion:** Evolution of season 6: Bill Carter, "Producer Says 'Sopranos' Will Have a Sixth Season," *New York Times*, June 18, 2003, www.nytimes.com /2003/06/18/business/producer-says-sopra nos-will-have-a-6th-season.html; Michael Schneider, "'Sopranos' to Sing for Sixth,' *Variety*, June 17, 2003, variety.com/2003/tv /news/sopranos-to-sing-for-sixth-1117 888092/; Michael Starr, "'Sopranos' Gang Up for Sixth Season," *New York Post*, June 18, 2003, nypost.com/2003/06/18/sopranos-ga ng-up-for-sixth-season/; Denise Martin, "Chase: No Encore for 'Sopranos,'" *Variety*, January 8, 2004, variety.com/2004/scene /markets-festivals/chase-no-encore-for-so pranos-1117898083/; James Endrst, "'Sopranos' Bumped to '06," *New York Daily News*, July 23, 2004, NYPL; Lawrence van Gelder, "New Life for 'Sopranos'?" *New York Times*, May 26, 2005, www.nytimes .com/2005/05/26/arts/arts-briefly.html; Joe Brescia, "A Seventh 'Sopranos'?" *New York Times*, June 20, 2005, www.nytimes .com/2005/06/20/arts/arts-briefly-a -seventh-sopranos.html; *Variety* staff, "'Sopranos' Gunning for Extra Episodes," *Variety*, August 11, 2005, variety.com/2005 /more/news/sopranos-gunning-for-extra -episodes-1117927407/.

193 **"While the 1950s . . .":** Stuart Levine, "Recipe for a Renaissance," *Variety*, June 15, 2005, variety.com/2005/tv/awards/recipe-for -a-renaissance-1117924501/.

194 **syndication deal:** Jacques Steinberg, "A&E Buys Rights to Rerun 'Sopranos," *New York Times*, February 1, 2005, www.nytimes.com /2005/02/01/arts/television/ae-buys-rights -to-rerun-39sopranos.html.

194 **"We used to talk about it . . .":** Denise Martin, "The Fat Lady Sings," *Variety*, January 15, 2006, variety.com/2006/scene/mar kets-festivals/koppel-news-too-soft-111793 6168/.

194 **"I remember once the idea was floated . . .":** *Talking Sopranos*, episode 64, June 14, 2021, youtu.be/PpP1MMw2jpQ.

194 **"Honestly, the last break . . .":** Bill Carter, "The Last Aria of Tony Soprano," *New York Times*, February 26, 2006, www.nytimes .com/2006/02/26/arts/television/the-last -aria-of-tony-soprano.html.

194 **"Some days you wish . . .":** Heath, "Garden State Warrior."

194 **"I have a little bit . . .":** Michael Starr, "'Sopranos' Creator Kills When 'Bored,'" *New York Post*, May 18, 2005, nypost.com /2005/05/18/sopranos-creator-kills-when -bored/.

195 **"The truth is . . .":** Author interview with Julianna Margulies, May 24, 2023.

195 **"I actually really . . .":** Ibid.

195 **"He really didn't . . .":** Miller, *Tinderbox*, 415–16.

195 **"I don't think it was that . . .":** Kornacki interview.

195 **"He never said . . .":** Miller, *Tinderbox*, 415–16.

195 **"He was a big mush ball . . .":** Margulies interview.

197 **"We were two days . . .":** Kashner and Kelly, *The Sopranos*, 26.

197 **"He said, work with Susan . . .":** Funaro interview.

197 **"I'll pick you . . .":** Iler interview.

198 **"It gave us a whole other look . . .":** Seitz & Sepinwall, *The Sopranos Sessions*, 577.

199 **"Tony's lack of forward progress . . .":** Sepinwall, *The Revolution Was Televised*, 46.

199 **"The Tony Soprano that emerges . . .":** David Blum, "The Sopranos," *New York Sun*, March 10, 2006, NYPL.

200 **season 6 premiere party:** Cara Buckley, "Home Court Advantage," *New York Times*, March 8, 2006, archive.nytimes.com/carpet bagger.blogs.nytimes.com/2006/03/08/home -court-advantage/.

200 **"The best series . . .":** Alessandra Stanley, "Brutality and Betrayal, with a Vengeance," *New York Times*, March 10, 2006, www.ny times.com/2006/03/10/arts/television/10sopr .html.

200 **season premiere drew:** Bill Carter, "Mob Boss Takes Hit; Housewife Implicated," *New York Times*, March 15, 2006, www .nytimes.com/2006/03/15/arts/television /mob-boss-takes-hit-housewife-implicated .html.

Chapter 18

201 **"the actors, specifically":** Seitz & Sepinwall, *The Sopranos Sessions*, 577.

201 **To that end:** salary negotiations: Michael Starr, "'Sopranos' in the Soup—Final-Season

Crisis Simmers for the Mob Opera Stars," *New York Post*, June 22, 2006, nypost.com/2006/06/22/sopranos-in-the-soup-final-season-crisis-simmers-for-the-mob-opera-stars/. Lawrence Van Gelder, "The Gang's All Here," *New York Times*, July 6, 2006, www.nytimes.com/2006/07/06/books/arts/arts-briefly.html.

201 **"By the end . . .":** Kashner and Kelly, *The Sopranos*, 42.

201 **"Toward the end of 'The Sopranos' . . .":** Egner, "David Chase on 'The Sopranos.'"

201 **"I can't see . . .":** Dan Fierman, "True Grit: James Gandolfini," *GQ*, October 26, 2010, www.gq.com/story/james-gandolfini-true-grit-sopranos?.

201 **knee injury:** surgery and delay: John Rockwell, "Surgery for Gandolfini Delays 'Sopranos' Finale," *New York Times*, July 14, 2006, www.nytimes.com/2006/07/14/arts/14arts.html; Shira Levine, "Knee-Whack Delays Finale," *amNew York*, July 14, 2006, NYPL.

202 **"I can't do this," Jim said:** Kashner and Kelly, *The Sopranos*, 50.

202 **"It was two fat . . .":** Ibid.

202 **"It was a lot easier . . .":** Iler interview.

202 **shoot in Miami:** Kamine, *On Locations*, 181–83.

203 **"He just wanted to keep . . .":** Kamine interview.

203 **"there was pin-drop silence . . .":** Kornacki interview.

203 **"It was very emotional . . .":** Seitz & Sepinwall, *The Sopranos Sessions*, 593.

203 **assembled at Holsten's:** Jonathan Miller, "Does Soprano Get Whacked? Does He Get a Banana Split?" *New York Times*, March 23, 2007, www.nytimes.com/2007/03/23/nyregion/23sopranos.html.

203 **"Normally when we . . .":** Iler interview.

204 **"It just felt . . .":** Seitz & Sepinwall, *The Sopranos Sessions*, 594.

204 **Kobold watch:** De Matteo interview, May 22, 2023; Gee interview.

204 **"He must have spent . . .":** Schirripa interview.

205 **"Because it was in Vegas . . .":** Imperioli, Schirripa, and Lerman, *Woke Up This Morning*, 436.

205 **"It's the middle . . .":** Sakharov interview.

205 **"Camera moves . . .":** Ibid.

205 **The last shot:** Imperioli, Schirripa, and Lerman, *Woke Up This Morning*, 436.

207 **"brought a lot of blue-collar . . .":** Steven Zeitchik, "'Sopranos' ' Last Hit," *Variety*, March 28, 2007, variety.com/2007/scene/vpage/sopranos-last-hit-1117962048/.

207 **"beginning of the end . . .":** Tom Teodorczuk, "Beginning of the End for the Best TV Ever," *Guardian*, April 8, 2007, www.theguardian.com/media/2007/apr/08/broadcasting.observerreview.

207 **Norman Mailer:** Alessandra Stanley, "This Thing of Ours, It's Over," *New York Times*, April 8, 2007, www.nytimes.com/2007/04/08/arts/television/08stan.html.

207 **"Maybe Archie Bunker . . .":** Jon Weisman, "'Sopranos' Readies Final Hit on Viewers," *Variety*, April 3, 2007, variety.com/2007/scene/features/sopranos-readies-final-hit-on-viewers-1117962478/.

207 **"I mean, c'mon, we did our best . . .":** *TV Guide*, April 2, 2007, NYPL.

207 **"It was summer . . .":** Kornacki interview.

207 **merely confused:** Finale reactions: *Variety* Staff, "So Long, 'Sopranos," *Variety*, June 10, 2007, variety.com/2007/tv/news/so_long_soprano-22985/; Whitney Friedlander, "David Chase Didn't Think the 'Sopranos' Finale Would Cause So Much Debate," *Variety*, April 14, 2015, variety.com/2015/tv/news/david-chase-sopranos-finale-1201472646/; Sepinwall, *The Revolution Was Televised*, 60–61.

208 **"So let's say . . .":** Sakharov interview.

208 **"I think *Breaking Bad*'s . . . ":** Kornacki interview.

208 **"I never thought it would create . . .":** Seitz & Sepinwall, *The Sopranos Sessions*, 590.

209 **"When I first saw the ending . . .":** Kashner and Kelly, *The Sopranos*, 63.

209 **fifteen nominations:** Emmys: Jacques Steinberg, "'Sopranos' Tops Drama Contenders for the Emmys," *New York Times*, July 20, 2007, www.nytimes.com/2007/07/20/arts/television/20emmy.html; Edward Wyatt, "Parting Gift: 'Sopranos' Wins Emmy for Drama," *New York Times*, September 17, 2007, www.nytimes.com/2007/09/17/arts/television/17emmy.html.

209 **OMG EVEN JAMES . . . :** *Variety* staff, "OMG even James Spader looked embarrassed but proved himself a class act," *Variety*, September 16, 2007, variety.com/2007/tv/news/omg-even-james-21884/.

209 **"It's been ten . . .":** Reuters, "SAG Awards: One Last Tribute to 'The Sopranos,'" *New York Times*, January 28, 2008, archive.nytimes.com/mediadecoder.blogs.nytimes.com/2008/01/28/sag-awards-one-last-tribute-to-the-sopranos/.

209 **"You know, at . . .":** Whitty, "James Gandolfini Looms Large."

Chapter 19

210 **"He didn't take anything . . .":** Karasawa interview.

210 **The engagement hit:** *Post* staff, "Tony Soprano Is Getting Hitched," *New York Post*, January 11, 2008, NYPL.

210 **"they both wore long . . .":** *Newsday* staff, "James Gandolfini Ties Knot," *Newsday*, September 1, 2008, NYPL.

210 **"they seemed OK . . .":** Gee interview.

210 **two-story colonial:** Tewksbury home: Veronica Slaght, "'Sopranos' Star James Gandolfini Buys home in Tewksbury," *Newark Star-Ledger*, September 24, 2009, www.nj.com/news/local/2009/09/gandolfini_buys_home_in_tewksb.html.

211 **solo dance show:** *Dining Alone*: Gia Kourlas, "One Dancer and 5 Solos in Studies of Character," *New York Times*, June 30, 2007, www.nytimes.com/2007/06/30/arts/dance/30tric.html.

211 **Bob Woodruff Family Fund benefit:** Jacques Steinberg, "O'Brien Performs Live, but Charity Benefits," *New York Times*, November 8, 2007, www.nytimes.com/2007/11/08/arts/08cnd-conan.html.

212 **"He was obviously compelled . . .":** Austin Smith, "Jail Visit," *New York Post*, August 31, 2007, nypost.com/2007/08/31/jail-visit/.

212 **subsequently awarded:** Tankleff resolution: Bruce Lambert, "With L.I. Murder Conviction Voided, the Same Old Question: Who Did It?," *New York Times*, December 24, 2007, www.nytimes.com/2007/12/24/nyregion/24tankleff.html; Mosi Secret, "Long Island Man Gets $3.4 Million for 17 Years in Jail," *New York Times*, January 7, 2014, www.nytimes.com/2014/01/08/nyregion/man-gets-3-4-million-for-17-years-in-jail.html; Maggie Astor, "Man Wrongly Convicted of Murdering Parents to Get $10 Million," *New York Times*, April 20, 2018, www.nytimes.com/2018/04/20/nyregion/martin-tankleff-settlement.html.

212 **"I live down . . .":** Albert Amateau, "Gandolfini Helped Community Fight Against Mega-Garage," *amNewYork*, July 3, 2013, www.amny.com/news/gandolfini-helped-community-fight-against-mega-garage/.

212 **"We couldn't get . . .":** Joseph Berger, "Using Celebrity Wattage to Fight City's Planned 'Garbage Garage,'" *New York Times*, November 15, 2009, www.nytimes.com/2009/11/16/nyregion/16garbage.html.

212 **"piece of crap":** Amateau, "Gandolfini Helped Community Fight Against Mega-Garage."

212 **"I spoke to him . . .":** Kate Sheehy, "Hit Man," *New York Post*, January 30, 2008, nypost.com/2008/01/30/hit-man/.

212 **"There's a lot of things . . .":** Heath, "Garden State Warrior."

212 **"He very much wanted . . .":** Richardson interview.

213 **made-for-cable movie:** *ABCD Camp*: Michael Fleming, "Gandolfini Returns to HBO for 'Camp,'" *Variety*, August 12, 2007, variety.com/2007/scene/markets-festivals/gandolfini-returns-to-hbo-for-camp-1117970112/; Pete Thamel, "'Conflicted Vaccaro Speaks at Harvard," *New York Times*, September 20, 2007, www.nytimes.com/2007/09/20/sports/ncaabasketball/20vaccaro.html.

213 **buddy action cop comedy:** *A Couple of Dicks*: Anne Thompson, "Robin Williams Sues Frank and Beans," *Variety*, October 19, 2018, variety.com/2008/biz/markets-festivals/robin-williams-sues-frank-and-beans-1117994311/.

213 **World War II drama:** *Miracle at St. Anna*: Nick Vivarelli, "TF1 Takes Spike Lee's 'St. Anna,'" *Variety*, October 15, 2007, variety.com/2007/film/news/tf1-takes-spike-lee-s-st-anna-1117974055/.

213 **Marvin Gaye biopic:** *Sexual Healing*: Tatiana Siegel, "Martin, Gandolfini Set for 'Healing,'" *Variety*, January 31, 2008, variety.com/2008/film/news/martin-gandolfini-set-for-healing-1117979961/; Michael Fleming, "F. Gary Gray to Direct 'Marvin' Movie," *Variety*, June 5, 2008, variety.com/2008/film/markets-festivals/f-gary-gray-to-direct-marvin-movie-1117986983/.

213 **"For a long time . . .":** Falco interview, May 17, 2023.

213 **"He saw things . . .":** Richardson interview.

213 **"Whether you agree . . .":** Whitty, "James Gandolfini Looms Large."

213 **"He really saw them . . .":** Richardson interview.

214 **"I grew up not so different . . .":** Bischoff, *James Gandolfini*, 147.

214 **"But because they . . .":** Richardson interview.

214 **documentary about these soldiers:** *Alive Day Memories* production: Bill Carter, "The Price of War, Front and Center," *New York*

Times, September 6, 2007, www.nytimes.com/2007/09/06/arts/television/06aliv.html; Addie Morfoot, "Gandolfini Saves 'Day,'" *Variety*, September 10, 2007, NYPL.

214 **"Jim was great . . .":** Miller, *Tinderbox*, 708.

214 **"We were in an East Village theater . . .":** Alpert interview.

215 **"And with wonder . . .":** Ibid.

215 **The film was titled:** *Alive Day Memories: Home from Iraq*, directed by Jon Alpert and Ellen Goosenberg Kent, Attaboy Films, 2007.

216 **"There was a real sincerity . . .":** Alpert interview.

216 **"He's an intense listener . . .":** *James Gandolfini: Tribute to a Friend.*

216 **"He was always self-critical . . .":** Alpert interview.

216 **"No doubt wanting . . .":** William Triplett, "War Weary," *Variety*, September 6, 2007, variety.com/2007/biz/opinion/war-weary-44995/.

217 **"Mike Mullen, who . . .":** Panel discussion, "James Gandolfini's Documentary Legacy."

217 **"Mr. Gandolfini functions . . .":** Ginia Bellafante, "When the War Comes Home," *New York Times*, September 8, 2007, www.nytimes.com/2007/09/08/arts/television/08aliv.html.

217 **"The whole fame thing . . .":** Richardson interview.

217 **"These films and their stories . . .":** Panel discussion, "James Gandolfini's Documentary Legacy."

217 **"He was very proud . . .":** Richardson interview.

217 **"And at that particular point . . .":** Alpert interview.

Chapter 20

218 **"All the fuss . . .":** Heilpern, "Curtains for Gandolfini."

218 **"He was with *M*A*S*H* . . .":** Deborah Sontag, "The Alpha Males of 'Carnage,'" *New York Times*, March 18, 2009, www.nytimes.com/2009/03/22/theater/22sont.html.

218 **"We were always chasing . . .":** Author interview with Nancy Sanders, May 14, 2024.

218 **complicated production:** *Where the Wild Things Are* production: Dennis Lim, "Conjuring Max's Wild World," *New York Times*, September 10, 2009, www.nytimes.com/2009/09/13/movies/13lim.html; "Stars Lined Up for 'Wild Things' film," UPI, May 4, 2006, www.upi.com/Entertainment_News/2006/05/04/Stars-lined-up-for-Wild-Things-film/33391146792172/.

219 **"It wasn't the . . .",** Editors of *McSweeney's*, *Heads On and We Shoot: The Making of "Where the Wild Things Are"* (San Francisco: McSweeney's Publishing, 2009), 46.

219 **"We needed the . . .":** Ibid., 48.

219 **"The process was . . .":** Ibid.

219 **"It was a bunch . . .":** Karasawa interview.

220 **"When Gandolfini didn't . . .":** McSweeney's, *Heads On and We Shoot*, 48.

220 **"Carol was a . . .":** Ibid.

220 **one of his finest:** *Where the Wild Things Are*, directed by Spike Jonze, Warner Bros., 2009.

220 **"When I saw that movie . . .":** Pulcini and Springer Berman interview.

221 **"To be honest, I don't . . .":** Melena Ryzik, "Once Tough Guy, Now Nurturer," *New York Times*, October 26, 2010, www.nytimes.com/2010/10/27/movies/27gandolfini.html.

221 **"This was really a family project . . .":** Author interview with Famke Janssen, May 26, 2023.

221 **"It's *him*, Jim Gandolfini . . .":** Author interview with John Magaro, May 16, 2023.

221 **"The script had been around . . .":** Janssen interview.

221 **"it's ice-cold . . .":** Magaro interview.

221 **"You're basically with a rock star . . .":** Janssen interview.

222 **"We shared this . . .":** Ibid.

222 **"Watching him was . . .":** Magaro interview.

222 **"He was not only . . .":** Janssen interview.

222 **a brilliant performance:** *Down the Shore*, directed by Harold Guskin, Jersey Shore Films, 2011.

222 **It wasn't seen at all until:** *Down the Shore* debut: Dave McNary, "'Potiche' to open Palm Springs," *Variety*, December 22, 2010, variety.com/2010/biz/markets-festivals/potiche-to-open-palm-springs-1118029415/.

222 **"extraordinary skill and sensitivity":** Elizabeth Weitzman, "Movie Reviews: 'Down the Shore,' 'The Brass Teapot,'" *New York Daily News*, April 4, 2013, www.nydailynews.com/2013/04/04/movie-reviews-down-the-shore-the-brass-teapot/.

223 **"why he's a genuine . . .":** *Variety* Staff, "Film Review: 'Down the Shore," *Variety*, January 9, 2011, variety.com/2011/film/reviews/down-the-shore-1117944263/.

223 **"okay with money . . .":** Bischoff, *James Gandolfini*, 155.
223 **"Michael had a . . .":** Magaro interview.
223 **"It was beautiful . . .":** Janssen interview.
224 **remake of the 1974 Gotham classic:** *Taking of Pelham 123* background: Michael Fleming, "Gandolfini Plays Mayor in 'Pelham,'" *Variety*, March 23, 2008, variety.com/2008/film/features/gandolfini-plays-mayor-in-pelham-1117982798/.
224 **"I would think it would be . . .":** Sam Roberts, "The Remaking of 'Pelham One Two Three' and New York, 35 Years Later," *New York Times*, April 18, 2009, www.nytimes.com/2009/04/19/nyregion/19pelham.html.
224 **a millionaire businessman turned politico:** *The Taking of Pelham 123*, directed by Tony Scott, Columbia Pictures, 2009.
225 **Lieutenant General George Miller:** *In the Loop* casting: Ali Jaafar, "Gandolfini, Coogan Join 'Loop,'" *Variety*, May 1, 2008, variety.com/2008/film/news/gandolfini-coogan-join-loop-1117984932/.
225 **"My whole thing . . .":** Author interview with Mimi Kennedy, May 15, 2023.
225 **"loosen it up . . .":** Ibid.
225 **"I wanted the actors . . .":** Sarah Lyall, "What's So Funny About War?" *New York Times*, July 16, 2009, www.nytimes.com/2009/07/19/movies/19lyal.html.
225 **"He brought complete . . .":** Kennedy interview.
226 **"*Jim! Tony!* It didn't matter . . .":** Ibid.
227 ***In the Loop* premiered:** Michael Jones, "IFC Gets 'In the Loop' at Sundance," *Variety*, January 22, 2009, variety.com/2009/film/markets-festivals/ifc-gets-in-the-loop-at-sundance-1117998965/.
227 **It hit theaters in July:** *In the Loop* release: Sam Thielman, "'In the Loop' July 13 Premiere," *Variety*, July 17, 2009, variety.com/2009/film/news/in-the-loop-july-13-premiere-1118006150/.
227 **"*In the Loop* changed . . .":** Armstrong interview, January 9, 2024.
227 **"He had a moral righteousness . . .":** Kennedy interview.
227 **"He was really trying to honor . . .":** Ibid.
227 **"He was generous . . .":** Ibid.
228 **next leading role:** *Welcome to the Rileys* background: Sharon Swart, "Scott Siblings Skewer Pics," *Variety*, February 7, 2008, variety.com/2008/film/markets-festivals/scott-siblings-skewer-pics-1117980390/.
228 **"I saw her . . .":** Melena Ryzik, "Once Tough Guy, Now Nurturer."
228 **"It was a kind of shedding . . .":** Author interview with Jake Scott, May 23, 2023.
228 **"I've never seen it . . .":** Ryzik, "Once Tough Guy."
229 **"I've seen people":** Ibid.
229 **"We met in . . .":** Scott interview.
229 **notes from those meetings:** Script meeting notes: Email from Jake Scott to Ken Hixon, "Notes from Gandolfini session," August 27, 2008, Ken Hixon Collection, Margaret Herrick Library, AMPAS.
229 **"In my experience . . .":** Scott interview.
229 **"You could never . . .":** Ibid.
230 **"The French Quarter being . . .":** Blow-up story: Ibid.
231 **"That was Jimmy . . .":** Ibid.
231 ***Rileys* took Jim:** *Rileys* release: Sharon Swart, "Apparition, Sony Welcome 'Rileys,'" *Variety*, March 14, 2010, variety.com/2010/film/markets-festivals/apparition-sony-welcome-rileys-1118016427/.
231 **"The only saving grace . . .":** Joe Neumaier, "'Welcome to the Rileys' Review: Kristen Stewart's Stripper Can't Be Saved by James Gandolfini," *New York Daily News*, October 29, 2010, www.nydailynews.com/2010/10/29/welcome-to-the-rileys-review-kristen-stewarts-stripper-cant-be-saved-by-james-gandolfini/.
231 **"I like to support . . .":** Robert Levin, "Gandolfini, Stewart Savor Low-Key Roles," *amNew York*, October 27, 2010, NYPL.
232 **"I think he kind of wanted . . .":** Armstrong interview, January 9, 2024.
232 **"sexy and scary . . .":** James Gandolfini, "James Gandolfini on Kristen Stewart in 'On the Road,'" *Variety*, November 26, 2012, variety.com/2012/film/awards/james-gandolfini-on-kristen-stewart-in-on-the-road-1118062462/.
232 **"completely down-to-earth . . .":** Bischoff, *James Gandolfini*, 152.

Chapter 21

233 **itself a transplant:** *God of Carnage* background: Doug Sturdivant, "The Art of Carnage," *Playbill*, March 31, 2009, playbill.com/article/the-art-of-carnage-com-159561; Armstrong interview, January 9, 2024.
233 **"I didn't know anything about it . . .":** Barbara Isenberg, "Actors Talk About Rhythm of 'God of Carnage,'" *Los Angeles Times*, April 10, 2011, www.latimes.com/entertainment/la-xpm-2011-apr-10-la-ca-god-of-carnage-20110410-story.html.

233 **"I don't know if they're going to move it . . .":** Heilpern, "Curtains for Gandolfini."
233 **"He loved the theater . . .":** Aston interview.
233 **"I hate to admit . . .":** Sontag, "Alpha Males of 'Carnage.'"
233 **"This is a play . . .":** Ibid.
234 **The cast was announced:** Gordon Cox, "Cast Set for 'God of Carnage,'" *Variety*, January 12, 2009, variety.com/2009/legit/news/cast-set-for-god-of-carnage-1117998386/.
234 **"I remember you from that audition . . .":** Author interview with Marcia Gay Harden, May 16, 2023.
234 **"Certainly he has a strong . . .":** Sontag, "Alpha Males of 'Carnage.'"
234 **"I appreciate the . . .":** Ibid.
234 **"No, I'm not . . .":** Heilpern, "Curtains for Gandolfini."
234 **"I think I was probably kind of arrogant . . .":** "Theater Talk: God of Carnage," CUNY TV Foundation, 2009, NYPL Theatre on Film Library.
234 **"The rehearsal process . . .":** Harden interview.
234 **"hundreds of pages . . .":** "Theater Talk: God of Carnage."
235 **"It keeps everybody on their toes . . .":** Sontag, "Alpha Males of 'Carnage.'"
235 **"I thought I'd lose weight . . .":** Isenberg, "Actors Talk."
235 **"I came in thinking . . .":** "Theater Talk: God of Carnage."
235 **"There was an incredible humility . . .":** Harden interview.
235 **"I don't want to make it out . . .":** Sontag, "Alpha Males of 'Carnage.'"
236 **"He didn't know what the button was . . .":** Harden interview.
236 **"Somehow I felt like an actor . . .":** Isenberg, "Actors Talk."
236 **"I loved doing . . .":** Sontag, "Alpha Males of 'Carnage.'"
236 ***The Three Stooges*:** Missy Schwartz, "Sean Penn Cast in 'The Three Stooges': Nyuck, nyuck, nyuck?," *Entertainment Weekly*, March 25, 2009, ew.com/article/2009/03/25/sean-penn-three/; Richardson interview.
236 **"We buckled over in laughter . . .":** Harden interview.
236 **"Everybody's a little different . . .":** "Theater Talk: God of Carnage."
237 **"People have no idea . . .":** Aston interview.
237 **"Never underestimate the . . .":** Ben Brantley, "Rumble in the Living Room," *New York Times*, March 22, 2009, www.nytimes.com/2009/03/23/theater/reviews/23carn.html.
237 **"dark and hilarious . . .":** John Lahr, "Turf Wars," *New Yorker*, March 23, 2009, www.newyorker.com/magazine/2009/03/30/turf-wars.
237 **"It was an extra . . .":** *New Yorker* (blog), "The Top Ten Moments in Theatre of 2009," *New Yorker*, December 15, 2009, www.newyorker.com/culture/the-new-yorker-blog/the-top-ten-moments-in-theatre-of-2009.
237 **"what I am":** *God of Carnage* commentary: Personal viewing, New York Public Library Theatre on Film Archive, recorded October 28, 2009.
238 **"grosses topped $700,000":** *God of Carnage* box office: *Variety* staff, "'West Side Story' Rocks Broadway," *Variety*, March 6, 2009, variety.com/2009/legit/news/west-side-story-rocks-broadway-1118000936/; Gordon Cox, "'God of Carnage' Hits $1 Million Mark," *Variety*, July 27, 2009, variety.com/2009/legit/news/god-of-carnage-hits-1-million-mark-1118006530/.
238 **cancellation of a Wednesday matinee:** Theatermania staff, "'God of Carnage' Cancels March 11 Matinee; James Gandolfini on Vocal Rest," Theatermania.com, March 11, 2009, www.theatermania.com/news/god-of-carnage-cancels-march-11-matinee-james-gandolfini-on-vocal-rest_18032/.
238 **"though sometimes they . . .":** Alex Witchel, "A Speakeasy Keeps Its Voice," *New York Times*, May 26, 2009, www.nytimes.com/2009/05/27/dining/27feed.html.
238 **"I used to go to him . . .":** Harden interview.
238 **"he started the show over . . .":** Karasawa interview.
238 **"Man, you are like . . .":** Abraham interview.
239 **Drama League Awards:** Gordon Cox, "Drama League Unveils Nominations," *Variety*, April 21, 2009, variety.com/2009/film/awards/drama-league-unveils-nominees-2-1118002658/.
239 **Tony Awards:** Patrick Healy, "'Billy Elliot' Leads Tony Nominations," *New York Times*, May 5, 2009, www.nytimes.com/2009/05/06/theater/theaterspecial/06tony.html; *Variety* staff, "2009 Tony Awards Nominations List," *Variety*, May 5, 2009, variety.com/2009/film/awards/2009-tony-awards-nominations-list-1118003190/; *New York Times* staff, "2009 Tony Award Winners," *New York Times*, May 4, 2009, www.nytimes.com/2009

/05/05/theater/theaterspecial/05tonyslist.html.

239 **"if you allow . . .":** "Theater Talk: God of Carnage."

239 **"For the record . . .":** Patrick Healy, "A Big Night for Broadway, and Especially for Billy," *New York Times*, June 7, 2009, www.nytimes.com/2009/06/08/theater/theaterspecial/08tony.html.

239 **six-week hiatus:** Dave Itzkoff, "'God of Carnage' Extends Run, Cast Intact," *New York Times*, June 2, 2009, www.nytimes.com/2009/06/03/theater/03arts-GODOFCARNAGE_BRF.html; Gordon Cox, "'Carnage' Cast to Return After Break," *Variety*, June 2, 2009, variety.com/2009/legit/news/carnage-cast-to-return-after-break-1118004445/; Dave Itzkoff, "How They Spent Their 'God of Carnage' Vacation," *New York Times*, August 26, 2009, www.nytimes.com/2009/08/27/theater/27carnage.html.

239 **topped $1 million:** Closing week box office: Gordon Cox, "Broadway Gets a Box Office Bump," *Variety*, November 16, 2009, variety.com/2009/legit/news/broadway-gets-a-box-office-bump-1118011415/.

239 **declined steeply:** New cast box office: Patrick Healy, "Audience and Box Office Drops at 'God of Carnage' as New Cast Takes Over," New York Times, November 23, 2009, archive.nytimes.com/artsbeat.blogs.nytimes.com/2009/11/23/audience-and-box-office-drops-at-god-of-carnage-as-new-cast-takes-over.

239 **new cast members:** Dave Itzkoff, "New 'God of Carnage' Cast Is Set," *New York Times*, October 15, 2009, archive.nytimes.com/artsbeat.blogs.nytimes.com/2009/10/15/new-god-of-carnage-cast-is-set/.

239 **"He couldn't have been nicer . . .":** NPR, "Gandolfini Through the Eyes of Those He Worked With," *Fresh Air*, June 20, 2013, www.npr.org/2013/06/20/193865792/gandolfini-through-the-eyes-of-those-he-worked-with.

239 **closing for good:** Gordon Cox, "'Carnage' to End Broadway Run," *Variety*, April 26, 2010, variety.com/2010/legit/news/carnage-to-end-broadway-run-1118018281/.

239 **touring production:** Patrick Healy, "'Peter and the Starcatcher to Go on National Tour Next Year," *New York Times*, May 14, 2012, archive.nytimes.com/artsbeat.blogs.nytimes.com/2012/05/14/peter-and-the-starcatcher-to-go-on-national-tour-next-year.

239 **Ahmanson Theatre in Los Angeles:** Gordon Cox, "Broadway Cast to Play 'God' in L.A.," *Variety*, January 12, 2011, variety.com/2011/legit/news/broadway-cast-to-play-god-in-l-a-1118030134/; Isenberg, "Actors Talk."

239 **"I was sincerely, genuinely happy . . .":** NPR, "Gandolfini Through the Eyes."

240 **spending most of their time:** Going bicoastal: Bischoff, *James Gandolfini*, 150.

240 **invited to join the Academy of Motion Picture Arts and Sciences:** Stuart Oldham, "Academy Invites 135 to Join for Membership," *Variety*, June 25, 2010, variety.com/2010/film/news/academy-invites-135-to-membership-8074/.

240 **"And the next minute . . .":** PageSix.com staff, "Gandolfini's a Blizzard Hero," Page Six, December 29, 2010, pagesix.com/2010/12/29/gandolfinis-a-blizzard-hero/.

240 **"A couple years before . . .":** Sanders interview, January 10, 2024.

241 **"MEN-U":** Richardson interview.

241 **"I think I can play someone . . .":** Heath, "Garden State Warrior."

241 **Researching the role as early:** Alessandra Stanley, "Where Old Television Goes to Its Final Reward," *New York Times*, July 2, 2004, www.nytimes.com/2004/07/02/movies/where-old-television-goes-to-its-final-reward.html.

241 **"He'd always wanted to go to Cuba . . .":** Richardson interview.

241 **"It won some . . .":** Ibid.

241 **another documentary:** *Wartorn* origins: Rob Owen, "Nevins Always Looking for Top Docs," *Variety*, November 8, 2010, variety.com/2010/tv/news/nevins-always-looking-for-top-docs-1118026827/.

241 **"One of the things that Jim really noticed . . .":** Richardson interview.

241 **"We talked to a lot of guys . . .":** Ryzik, "Once Tough Guy."

242 **"I really liked traveling with him . . .":** Alpert interview.

242 **"Then we lost the USO guys . . .":** Richardson interview.

242 **"While it wasn't the heat of the war . . .":** Panel discussion, "James Gandolfini's Documentary Legacy."

242 **"The generosity of the time . . .":** Alpert interview.

242 **That genuineness and generosity:** *Wartorn: 1861–2010*, directed by Jon Alpert, Ellen Goosenberg Kent, and Matthew O'Neill, Attaboy Films, 2010.

243 **screened at the Pentagon; "powerful and tough":** Ted Johnson, "Pentagon Embraces HBO's 'Wartorn," *Variety*, November 11,

2010, variety.com/2010/biz/opinion/pentagon-embraces-hbos-wartorn-38393/.

243 **"quietly devastating, haunting . . .":** Mike Hale, "A Searching Look at Combat Wounds to the Spirit," *New York Times*, November 10, 2010, www.nytimes.com/2010/11/11/arts/television/11wartorn.html.

243 **"Together, these documentaries . . .":** Brian Lowry, "Wartorn: 1861-2010," *Variety*, November 10, 2010, variety.com/2010/tv/reviews/wartorn-1861-2010-1117944028/.

243 **"General [Peter] Chiarelli . . .":** Richardson interview.

243 **"He really was most enthusiastic . . .":** Alpert interview.

244 **star-studded video; "We got those . . .":** Karu F. Daniels, "New York Knicks Used a Secret Spin-Off Episode of 'The Sopranos' to Try Get LeBron James to Join the Team," *New York Daily News*, April 29, 2021, www.nydailynews.com/snyde/ny-the-knicks-the-sopranos-edie-falco-lebron-james-20210430-swj4pro735gm7gwemhsospjxc4-story.html.

244 **not seen publicly:** James video uncovered: Dustin Nelson, "Watch James Gandolfini Reprise His *Sopranos* role in Unearthed Video Trying to Woo LeBron James to the Knicks," *Entertainment Weekly*, April 16, 2024, ew.com/james-gandolfini-tony-soprano-lebron-james-knicks-recruitment-video-8634402.

244 **"never really spoke to me . . .":** Iler interview.

244 **"I think it was 2010 . . .":** Curatola interview.

Chapter 22

246 **"People say 'Oh . . .":** Nicole Sperling, "James Gandolfini Dies: A Last Interview with Tony Soprano," *Los Angeles Times*, June 20, 2013, www.latimes.com/entertainment/movies/la-xpm-2013-jun-20-la-et-mn-james-gandolfini-dies-last-interview-20130619-story.html.

246 **"I like the character parts . . .":** Fierman, "True Grit."

246 **"I was like, there's no one . . .":** Pulcini and Springer Berman interview.

247 **New York–based television writer:** Craig Gilbert background: Laurie Winer, "Reality Replay," *New Yorker*, April 18, 2011, www.newyorker.com/magazine/2011/04/25/reality-replay.

247 **"I thought, why . . .":** Pulcini and Springer Berman interview.

248 **"He knocked on . . .":** *James Gandolfini: Tribute to a Friend.*

248 **"He's a wonderful . . .":** Roger Friedman, "James Gandolfini on the Louds and 'American Family' Director Craig Gilbert," *Showbiz 411*, April 30, 2011, www.showbiz411.com/2011/04/30/james-gandolfini-on-the-louds-and-american-family-director-craig-gilbert.

249 **"I'm sure he . . .":** Pulcini and Springer Berman interview.

249 **"But his instincts . . .":** Ibid.

249 **"You meet a . . .":** *James Gandolfini: Tribute to a Friend.*

249 **"he was very positive . . ."; huge arrangement:** Pulcini and Springer Berman interview.

250 **no less impressive:** *Cinema Verite*, directed by Shari Springer Berman and Robert Pulcini, HBO Films, 2011.

250 **"Gandolfini lends Gilbert . . .":** Richard Brody, "Reel Life," *New Yorker*, August 5, 2013, www.newyorker.com/magazine/2013/08/12/reel-life.

250 **championed as equal:** Oscar comparison: Richard Brody, "Movie of the Week: 'Cinema Verite," *New Yorker*, archived December 31, 2014, www.newyorker.com/culture/richard-brody/movie-week-cinema-verite.

250 **"I just couldn't . . .":** Pulcini and Springer Berman interview.

251 **"Those were very sensitive men . . .":** Author interview with Mark Armstrong, May 14, 2024.

251 **Bruce Willis was originally:** *Violet & Daisy* casting: Brendan Bettinger, "Bruce Willis and Danny Trejo in Talks to Join Carey Mulligan and Saoirse Ronan for VIOLET & DAISY," *Collider*, August 19, 2010, collider.com/violet-and-daisy-bruce-willis-danny-trejo/; Dave McNary and Justin Kroll, "Killer Gigs for Gandolfini, Ronan," *Variety*, September 13, 2010, variety.com/2010/film/markets-festivals/killer-gigs-for-ronan-gandolfini-1118024066/.

251 **"Fortunately, [Gandolfini] got . . .":** Fletcher interview.

251 **"I'm going to die . . .":** *Violet & Daisy*, directed by Geoffrey Fletcher, Magic Violet, 2011,

251 **"After seeing the film . . .":** Fletcher interview.

251 **"There's a scene . . .":** Armstrong interview, January 9, 2024.

252 **"He was warm . . .":** Fletcher interview.

252 **"bringing a soul . . .":** Peter Debruge, "Violet & Daisy," *Variety*, September 16, 2011, variety.com/2011/film/markets-festivals/violet-daisy-1117946120/.

252 **"finally acquired":** Dave McNary, "Cinedigm Seeing 'Violet,'" *Variety*, November 12, 2012, variety.com/2012/film/news/cinedigm-seeing-violet-1118062116/.

252 **"Gandolfini scoops up . . .":** Joe Neumaier, "'Violet & Daisy,' Movie Review," *New York Daily News*, June 6, 2013, www.nydailynews.com/2013/06/06/violet-daisy-movie-review/.

252 **"weary ease":** A. O. Scott, "Young Femmes Fatales, Doing Their Job," *New York Times*, June 6, 2013, www.nytimes.com/2013/06/07/movies/violet-daisy-by-geoffrey-fletcher.html.

252 **"another indelible portrait . . .":** Matt Zoller Seitz, "Violet & Daisy," RogerEbert.com, June 7, 2013, www.rogerebert.com/reviews/violet-and-daisy-2013.

252 **"He was always hard on himself . . .":** Armstrong interview, May 14, 2024.

252 **"It was originally titled":** *Not Fade Away* original title: Dave McNary, "Gandolfini, Chase Reconnect at 'Twylight,'" *Variety*, January 24, 2011, variety.com/2011/film/news/gandolfini-chase-reconnect-at-twylight-1118030784/.

253 **had to helm it himself:** Chase choosing to direct: Gee interview.

253 **"I think David would admit this . . .":** Magaro interview.

253 **"there weren't that many candidates . . .":** Seitz & Sepinwall, *The Sopranos Sessions*, 607.

253 **"I knew this . . .":** Moore, "Gandolfini Remembers."

253 **"As a kid . . .":** Whitty, "James Gandolfini Looms Large."

254 **"David can write . . .":** David Carr, "'Sopranos' Alumni, Back in Jersey," *New York Times*, December 5, 2012, www.nytimes.com/2012/12/09/movies/inside-not-fade-away-from-david-chase.html.

254 **"Working with him on . . .":** *James Gandolfini: Tribute to a Friend*.

254 **"very easy between . . .":** Gee interview.

254 **"He was a pleasure . . .":** Seitz & Sepinwall, *The Sopranos Sessions*, 607.

254 **"Jim came into . . .":** Magaro interview.

255 **"go back to doing . . .":** Richard Corliss, "David Chase's *Not Fade Away*: A Musical Memoir from the *Sopranos* Boss," *Time*, December 19, 2012, entertainment.time.com/2012/12/19/david-chases-not-fade-away-a-musical-memoir-from-the-sopranos-boss/.

255 **"wonderful as ever":** Stephen Holden, "Playing with the Band When the Music Meant Everything," *New York Times*, December 20, 2012, www.nytimes.com/2012/12/21/movies/not-fade-away-directed-by-david-chase.html.

255 **"knockout supporting performance":** Ronnie Scheib, "Not Fade Away," *Variety*, October 6, 2012, variety.com/2012/film/reviews/not-fade-away-1117948487/.

255 **"his little chuckle":** *Not Fade Away*, directed by David Chase, Chase Films / Paramount Vantage, 2012.

255 **"He just stands there . . .":** Magaro interview.

255 **"had some overtones . . .":** Rachel Dodes, "Tony Sopranos Slips Back into a Bathrobe," *Wall Street Journal*, November 22, 2012, www.wsj.com/articles/SB10001424127887324851704578132982908409260.

256 **"would do anything for Brad . . .":** Armstrong interview, January 9, 2024.

256 **"You put all the mob guys . . .":** Moore, "Gandolfini Remembers."

256 **"Mickey is Tony Soprano":** *Killing Them Softly*, directed by Andrew Dominik, Annapurna Pictures, 2012.

257 **"rancid swagger":** A. O. Scott, "One Bad Turn Deserves Another," *New York Times*, November 29, 2012, www.nytimes.com/2012/11/30/movies/killing-them-softly-with-brad-pitt-from-andrew-dominik.html.

257 **"All of Gandolfini's scenes . . .":** Ty Burr, "'Killing Them Softly' Cast Stands Out," *Boston Globe*, November 28, 2012, www.boston.com/uncategorized/noprimarytagmatch/2012/11/28/killing-them-softly-cast-stands-out/.

257 **"Harvey Weinstein called . . .":** Ryan Parker, "James Gandolfini Once Threatened to 'Beat the F***' Out of Harvey Weinstein," *Hollywood Reporter*, June 18, 2020, www.hollywoodreporter.com/news/general-news/james-gandolfini-threatened-beat-f-harvey-weinstein-1299057/.

257 **fiftieth birthday:** *Page Six* staff, "Jolly 50th for Gando," *New York Post*, September 20, 2011, pagesix.com/2011/09/20/jolly-50th-for-gando/.

257 **"I don't know, I just . . .":** Whitty, "James Gandolfini Looms Large."

257 **"He didn't want to do TV . . .":** Sanders interview, January 10, 2024.

257 **"a politically incorrect cab driver . . .":** Michael Schneider, "James Gandolfini Plotting Potential Return to HBO," *Variety*,

May 5, 2010, variety.com/2010/tv/news/james-gandolfini-plotting-potential-return-to-hbo-15803/.

258 **"He was always looking . . .":** Armstrong interview, January 9, 2024.

258 ***Eating with the Enemy*:** Stuart Levine, "Healy on Board as 'Enemy' Scribe," *Variety*, October 12, 2011, variety.com/2011/tv/news/healy-on-board-as-enemy-scribe-1118044318/.

258 **Peter Tolan:** Cynthia Littleton, "Fox Collars David Shore–Peter Tolan Drama," *Variety*, September 27, 2012, variety.com/2012/tv/news/fox-collars-david-shore-peter-tolan-drama-1118059974/.

258 ***Escape from Planet Earth*:** Dave McNary, "Voice Cast Set for 'Planet Earth,'" *Variety*, August 2, 2011, variety.com/2011/film/news/voice-cast-set-for-planet-earth-1118040772/.

258 ***Extremely Loud and Incredibly Close*:** Yahoo! Lifestyle staff, "Stars Cut from Movies," Yahoo.com, June 21, 2012, web.archive.org/web/20130929150536/http://au.lifestyle.yahoo.com/general/galleries/photo/-/14006962/stars-cut-from-movies/14006974/.

258 ***The Office*:** Andrew Wallenstein, "Big Names Eyed for 'Office' Openings," *Variety*, June 27, 2011, variety.com/2011/tv/news/big-names-eyed-for-office-openings-1118039155/.

258 **"HBO paid him . . .":** Hannah Sparks, "James Gandolfini Was Paid $3M to Turn Down Role in 'The Office,'" *New York Post*, July 14, 2021, nypost.com/2021/07/14/james-gandolfini-was-paid-3m-to-turn-down-the-office-role/.

258 **"I think he always wanted to be . . .":** Magaro interview.

258 **"I watch stupid comedies . . .":** Ryzik, "Once Tough Guy.").

258 **casting his feature film *The Incredible Burt Wonderstone*:** Jeff Sneider, "Gandolfini in Talks for 'Wonderstone,'" *Variety*, October 29, 2011, variety.com/2011/film/news/gandolfini-in-talks-for-wonderstone-1118045275/.

259 **"Why do you guys want me . . .":** Scardino interview.

259 **"He's such an honest actor . . .":** Ibid.

259 **"I need you to dump . . .":** *The Incredible Burt Wonderstone*, directed by Don Scardino, New Line Cinema, 2013.

260 **"Once we started . . ."; last day story:** Scardino interview.

260 **"Gandolfini attacks his . . .":** Joe Leydon, "SXSW Review: 'The Incredible Burt Wonderstone,'" *Variety*, March 9, 2013, variety.com/2013/film/reviews/sxsw-film-review-the-incredible-burt-wonderstone-1200006361/.

261 **"James Gandolfini has . . .":** Stephen Holden, "Sleepwalking Magician Pulls a New Self Out of a Hat," *New York Times*, March 14, 2013, www.nytimes.com/2013/03/15/movies/the-incredible-burt-wonderstone-with-steve-carrell.html.

261 **even smaller role:** *Zero Dark Thirty*, directed by Kathryn Bigelow, Columbia Pictures, 2012.

261 **"It wasn't a big part . . .":** Moore, "Gandolfini Remembers."

261 **"It's a movie. And . . .":** Ted Johnson, "Leon Panetta on 'Zero Dark Thirty': 'A Good Movie,'" *Variety*, February 2, 2013, variety.com/2013/biz/opinion/leon-panetta-on-zero-dark-thirty-a-good-movie-35922/.

261 **"I sent a note . . .":** Page Six staff, "James Gandolfini Apologizes to Leon Panetta," *New York Post*, January 10, 2013, pagesix.com/2013/01/10/james-gandolfini-apologizes-to-leon-panetta/.

262 **"I did all those things . . .":** Whitty, "James Gandolfini Looms Large."

262 **"I think what made his performance . . .":** Author interview with Nicole Holofcener, May 12, 2023.

262 ***Please Give*:** Tim Robey, "Nicole Holofcener Interview: 'Gandolfini Was Perfect—Belly and All,'" *Telegraph*, October 19, 2013, www.telegraph.co.uk/culture/film/10382463/Nicole-Holofcener-interview-Gandolfini-was-perfect-belly-and-all.html.

262 **"That performance was really him . . .":** Author interview with Julia Louis-Dreyfus, May 22, 2023.

262 **"He was terrified . . .":** Sanders interview, January 10, 2024.

262 **"I don't get called . . .":** Nicole Sperling, "James Gandolfini's 'Not Fade Away' Performance Honors His Late Father," *Los Angeles Times*, December 21, 2012, www.latimes.com/entertainment/movies/moviesnow/la-et-mn-james-gandolfini-not-fade-away-20121222-story.html.

263 **"I was really surprised . . .":** Holofcener interview.

263 **"I feel like you don't . . .":** Trailer conversation: Ariel Levy, "Nicole Holofcener's Human Comedies," *New Yorker*, July 30, 2018, www.newyorker.com/magazine/2018

/08/06/nicole-holofceners-human-comedies.

263 **"He was nervous . . .":** Holofcener interview.

264 **"We had a scene in bed . . .":** Louis-Dreyfus interview.

264 **"What I loved . . .":** *James Gandolfini: Tribute to a Friend.*

264 **"He was really attentive . . .":** Holofcener interview.

264 **"He brought total honesty . . .":** Louis-Dreyfus interview.

264 **"Got any money?":** *Enough Said*, directed by Nichole Holofcener, Fox Searchlight Pictures, 2013.

265 **"My saddest moment . . .":** Armstrong interview, January 9, 2024.

Chapter 23

266 **"We were working . . .":** Aston interview.

266 **Vincent Thomas Bridge:** Death of Tony Scott: Chelsea J. Carter and JD Cargill, "Official: Director Tony Scott Left Notes in Car, Office Before His Apparent Suicide," CNN, August 21, 2012, www.cnn.com/2012/08/20/showbiz/obit-tony-scott/index.html.

266 **"The two of us going . . .":** Falco interview, May 17, 2023.

266 **"He was just . . .":** Falco interview, March 29, 2024.

267 **"I hadn't seen Jim . . .":** Schirripa interview.

267 **"Just stay away! . . .":** *Nicky Deuce*, directed by Jonathan A. Rosenbaum, MarVista Entertainment, 2013.

267 **"and I love . . .":** Nigel M. Smith, "Elaine Stritch on (Not) Wearing Pants, Being Hungover With James Gandolfini and Hating the Title of Her New Documentary," *IndieWire*, April 19, 2013, www.indiewire.com/news/general-news/tribeca-elaine-stritch-on-not-wearing-pants-being-hungover-with-james-gandolfini-and-hating-the-title-of-her-new-documentary-39225/.

267 **"If we'd both met . . .":** *Elaine Stritch: Shoot Me*, directed by Chiemi Karasawa, isotope-films, 2013.

268 **"probably one hundred people . . .", IVF:** Karasawa interview.

268 **"I was asking about Michael . . .":** Duffy interview.

268 **"He liked living in LA . . .":** Author interview with Nancy Sanders, January 23, 2024.

268 **"Hey, have you . . .":** Imperioli, Schirripa, and Lerman, *Woke Up This Morning*, 478.

268 **"He was happy . . .":** Schirripa interview.

269 **"He was heavier . . .":** Karasawa interview.

269 **"300-pound Woody Allen":** Sperling, "James Gandolfini Dies."

269 **"what really interested . . .":** Richardson interview.

269 ***"Big Dead Place* . . .":** Armstrong interview, January 9, 2024.

269 **adaptation of the BBC series:** *Criminal Justice/The Night Of*: Stuart Levine, "HBO Orders Drama Pilot Based on 'Criminal Justice,'" *Variety*, September 19, 2012, variety.com/2012/tv/news/hbo-orders-drama-pilot-based-on-criminal-justice-1118059458/.

269 **"Since we originally thought of it . . .":** Miller, *Tinderbox*, 758.

270 **From Schoolhouse to Jailhouse:** Alpert interview.

270 **"I have dyslexia . . .":** Panel discussion, "James Gandolfini's Documentary Legacy."

270 **"He would have been the narrator . . .":** Richardson interview.

270 **"I guarantee you . . .":** Aston interview.

271 **"Those were not . . .":** Ibid.

271 **"It was almost . . .":** Bischoff, *James Gandolfini*, 187.

271 **"I was a big fan . . .":** Denis Hamill, "James Gandolfini Made Final Film and Good Friends in Brooklyn," *New York Daily News*, June 22, 2013, www.nydailynews.com/2013/06/22/james-gandolfini-made-final-film-and-good-friends-in-brooklyn/.

272 **"I pranced in . . .":** Ibid.

272 **"There's a scene where . . .":** Ethan Sacks, "Actors Who Worked with James Gandolfini on 'The Drop' Were in Awe of the Late Actor," *New York Daily News*, September 7, 2014, www.nydailynews.com/entertainment/movies/tom-hardy-noomi-rapace-james-gandolfini-article-1.1926977.

272 **He's funny in the picture:** *The Drop*, directed by Michaël R. Roskam, Fox Searchlight Pictures, 2014.

272 **"I felt after Sopranos . . .":** Bracco interview.

272 **New projects were continuing to line up:** *Criminal Justice*, *Bone Wars*, *Big Dead Place*: Nellie Andreeva, "'Criminal Justice' Starring James Gandolfini Greenlighted at HBO as Limited Series," *Deadline*, May 13, 2013, deadline.com/2013/05/criminal-justice-starring-james-gandolfini-greenlighted-at-hbo-as-limited-series-497895/.

272 **picked up the *Taxi-22*:** Nellie Andreeva, "CBS to Adapt Canadian Comedy Series 'Taxi-22' with James Gandolfini Producing," *Deadline*, June 6, 2013, deadline.com/2013

/06/cbs-to-adapt-canadian-comedy-series-taxi-22-with-james-gandolfini-producing-514467/.

272 **"It was a little premiere . . .":** Schirripa interview.

273 **"was in a wonderful . . .":** Imperioli, Schirripa, and Lerman, *Woke Up This Morning*, 479.

273 **Taormina Film Fest:** Nick Vivarelli, "'Lone Ranger' to Close Taormina Fest," *Variety*, June 11, 2013, variety.com/2013/film/global/lone-ranger-to-close-taormina-fest-1200495154/.

273 **family vacation**: Rome trip: Casey Tolan, Larry McShane, and Nancy Dillon, "James Gandolfini Dead at 51: One of the Last Pictures of Actor Shows Him Looking Healthy," *New York Daily News*, June 21, 2013, www.nydailynews.com/2013/06/21/james-gandolfini-dead-at-51-one-of-the-last-pictures-of-actor-shows-him-looking-healthy/; Steve Scherer, "Sopranos Star Had 'Wonderful' Last Day with Son: Friend," Reuters, June 21, 2003, www.reuters.com/article/centertainment-us-gandolfini-autopsy-idCABRE95K0BY20130621.

274 **"It's eerie because . . .":** Corky Siemaszko and Edgar Sandoval, "Photo Exclusive: James Gandolfini Ironically Looked at Book of the Dead Hours Before Dying," *New York Daily News*, June 24, 2013, www.nydailynews.com/news/national/gandolfini-mourned-woman-cast-article-1.1381276.

Chapter 24

275 **Michael Gandolfini found his father:** Details of Gandolfini's death: ABC News staff, "James Gandolfini's Son Witnessed Dad in Cardiac Arrest," ABC News, June 20, 2013, abcnews.go.com/Entertainment/james-gandolfinis-son-witnessed-dad-cardiac-arrest/story?id=19444093; *New York Post* staff, "Doctor Recounts Frantic 40-Minute Bid to Save James Gandolfini After Teen Son Calls for Help," *New York Post*, June 20, 2013, nypost.com/2013/06/20/doctor-recounts-frantic-40-minute-bid-to-save-james-gandolfini-after-teen-son-calls-for-help/.

275 **"The resuscitation maneuvers . . .":** Reuters staff, "James Gandolfini Dead at 51: Rome Doctors Tried to Save 'Sopranos' Star's Life for 40 Minutes," *New York Daily News*, June 20, 2013, www.nydailynews.com/2013/06/20/james-gandolfini-dead-at-51-rome-doctors-tried-to-save-sopranos-stars-life-for-40-minutes/.

275 **autopsy found:** Dave Itzkoff, "Autopsy on Gandolfini Finds Actor Died of 'Natural Causes,' Family Spokesman Says," *New York Times*, June 21, 2013, archive.nytimes.com/artsbeat.blogs.nytimes.com/2013/06/21/autopsy-on-gandolfini-finds-actor-died-of-natural-causes-family-spokesman-says; Denis Hamill and Larry McShane, "James Gandolfini's Sister Identifies Body in Rome as Autopsy Confirms Heart Attack Killed 'Sopranos' Star," *New York Daily News*, June 22, 2013, www.nydailynews.com/2013/06/22/james-gandolfinis-sister-identifies-body-in-rome-as-autopsy-confirms-heart-attack-killed-sopranos-star.

275 **"I remember I kind . . .":** Sanders interview, January 23, 2024.

275 **"It is with . . .":** ABC News staff, "James Gandolfini's Son Witnessed Dad in Cardiac Arrest."

275 **Marcy caught:** Bischoff, *James Gandolfini*, 175.

276 **"He was a genius . . .":** Dave Itzkoff, "Reactions to the Death of James Gandolfini," *New York Times*, June 20, 2013, archive.nytimes.com/artsbeat.blogs.nytimes.com/2013/06/20/reactions-to-the-death-of-james-gandolfini.

276 **"I was in my house . . .":** Falco interview, March 29, 2024.

276 **"I felt my legs . . .":** Schirripa interview.

276 **"I was at a poker table . . .":** Iler interview.

276 **"She goes *Chiem* . . . ":** Karasawa interview.

276 **"When I heard . . .":** Margaret Eby, "Kristen Stewart Talks James Gandolfini's Death: 'Every Memory Flooded Back and Gutted Me,'" *New York Daily News*, June 25, 2013, www.nydailynews.com/2013/06/25/kristen-stewart-talks-james-gandolfinis-death-every-memory-flooded-back-and-gutted-me/.

277 **"gutted by this loss . . .":** *Variety* staff, "Brad Pitt: Gandolfini Was a 'Ferocious Actor,'" *Variety*, June 20, 2013, variety.com/2013/film/news/brad-pitt-gandolfini-was-a-ferocious-actor-1200500034/.

277 **"I worked with Jim . . .":** Itzkoff, "Reactions to the Death."

277 **"His little boy . . .":** Larry McShane, "Travolta Will Look Out for His Pal's Kids," *New York Daily News*, June 22, 2013, NYPL.

277 **"It just didn't . . .":** *James Gandolfini: Tribute to a Friend.*

277 **"I'll always remember Edie . . .":** Karasawa interview.

277 **"I wasn't as shocked . . .":** Seitz & Sepinwall, *The Sopranos Sessions*, 613.

277 **"He was a larger-than-life . . .":** Lurie interview, June 29, 2023.

277 **"How could that be . . .":** Abraham interview.

277 **"He was the healthiest . . .":** Sanders interview, January 23, 2024.

277 **"When he passed away . . .":** Schirripa interview.

278 **Governor Chris Christie:** Leslie Larson, "Christie: Jersey Flags Half-Staff," *New York Daily News*, June 22, 2013, NYPL.

278 **"James Gandolfini was a fine actor . . .":** Frank Rosario, "Jersey Town Mourns Loss of 'Regular Guy' Gandolfini," *New York Post*, June 20, 2013, nypost.com/2013/06/20/jersey-town-mourns-loss-of-regular-guy-gandolfini/.

278 **"out of respect for him":** Holsten's tribute: Frank Rosario, "'Reserved': Gandolfini Mourned at Holsten's Ice-Cream Parlor Where Last 'Sopranos' Scene Was Shot," *New York Post*, June 20, 2013, nypost.com/2013/06/20/reserved-gandolfini-mourned-at-holstens-ice-cream-parlor-where-last-sopranos-scene-was-shot/.

278 **Satin Dolls:** Corky Siemaszko, "James Gandolfini Dead at 51: Jersey Club Used as the Bada Bing! on 'Sopranos' Honors Late Actor," *New York Daily News*, June 20, 2013, www.nydailynews.com/2013/06/20/james-gandolfini-dead-at-51-jersey-club-used-as-the-bada-bing-on-sopranos-honors-late-actor/.

278 **But the biggest Jersey tribute:** Ethan Sacks, "James Gandolfini Dead at 51: Bruce Springsteen and the E Street Band Dedicate Performance to Late Actor," *New York Daily News*, June 21, 2013, www.nydailynews.com/2013/06/21/james-gandolfini-dead-at-51-bruce-springsteen-and-the-e-street-band-dedicate-performance-to-late-actor.

279 **"Dimming the lights is a special . . .":** Larry McShane, "James Gandolfini Remembered as Broadway Theaters Plan to Dim Marquees Wednesday in Late Actor's Honor," *New York Daily News*, June 25, 2013, www.nydailynews.com/entertainment/broadway-dim-marquees-james-gandolfini-article-1.1382055.

279 **"In an Exclusive . . .":** Levine, "Exclusive Interview!"

279 **The *New York Daily News* followed:** *New York Daily News*, June 20, 2013, NYPL.

279 **the *New York Post* went:** *New York Post*, June 20, 2013, NYPL.

279 **accused of stealing:** Watch theft: David K. Li and Julia Marsh, "Tony's Rolex Swiped," *New York Post*, August 8, 2013, NYPL; Jason Silverstein, "Paramedic Allegedly Stole James Gandolfini's $3,000 Rolex Watch as Actor Lay Dying in Rome," *New York Daily News*, May 17, 2016, www.nydailynews.com/news/national/paramedic-allegedly-stole-james-gandolfini-rolex-actor-died-article-1.2639688; Chris Perez, "Tony's Time Bandit," *New York Post*, May 18, 2016, NYPL.

279 **Sandra Lee:** Rebecca Rosenberg, "Cuomo's Girlfriend Staying in Rome Suite Where James Gandolfini Suffered Fatal Heart Attack," *New York Post*, June 22, 2013, nypost.com/2013/06/22/cuomos-girlfriend-staying-in-rome-suite-where-james-gandolfini-suffered-fatal-heart-attack/; Corinne Lestch and Larry McShane, "Gov. Cuomo's Girlfriend Sandra Lee Stayed in Same Rome Hotel Room as James Gandolfini Following 'Sopranos' Star's Death," *New York Daily News*, June 22, 2013, www.nydailynews.com/entertainment/tv-movies/sandra-lee-stayed-room-gandolfini-article-1.1379838.

279 **"Gandolfini guzzled four . . .":** Rebecca Rosenberg, Jamie Schram, and Dan McCleod, "Deadly Bada-Binge for Tony," *New York Post*, June 21, 2013, NYPL.

279 **"the piña coladas . . .":** Jenn Harris, "James Gandolfini May Have Had Prawns, Foie Gras the Night He Died; So?," *Los Angeles Times*, June 21, 2013, www.latimes.com/food/dailydish/la-dd-james-gandolfini-last-meal-20130621-story.html.

280 **"and he was very happy . . .":** ABC News staff, "James Gandolfini's Son Witnessed Dad in Cardiac Arrest."

280 **"He was the American actor . . .":** Nick Vivarelli, "Gandolfini Mourned at Italian Festival as New Details Emerge," *Variety*, June 20, 2013, variety.com/2013/film/news/taormina-to-pay-tribute-to-james-gandolfini-1200500001/.

280 **"an actor who had in two decades . . .":** *Variety* staff, "James Gandolfini Tribute Closes Out Taormina Fest," *Variety*, June 24, 2013, variety.com/2013/film/markets-festivals/james-gandolfini-tribute-closes-out-taormina-fest-1200501273/.

280 **"In Italy it can take . . .":** Rebecca Rosenberg, "Gandolfini's Funeral Will Be Held in NY, Autopsy Confirms Heart Attack as Cause of Death," *New York Post*, June 21, 2013, nypost.com/2013/06/21/gandolfinis-funeral-will-be-held-in-ny-autopsy-confirms-heart-attack-as-cause-of-death/.

280 **Gandolfini's remains:** Cynthia Littleton, "Clintons Help Gandolfini Family Speed Return of Body to U.S.," *Variety*, June 23, 2013, variety.com/2013/tv/news/clintons-help-gandolfini-family-speed-return-of-body-to-u-s-1200500972/; amNY/Reuters, "'Tony' Heads Home," amNewYork, June 24, 2013, NYPL; Philip Messing, "Gandolfini's Body Arrives in Native New Jersey from Rome," *New York Post*, June 23, 2013, nypost.com/2013/06/23/gandolfinis-body-arrives-in-native-new-jersey-from-rome/; Rebecca Rosenberg, "James Gandolfini's Body Flown by Private Jet Home to New Jersey from Rome Before NYC Funeral," *New York Post*, June 24, 2013, nypost.com/2013/06/24/james-gandolfinis-body-flown-by-private-jet-home-to-new-jersey-from-rome-before-nyc-funeral/.

280 **family wake:** Chelsia Rose Marcius, Erik Badia, and Larry McShane, "James Gandolfini's Widow, Baby, Family and Friends Arrive in NJ for Private Wake," *New York Daily News*, June 26, 2013, www.nydailynews.com/entertainment/gossip/gandolfini-loved-arrive-nj-wake-article-1.1383398.

280 **the public service:** Funeral announcement: Adam W. Kepler, "Gandolfini Funeral to Be Held at St. John the Divine in Manhattan," *New York Times*, June 24, 2013, archive.nytimes.com/artsbeat.blogs.nytimes.com/2013/06/24/gandolfini-funeral-to-be-held-at-st-john-the-divine-in-manhattan/.

280 **"St. John's is the fourth-largest . . .":** Joan Acocella, "Gandolfini: The Goodbye," *New Yorker*, June 30, 2013, www.newyorker.com/culture/culture-desk/gandolfini-the-goodbye.

280 **More than fifteen hundred friends:** Funeral: James Barron, "Mourners Fill Cathedral to Remember Gandolfini," *New York Times*, June 27, 2013, www.nytimes.com/2013/06/28/nyregion/mourners-gather-to-pay-tribute-to-gandolfini.html; Scott Foundas, "James Gandolfini Remembered for 'Huge Heart and Spirit' at Funeral," *Variety*, June 27, 2013, variety.com/2013/tv/news/james-gandolfini-remembered-for-huge-heart-and-spirit-at-funeral-1200502478/; Erik Badia and Larry McShane, "James Gandolfini Funeral: Son Michael Gandolfini Carries Father's Casket to Final Resting Place," *New York Daily News*, June 28, 2013, www.nydailynews.com/2013/06/28/james-gandolfini-funeral-son-michael-gandolfini-carries-fathers-casket-to-final-resting-place/; Tara Palmeri, "Stars, Politicians, Friends and Family Pack 1,500 Seat Funeral for 'Sopranos' Star James Gandolfini," *New York Post*, June 27, 2013, nypost.com/2013/06/27/stars-politicians-friends-and-family-pack-1500-seat-funeral-for-sopranos-star-james-gandolfini/.

280 **"We thought we walked into . . .":** Pastore interview.

280 **"It was like a scene we shot . . .":** *James Gandolfini: Tribute to a Friend.*

280 **"I was like, *Jim's gone* . . .":** Iler interview.

280 **"My husband was . . .":** Badia and McShane, "James Gandolfini Funeral."

280 **"the most giving . . .":** Matt Zoller Seitz, "Publicly Mourning a Private Man: Seitz on the Funeral of James Gandolfini," *Vulture*, June 27, 2013, www.vulture.com/2013/06/matt-zoller-seitz-on-james-gandolfinis-funeral.html.

280 **"Close your eyes . . .":** Badia and McShane, "James Gandolfini Funeral."

280 **"These were liberating words . . .":** Read during Aston interview.

282 **"I don't want to lose . . .":** Palmeri, "Stars, Politicians, Friends and Family Pack 1,500 Seat Funeral for 'Sopranos' Star James Gandolfini."

282 **"I don't like speaking . . .":** Seitz & Sepinwall, *The Sopranos Sessions*, 613.

282 **"I am so honored . . .":** *Variety* staff, "'Sopranos' Creator David Chase's Eulogy for James Gandolfini," *Variety*, June 27, 2013, variety.com/2013/tv/news/james-gandolfini-funeral-read-sopranos-creator-david-chases-eulogy-1200502711/.

282 **"I watched Deb . . .":** Karasawa interview.

282 **"We all went to a restaurant . . .":** Margulies interview.

282 **"They were putting the coffin . . .":** *James Gandolfini: Tribute to a Friend.*

283 **salute at the primetime Emmys:** Jon Weisman, "Gandolfini, Monteith, Stapleton, Winters and Goldberg to Receive Special Tributes at Emmys," *Variety*, September 16, 2013, variety.com/2013/tv/awards/gandolfini-monteith-stapleton-winters-and-goldberg-to-receive-special-tributes-at-emmys-1200613466/.

283 **Wounded Warrior Project's:** Maane Khatchatourian, "'The Sopranos' Honor Wounded

Warriors, Late James Gandolfini," *Variety*, October 11, 2013, variety.com/2013/scene/news/the-sopranos-honor-wounded-warriors-late-james-gandolfini-1200714936/.

283 **"James Gandolfini Way":** Park Ridge tribute: Associated Press, "'Sopranos' Stars Gather as N.J. Town Honors James Gandolfini," *Variety*, December 2, 2013, variety.com/2013/tv/news/james-gandolfini-sopranos-1200909628/.

284 **"the day Jim died . . .":** Panel discussion, "James Gandolfini's Documentary Legacy."

284 **"The family has been asking . . .":** Alpert interview.

284 ***Taxi-22* finally moved:** Nellie Andreeva, "John Leguizamo to Star in CBS Pilot 'Taxi-22,' Passion Project of James Gandolfini," Deadline, January 22, 2015, deadline.com/2015/01/john-leguizamo-cast-taxi-22-cbs-comedy-pilot-james-gandolfini-1201356248/.

284 **"I can't imagine us airing . . .":** *Daily News* staff, "James Gandolfini's 'Criminal Justice' Pilot Won't Air on HBO, Network Announces," *New York Daily News*, July 26, 2013, www.nydailynews.com/2013/07/26/james-gandolfinis-criminal-justice-pilot-wont-air-on-hbo-network-announces/.

284 **"I loved James and . . .":** Miller, *Tinderbox*, 759.

284 **take over the role:** Recasting: *Criminal Justice*: Bill Carter, "De Niro to Replace James Gandolfini in HBO Drama," *New York Times*, September 26, 2013, www.nytimes.com/2013/09/27/business/media/de-niro-to-replace-james-gandolfini-in-hbo-drama.html; Debra Birnbaum, "Steve Zaillian Brings Film-Style Grittiness to HBO Series 'The Night Of,'" *Variety*, July 13, 2016, variety.com/2016/tv/features/hbo-night-of-director-steve-zallian-1201812916/.

284 **"John was like . . .":** Armstrong interview, January 9, 2024.

284 **"I didn't know how big . . .":** John Koblin, "In 'The Night Of,' John Turturro Picks Up Where James Gandolfini Left Off," *New York Times*, July 1, 2016, www.nytimes.com/2016/07/03/arts/television/in-the-night-of-john-turturro-picks-up-where-james-gandolfini-left-off.html.

285 **research the role:** Shayna Jacobs, "EXCLUSIVE: John Turturro Appears in Manhattan Criminal Court to Observe Proceedings Ahead of Role in HBO Miniseries 'Criminal Justice,'" *New York Daily News*, August 5, 2014, www.nydailynews.com/entertainment/tv/john-turturro-appears-manhattan-court-observe-proceedings-article-1.1892535.

285 **briefly resurrected *Big Dead Place*:** Elizabeth Wagmeister, "James Gandolfini's 'Big Dead Place' Revived at HBO with 'Sopranos' Alum Timothy Van Patten Attached," January 21, 2016, variety.com/2016/tv/news/james-gandolfini-big-dead-place-hbo-drama-1201685566/.

285 **premiered *Enough Said*:** Daniel Beekman, "The Ghost of Gandolfini," *New York Post*, July 17, 2013, NYPL; Justin Chang, "Film Review: *Enough Said*," *Variety*, September 7, 2013, variety.com/2013/film/markets-festivals/enough-said-review-toronto-1200603239/.

285 **"Obviously, Jim is . . .":** Ramin Setoodeh, "James Gandolfini Remembered at 'Enough Said' New York Premiere," *Variety*, September 17, 2013, variety.com/2013/film/news/james-gandolfini-remembered-at-enough-said-new-york-premiere-1200614880/.

285 **"This movie will . . .":** A. O. Scott, "The Woman Who Knew Too Much," *New York Times*, September 17, 2013, www.nytimes.com/2013/09/18/movies/enough-said-stars-james-gandolfini-and-julia-louis-dreyfus.html.

285 **"Gandolfini, without bullying . . .":** David Denby, "Drifting," *New Yorker*, September 30, 2013, www.newyorker.com/magazine/2013/10/07/drifting.

285 **"What a treat . . .":** Joe Neumaier, "'Enough Said,' Movie Review," *New York Daily News*, September 18, 2013, www.nydailynews.com/2013/09/18/enough-said-movie-review/.

285 **"The counterpoint between . . .":** A. O. Scott, "Quiet Bartender's Secret," *New York Times*, September 11, 2014, www.nytimes.com/2014/09/12/movies/the-drop-unfolds-in-a-brooklyn-underworld.html.

285 **"Gandolfini is on . . .":** Joe Neumaier, "'The Drop,' James Gandolfini's Final Film, Provides Worthy Sendoff to Late, Great Actor," *New York Daily News*, August 6, 2014, www.nydailynews.com/entertainment/movies/james-gandolfini-final-film-article-1.1894465.

285 **"Unsurprisingly, . . .":** Justin Chang, "Toronto Film Review: 'The Drop,'" September 5, 2014, variety.com/2014/film/festivals/toronto-film-review-the-drop-1201299293/.

286 **"This is a show . . .":** Seitz & Sepinwall, *The Sopranos Sessions*, 613.

286 **200 percent:** Pandemic viewing: Mike Hale, "A Pandemic Bonus: Catch These TV

Shows While They're Still Free," *New York Times*, April 21, 2020, www.nytimes.com/2020/04/21/arts/television/free-shows.html; Pope, "The Making of Michael Gandolfini."

286 **"rewatch" podcast:** *Talking Sopranos*: Margy Rochlin, "How Two 'Sopranos' Wise Guys Launched a Podcast from Their Coronavirus Quarantine," *Los Angeles Times*, April 9, 2020, www.latimes.com/entertainment-arts/tv/story/2020-04-09/coronavirus-quarantine-talking-sopranos-podcast-michael-imperioli-steve-schirripa; Mike Fleming Jr., "'Talking Sopranos' Duo Michael Imperioli and Steve Schirripa Score Book Deal with William Morrow," Deadline, September 17, 2020, deadline.com/2020/09/talking-sopranos-michael-imperioli-steve-schirripa-book-deal-william-morrow-1234578849/.

286 **"The show's depiction . . .":** Willy Staley, "Why Is Every Young Person in America Watching 'The Sopranos'?," *New York Times*, September 29, 2021, www.nytimes.com/2021/09/29/magazine/sopranos.html.

286 **"Even if I did it . . .":** Associated Press, "David Chase Intrigued by 'Sopranos' Prequel Idea," *New York Daily News*, November 5, 2014, www.nydailynews.com/entertainment/tv/david-chase-intrigued-sopranos-prequel-idea-article-1.2000336.

287 **Deadline reported:** Many Saints casting: Mike Fleming Jr., "'Sopranos' Prequel Film Finds Young Tony: Michael Gandolfini Is Chip off Old Block," Deadline, January 22, 2019, deadline.com/2019/01/the-sopranos-prequel-movie-michael-gandolfini-tony-soprano-james-gandolfini-the-many-saints-of-newark-james-gandolfini-david-chase-1202539160/.

287 **"I think David . . .":** *Talking Sopranos*, episode 78, September 20, 2021.

287 **"My dad really . . .":** Pope, "The Making of Michael Gandolfini."

288 **"I had this . . .":** Ibid.

288 **"He was a big . . .":** De Matteo interview, March 22, 2024.

288 **"I miss him every day . . .":** Van Zandt interview.

288 **"This is the time . . .":** Alpert interview.

288 **"I loved James with . . .":** Aston interview.

289 **twentieth-anniversary:** Daniel D'Addario, "'The Sopranos' 20th Anniversary Reunion: Cast, Producers Remember James Gandolfini," *Variety*, January 9, 2019, variety.com/2019/scene/news/sopranos-20th-anniversary-panel-david-chase-steven-van-zandt-1203104405/.

289 **"As soon as . . .":** Iler interview.

INDEX

ABOUT THE AUTHOR

Photo by Nick Dryden

Jason Bailey is a film critic, historian, and the author of five previous books, including *Richard Pryor: American Id* and *Fun City Cinema: New York City and the Movies that Made It*. His work has appeared in the *New York Times*, *Vanity Fair*, Vulture, Bloomberg, *Rolling Stone*, *Time*, Slate, and more. He lives in the Bronx with his wife, two daughters, two cats, and dog.